NTC's Anthology of Nonfiction

Jane Bachman Gordon

Karen Kuehner

NTC *Publishing Group*
Lincolnwood, Illinois USA

Executive Editor: John T. Nolan
Developmental Editor: Marisa L. L'Heureux
Cover and interior design: Ophelia M. Chambliss
Cover art: June Rothman
Production Manager: Rosemary Dolinski

Acknowledgments for permission to reprint literary selections begin on page 467, which is to be considered an extension of this copyright page.

Contents

—w—

Preface

—ɯ—

$\mathcal{S}$ome centuries, some countries seem inextricably associated with certain literary genres: the lyric and Romantic poetry written in Tang dynasty China during the eighth and ninth centuries and in early-nineteenth-century England; the drama—both comedy and tragedy—of fifth century B.C. Athens or of Elizabethan England; and the novels written in France, England, and the United States during the nineteenth and early twentieth centuries.

What might literary historians three hundred years hence consider the most significant genre of the latter half of the twentieth century? Poetry? Drama? Novels? Contemporary critics such as Tom Wolfe and Donald Hall make a strong case for nonfiction. Certainly an astonishing number of talented modern writers have chosen to write nonfiction. Some few follow the style and structure established by Michel de Montaigne, the sixteenth-century Frenchman credited with developing the form; such writers muse in one direction and then another about a particular idea, a specific oddity. Others, chiefly but not exclusively journalists, produce highly readable, objective exposition in the tradition of newspaper or magazine feature writers. An increasing number write pieces in which the subjective I/eye is central. And what do these authors write about? Their subjects range from travel to childhood experiences to frogs; their modes range from narration to exposition to argumentation; their manner of development, from comparison and contrast to analysis to definition; their style, from the minimal to the highly structured; their diction, from the plain to the florid; their tone, from the serious to the comic.

Despite the manifest accomplishments of these contemporary writers, the extent to which they are unknown in many English classrooms is astonishing—especially in light of what we know about student reading habits. Virtually every English instructor has heard the following responses to a reading assignment: "Is this true?" "Did this really happen?" And the motivation for these questions seems to be that what is real can be trusted. Thus, when students are asked what they prefer to read in their leisure time, an overwhelming number do not cite the latest novels, the newest play, or the most recent book of poetry. Students read nonfiction, typically in magazines or newspapers. And they seem to read it not to discover what might be, but to discover what is or what was or what will be.

This book of nonfiction is a response to students' interests and preferences. Instead of organizing the essays in chronological order, we have focused on certain areas of interest about which some talented and provocative writers have something to say. In such chapters as **Ancestors and Families, Working, Sports, Nature, Science and Technology, Values, Travel,** and **Writers on Writing,** you will find between five and seven essays—some of them contradictory, some of them complementary, all of them by authors worth getting to know.

THE CHOICE OF SELECTIONS

In choosing the essays in this book, we were guided by the following four criteria:

1. **Do the essays cover a wide variety of subjects?** Although virtually any subject can be—and has been—the object of an essayist's interest, areas such as sports or science have been little explored, perhaps because traditional essayists had little interest in such topics or because they thought their readers would not respond to them. Today's readers, however, *are* interested, as the sales of magazines devoted to those topics attest. If you think that technology couldn't possibly be interesting, read Daniel Boorstin's essay on the development of timepieces.

2. **Will the essays appeal to a significant number of readers?** We recognize that not all of you will be interested in every category or, indeed, every essay. We feel certain, however, that you will find many essays here that will appeal to you or provoke you, even in areas that may surprise you. If you have never been particularly interested in nature or travel, read Annie Dillard or Paul Theroux. We think you'll be surprised and amazed.

3. **Is each author's writing style vivid and compelling?** Through its choice of subject, point of view, accessible organization, sentence variety, and precise or surprising diction, good writing compels you to read on—no matter what the subject or your interest in it. Good writing can make any topic attractive. Try the sports piece by Dave Barry and just *try* to suppress a giggle or a guffaw.

4. **Does the author have a strong and discernible point of view?**
   It is as true today as it was when Montaigne first developed the essay form: one happy by-product of reading essays is the opportunity to get to know the authors—their prejudices, opinions, aspirations, doubts. If you have ever wondered what it would be like to grow up a "stranger in a strange land," try Amy Tan or Simon J. Ortiz. Or if you have ever wondered what it was like to be the victim of the end of an era, read Galsworthy's essay on the demise of his bootmaker.

We believe that no matter what your preferences, you will find that each of the essays fulfills these four criteria.

The Objectives of the Book

In compiling these essays, we kept two primary objectives in mind: (1) *to increase your awareness of the diversity of nonfiction*, and (2) *to promote your ability to respond to nonfiction*. Since you regularly read nonfiction in nearly all your courses, many English instructors concentrate on the teaching of novels, short stories, drama, and poetry. Thus, many of you may have little guided experience with essays, particularly contemporary essays, and even less practice in responding to them. Through the various questions in this book, we encourage you to discuss and to write about what you have read and how your feel or think about it.

Features of the Text

In each of the eight parts of this book, you will find the following features:

- The **Preview** presents an introduction to the topic and a brief overview of each of the essays included.

- The *introduction* to each selection consists of two sections: the first is a biographical sketch of the author; the second, **Looking Ahead**, is a succinct overview of the featured work that encourages you to consider certain points as you read.

- **Footnotes** explain foreign words and phrases, historical or literary allusions, or terms critical to an understanding of the work.

- **Looking Back** consists of a series of analytical, interpretive, or evaluative discussion questions about the selection itself.

- **Looking Into** contains specific suggestions for writing that either send you into the selection or into your own life and experiences.

- **Looking Around**, the section that appears at the end of each part, features a number of questions that ask you to go on to more advanced critical thinking skills—those of comparison and contrast, analysis, or synthesis.

The sixteenth-century English essayist Francis Bacon once wrote:

> Some books are to be tasted, others to be swallowed, and some few to be chewed and digested; that is, some books are to be read only in parts; others to be read but not curiously; and some few to be read wholly, and with diligence and attention.

We hope that you will regard this book as belonging in Bacon's third category and that you will read "with diligence and attention," for just as there are categories of books, so, too, are there categories of readers. To take a metaphor from the world of sports or the arts, we urge you to become not a *spectator* but a *participant* in your reading of these essays. Some you will "get" on a first reading; others may require a closer look, perhaps even a rereading, before you can respond thoroughly to the author's ideas. We assure you that the effort—like the essays—will be worth it.

ACKNOWLEDGMENTS

The authors wish to thank John T. Nolan and Marisa L. L'Heureux at NTC Publishing Group for encouraging us to undertake this project; for contributing significantly to its shape; and for being unfailingly good-humored during its completion.

PART 1
Ancestors and Families

—m—

However constructed, the traditional kinship group has usually provided those who live in it with security, identity, and indeed with their entire scheme of activities and beliefs. The nameless billions of hunter-gatherers who have lived and died over the past several million years have been embedded in kinship groups, and when people started to farm about ten thousand years ago their universe remained centered on kinship.

* * *

The family is still the crucible. It still provides the most intense, intimate, and permanent relationships most of us will ever have; and this is not likely to change. There may even be, as many scientists believe, a basic human need for kinship. Perhaps, like other animals, we are "wired for attachment."

Alex Shoumatoff from *The Mountain of Names*

We all carry within us the genes of our parents, many genes of our grandparents, and even some of our great grandparents, but we also inherit a culture. Or, if we do not grow up with our birth parents, we adopt a culture that is a part of who we are. Why is it important to probe our own cultural background? To understand the lives of others? To search for links between our humanness and the humanness of others? These are only a few of the questions it is possible to ask, and to try to answer, while reading this section.

In "Searching for Ancestors," Barry Lopez writes of a quest for ancestors who are forebears of part of the land we know as North America. Russell Baker reminisces about boyhood summers with his family in Virginia in "Summer Beyond Wish." Beverly Hungry Wolf tells of the values of learning from her ancestors, and Jill Nelson writes about her love of a special place.

In "Good Housekeeping," Bailey White recounts the story of the preparations for a memorable family Thanksgiving. David Mamet recalls the circumstances surrounding a gift from his father in "The Watch," and Maxine Hong Kingston composes a revealing portrait of her mother in an excerpt from *Woman Warrior*.

Searching for Ancestors

BARRY LOPEZ

Barry Lopez's writing focuses chiefly on the environment and natural history. For *Of Wolves and Men* (1978) he received the John Burroughs Medal for distinguished natural history writing, the Christopher Medal for humanitarian writing, and the Pacific Northwest Booksellers Award for excellence in nonfiction, as well as an American Book Award nomination.

Arctic Dreams: Imagination and Desire in a Northern Landscape (1986) also won several awards, among them a nomination for an award from the National Book Critics Circle, a place on the *New York Times* best book list, and an American Library Association notable book citation.

Lopez was born in Port Chester, New York, in 1945. He graduated *cum laude* with a B.A. from the University of Notre Dame in 1966 and received his M.A. in teaching in 1968. He did some graduate study at the University of Oregon in 1968–1969.

He won an Award in Literature from the American Academy and Institute of Arts and Letters for the body of his work in 1986 and received a Guggenheim Fellowship in 1987. His other works include *Desert Notes: Reflections in the Eye of a Raven* (1976), *Winter Count* (1981), *Crow and Weasel* (1990), and *Field Notes: The Grace Note of the Canyon Wren* (1994), all fiction. *Crossing Open Ground* (1988) and *The Rediscovery of North America* (1991) are essay collections.

Looking Ahead

In this essay, which was taken from a collection entitled *Crossing Open Ground* (1988), Lopez writes about the Anasazi, a prehistoric people who lived in the Southwest United States. Originally seminomadic, they settled into farming communities about two thousand years ago. Here Lopez explores their culture and his feelings about these "ancient ones." As you read, think about Lopez's reasons for writing about these people.

1   *I* am lying on my back in northern Arizona. The sky above, the familiar arrangement of stars at this particular latitude on a soft June evening, is comforting. I reach out from my sleeping bag, waiting for sleep, and slowly brush the Kaibab Plateau, a grit of limestone 230 million years old. A slight breeze, the settling air at dusk, carries the pungent odor of blooming cliffrose.

2   Three of us sleep in this clearing, on the west rim of Marble Canyon above the Colorado River. Two archaeologists and myself, out hunting for tangible remains of the culture called Anasazi. The Anasazi abandoned this particular area for good around A.D. 1150, because of drought, deteriorating trade alliances, social hostilities—hard to say now. But while they flourished, both here and farther to the east in the austere beauty of canyons called de Chelly and Chaco, they represented an apotheosis in North American culture, like the Hopewell of Ohio[1] or the horse-mounted Lakota of the plains in the last century.

3   In recent years the Anasazi have come to signify prehistoric Indians in the same way the Lakota people have been made to stand for all historic Indians. Much has been made of the "mystery" of their disappearance. And perhaps because they seem "primitive," they are too easily thought of as an uncomplicated people with a comprehensible culture. It is not, and they are not. We know some things about them. From the start they were deft weavers, plaiting even the utensils they cooked with. Later they became expert potters and masons, strongly influencing cultures around them. They were clever floodwater farmers. And astronomers; not as sophisticated as the Maya, but knowledgeable enough to pinpoint the major celestial events, to plant and celebrate accordingly.

4   They were intimate with the landscape, a successful people. Around A.D. 1300 they slipped through a historical crevice to emerge (as well as we know) as the people now called Hopi and Zuni, and the pueblo peoples of the Rio Grande Valley—Keres, Tiwa, Tewa.

5   On a long, dry June day like this, hundreds of tourists wander in fascination at Mesa Verde and Pueblo Bonito;[2] and I am out here on the land the Anasazi once walked—here with two people who squat down to look closely at the land itself before they say anything about its former inhabitants. Even then they are reticent. We are camped here amid the indige-

---

1   **Hopewell of Ohio:** mound builders who lived in the Ohio Valley and left a variety of earthworks.
2   **Mesa Verde and Pueblo Bonito:** Mesa Verde is a national park in Colorado and the site of Anasazi cliff dwellings. Pueblo Bonito is a site in Chaco Culture National Historical Park in New Mexico. The pueblo has five hundred rooms.

nous light siennas and dark umbers, the wild red of ripe prickly pear fruit, the dull silver of buffalo berry bushes, the dark, luminous green of a field of snakegrass.

6   We inquire after the Anasazi. Because we respect the spiritual legacy of their descendants, the Hopi. Because of the contemporary allure of Taos. Because in our own age we are "killing the hidden waters" of the Southwest, and these were a people who took swift, resourceful advantage of whatever water they could find. Because of the compelling architecture of their cliff dwellings, the stunning placement of their homes in the stone walls of Betatakin,[3] as if set in the mouth of an enormous wave or at the bottom of a towering cumulus cloud. We make the long automobile trip to Hovenweep[4] or the hike into Tsegi Canyon to gaze at Keet Seel.[5] It is as though we believed *here* is a good example, here are stories to get us through the night.

7 Some eight thousand years ago, after the decline of the Folsom and Clovis hunters, whose spearpoints are still found in the crumbling arroyos of New Mexico, a culture we know very little about emerged in the Great Basin. Archaeologists call it simply the Desert Culture. Some two thousand years ago, while Rome was engaged in the Macedonian wars, a distinct group of people emerged from this complex. They were called Anasazi from the Navajo *anaasázi*, meaning "someone's ancestors." Their culture first appeared in the Four Corners country, where Utah, Arizona, New Mexico, and Colorado meet. By this time (A.D. 1) they were already proficient weavers and basketmakers, living a mixed agricultural hunter-gatherer life and dwelling in small groups in semisubterranean houses. Archaeologists call this period, up to about A.D. 700, the Basket Maker Period. It was followed by a Pueblo Period (A.D. 700–1598), during which time the Anasazi built the great cliff and pueblo dwellings by which most of us know them.

8   Archaeologists divide the Anasazi occupation geographically into three contemporary traditions—Kayenta, Chaco, and Mesa Verde. Here, where I have rolled my sleeping bag out this June evening, Kayenta Anasazi lived, in an area of about ten thousand square miles bounded by the Henry

---

3   **Betatakin:** cliff dwellings at the Navajo National Monument in northeast Arizona. The inhabitants were Kayenta Anasazi. *Betatakin* means "ledge house" in Navajo.
4   **Hovenweep:** a national monument in southwest Colorado and southeast Utah.
5   **Tsegi Canyon . . . Keet Seel:** Tsegi Canyon is in the Navajo National Monument and the site of Betatakin and Keet Seel, the largest cliff dwelling in Arizona.

Mountains in Utah, the Little Colorado River to the south, Grand Canyon to the west, and Chinle Wash, near the New Mexico border, to the east. This part of the Anasazi country has long been of interest to Robert Euler, the research anthropologist at Grand Canyon National Park. He lies quietly now a few yards away from me, in the night shadow of a large juniper tree. From here, at the lip of Marble Canyon and the old edge of Anasazi territory, amid the very same plants the Anasazi took such perceptive advantage of—threads of the yucca leaf to be made into snares; the soft, shreddy bark of the cliffrose to absorb the flow of blood; delicate black seeds of rice grass to eat—from here, with the aid of an observer like Euler, it is possible to imagine who these people might have been, to make some cautious surmise about them and the meaning they may have for us, who wistfully regard them now as mysterious and vanished, like the Eskimo curlew.

9   We go toward sleep this evening—Euler, a colleague named Trinkle Jones, and myself—restless with the bright, looming memory of a granary we have located today, a small storage structure below a cliff edge that has been visited only by violet-green swallows and pack rats since its Anasazi owners walked away some eight hundred years ago. It is like a piece of quartz in the mind.

10 In a quiet corner of the national park's health clinic on the south rim of the Grand Canyon, an entire wall of Euler's modest office is covered by books. A small slip of paper there reads:

> These are not books, lumps of lifeless paper, but *minds* alive on the shelves. From each of them goes out its own voice, as inaudible as the streams of sound conveyed day and night by electric waves beyond the range of our physical hearing; and just as the touch of a button on our set will fill the room with music, so by taking down one of these volumes and opening it, one can call into range the far distant voice in time and space, and hear it speaking to us, mind to mind, heart to heart.
>
> Gilbert Highet

11   Highet was a classics scholar. The words reflect his respect for the ideas of other cultures, other generations, and for the careful deliberations of trained minds. Euler is in this mold; keen and careful, expert in his field, but intent on fresh insight. At fifty-seven, with an ironic wit, willing to listen attentively to the ideas of an amateur, graciously polite, he is the sort of man you wish had taught you in college.

12   Of the Anasazi he says: "It is relatively easy to see *what* they did, but why did they do these things? What were their values? What were the fundamental relationships between their institutions—their politics, economics, religion? All we can do is infer, from what we pick up on the ground."

13   To elucidate the Anasazi, Euler and his colleagues have taken several ingenious steps in recent years. In the 1920s a man named Andrew Douglass pioneered a system of dating called dendrochronology. By comparing borings from timbers used in Anasazi dwellings, Douglass and his successors eventually constructed a continuous record of tree-ring patterns going back more than two thousand years. The measurements are so precise that archaeologists can, for instance, tell that a room in a particular dwelling in Chaco Canyon was roofed over in the spring or summer of 1040 with timbers cut in the fall or winter of 1039.

14   Using dendrochronology as a parallel guide in time, archaeologists have been able to corroborate and assemble long sequences of pottery design. With the aid of radiocarbon dating, obsidian hydration dating,[6] and a technique called thermoluminescence,[7] they have pinned down dates for cooking fires and various tools. By determining kinds of fossil pollens and their ratios to each other, palynologists[8] have reconstructed former plant communities, shedding light on human diets at the time and establishing a history of weather patterns.

15   With such a convergence of dates and esoteric information, archaeologists can figure out when a group of people were occupying a certain canyon, what sort of meals they were eating, what kind of animals and plants were present there, and how they were adapting their farming methods and living patterns to cope with, say, several years of heavy rainfall. With more prosaic techniques—simple excavation and observation—much more becomes clear: details and artifacts of personal adornment; locally traded items (beans and squash for tanned deerskin) and distant trade patterns (turquoise for abalone shell beads from California or copper bells from Mexico); and prevalent infirmities and diseases (arthritis, iron-deficiency anemia).

16   As much as one can learn, however—the Anasazi were a short people with straight black hair, who domesticated turkeys for a supply of feathers, which they carefully wrapped around string and wove together to make

---

6 **obsidian:** Obsidian is a volcanic glass that can be dated by using advanced scientific methods.

7 **thermoluminescence:** phosphorescence produced by heating.

8 **palynologists:** scientists who study spores and pollen.

blankets—the information seems hollow when you are standing in the cool silence of one of the great kivas[9] at Mesa Verde. Or staring at the stone that soars like a cathedral vault above White House Ruin in Canyon de Chelly. Or turning an Anasazi flute over in your hands. The analytic tools of science can obscure the fact that these were a people. They had an obvious and pervasive spiritual and aesthetic life, as well as clothing made of feathers and teeth worn down by the grit in their cornmeal. Their abandoned dwellings and ceremonial kivas would seem to make this clear. This belief by itself—that they were a people of great spiritual strength—makes us want to know them, to understand what they understood.

[17] The day Euler and Jones discovered the intact granary, with its handful of tiny corncobs, I was making notes about the plants and animals we had encountered and trying to envision how water fell and flowed away over this parched land. Euler had told me the area we were traversing was comparable to what the Anasazi had known when they were here, though it was a little drier now. Here then was buffalo berry, which must have irritated their flesh with the white powder beneath its leaves, as it did mine. And apache plume, from whose stout twigs the Anasazi made arrows. And a species of sumac, from the fruits of which they made a sweet lemonade. Dogbane, from whose fibrous stems they wove sandals, proof against scorpions, cactus spines, and the other sharp and pointed edges of this country.

[18] One afternoon I came on the remains of a mule deer killed by a mountain lion and thought the Anasazi, eminently practical, must have availed themselves of such meat. And I considered the sheltered, well-stocked dwellings of the pack rat, who may have indicated to the newly arrived Anasazi the value of providence and storage.

[19] Such wandering is like an interrogation of the landscape, trying by means of natural history and analog to pry loose from it a sense of a people who would be intimate with it—knowledgeable of the behavior of its ground and surface water, its seven-year cycle of piñon nut production, the various subtle euphonies of whirring insects, bumblebees, and hummingbirds on a June afternoon—a people reflective of its order.

[20] Euler stood by me at one point when I asked about a particular plant—did they parch, very carefully, the tiny seeds of this desert plume in fiber baskets over their fires?—and said that their botany was so good they probably made use of everything they could digest.

---

9 **kivas:** large chambers, often partly or wholly underground, used for religious ceremonies.

21   They made mistakes, too, if you want to call them that: farmed one area too intensively and ruined the soil; cut down too many trees with their stone axes for housing and firewood and abetted erosion; overhunted. But they survived. They lived through long droughts and took advantage of years of wetness to secure their future. One of the great lessons of the Anasazi is one of the great lessons of all aboriginal peoples, of human ecology in general: Individuals die—of starvation, disease, and injury; but the population itself—resourceful, practical, determined—carries on through nearly everything. Their indomitable fierceness is as attractive as the power we imagine concentrated in their kivas.

22   With the Anasazi, however, you must always turn back and look at the earth—the earth they farmed and hunted and gathered fruits and nuts and seeds upon—and to the weather. The Anasazi responded resourcefully and decisively to the earth and the weather that together made their land. If they were sometimes victims of their environment through drought or epidemic disease, they were more often on excellent terms with it. Given a slight advantage, as they were about A.D. 600 and again about A.D. 1150, when food was abundant at the peak of the Southwest's 550-year moisture cycle, their culture flourished. Around A.D. 600 they developed pottery, the cultivated bean, and the bow and arrow. In the bean was an important amino acid, lysine, not available in the corn they cultivated. Their diet improved dramatically. By 1150 the Anasazi were building pueblos with three-story, freestanding walls, and their crafts were resurgent during this "classic" period. We can only wonder what might have happened at the next climatic, in 1700—but by then the hostile Spanish were among them.

23   The rise and fall of Anasazi fortunes in time with the weather patterns of the region is clear to most historians. What is not clear is how much of a role weather played in the final retreat of the Anasazi in A.D. 1300 from areas they had long occupied—Mesa Verde, southern Black Mesa, Chaco Canyon. Toward the end, the Anasazi were building what seem to be defensive structures, but it is unclear against whom they were defending themselves. A good guess is that they were defending themselves against themselves, that this was a period of intense social feuding. The sudden alteration of trading relationships, social and political realignment in the communities, drought—whatever the reasons, the Anasazi departed. Their descendants took up residence along the Rio Grande, near springs on the Hopi mesas, and on tributaries of the Little Colorado where water was more dependable. Here, too, they developed farming techniques that were not so harmful to the land.

24 For many in the Southwest today the Anasazi are a vague and nebulous passage in the history of human life. For others, like Euler, they are an intense reflection of the land, a puzzle to be addressed the way a man might try to understand the now-departed curlew.[10] For still others they are a spiritual repository, a mysterious source of strength born of their intimacy with the Colorado Plateau.

25 To wonder about the Anasazi today at a place like the Grand Canyon is to be humbled—by space and the breadth of time—to find the Anasazi neither remote nor primitive, but transcendent. The English novelist J. B. Priestley once said that if he were an American he would make the final test of whatever men chose to do in art and politics a comparison with this place. He believed that whatever was cheap and ephemeral would be revealed for what it was when stood up against it. Priestley was an intellectual, but he had his finger on an abiding aboriginal truth: If something will not stand up in the land, then it doesn't belong there. It is right that it should die. Most of us are now so far removed from either a practical or an aesthetic intimacy with North America that the land is no longer an arbiter for us. And a haunting sense that this arrangement is somewhat dangerous brings us to stare into the Grand Canyon and to contemplate the utter honesty of the Anasazi's life here.

26 In 1906, with some inkling that North America was slowly being stripped of the evidence of its aboriginal life and that a knowledge of such life was valuable, Congress passed a protective Antiquities Act. The impulse in 1979 to pass a much stronger Archaeological Resources Act was different. Spurred on by escalating prices for Anasazi artifacts, thieves had been systematically looting sites for commercial gain. The trend continues. A second serious current threat to this human heritage is the small number of tourists who, sometimes innocently, continue to destroy structures, walk off with artifacts, and deface petroglyphs.[11] More ominously, the national parks and monuments where most Anasazi sites are now found operate on such restricted budgets that they are unable to adequately inventory, let alone protect, these cultural resources.

27 Of the Grand Canyon's two thousand or more aboriginal sites only three have been both excavated and stabilized. Of its 1.2 million acres, 500,000 have never even been visited by an archaeologist or historian. In

---

10   **curlew:** type of shore bird.
11   **petroglyphs:** drawings or carvings on rock made by a prehistoric artist.

the summer of 1981 an unknown person or persons pushed in the wall of an Anasazi granary on the Colorado River at the mouth of Nankoweap Canyon, one of the most famous sites in the park.

[28]   The sites, which people come so far every year to visit, are more vulnerable every year.

[29]   On a helicopter reconnaissance in September 1981, part of a long-term project to locate and describe aboriginal sites in the park, Trinkle Jones found what she thought was a set of untouched ruins in the west rim of Marble Canyon. It was almost a year before she and Euler could get there to record them, on a trip on which I accompanied them.

[30] Euler is glad to get out into the country, into the canyons that have been the focus of his work since 1960. He moves easily through the juniper-piñon savannahs, around the face of a cliff and along narrow trails with a practiced stride, examining bits of stone and brush. His blue eyes often fill with wonder when he relates bits of Anasazi history, his right hand sometimes turning slowly in the air as he speaks, as if he were showing you a rare fruit. He tells me one night that he reveres the land, that he thinks about his own footprints impressed in the soil and on the plants, how long before there will be no trace.

[31]   Euler is a former college president, an author and editor, has been on several university faculties and a codirector of the Black Mesa Archaeological Project, working one step ahead of Peabody Coal's drag buckets. The Park Service, so severely hampered by its humiliating lack of funds, is fortunate, at least, to be able to retain such men.

[32]   The granaries Jones found prove, indeed, to be untouched. Over a period of several days we map and describe nine new ruins. The process is somewhat mechanical, but we each take pleasure in the simple tasks. As the Anasazi had a complicated culture, so have we. We are takers of notes, measurers of stone, examiners of fragments in the dust. We search for order in chaos wherever we go. We worry over what is lost. In our best moments we remember to ask ourselves what it is we are doing, whom we are benefiting by these acts. One of the great dreams of man must be to find some place between the extremes of nature and civilization where it is possible to live without regret.

[33] I lie in my sleeping bag, staring up at the Big Dipper and other familiar stars. It is surprisingly cool. The moon has risen over the land of the Navajo nation to the east. Bats flutter overhead, swooping after moths. We are the only people, I reflect, who go to such lengths to record and preserve the past. In the case of the Anasazi it is not even our own past. Until recently

Indians distrusted this process. When Andrew Douglass roamed the Southwest looking for house timbers to core to establish his dendrochronologies, he was required to trade bolts of velveteen for the privilege and to close off every drill hole with a piece of turquoise.

34   I roll on my side and stare out into the canyon's abyss. I think of the astonishing variety of insects and spiders I have seen today—stinkbugs inverted in cactus flowers, butterflies, tiny biting gnats and exotic red velvet ants, and on the ceiling of an Anasazi granary a very poisonous brown recluse spider. For all the unrelieved tedium there might seem to be in the miles of juniper-piñon savannah, for all the cactus spines, sharp stones, strong light, and imagined strikes of rattlesnakes, the land is replete with creatures, and there is a soft and subtle beauty here. Turn an ash-white mule deer antler over, and its underside, where it has lain against the earth, is flushed rose. Yellow pollen clings to the backs of my hands. Wild grasses roll in the wind, like the manes of horses. It is important to remember that the Anasazi lived in a place, and that the place was very much like the place I lie in tonight.

35   The Anasazi are a reminder: Human life is fundamentally diverse and finally impenetrable. That we cannot do better than a crude reconstruction of their life on the Colorado Plateau a thousand years ago is probably to our advantage, for it steers us away from presumption and judgment.

36   I roll over again and look at the brightening stars. How fortunate we all are, I think, to have people like Euler among us, with their long-lived inquiries; to have these bits of the Anasazi Way to provoke our speculation, to humble us in this long and endless struggle to find ourselves in the world.

37   The slow inhalation of light that is the fall of dusk is now complete. The stars are very bright. I lie there recalling the land as if the Anasazi were something that had once bloomed in it.

Looking Back

1. Lopez has learned a great deal about a people who are not his ancestors but in whom he has a deep interest. What might be some reasons for this interest?

2. In paragraph 3, Lopez makes a distinction between prehistoric Indians such as the Anasazi and historic Indians such as the Lakota. Discuss what distinguishes these two groups, historic and prehistoric.

3. Reread paragraph 25 in which Lopez tells of J. B. Priestley's thoughts about the Grand Canyon. Think of an example of something that would be revealed as "cheap and ephemeral" "when stood up against" the Grand Canyon.

4. An *arbiter* is someone or something having the power to judge or decide. What does Lopez mean when he says in paragraph 25 that the land is not an arbiter now?

5. Reread paragraph 32. In a small group, discuss what you think Lopez means by the last sentence.

6. Robert Euler says that we can only infer or guess at the values of the Anasazi. Why is it important to do so?

Looking Into

1. Working with other members of a small group, write one or two persuasive paragraphs telling why it is important to study past civilizations.

2. Write two descriptive paragraphs about a place out-of-doors—rural, suburban, or urban—that you know well. Include sensory details.

3. Reread paragraph 35 and use it as the basis for an essay on what the author means when he says that life is "impenetrable."

Summer Beyond Wish

RUSSELL BAKER

Russell Baker's "Observer" column has appeared in the *New York Times* since 1962, and in 1993 he became known to many as host of television's Masterpiece Theatre.

Baker was born in Loudoun County, Virginia, in 1925. His father died at the age of thirty-three, and Russell and one of his younger sisters (the other stayed with relatives) lived with his mother in various places in Virginia and New Jersey and in Baltimore. Much of his early life is chronicled in the autobiographical *Growing Up* (1982), which won him a second Pulitzer Prize. His first Pulitzer was awarded in 1979 for distinguished commentary.

Baker graduated from Johns Hopkins University in 1947 and went to work for the *Baltimore Sun* from 1947–1954. He was London bureau chief in 1953–1954. He then went to work for the *New York Times* and was a member of the Washington, D.C., bureau for eight years where he covered the White House, the State Department, and Congress. Several collections of his columns have been published, among them *There's a Country in My Cellar* (1990) from which "Summer Beyond Wish" is taken.

Looking Ahead

Here Russell Baker writes of an unforgettable boyhood summer with his family in which "nothing of consequence happened." Notice the details that convey a sense of the period in which Baker grew up.

1   *A* long time ago I lived in a crossroads village of northern Virginia and during its summer enjoyed innocence and never knew boredom, although nothing of consequence happened there.

2   Seven houses of varying lack of distinction constituted the community. A dirt road meandered off toward the mountain where a bootleg still[1]

---

1   **bootleg still:** illegal apparatus for distilling alcoholic liquor.

supplied whiskey to the men of the countryside, and another dirt road ran down to the creek. My cousin Kenneth and I would sit on the bank and fish with earthworms. One day we killed a copperhead which was baking on a rock nearby. That was unusual.

3   The heat of the summer was mellow and produced sweet scents which lay in the air so damp and rich you could almost taste them. Mornings smelled of purple wisteria, afternoons of the wild roses which tumbled over stone fences, and evenings of honeysuckle.

4   Even by standards of that time it was a primitive place. There was no electricity. Roads were unpaved. In our house there was no plumbing. The routine of summer days was shaped by these deficiencies. Lacking electric lights, one went early to bed and rose while the dew was still in the grass. Kerosene lamps were cleaned and polished in an early-morning hubbub of women, and children were sent to the spring for fresh water.

5   This afforded a chance to see whether the crayfish population had multiplied. Later, a trip to the outhouse would afford a chance to daydream in the Sears, Roebuck catalog, mostly about shotguns and bicycles.

6   With no electricity, radio was not available for pacifying the young. One or two people did have radios that operated on mail-order batteries about the size of a present-day car battery, but these were not for children, though occasionally you might be invited in to hear "Amos 'n' Andy."[2]

7   All I remember about "Amos 'n' Andy" at that time is that it was strange hearing voices come out of furniture. Much later I was advised that listening to "Amos 'n' Andy" was racist and was grateful that I hadn't heard much.

8   In the summer no pleasures were to be had indoors. Everything of delight occurred in the world outside. In the flowers there were hummingbirds to be seen, tiny wings fluttering so fast that the birds seemed to have no wings at all.

9   In the heat of midafternoon the women would draw the blinds, spread blankets on the floor for coolness and nap, while in the fields the cattle herded together in the shade of spreading trees to escape the sun. Afternoons were absolutely still, yet filled with sounds.

10   Bees buzzed in the clover. Far away over the fields the chug of an ancient steam-powered threshing machine could be faintly heard. Birds rustled under the tin of the porch roof.

---

2   **Amos 'n' Andy:** a popular radio show depicting African Americans, thought by many to be demeaning, in part because the actors were white and spoke in dialect.

11   Rising dust along the road from the mountains signaled an approaching event. A car coming. "Car's coming," someone would say. People emerged from houses. The approaching dust was studied. Guesses were hazarded about whom it might contain.

12   Then—a big moment in the day—the car would cruise past.

13   "Who was it?"

14   "I didn't get a good look."

15   "It looked like Packy Painter to me."

16   "Couldn't have been Packy. Wasn't his car."

17   The stillness resettled itself as gently as the dust, and you could wander past the henhouse and watch a hen settle herself to perform the mystery of laying an egg. For livelier adventure there was the field that contained the bull. There, one could test his courage by seeing how far he dared venture before running back through the fence.

18   The men drifted back with the falling sun, streaming with heat and fatigue, and washed in tin basins with water hauled in buckets from the spring. I knew a few of their secrets, such as who kept his whiskey hidden in a Mason jar behind the lime barrel, and what they were really doing when they excused themselves from the kitchen and stepped out into the orchard and stayed out there laughing too hard.

19   I also knew what the women felt about it, though not what they thought. Even then I could see that matters between women and men could become very difficult and, sometimes, so difficult that they spoiled the air of summer.

20   At sunset people sat on the porches. As dusk deepened, the lightning bugs came out to be caught and bottled. As twilight edged into night, a bat swooped across the road. I was not afraid of bats then, although I feared ghosts, which made the approach of bedtime in a room where even the kerosene lamp would quickly be doused seem terrifying.

21   I was even more afraid of toads and specifically of the toad which lived under the porch steps and which everyone assured me would, if touched, give me warts. One night I was allowed to stay up until the stars were in full command of the sky. A woman of great age was dying in the village and it was considered fit to let the children stay abroad into the night. As four of us sat there we saw a shooting star and someone said, "Make a wish."

22   I did not know what that meant. I didn't know anything to wish for.

Looking Back

1. The author says he "never knew boredom." What were some of the activities that he enjoyed as a boy?

2. Which of the following does Baker use to make his descriptions vivid: sensory language, active verbs, vivid modifiers, figurative language—similes, metaphors, hyperbole?

3. What does Baker's last sentence imply about him as a boy?

4. The author seems to have been an observant child. Give some examples of this.

Looking Into

1. In a short paper, write about one of your memorable childhood summers or about one memorable incident in a childhood summer.

2. Take a poll of class members to find out the one important thing each person would wish for, excluding material possessions. Design a system to protect the privacy of class members, compile the results, and then present your findings to the class. Work with a small group to complete this assignment.

Learning from My Grandmothers

BEVERLY HUNGRY WOLF

Beverly Hungry Wolf is a member of the Blood tribe of the Blackfoot people and lives in British Columbia. She was born in Alberta in 1950, the daughter of Edward and Ruth (Beebe) Little Bear. Her father is an artist.

She attended Lethbridge College, has been a teaching assistant at St. Mary's Indian School on the Blood Reservation in Alberta, and, with her husband, Adolf Hungry Wolf, founded Good Medicine Books, a publishing company.

Among the books she has written with her husband are *Shadows of the Buffalo: A Family Odyssey Among the Indians* (1983) and *Indian Tribes of the Northern Rockies* (1991). She and her husband also edited *Children of the Sun: Stories by and about Indian Kids* (1989).

The Ways of My Grandmothers (1980), from which the excerpt in this book was taken, is largely a collection of reminiscences by older Blackfoot women and includes a detailed description of a tipi and instructions for cleaning and cooking game.

Looking Ahead

In the acknowledgements of her book, Beverly Hungry Wolf says that "by tribal custom, all the old women of the past are my grandmothers." In this excerpt she tells of her desire to learn the old ways of her people and of how her efforts to do so were sometimes discouraged.

[1]   There is a special thrill to waking up in a tipi. I think this has helped make tipi living so popular among many different people in recent years. Even among Indians there is a revival of using tipis at tribal encampments. Tipis are an aesthetic link to our ancestral past, as well as being handsome and practical dwellings to camp in.

2   This is greatly magnified when the tipi is part of a traditional holy camp, like the Sun Dance[1] of my people. We still camp according to families and bands, as part of a large tribal circle. That circle always includes most of our elders, who look forward to this annual event all year long. In addition, the circle seems to grow larger each year as more and more of our young people discover the spiritual strength that can be gained from this experience.

3   I love to wake up on an early summer morning to hear some old person singing in one of the lodges. Another old person will go around the camp circle to announce the day's events, and to add some words of advice and encouragement. This is our traditional form of news and information broadcasting.

4   But the best part of the Sun Dance encampment is that I get to visit with all my different grandmothers—my actual relatives as well as those elders with whom I have become close friends. The Sun Dance encampment makes them feel really close to their old manner of living, so this is the best time for me to learn my grandmothers' ways. I try to prepare everything for my own household as well as I can before the Sun Dance, so that I will have lots of time to spend in helping and learning with my grandmothers. They are always glad to have someone come by and do little chores for them, and this is the best way to learn how to do traditional chores right.

5   I admire the dedication that my grandmothers show for their traditional ways. It makes me realize how really hard it is to overcome the way we younger people have been raised. Nowadays we have the freedom to keep on with the modern ways, or to live by our traditional ways, if we want to. Until recently, our younger generations were not given this choice to make. But still it is hard to decide which values to use in making decisions about the ways of life we want to follow. And all the time our elders are passing away and taking their traditional knowledge with them.

6   Many of our young people have a very confused idea of what it is to really be an Indian. Even though they are free to learn about their traditions—in school they are even encouraged and taught to do so—many of them just don't seem to want anything to do with our old ways. All the

---

1 **Sun Dance:** a religious ceremony held in the middle of summer, consisting in part of the retelling of legends.

many generations of government and missionary propaganda against our old ways cannot be overcome in a few short years.

7   For instance, many young people have no knowledge about our tribal medicine bundles except to fear them. They don't understand that these bundles are sacred symbols through which our people are meant to be helped and educated. Even the children of people who are keepers of such bundles often know nothing about them, except that they are supposed to keep away. I cannot say that the parents are of any help, either, in cases like this. Perhaps because many parents are just starting to learn our old ways, too, they don't know enough to teach their children yet. Our young people need a lot of encouragement and guidance to learn about these things and to try some of them.

8   I recall that when I first started asking my grandmothers about their old ways they sometimes discouraged me and made me feel silly for having such interests. When I first started wearing long skirts and dresses even my own grandmother told me that I should stop. "You look like an old lady," she told me. Even though their belief in these traditions was very strong, they had been made to feel that there was no future in this world for their children and grandchildren if they didn't put these old ways aside.

9   But once my grandmothers saw that I was sincere in wanting to learn their old ways they were very encouraging. They didn't think any of us younger girls cared about cutting up meat properly to dry, or about putting soles on moccasins so that they wear well. I think it pleased them to know that they had something very special to offer us young people, even if it took a while for them to believe that times had changed enough to make us young people want to learn.

10 I think history about Indians has often neglected the women. We get the impression that women just did their daily work and drudgery and had nothing to look forward to or talk about. When I was young I used to think that the old-time Indian women were sold and treated like slaves, because that's what the books said. I have found out that among some tribes the women were not too well treated, but among others they were equal to the men and among some they even served as chiefs and leaders.

11 Actually, when you judge the traditional lives of my grandmothers by modern values you could, indeed, say that they had hard lives and were much mistreated. The modern woman would rebel against carrying loads of firewood home in the middle of a cold winter while her husband sat inside the house smoking and entertaining his friends. Yet my grandmothers did it for as long as they could walk, and they were not known to complain. They brought water, too, from the holes that they chopped into the

frozen river. But my grandfathers, in turn, spent countless frozen days and nights out on those same cold winter days, seeking food to kill and bring home; or defending their families from prowling enemies; or hiking several hundred miles to bring home needed horses and social honor. Times have changed so much that we can barely imagine the daily challenges faced by our forefathers. For that reason it is pretty hard to make any judgments about the ways they did things.

12   Let me just say that in the culture of my people the work of the women was generally respected and honored, for the men knew very well that they could not live without them. The people of the past thought it a great honor that the women should bear and rear the children, ensuring that there would be people in the future. Equally honorable was the women's work of creating the lodges that made the homes, taking them up and down when camp moved, heating them, and providing the bedding and clothing for the household members. In the social life of my grandmothers, a household was judged not only by the bravery and generosity of the man, but also by the kindness and work habits of the woman. Even the wife of a poor man could find honor among the people by being a good housekeeper.

13   This traditional life of housekeeping was passed from mother to daughter through daily experience, not in classrooms or from books. That is why I feel that the Sun Dance encampment is so important for the young among my people. That is also why I feel that young women should offer their help and friendship to the old. What better way is there to learn which wood burns best in a fire, and which kind of meat is best to roast? How else would I know that one of the finest rewards for being an old woman comes from going outside the camp circle early each morning, to face the rising sun and call out the names of all the children, grandchildren, great-grand-children, and friends, during a prayer that shows the old woman's thankfulness and humbleness before the Creator, and brings cheerful tears into the eyes of all those in the camp who can hear?

Looking Back

1. The author writes that "it is hard to decide which values to use in making decisions about the ways of life we want to follow." What has she done to help her make these decisions?

2. What is the value in keeping alive the skills and traditions of one's ancestors? Is such an attempt merely a nostalgic, and often fruitless, desire to return to the past, or is it something else? Explain.

3. In a small group discuss the similarities and the differences in the ways grandmothers are treated in the author's culture and in your culture.

Looking Into

1. Do you have any customs, celebrations, or sayings in your family that are handed down from your grandparents? If so, write about them in a short paper.

2. As a group, make a list of some important things that you will want to remember to tell your children. You may want to start with some of the things that you think you do well. Present your list to the rest of the class.

3. Describe the author's attitude toward the Indian past. Does she seem nostalgic, unsentimental, bitter, romantic? Write a paragraph or two in which you analyze the author's tone in this excerpt.

An Island on an Island

JILL NELSON

Jill Nelson grew up on New York's Upper West Side and graduated from the City College of New York and Columbia Journalism School. Her work has appeared in *Essence, USA Weekend, The Village Voice, Ms.,* and the *New York Times. Volunteer Slavery: My Authentic Negro Experience* (1993) is the story of her four years at *The Washington Post Sunday Magazine* and her reflections on her career and her heritage. She divides her time between Martha's Vineyard and New York.

Looking Ahead

In this article, which appeared in the *New York Times,* Nelson writes of why she cherishes a special place on Martha's Vineyard, a popular island summer resort.

—————ɱ——

1   *O*ak Bluffs, Mass.—I wake up at dawn in book-tour panic. What city am I in? What time is it? Have I slept through a major media market, left a zillion book buyers hanging—finally, after two months on the road, blown it? Lying here, I try to unscramble a tired brain before opening exhausted eyes. The acrid-sweet scent of salt drifts into my nostrils, the seductive back and forth of waves stroking sand curls into my ears, and even before I open my eyes I know I am home at last, on Martha's Vineyard.

2   Thanks to the presence of the Clintons and their entourage, the island where "Jaws" was filmed is under attack by media sharks. (It's happened before.) Big city reporters in leisure wear do live broadcasts from one of the six small towns that make up Martha's Vineyard. Hype, anticipation and paranoia reign. I wonder if the man outside my window, who has tended the flowers in Ocean Park for decades, is himself or a member of the Secret Service in disguise.

3   But I know who I am. Here, I am first myself, my mother's daughter, my daughter's mother, and then everything else. It is as it has been for 38

years; a homecoming. Growing up in New York City, we lived in apartments and moved as often as upward mobility allowed. In the city, home was a temporary shelter until something bigger and better came along. Knowing that we could not dig our roots into the earth, we wrapped them around ourselves and each other and waited until summer came.

[4] My parents first came to the Vineyard in 1956, when I was 3. My mother tells the story of how they rented a ramshackle house in the Highlands, the twisting hill community above the harbor, part of the town of Oak Bluffs, where black people first formed a summer community in the early part of the century.

[5] Oak Bluffs is like a fun-house mirror of the black middle class: here, the images expand, multiply, into a world. The children of lawyers, doctors, school teachers, engineers, Ph.D's, business people and dentists are the rule, not the exception. No one ever chants, "I am somebody." That goes without saying. If you weren't, you couldn't hang.

[6] Affirmation comes from many places, one of which is seeing yourself reflected in the world around you, in a sense of commonality, in the very unspecialness of knowing there are thousands of other folks pretty much like you in hollering distance. Nine months of the year I lived in a world where this was not the case. Where being black, bourgeois, going to private school and having parents who were hard-working professionals was perceived as aberrant. Positive, but aberrant nonetheless.

[7] It is lonely growing up as one of a few dozen black students in a school of hundreds, or the only black people in a building of thousands, living on Manhattan island in a city of seven million people where there is no certain place, no piece of land, where middle-class black people own land, live in houses, put down their roots.

[8] "It rained all week long," my mother will say of our first visit here, laughing. "But we fell in love with the island."

[9] Me, I remember splashing around in the rain with my brothers and sister, free, safe, muddy, and not having to ask permission to go outside or having to ride down in an elevator, an absence of all the fearful things city kids must know about. But these memories may be more elaborations on a tale oft heard than what was. I know what my parents fell in love with. The neat shingled houses with elaborate ornamentation on porches and eaves, the tiny, intricate, gingerbread cottages in the Campgrounds, a world all its own until Illumination Night, when each house is festooned with colored lanterns and lights and it seems the whole island wanders through, awestruck.

[10] The red, gray and ochre cliffs of Gay Head, which we used to scramble

down as children on our way to long days spent on the beach and cookouts with driftwood fires late into the night. The cliffs are now off-limits, protected, as they should be, from human erosion. But the water remains icy sparkling, somehow magical, the mussels pulled from submerged rocks as fat and sweet as ever.

11   Now, in deference to the land, we no longer cook on the beach. Instead we go to the Aquinnah Shop, founded in the early 1940's by Napoleon Madison, a member of the Wampanoag Tribe, the Island's original inhabitants. There we eat blackened bluefish burgers, washed down with a slice of superlative strawberry rhubarb pie baked by Luther Madison, Napoleon's son and the chief medicine man of the Wampanoag.

12   Like a New England dinner of steamers, sugary island-grown corn on the cob, new potatoes and lobster cooked in one big pot, the famous, infamous and regular folk blend together in a delicious island stew. The roux that holds us together is our love for the Vineyard, its sense of peace, solitude and acceptance.

13   We come to the Vineyard every summer. As children, the four of us would prepare for the long car trip judiciously, hoarding bags of penny candy and comic books. By the time we were, at best, a few hours out of the city, the candy was gone, comics were read, counting-the-license-plate game was played and the squabbling was in full swing. We fought about whatever: who was hogging the space in the back seat, who ate the last half sandwich, what radio station to listen to, who was the better group, the Temptations or the Marvelettes.

14   Now, I think the bickering was merely a prelude to entering nirvana, interstate purgatory before boarding the ferry to heaven. All summer long we rode bikes, swam in the ocean every day, went fishing, crabbing, had cookouts on the beach, picked wild blueberries, occasionally got poison ivy. We were free against the backdrop, the beauty of the island itself: winding roads, surprising views, a multitude of beaches, each with its own particular smell, taste, surf.

15   The Vineyard. The Vineyard. The Vineyard. It's like some geo-spiritual mantra chanted nine mouths of the year for nearly a lifetime; a lifeline. If I have a home, it is here, off Cape Cod, in the town of Oak Bluffs, in the house my parents bought 30 years ago.

16   I have lived many lives here. As a child with pigtails, my mother taught me to swim at the beach across the street from our house. "Stroke, down, breathe. Stroke, down, breathe," she chanted. I thought I would never get it, sinking, and then suddenly I was skimming through the water, forever. I rode the Flying Horses carousel until I could snatch eight rings with one finger.

[17] Here, I was a plump adolescent who one summer insisted on wearing a beige, waterproof, knee-length trench coat everywhere, including the beach. I had my first kiss here, at a yard party strung with Japanese lanterns, bestowed wetly by a young man whose name is irrelevant but whose appropriate nickname, Chubby Lips, is unforgettable. I went sailing and learned to dive for mussels, to boil perfect lobster and to scale, gut and fillet fish. When big changes came—when I had my daughter, had a broken heart, decided to quit my job at the *Washington Post,* finally sold my book—I came here to get sane.

[18] I lie in bed, smiling, looking at the ancient wallpaper of entwined roses. Here, familiarity breeds contentment. I climb out of bed and walk through my mother's silent house, where everything has both a place and meaning. I search for pictures, a vase from Grenada, a sweater always left hanging, my daughter's clogs by the staircase. I find them all. I sit on the wicker porch swing and watch the ocean, wave occasionally as friends, parents of friends, stride by on their morning constitutional. I check the flower and vegetable gardens, note weeding to be done. Finally, I go for an early morning dip, swim in the path the sun makes along the cold, salty water.

[19] That first morning, I walk through the town of Oak Bluffs, searching for and finding the familiar. The houses of the Finleys, Overtons, Thornes, Thomases, Smiths. The tennis and basketball courts; Waban Park, where as children we chased my father's golf balls, four for a penny; the Oak Bluff Public Library on the corner of Circuit Avenue, the main street where I have borrowed hundreds of books and now people borrow mine.

[20] Unfortunately, it is too early to get a peppermint-stick ice cream cone from Cozy's, or succulent clams from the Clam Bar, or whatever's cooking at Lobster in the Bluffs. I settle for doughnuts from the Old Stone Bakery, happily munch my way through Ocean Park, past the gazebo where the island band plays on summer Sundays, toward home.

[21] Entering, the screen door slams behind me and my mother calls from the kitchen, "Star? Is that you?" It is a nickname earned this summer, since my book was published. It is said lovingly, teasingly. It does not connote any change in family status. No one ever says, "Star, can I fetch you something?" or "Star, shall I peel you a grape?" Instead, it's the same old same old. "Star, would you do the dishes? Go to the grocery? Weed the garden?" This is as it should be.

[22] The wonderful thing about the Vineyard is that most everyone believes you're going to do well, though sometimes they're not quite sure in what or when or maybe it is that they don't care. It's what is expected, what everyone before you did and after you will do. If the black summer

community on Martha's Vineyard forms its own world, it is a world absent the assumptions of inferiority rife elsewhere. It is, I think, the absence of burden of carrying around both the negative assumptions of others, and my own. On the Vineyard, as the old spiritual goes, I can lay my burdens down.

23   Here, there is no feeling of unearned, condescending specialness so often bestowed on successful African-Americans by others, that "Golly, gosh, you're not like most black people. You're different."

24   Here, fourth and fifth generations of college graduates, advisers to presidents, writers, politicians and artists tend neat shingled houses, plant tomatoes, swim early each morning with the rest of the Polar Bears, mow lawns, have cocktail parties, play cards and tennis and talk politics and stuff. Just like everybody else. The phenomenon is that there is no phenomenon. Quiet as it's kept, this is nothing new. I'm just a link in the chain.

25   On Aug. 14, in the yard of my mother's house, we celebrated her 75th birthday. We pitched a tent, hung balloons and, since 7 in the morning, made trays of canapés. By twilight the lawn was filled with laughing, talking people, champagne glasses in hand. My mother held forth, a diminutive diva in black and silver. Miles Davis's "So What" floated through the particular air of twilight.

26   We waited until dark to pass out sparklers, lighting them on cue. My niece, Olivia, and the other children raced around the yard, squealing as white sparks flew, delighting in that remembered time when the adults, slightly high and talking intently, forgot all about them. The faces of friends and family, ages 3 to 83, glowed and became childish as sparklers sprouted from fingertips, lighting up the night and their peaceful faces. Whirling our torches in the air, we sang "Happy Birthday," cradled by the ocean on one side, the island on the other, roots firmly sunk.

27   Someone called out, "And many more," and I smiled, knowing that there will be. We are here, we have roots. We are not Halley's Comet, visible only every 75 years.

Looking Back

1. This article moves back and forth in time between past and present. Comment on the effectiveness of this structure.

2. Nelson writes from the perspective of an African American. How does this perspective influence her view of Martha's Vineyard?

3. Nelson says that "affirmation comes from many places, one of which is seeing yourself reflected in the world around you, in a sense of commonality, in the very unspecialness of knowing there are thousands of other folks pretty much like you. . . ." In a small group discuss what she means by "affirmation," whether affirmation is important, and whether what she writes about affirmation is true for the members of the discussion group.

4. Reread the quotation above. Could this statement apply to Beverly Hungry Wolf as well? Explain.

Looking Into

1. Nelson writes of the many things that make Martha's Vineyard special to her, including the geography, the food, and her mother's house. Think about these same types of things that make your surroundings unique and tell about them in a short paper or poem.

2. Write a short description of your ideal community. Where would it be located? What kinds of houses would it have? Who else would live there? What would you do during the day?

Good Housekeeping

BAILEY WHITE

Bailey White lives with her mother, Rose, in Thomasville, Georgia, where she teaches first grade, writes, and delivers commentaries on National Public Radio about rural life in the south and eccentric relatives.

Her late father, Robb White, was also a writer, but since he lived in California much of his life, the family seldom saw him. Bailey White graduated from Florida State University in 1973, moved to California, and then returned to live in Georgia. "Good Housekeeping" is from *Mama Makes Up Her Mind* (1993), parts of which appeared in various magazines or were heard on NPR's "All Things Considered."

Looking Ahead

In this essay, White writes about a memorable Thanksgiving. Analyze how she achieves her tone.

1   *I*t was the middle of November, just a month before the wedding, when my mother announced that she was going to invite the family of our cousin's bride to Thanksgiving dinner at our house.

2   "They need to get to know us on our own ground," she said. She rared back in her reclining chair. "You girls can help with the cooking. Let's see, there will be ten of us, and six of those Mitchells" (the bride's family).

3   My mother was sitting in the kitchen, dammed in by stacks of old *Natural History* magazines. Behind her a bowl of giant worms, night crawlers, was suspended from the ceiling. She uses worm castings as an ingredient in her garden compost, and she keeps the worms in the kitchen so she can feed them food scraps.

4   My sister and I didn't say anything for a while. I watched the worms. Every now and then one of them would come up to the edge of the bowl, loop himself out, swag down—where he would hang for an instant, his coating of iridescent slime gleaming—and then drop down like an arrow

into another bowl on the floor. My mother had an idea that the worms missed the excitement of a life in the wild, and she provided this skydiving opportunity as an antidote for boredom.

5   My sister was eyeing the jars of fleas on the kitchen counter, part of an ongoing experiment with lethal herbs.

6   Those worms, or their ancestors, had been there my whole life, but somehow, until this moment, it had not seemed odd to have a bowl of night crawlers getting their thrills in the kitchen.

7   "Worms," I whispered to myself.

8   "Fleas," my sister whispered.

9   My eyes fell on a rusty 1930s Underwood typewriter under the kitchen sink. It had been there as long as I could remember, the G key permanently depressed, the strike arm permanently erect. My sister and I exchanged a look.

10   "What is that typewriter doing under the sink?" I asked flatly.

11   "Why on our own ground?" said my sister.

12   "Let's see, we'll have your Aunt Thelma's sweet potato crunch, and Corrie Lou's cranberry mold," my mother said.

13   Beside the typewriter was a guide to the vascular flora of the Carolinas, a turtle skull, and a dog brush. There were hairs in the dog brush, black hairs. Our dog Smut had died fifteen years ago. I thought about the typewriter, the turtle skull, and the dog brush. I thought about the worms. I thought about the bride's family—nice people, we were told, from Bartow County—walking into this house on Thanksgiving Day.

14   "Welcome to our home," my mother would say. And she would lead them over the stacks of books, through the musty main hall, and into a twilight of clutter. They would clamp their arms to their sides and creep behind her with their tight lips and furtive eyes, past rooms with half-closed doors through which they would glimpse mounds of moldy gourds, drying onions spread on sheets of newspaper, broken pottery in stacks, and, amazingly preserved, my grandfather's ship model collection. From one room a moth-eaten stuffed turkey would blindly leer out at them. "Storage!" my mother would explain cheerfully.

15   The guests would be settled on the front porch, where they would gaze hollowly down into the garden while our mother explained the life cycle of the solitary wasp who made his home in one of the porch columns. My sister and I would pass around plates of olives and cheese brightly, trying to keep a lilt in our voices and making the guests feel "at home."

16   "You can't do it!" my sister exploded. "We can never get ready in time!"

17 "What is there to get ready?" our mother asked innocently. "Just the food, and we'll do that ahead of time. You should always do the food ahead of time, girls," she instructed us. "Then you can enjoy your guests."

18 "Mama!" my sister wailed. "Just look at this place!" She gestured wildly.

19 "What's wrong with it?" My mother peered out at the room through a haze of dust. Behind her, another worm dropped.

20 "Just look!" Louise threw her arms wide. "The clutter, the filth . . ." She spied the rows of jars on the counter. ". . . The fleas!"

21 "Don't worry about the fleas, Louise," our mother reassured her. "I am working on a new concoction, based on myrtle and oil of pennyroyal.[1] I may have the fleas under control by Thanksgiving."

22 Louise sank into a chair and looked our mother in the eye. "Mama," she began, "it's not just the fleas. It's . . ."

23 But I had come to my senses.

24 "Stop, Louise," I said. "Get up. We've got a weekend. We'll start on Saturday."

25 Louise arrived at dawn, the Saturday before Thanksgiving, loaded down with vacuum cleaners, extra bags and filters, brooms, mops, and buckets. Mama was sitting in her chair in the kitchen, eating grits and making feeble protestations. "You girls don't have to do this, Bailey. I'll sweep up Wednesday afternoon. Then on Thursday there will just be the cooking."

26 "I know, Mama," I said, "but we want to do a good job. We want to really straighten up. You'll be glad when it's all done. Eat your grits." I didn't want her to see Louise staggering out with the first load for the dump: a box of rotten sheets, some deadly appliances from the early days of electricity, and an old mechanical milking machine with attachments for only three teats.

27 Mama would not let us throw out a box of old photographs we found under the sofa—"I may remember who those people are some day"—or the lecherous old stuffed turkey with his hunched-up back and his bad-looking feet. "It was one of Ralph's earliest taxidermy efforts," she said, fondly stroking the turkey's bristling feathers down. And she let us haul off boxes of back issues of the *Journal of the American Gourd Growers' Association* only if we promised to leave them stacked neatly beside the dumpster for others to find. But she got suspicious when she caught Louise with the typewriter.

---

1 **oil of pennyroyal:** oil from the pennyroyal plant; used medicinally.

28   "Where are you going with that typewriter, Louise?" she asked.

29   "We're going to throw it away, Mama."

30   "You can't throw it away, Louise. It's a very good typewriter!"

31   Louise was getting edgy. "Mama, it's frozen up with rust and clogged with dust. None of the moving parts moves. And they don't make ribbons to fit those old typewriters anymore."

32   "Nonsense," said Mama. "You put that typewriter down, Louise. It just needs a little squirt of oil. Bring me the WD-40."

33   Louise put the typewriter down with a *clunk.* I brought a can of WD-40, with the little red straw to aim the spray. Mama put on her glasses, pursed her lips, and peered into the typewriter. *Skeet! Skeet!* She went to work with the WD-40 and a tiny, filthy rag. "You girls are throwing away too much," she said.

34   By midafternoon we began to feel that we were making progress. We could see out the windows, and we had several rooms actually in order. We had found our brother's long-lost snakeskin collection and the shoes our great-aunt Bertie had worn at her wedding; a dusty aquarium containing the skeletons of two fish; and under a tangle of dried rooster-spur peppers and old sneakers, a rat trap with an exquisitely preserved rat skeleton, the tiny bright-white neck bones delicately pinched. "Just like Pompeii," Mama marveled.

35   By the end of the day we had cleared the house out. What had not been thrown away was in its place. I had dropped a drawer on my foot, and Louise was in a bad mood. Mama's glasses were misted with WD-40. We sat down in the kitchen and drank tea.

36   "What I want to know is, where are the priceless heirlooms?" asked Louise. "You read about people cleaning out their attics and finding 200-year-old quilts in perfect condition, old coins, cute kitchen appliances from the turn of the century, Victorian floral scenes made of the hair of loved ones. What kind of family are we? All we find is bones of dead animals and dried-up plants. Where are the Civil War memorabilia, the lost jewels, the silk wedding dresses neatly packed away in linen sheets and lavender?"

37   "Well," said Mama, "you found your brother's snakeskins. And I think this rat skeleton is fascinating. How long must it have been there?"

38   "Don't ask," moaned Louise. "I'm going home."

39   On Sunday we dusted everything, swept, vacuumed and mopped the floors, washed the windows, and laundered the curtains, rugs, and slipcovers. By nightfall the house was ready.

40   "You girls have certainly struck a blow," Mama congratulated us. "This place is as clean as a morgue." We left her sitting in her chair with the worms, the typewriter, and the last three surviving fleas.

41   I walked out with Louise. "She looks a little forlorn," I said.

42   "She'll get used to it," Louise declared. "And the Mitchells will never dream that we are peculiar!"

43   Thanksgiving morning. Louise and I divided up the cooking. She made the sweet potato soufflé and the squash casserole, and I cooked the turkey and made bread. Mama spent the morning in her garden picking every last English pea, even the tiniest baby ones, because we knew we would have our first freeze that night.

44   At ten o'clock we set the table. For a centerpiece Mama put some pink and white sasanquas to float in a crystal bowl, and the low autumn light came slanting in through the windows onto the flowers and the bright water. We had built a fire in the stove, and the heat baked out the hay-field fragrance of the bunches of artemisia hung to dry against the walls. The floors gleamed. The polished silverware shone. Beneath the sweet fall smells of baking bread and sasanquas and drying herbs I could just detect the faintest whiff of Murphy Oil Soap. Louise and I stood in the middle of the living room and gazed.

45   "The furniture looks startled," Louise said.

46   "It's beautiful," I said. "And here they are."

47   "Welcome to our home. We're so glad you could come," Mama was saying to the Mitchells. "Come out onto the porch. You will be interested to see the wasp who lives there. It's a solitary wasp, quite rare . . . I know it looks a bit cleared out in here; my girls have been cleaning. Bailey, Louise, come and meet these Mitchells."

48   We sat on the porch for a while, bundled in coats, and watched the last petals of the sasanquas drift to the ground. Mr. Mitchell examined the neat, round hole of the solitary wasp with some interest.

49   "Do you have a knowledge of the hymenoptera,[2] Mr. Mitchell?" Mama asked. And she was off.

50   Mrs. Mitchell had smiley eyes and a knowing look. She leaned over to Louise and me. "It's the cleanest house I've ever seen," she whispered. We were friends. Louise and I took her to the kitchen to help with the food.

51   Other guests arrived—our brother and his family, aunts and uncles, and the bridal couple. The house was full of talk and laughter. We brought out food and more food. Everyone sat down.

52   Then, "Where's Daddy?" asked the bride.

53   Sure enough, an empty chair . . . two empty chairs.

54   "Where's Mama?" asked Louise.

---

2 **hymenoptera:** an order of insects that includes wasps.

55   "On the porch?"

56   No..

57   "In the kitchen?"

58   No.

59   "Everyone please start. The food will get cold," I said. "I'll go find them."

60   Outside, the temperature was dropping. This was the last day the garden would be green. I wandered along the path, following the scent of bruised basil until I heard voices way in the back of the yard.

61   Mr. Mitchell: ". . . and this is?"

62   "*Franklinia altamaha,* Mr. Mitchell, and quite a spectacular specimen, if I do say so."

63   "The famous Lost Franklinia of John Bartram,"[3] Mr. Mitchell murmured reverently, gazing up into its branches. "I have never seen one."

64   The sun shining through the crimson leaves of the Franklinia lit up the air with a rosey glow. Mr. Mitchell was holding her arm in his and gesturing with her walking stick. She was cradling some stalks of red erythrina berries in their black pods.

65   Mr. Mitchell turned slowly and looked over the garden. "Silver bell, shadbush, euonymous, blood-root, trillium"—he named them off. "Mrs. White, I've been collecting rare plants and heirloom seeds all my life, and I've never seen anything to equal this."

66   "It's an old lady's pleasure, Mr. Mitchell," said my mother. "Now wait till I take you to the dump and show you my bones. Louise threw them out," she whispered hoarsely, "but I know right where they are. We'll get them tomorrow, if you're interested. You will be kind enough not to mention it to my girls."

67   "It would be my extreme pleasure to see your collection of bones, Mrs. White," said Mr. Mitchell. And slowly he led her out of the pink glow and back to the party.

68   The next day Louise came over, and we went to sit in the kitchen and drink hot chocolate with Mama and congratulate ourselves on a job beautifully done. But Mama was not in her chair. There was a note on the kitchen table. It was typewritten. Every letter was clear and black and even.

> Sorry I missed you girls. Mr. Mitchell and I have gone on a little errand. Make yourselves some hot chocolate.
>
> Love,
> Mama

---

3 **John Bartram:** eighteenth-century American botanist.

Looking Back

1. The *tone* of a work is the author's attitude toward his or her subject. What is the tone of this essay? Give at least three examples of details that contribute to the tone.

2. How would you describe the relationships depicted here?

3. Give some examples of the eccentricity of the mother in this selection.

4. Is a concern for what other people think (in this case, the Mitchells) a sign of weakness or of thoughtfulness? Explain.

Looking Into

1. The priorities of family members are often not the same. Think of a time when this was true of the people with whom you live and write about the result.

2. The writer and her sister worry about what the Mitchells will think of them, their mother, and their house. Pretend you are Louise (or Louise and Bailey's brother) and write a journal entry in which you record what you fear the Mitchells might think.

The Watch

DAVID MAMET

David Mamet is a playwright, director, and screenwriter. He was born in Chicago in 1947 and grew up on Chicago's South Side. After his parents were divorced, he lived with his mother in a suburb of Chicago and went to a private school.

He attended the Neighborhood Playhouse School of the Theater in New York in 1968–1969 and received his B.A. from Goddard College in Plainfield, Vermont. He was one of the founders of the St. Nicholas Theater Company in Chicago in 1973, a teaching fellow at Yale University in 1976–1977, associate artistic director for the Goodman Theatre for the 1978–1979 season, and a guest lecturer at New York University in 1981.

His plays include *Sexual Perversity in Chicago* and *American Buffalo*, each of which won a Joseph Jefferson Award in 1975 and 1976, respectively, *Duck Variations*, *A Life in the Theater*, *The Water Engine*, *The Woods*, *Lakeboat*, *Lone Canoe*, and *Oleanna*, which he also directed.

Glengarry Glen Ross, which is set in a real-estate office, won a Pulitzer Prize in drama and a New York Drama Critics' Circle Award in 1984. Mamet also wrote the screenplay for the 1981 film *The Postman Always Rings Twice* and the 1982 film *The Verdict*, starring Paul Newman.

Looking Ahead

Notice how Mamet builds suspense in this essay about an event in his life that left him surprised, uneasy, and puzzled.

1   The Chicago in which I wanted to participate was a workers' town. It was, and, in my memory, is, the various districts and the jobs that I did there: factories out in Cicero or down in Blue Island—the Inland Steel plant in East Chicago; Yellow Cab Unit Thirteen on Halsted.

2   I grew up on Dreiser and Frank Norris and Sherwood Anderson,[1] and

---

1   **Dreiser, Frank Norris, and Sherwood Anderson:** authors who lived in and sometimes wrote about Chicago in the nineteenth and early twentieth centuries.

I felt, following what I took to be their lead, that the bourgeoisie was not the fit subject of literature.

3   So the various jobs paid my rent, and showed me something of life, and they were irrefutable evidence of my escape from the literarily unworthy middle class. For not only was I a son of the middle class, I was, and perhaps I still am, the *ne plus ultra* of that breed: a Nice Jewish Boy. And, as that Nice Jewish Boy, I went to college.

4   I went to college in the East, at a countercultural institution, a year-round camp, really, where I and those of my class griped about the war and took ourselves quite seriously.

5   The college was in the very lovely midst of nowhere in New England. It was ten miles from the nearest town; those who did not possess either an auto or a good friend with an auto were under a *de facto* house arrest on the college grounds.

6   I did not have an auto. My father was the child of immigrants, born right off the boat. He had sent his first-born son, in effect, to finishing school, and it never would have occurred to him to compound this enormity by supplying that son with the sybaritic indulgence of a car.

7   Neither would it have occurred to me to expect the same. However, I had been told, from what seems to me to've been my earliest youth, that, on my graduation from college, I'd be given a convertible.

8   It was not any car that I'd receive, it was *the convertible*. How this notion got started, I don't know. But my grandmother said it, and my father said it, and I looked forward to it as a fixed point in my life.

9   Was it a bribe, was it to be a reward? I don't know. It was an out-of-character assurance on my father's part; for he was capable of generosity, and, indeed, on occasion, of real lavishness, but both, in my memory, were much more likely to stem from impulse than from a thought-out plan. However, he had promised it, and not only had the family heard it, but we joked about it and it became, it seemed, part of our family phrase book; e.g., "Study hard, or you won't get into college, and then you know what you aren't going to get."

10   So much that I forgot about it. It was nothing to long for, or even, truly, to anticipate. The one event would bring about the other, as retirement, the agreed-upon pension—not a subject for anticipation, or, even, on receipt, for gratitude, but the correct conclusion of an agreement.

11 It was my final year at college. Graduation was to come in May, and in the preceding November I would turn twenty-one. In three and a half years at college I had learned not a damned thing. I had no skills, nor demonstrable talents. Upon graduation I would be out in the world with no money, nor

prospects, nor plan. Not only did I not care, I had given it no thought at all; and I believe I assumed that some happy force would intervene and allow me to spend the rest of my life in school.

12   Just before the Thanksgiving break my father called. He told me he was looking forward to my return to Chicago for the holiday. Now, this was news to me, as we had not discussed my coming to Chicago, and I'd made plans to spend the long weekend with friends in the East. But, no, he said, the holiday fell two days from my birthday, and it was important for him that I be back home.

13   I tried to beg off, and he persevered. He pressed me to come home, and told me that it was essential, as he *had* something for me. He was sending me a ticket, and I had to come.

14   Well. There I was. It was *the convertible,* and my father had remembered his promise, and was calling to tell me that he was about to make good on his pledge.

15   I left the phone booth smiling, and quite touched. I told my friends I would be flying to Chicago, but I would be driving back. I flew to O'Hare and took a bus downtown, and took a city bus to the North Side.

16   On the plane and on the buses I rehearsed both my gratitude and my surprise. Surprise, I knew, was difficult to counterfeit, and this troubled me. I would hate to disappoint my father, or to give him less than what he might consider his just due for the award of a magnificent gift.

17   But no, I thought, no. The moment boded well to sweep us up in sentiment free of hypocrisy on either of our parts. For was he not the child of immigrants? And was he not raised in poverty, in the Depression, by his mother, my beloved grandmother, and had we not heard countless times, my sister and I, of their poverty, and our ingratitude? And here before us was a ceremony of abundance . . . a ceremony, finally, of manhood. It was my twenty-first birthday; I was graduating from college.

18   I got off the Broadway bus, and walked down the side street, rehearsing all the while, and there, across from his building, was the car.

19   No. I had doubted. I realized that as I saw the car. No, I would admit it. To my shame. I'd doubted him. How could I have doubted? What other reason would he have had for his insistence, his almost pleading that I come back home? Of course it was the car; and I was ashamed I had doubted him. I looked at the car from across the street.

20   It was a Volkswagen convertible. It was a tricked-out model called the Super Beetle. It had outsized bubble skirts and wheels, and it was painted with broad racing stripes. I seem to remember a metallic black, with stripes of yellow and orange. I chuckled. I'm not sure what sort of a vehicle I'd expected—perhaps I'd thought he'd take me shopping, down on Western

Avenue, and we'd be buyers together, at the horse fair. I don't know what I expected from him, but when I saw that Beetle, I was moved. It was, I thought, a choice both touching and naïve. It seemed that he had tried to put himself in the place of his son. It was as if he'd thought, What sort of car would the youth of today desire? And there was his answer, across the street.

21   I thought, No, that's not my style, and then reproached myself. And I was worthy of reproach. For the gift was magnificent, and, with the gift, his effort to understand me—*that* was the gift, the magnificent gift. Rather than insist that I be like him, he'd tried to make himself like me. And if my chums thought that the car was somewhat obvious, well, they could go to hell. For I was not some kid in the schoolyard who could be embarrassed by his parents; I was a man, and the owner of a valuable possession. The car could take me to work, it could take me from one city to the next, and finally, my father'd given it to me.

22   As I walked close to it I saw the error of my momentary reluctance to appreciate its decoration. It was truly beautiful. That such a car would not have been my first choice spoke to the defects not of the car, but of my taste.

23   I remember the new car sticker on the window, and I remember thinking that my dad must have expected me to come into the building by the other door, or he wouldn't have left the gift out here so prominently. Or did he mean me to see it? That was my question, as I rode the elevator up.

24   He met me at the door. There was the table, laid out for a party in the living room beyond. Did he look wary? No. I wondered whether to say which route I had taken home, but, no, if he'd wanted to test me, he would ask. No. It was clear that I wasn't supposed to've seen the car.

25   But why would he have chanced my spotting it? Well, I thought, it's obvious. They'd delivered the car from the showroom, and he'd, carefully, as he did all things, instructed them on where it should be parked, and the car salesman had failed him. I saw that this could present a problem: if we came out of the building on the side opposite from where the car was parked—if we began what he would, doubtless, refer to as a simple walk, and could not *find* the car (which, after all, would not be parked where he'd directed it should be), would it be my place to reveal I'd *seen* it?

26   No. For he'd be angry then, at the car salesman. It would be wiser to be ignorant, and not be part of that confluence which spoiled his surprise. I could steer our progress back into the building by the other door. Aha. Yes. That is what I'd do.

27   There was another possibility: that we would leave the building by the door *near* the car, and that he'd come across it in the unexpected place,

and be off-guard. But that need not be feared, as, if I stayed oblivious to his confusion for the scantiest second, he would realize that my surprise would in no way be mitigated by the car's location. He would improvise, and say, "Look here!" That he'd surely have words with the car dealership later was not my responsibility.

28   We sat down to dinner. My father, my stepmother, my half-siblings, and several aunts. After the meal my father made a speech about my becoming a man. He told the table how he'd, in effect, demanded my return as he had something to give me. Then he reached in the lapel pocket of his jacket, draped over the back of his chair, and brought out a small case. Yes, I thought, this is as it should be. There's the key.

29   Some further words were said. I took the case, and fought down an impulse to confess that I knew what it contained, et cetera, thus finessing the question of whether or not to feign surprise. I thanked him and opened the case, inside of which there was a pocket watch.

30   I looked at the watch, and at the case beneath the watch, where the key would be found. There was no key. I understood that this gift would be in two parts, that *this* was the element of the trip that was the surprise. I'd underestimated my father. How could I have thought that he would let an opportunity for patriarchal drama drift by unexploited.

31   No mention had been made of the car. It was possible, though unlikely, that he thought I'd forgotten that the car was owing to me; but in *any* case, and even if, as was most likely, I had returned to Chicago expecting the car, such hopes would indeed be dashed before they would be realized. He would make me the present of the watch, and, then, the party would go on, and at some point, he'd say, "Oh, by the way . . ." and draw my attention to the key, secreted in the lining of the watch case, or he'd suggest we go for a walk.

32   Once again, he would keep control. Well, that was as it should be, I thought. And a brand-new car—*any* car—was not the sort of present that should be given or accepted lightly, and if he chose to present the gift in his own way, it came not primarily from desire for control, but from a sense on his part of drama, which is to say, of what was fitting. I thought that that was fine.

33   That I had, accidentally, discovered the real present parked outside was to my advantage. It allowed me to feign, no, not to feign, to *feel* true gratitude for the watch he had given me. For, in truth, it was magnificent.

34   It was an Illinois pocket watch. In a gold Hunter case. The case was covered with scrollwork, and, in a small crest, it had my initials. The back of the case had a small diamond set in it. There was a quite heavy gold chain. In all, it was a superb and an obviously quite expensive present.

35   I thanked him for it. He explained that it was a railroad watch, that is, a watch made to the stringent standards called for by the railroads in the last century. The railroads, in the days before the radio, relied exclusively upon the accuracy of the railroaders' watches to ensure safety. Yes. I understood. I admired the watch at length, and tried it in various of my pockets, and said that, had I known, I would have worn a vest.

36   As the party wound down, I excused myself from the table, and took the watch and the case into a back room, where I pried up the lining of the case to find the key.

37   But there was no key, and there was, of course, no car; and, to one not emotionally involved, the presence of a convertible with a new-car sticker on the street is not worthy of note.

38 I pawned the watch many times; and once I sold it outright to the pawnbroker under the El on Van Buren Street.

39   He was a man who knew my father, and, several years after I'd sold it, I ran into him and he asked if I'd like my watch back. I asked why such a fine watch had lain unsold in his store, and he said that he'd never put it out, he'd kept it for me, as he thought someday I'd like it back. So I redeemed it for what I had sold it for.

40   I wore it now and then, over the years, with a tuxedo; but, most of the time, it stayed in a box in my desk. I had it appraised at one point, and found it was, as it looked, valuable. Over the years I thought of selling it, but never did.

41   I had another fantasy. I thought, or *felt*, perhaps, that the watch was in fact a token in code from my father, and that the token would be redeemed after his death.

42   I thought that, *after his death,* at the reading of his will, it would be shown that he'd never forgotten the convertible, and that the watch was merely a test; that if I would *present* the watch to his executors—my continued possession of it a sign that I had never broken faith with him—I would receive a fitting legacy.

43   My father died a year ago, may he rest in peace.

44   Like him I have turned, I'm afraid, into something of a patriarch, and something of a burgher. Like him I am, I think, overfond of the few difficulties I enjoyed on my travels toward substantiality. Like him I will, doubtless, subject my children, in some degree, to my personality, and my affection for my youth.

45   I still have the watch, which I still don't like; and, several years ago I bought myself a convertible, which, I think, I never drive without enjoyment.

Looking Back

1. Does the author seem to have had a life of deprivation or privilege? What does his attitude toward his background seem to be?

2. What is the central mystery of this reminiscence, and why is it never explained? How is this mystery connected to the author's frequent fantasies?

3. What can you infer were and are the author's feelings about his father?

4. Would you have done as the author did and accepted the watch without question? Why, or why not?

Looking Into

1. Write an article that could be printed in a newspaper about a disappointing gift you have received. Try to build suspense as Mamet does.

2. With a small group, write a summary of this essay in one paragraph of eight to ten sentences.

3. Write a paragraph about a gift you would like to give a child of yours when he or she graduates from high school or college.

from Woman Warrior

MAXINE HONG KINGSTON

Maxine Hong Kingston's mother, Ying Lan, was a midwife, a field hand, and a laundry worker. Her father, Tom, was a scholar, manager of a gambling house, and a laundry worker. Hong Kingston was born in Stockton, California, in 1940 and graduated from the University of California, Berkeley, in 1962. She received a teaching certificate in 1965, and since then she has been an English teacher in California and Hawaii and a writer.

The Woman Warrior: Memories of a Girlhood Among Ghosts, from which the selection in this book was taken, won the National Book Critics Circle Award for general nonfiction in 1976 and was named one of the top ten non-fiction works of the decade by *Time* in 1979. *China Men* (1980) won an American Book Award in 1981 and was named a notable book by the American Library Association in 1980.

In addition to the two books mentioned, she has written *Hawaii One Summer* (1987) and *Tripmaster Monkey: His Joke Book* (1988). She has also written many articles and stories for various publications.

Looking Ahead

In the book from which this excerpt is taken, Maxine Hong Kingston writes of the old "ghosts" her Chinese-born parents brought with them in the form of beliefs, traditions, and stories—all familiar to her from her childhood—and the "ghosts" she faced in growing up as a child of immigrant parents. Here she recounts a talk with her mother where some of those "ghosts" reappear.

1 *W*hen I last visited my parents, I had trouble falling asleep, too big for the hills and valleys scooped in the mattress by child-bodies. I heard my mother come in. I stopped moving. What did she want? Eyes shut, I pictured my mother, her white hair frizzy in the dark-and-light doorway, my hair white now too, Mother. I could hear her move furniture about. Then

she dragged a third quilt, the thick, homemade Chinese kind, across me. After that I lost track of her location. I spied from beneath my eyelids and had to hold back a jump. She had pulled up a chair and was sitting by the bed next to my head. I could see her strong hands in her lap, not working fourteen pairs of needles. She is very proud of her hands, which can make anything and stay pink and soft while my father's became like carved wood. Her palm lines do not branch into head, heart, and life lines like other people's but crease with just one atavistic fold. That night she was a sad bear; a great sheep in a wool shawl. She recently took to wearing shawls and granny glasses, American fashions. What did she want, sitting there so large next to my head? I could feel her stare—her eyes two lights warm on my graying hair, then on the creases at the sides of my mouth, my thin neck, my thin cheeks, my thin arms. I felt her sight warm each of my bony elbows, and I flopped about in my fake sleep to hide them from her criticism. She sent light at full brightness beaming through my eyelids, her eyes at my eyes, and I had to open them.

2   "What's the matter, Mama? Why are you sitting there?"

3   She reached over and switched on a lamp she had placed on the floor beside her. "I swallowed that LSD pill you left on the kitchen counter," she announced.

4   "That wasn't LSD, Mama. It was just a cold pill. I have a cold."

5   "You're always catching colds when you come home. You must be eating too much *yin*. Let me get you another quilt."

6   "No, no more quilts. You shouldn't take pills that aren't prescribed for you. 'Don't eat pills you find on the curb,' you always told us."

7   "You children never tell me what you're really up to. How else am I going to find out what you're really up to?" As if her head hurt, she closed her eyes behind the gold wire rims. "Aiaa," she sighed, "how can I bear to have you leave me again?"

8   How can I bear to leave her again? She would close up this room, open temporarily for me, and wander about cleaning and cleaning the shrunken house, so tidy since our leaving. Each chair has its place now. And the sinks in the bedrooms work, their alcoves no longer stuffed with laundry right up to the ceiling. My mother has put the clothes and shoes into boxes, stored against hard times. The sinks had been built of gray marble for the old Chinese men who boarded here before we came. I used to picture modest little old men washing in the mornings and dressing before they shuffled out of these bedrooms. I would have to leave and go again into the world out there which has no marble ledges for my clothes, no quilts made from our own ducks and turkeys, no ghosts of neat little old men.

⁹   The lamp gave off the sort of light that comes from a television, which made the high ceiling disappear and then suddenly drop back into place. I could feel that clamping down and see how my mother had pulled the blinds down so low that the bare rollers were showing. No passer-by would detect a daughter in this house. My mother would sometimes be a large animal, barely real in the dark; then she would become a mother again. I could see the wrinkles around her big eyes, and I could see her cheeks sunken without her top teeth.

¹⁰   "I'll be back again soon," I said. "You know that I come back. I think of you when I'm not here."

¹¹   "Yes, I know you. I know you now. I've always known you. You're the one with the charming words. You have never come back. 'I'll be back on Turkeyday,' you said. Huh."

¹²   I shut my teeth together, vocal cords cut, they hurt so. I would not speak words to give her pain. All her children gnash their teeth.

¹³   "The last time I saw you, you were still young," she said. "Now you're old."

¹⁴   "It's only been a year since I visited you."

¹⁵   "That's the year you turned old. Look at you, hair gone gray, and you haven't even fattened up yet. I know how the Chinese talk about us. 'They're so poor,' they say, 'they can't afford to fatten up any of their daughters.' 'Years in America,' they say, 'and they don't eat.' Oh, the shame of it—a whole family of skinny children. And your father—he's so skinny, he's disappearing."

¹⁶   "Don't worry about him, Mama. Doctors are saying that skinny people live longer. Papa's going to live a long time."

¹⁷   "So! I knew I didn't have too many years left. Do you know how I got all this fat? Eating your leftovers. Aiaa, I'm getting so old. Soon you will have no more mother."

¹⁸   "Mama, you've been saying that all my life."

¹⁹   "This time it's true. I'm almost eighty."

²⁰   "I thought you were only seventy-six."

²¹   "My papers are wrong. I'm eighty."

²²   "But I thought your papers are wrong, and you're seventy-two, seventy-three in Chinese years."

²³   "My papers are wrong, and I'm eighty, eighty-one in Chinese years. Seventy. Eighty. What do numbers matter? I'm dropping dead any day now. The aunt down the street was resting on her porch steps, dinner all cooked, waiting for her husband and son to come home and eat it. She closed her eyes for a moment and died. Isn't that a wonderful way to go?"

²⁴   "But our family lives to be ninety-nine."

25   "That's your father's family. My mother and father died very young. My youngest sister was an orphan at ten. Our parents were not even fifty."

26   "Then you should feel grateful you've lived so many extra years."

27   "I was so sure you were going to be an orphan too. In fact, I'm amazed you've lived to have white hair. Why don't you dye it?"

28   "Hair color doesn't measure age, Mother. White is just another pigment, like black and brown."

29   "You're always listening to Teacher Ghosts, those Scientist Ghosts, Doctor Ghosts."

30   "I have to make a living."

31   "I never do call you Oldest Daughter. Have you noticed that? I always tell people, 'This is my Biggest Daughter.'"

32   "Is it true then that Oldest Daughter and Oldest Son died in China? Didn't you tell me when I was ten that she'd have been twenty; when I was twenty, she'd be thirty?" Is that why you've denied me my title?"

33   "No, you must have been dreaming. You must have been making up stories. You are all the children there are."

34   (Who was that story about—the one where the parents are throwing money at the children, but the children don't pick it up because they're crying too hard? They're writhing on the floor covered with coins. Their parents are going out the door for America, hurling handfuls of change behind them.)

35   She leaned forward, eyes brimming with what she was about to say: "I work so hard," she said. She was doing her stare—at what? My feet began rubbing together as if to tear each other's skin off. She started talking again, "The tomato vines prickle my hands; I can feel their little stubble hairs right through my gloves. My feet squish-squish in the rotten tomatoes, squish-squish in the tomato mud the feet ahead of me have sucked. And do you know the best way to stop the itch from the tomato hairs? You break open a fresh tomato and wash yourself with it. You cool your face in tomato juice. Oh, but it's the potatoes that will ruin my hands. I'll get rheumatism washing potatoes, squatting over potatoes."

36   She had taken off the Ace bandages around her legs for the night. The varicose veins stood out.

37   "Mama, why don't you stop working? You don't have to work anymore. Do you? Do you really have to work like that? Scabbing in the tomato fields?" Her black hair seems filleted with the band of white at its roots. She dyed her hair so that the farmers would hire her. She would walk to Skid Row and stand in line with the hobos, the winos, the junkies, and the Mexicans until the farm buses came and the farmers picked out the workers they wanted. "You have the house," I said. "For food you have Social

Security. And urban renewal must have given you something. It was good in a way when they tore down the laundry. Really, Mama, it was. Otherwise Papa would never have retired. You ought to retire too."

38   "Do you think your father wanted to stop work? Look at his eyes; the brown is going out of his eyes. He has stopped talking. When I go to work, he eats leftovers. He doesn't cook new food," she said, confessing, me maddened at confessions. "Those Urban Renewal Ghosts gave us moving money. It took us seventeen years to get our customers. How could we start all over on moving money, as if we two old people had another seventeen years in us? Aa"—she flipped something aside with her hand—"White Ghosts can't tell Chinese age."

39   I closed my eyes and breathed evenly, but she could tell I wasn't asleep.

40   "This is terrible ghost country, where a human being works her life away," she said. "Even the ghosts work, no time for acrobatics. I have not stopped working since the day the ship landed. I was on my feet the moment the babies were out. In China I never even had to hang up my own clothes. I shouldn't have left, but your father couldn't have supported you without me. I'm the one with the big muscles."

41   "If you hadn't left, there wouldn't have been a me for you two to support. Mama, I'm really sleepy. Do you mind letting me sleep?" I do not believe in old age. I do not believe in getting tired.

42   "I didn't need muscles in China. I was small in China." She was. The silk dresses she gave me are tiny. You would not think the same person wore them. This mother can carry a hundred pounds of Texas rice up- and downstairs. She could work at the laundry from 6:30 a.m. until midnight, shifting a baby from an ironing table to a shelf between packages, to the display window, where the ghosts tapped on the glass. "I put you babies in the clean places at the laundry, as far away from the germs that fumed out of the ghosts' clothes as I could. Aa, their socks and handkerchiefs choked me. I cough now because of those seventeen years of breathing dust. Tubercular handkerchiefs. Lepers' socks." I thought she had wanted to show off my baby sister in the display window.

43   In the midnight unsteadiness we were back at the laundry, and my mother was sitting on an orange crate sorting dirty clothes into mountains—a sheet mountain, a white shirt mountain, a dark shirt mountain, a work-pants mountain, a long underwear mountain, a short underwear mountain, a little hill of socks pinned together in pairs, a little hill of handkerchiefs pinned to tags. Surrounding her were candles she burned in daylight, clean yellow diamonds, footlights that ringed her, mysterious masked mother, nose and mouth veiled with a cowboy handkerchief. Before undoing the bundles, my mother would light a tall new candle, which was a

luxury, and the pie pans full of old wax and wicks that sometimes sputtered blue, a noise I thought was the germs getting seared.

44   "No tickee, no washee, mama-san?" a ghost would say, so embarrassing.

45   "Noisy Red-Mouth Ghost," she'd write on its package, naming it, marking its clothes with its name.

46   Back in the bedroom I said, "The candles must have helped. It was a good idea of yours to use candles."

47   "They didn't do much good. All I have to do is think about dust sifting out of clothes or peat dirt blowing across a field or chick mash falling from a scoop, and I start coughing." She coughed deeply. "See what I mean? I have worked too much. Human beings don't work like this in China. Time goes slower there. Here we have to hurry, feed the hungry children before we're too old to work. I feel like a mother cat hunting for its kittens. She has to find them fast because in a few hours she will forget how to count or that she had any kittens at all. I can't sleep in this country because it doesn't shut down for the night. Factories, canneries, restaurants—always somebody somewhere working through the night. It never gets done all at once here. Time was different in China. One year lasted as long as my total time here; one evening so long, you could visit your women friends, drink tea, and play cards at each house, and it would still be twilight. It even got boring, nothing to do but fan ourselves. Here midnight comes and the floor's not swept, the ironing's not ready, the money's not made. I would still be young if we lived in China."

48   "Time is the same from place to place," I said unfeelingly. "There is only the eternal present, and biology. The reason you feel time pushing is that you had six children after you were forty-five and you worried about raising us. You shouldn't worry anymore, though, Mama. You should feel good you had so many babies around you in middle age. Not many mothers have that. Wasn't it like prolonging youth? Now wasn't it? You mustn't worry now. All of us have grown up. And you can stop working."

49   "I can't stop working. When I stop working, I hurt. My head, my back, my legs hurt. I get dizzy. I can't stop."

50   "I'm like that too, Mama. I work all the time. Don't worry about me starving. I won't starve. I know how to work. I work all the time. I know how to kill food, how to skin and pluck it. I know how to keep warm by sweeping and mopping. I know how to work when things get bad."

51   "It's a good thing I taught you children to look after yourselves. We're not going back to China for sure now."

52   "You've been saying that since nineteen forty-nine."

53   "Now it's final. We got a letter from the villagers yesterday. They asked if it was all right with us that they took over the land. The last uncles have been

killed so your father is the only person left to say it is all right, you see. He has written saying they can have it. So. We have no more China to go home to."

54   It must be all over then. My mother and father have stoked each other's indignation for almost forty years telling stories about land quarrels among the uncles, the in-laws, the grandparents. Episodes from their various points of view came weekly in the mail, until the uncles were executed kneeling on broken glass by people who had still other plans for the land. How simply it ended—my father writing his permission. Permission asked, permission given twenty-five years after the Revolution.

55   "We belong to the planet now, Mama. Does it make sense to you that if we're no longer attached to one piece of land, we belong to the planet? Whenever we happen to be standing, why, that spot belongs to us as much as any other spot." Can we spend the fare money on furniture and cars? Will American flowers smell good now?

56   "I don't want to go back anyway," she said. "I've gotten used to eating. And the Communists are much too mischievous. You should see the ones I meet in the fields. They bring sacks under their clothes to steal grapes and tomatoes from the growers. They come with trucks on Sundays. And they're killing each other in San Francisco." One of the old men caught his visitor, another old fellow, stealing his bantam; the owner spotted its black feet sticking out of his guest's sweater. We woke up one morning to find a hole in the ground where our loquat tree had stood. Later we saw a new loquat tree most similar to ours in a Chinese neighbor's yard. We knew a family who had a sign in their vegetable patch: "Since this is not a Communist garden but cabbages grown by private enterprise, please do not steal from my garden." It was dated and signed in good handwriting.

57   "The new immigrants aren't Communists, Mother. They're fugitives from the real Communists."

58   "They're Chinese, and Chinese are mischievous. No, I'm too old to keep up with them. They'd be too clever for me. I've lost my cunning, having grown accustomed to food, you see. There's only one thing that I really want anymore. I want you here, not wandering like a ghost from Romany. I want every one of you living here together. When you're all home, all six of you with your children and husbands and wives, there are twenty or thirty people in this house. Then I'm happy. And your father is happy. Whichever room I walk into overflows with my relatives, grandsons, sons-in-law. I can't turn around without touching somebody. That's the way a house should be." Her eyes are big, inconsolable. A spider headache spreads out in fine branches over my skull. She is etching spider legs into the icy bone. She pries open my head and my fists and crams into them responsibility for time, responsibility for intervening oceans.

59   The gods pay her and my father back for leaving their parents. My grandmother wrote letters pleading for them to come home, and they ignored her. Now they know how she felt.

60   "When I'm away from here," I had to tell her, "I don't get sick. I don't go to the hospital every holiday. I don't get pneumonia, no dark spots on my x-rays. My chest doesn't hurt when I breathe. I can breathe. And I don't get headaches at 3:00. I don't have to take medicines or go to doctors. Elsewhere I don't have to lock my doors and keep checking the locks. I don't stand at the windows and watch for movements and see them in the dark."

61   "What do you mean you don't lock your doors?"

62   "I do. I do. But not the way I do here. I don't hear ghost sounds. I don't stay awake listening to walking in the kitchen. I don't hear the doors and windows unhinging."

63   "It was probably just a Wino Ghost or a Hobo Ghost looking for a place to sleep."

64   "I don't want to hear Wino Ghosts and Hobo Ghosts. I've found some places in this country that are ghost-free. And I think I belong there, where I don't catch colds or use my hospitalization insurance. Here I'm sick so often, I can barely work. I can't help it, Mama."

65   She yawned. "It's better, then, for you to stay away. The weather in California must not agree with you. You can come for visits." She got up and turned off the light. "Of course, you must go, Little Dog."

66   A weight lifted from me. The quilts must be filling with air. The world is somehow lighter. She has not called me that endearment for years—a name to fool the gods. I am really a Dragon, as she is a Dragon, both of us born in dragon years. I am practically a first daughter of a first daughter.

67   "Good night, Little Dog."

68   "Good night, Mother."

69   She sends me on my way, working always and now old, dreaming the dreams about shrinking babies and the sky covered with airplanes and a Chinatown bigger than the ones here.

Looking Back

1. What are the varying moods of the author's mother as she sits by her daughter's bed?

2. The author's mother says that when she stops working she hurts and gets dizzy. What other reasons might she have for continuing to work?

3. With which person are you more sympathetic, the daughter or her mother?

4. What are some ways in which both mother and daughter are haunted by the past?

Looking Into

1. Interview a partner about a stressful or humorous family situation that person has been in. Write an article based on the interview.

2. With a partner, write a dialogue that might take place between the mothers in "Good Housekeeping" and in the excerpt from *Woman Warrior.*

3. Pretend you are the mother in this selection. Write a diary entry in which you elaborate on the narrator's remark that "the gods pay her and my father back for leaving their parents" (paragraph 59).

Looking Around

1. What do the families in this section have in common? Write a paper in which you describe the chief differences among the families described and what might account for these differences.

2. Research the Native Americans who once lived in the area in which you now live. Is anything known about their kinship groups? If so, what? Write a brief report.

3. Many people seek to maintain close ties with the ethnic or cultural group from which they are descended, while others seem to try to sever those ties. Write about advantages and disadvantages of each way of thinking.

4. What are some of the recurrent problems and themes that characterize families? State your opinions in a short paper.

5. Do you think our society reveres ancestors and families, or does it tend to value other things more highly? Explain in an essay.

6. In a paper, discuss which families in this unit you would particularly like to visit and why.

PART 2
Working

—ᴍ—

$\mathcal{A}$s I preferred some things to others, and especially valued my freedom, as I could fare hard and yet succeed well, I did not wish to spend my time in earning rich carpets or other fine furniture, or delicate cookery, or a house in the Grecian or the Gothic style just yet. If there are any to whom it is no interruption to acquire these things, and who know how to use them when acquired, I relinquish to them the pursuit. Some are "industrious," and appear to love labor for its own sake, or perhaps because it keeps them out of worse mischief; to such I have at present nothing to say. Those who would not know what to do with more leisure than they now enjoy, I might advise to work twice as hard as they do,—work till they pay for themselves, and get their free papers. For myself I found that the occupation of a day-laborer was the most independent of any, especially as it required only thirty or forty days in a year to support one. The laborer's day ends with the going down of the sun, and he is then free to devote himself to his chosen pursuit, independent of his labor; but his employer, who speculates from month to month, has no respite from one end of the year to the other.

In short, I am convinced, both by faith and experience, that to maintain one's self on this earth is not a hardship but a pastime, if we will live simply and wisely. . . .

Henry David Thoreau from *Walden*

"Blessed is he who has found his work," wrote Thomas Carlyle, "let him ask no other blessedness." In an age that knows too well the meaning of words such as "downsizing" and "outplacement," few would disagree, except perhaps to wish that Carlyle had included women in his statement. Carlyle was talking about finding satisfying work, work to which one is suited, work that seems a "pastime," in Thoreau's words.

Work, after all, is how we must maintain ourselves, our children, and, sometimes, our parents unless we have inherited the means to do so. Most of us will work from thirty to fifty years of our lives. The selections in this section are about the necessities, virtues, satisfactions, and struggles surrounding work.

In the essay "Quality," John Galsworthy writes of a time when boots were custom-made for gentlemen and of the pride with which a pair of bootmakers regarded the results of their work. In an excerpt from *Moving the Mountain: Women Working for Social Change,* Jessie de la Cruz tells of her efforts to improve the lives of women farmworkers in the 1960s.

Naomi Shihab Nye, in "Maintenance," explores ideas that Thoreau might have found interesting about having possessions and caring for them. In his biographical essay, "Imelda," Richard Selzer, himself a physician, writes of a doctor who was one of his teachers and of the man's self-discipline and an astonishing act of humanity.

In the excerpt from *Strikes Have Followed Me All My Life,* Emma Mashinini, a South African, tells of caring for three children, working in a garment factory, and rising to supervisor and shop steward. "Memorandum" by E. B. White is the work of an individual who certainly had too much to do but who found his chosen pursuit in the labor of writing.

Quality

JOHN GALSWORTHY

John Galsworthy is best known for his short stories and for his Forsyte novels, the first of which appeared in 1906. *The Man of Property* was followed by *In Chancery* (1920) and *To Let* (1921), which with two interludes appeared as *The Forsyte Saga* in 1922. A television serial based on *The Forsyte Saga,* which follows the fortunes of three generations, was produced in 1967.

Galsworthy wrote many other novels, stories, and essays and was also a poet. In addition, he wrote twenty-five plays, many of which were successfully produced.

Galsworthy was born in Surrey, England, in 1867 into a well-to-do family. He was trained as a lawyer at Oxford and was then sent in 1891 on a series of voyages to survey the family's business concerns abroad. On one such journey in 1892, he met Joseph Conrad, who was first mate on the ship *Torrens.* Conrad was as yet unpublished, but he influenced Galsworthy to turn to writing. Galsworthy had already found the practice of law dull, and despite his father's objections, he decided to become an author.

In 1905 he married Ada Cooper Galsworthy, who had been unhappily married to Arthur Galsworthy, a cousin to John, and she greatly encouraged his writing efforts. He received the Order of Merit in 1929 and the Nobel Prize for literature in 1932. Much of his work deals with social and moral issues, often setting the rich against the poor and showing the effects of poverty.

He died at Grove Lodge, Hampstead, London, in 1933.

Looking Ahead

Galsworthy's life spanned the years before and after the end of the nineteenth century, and he deals here with the demise of the artisan and the rise of mass production in his account of two German bootmakers in a London of a bygone time.

¹ *I* knew him from the days of my extreme youth, because he made my father's boots; inhabiting with his elder brother two little shops let into one, in a small by-street—now no more, but then most fashionably placed in the West End.¹

² That tenement had a certain quiet distinction; there was no sign upon its face that he made for any of the Royal Family—merely his own German name of Gessler Brothers; and in the window a few pairs of boots. I remember that it always troubled me to account for those unvarying boots in the window, for he made only what was ordered, reaching nothing down, and it seemed so inconceivable that what he made could ever have failed to fit. Had he bought them to put there? That, too, seemed inconceivable. He would never have tolerated in his house leather on which he had not worked himself. Besides, they were too beautiful—the pair of pumps, so inexpressibly slim, the patent leathers with cloth tops, making water come into one's mouth, the tall brown riding boots with marvellous sooty glow, as if, though new, they had been worn a hundred years. Those pairs could only have been made by one who saw before him the Soul of Boot—so truly were they prototypes incarnating the very spirit of all foot-gear. These thoughts, of course, came to me later, though even when I was promoted to him, at the age of perhaps fourteen, some inkling haunted me of the dignity of himself and brother. For to make boots—such boots as he made—seemed to me then, and still seems to me, mysterious and wonderful.

³ I remember well my shy remark, one day, while stretching out to him my youthful foot:

⁴ "Isn't it awfully hard to do, Mr. Gessler?"

⁵ And his answer, given with a sudden smile from out of the sardonic redness of his beard: "Id is an Ardt!"

⁶ Himself, he was a little as if made from leather, with his yellow crinkly face, and crinkly reddish hair and beard, and neat folds slanting down his cheeks to the corners of his mouth, and his guttural and one-toned voice; for leather is a sardonic substance, and stiff and slow of purpose. And that was the character of his face, save that his eyes, which were gray-blue, had in them the simple gravity of one secretly possessed by the Ideal. His elder brother was so very like him—though watery, paler in every way, with a great industry— that sometimes in early days I was not quite sure of him until the interview was over. Then I knew that it was he, if the words, "I will ask my brudder," had not been spoken; and, that, if they had, it was his elder brother.

---

1 **West End:** area of London.

7   When one grew old and wild and ran up bills, one somehow never ran them up with Gessler Brothers. It would not have seemed becoming to go in there and stretch out one's foot to that blue iron-spectacled glance, owing him for more than—say—two pairs, just the comfortable reassurance that one was still his client.

8   For it was not possible to go to him very often—his boots lasted terribly, having something beyond the temporary—some, as it were, essence of boot stitched into them.

9   One went in, not as into most shops, in the mood of: "Please serve me, and let me go!" but restfully, as one enters a church; and, sitting on the single wooden chair, waited—for there was never anybody there. Soon, over the top edge of that sort of well—rather dark, and smelling soothingly of leather—which formed the shop, there would be seen his face, or that of his elder brother, peering down. A guttural sound, and the tip-tap of bast[2] slippers beating the narrow wooden stairs, and he would stand before one without coat, a little bent, in leather apron, with sleeves turned back, blinking—as if awakened from some dream of boots, or like an owl surprised in daylight and annoyed at this interruption.

10   And I would say: "How do you do, Mr. Gessler? Could you make me a pair of Russia leather[3] boots?"

11   Without a word he would leave me, retiring whence he came, or into the other portion of the shop, and I could continue to rest in the wooden chair, inhaling the incense of his trade. Soon he would come back, holding in his thin, veined hand a piece of gold-brown leather. With eyes fixed on it, he would remark: "What a beaudiful biece!" When I, too, had admired it, he would speak again. "When do you wand dem?" and I would answer: "Oh! As soon as you conveniently can." And he would say: "To-morrow ford-nighd?" Or if he were his elder brother: "I will ask my brudder!"

12   Then I would murmur: "Thank you! Good-morning, Mr. Gessler." "Goot-morning!" he would reply, still looking at the leather in his hand. And as I moved to the door, I would hear the tip-tap of his bast slippers restoring him, up the stairs, to his dream of boots. But if it were some new kind of foot-gear that he had not yet made me, then indeed he would observe ceremony—divesting me of my boot and holding it long in his hand, looking at it with eyes at once critical and loving, as if recalling the glow with which he had created it, and rebuking the way in which one had disorganized this masterpiece. Then, placing my foot on a piece of paper, he

---

2 **bast:** strong fiber made from ramie, hemp, or jute and woven.
3 **Russia leather:** a fine leather, often dyed dark red; originally produced in Russia.

would two or three times tickle the outer edges with a pencil and pass his nervous fingers over my toes, feeling himself into the heart of my requirements.

13   I cannot forget that day on which I had occasion to say to him: "Mr. Gessler, that last pair of town walking-boots creaked, you know."

14   He looked at me for a time without replying, as if expecting me to withdraw or qualify the statement, then said:

15   "Id shouldn'd 'ave greaked."

16   "It did, I'm afraid."

17   "You goddem wed before dey found demselves?"

18   "I don't think so."

19   At that he lowered his eyes, as if hunting for memory of those boots, and I felt sorry I had mentioned this grave thing.

20   "Zend dem back!" he said; "I will look at dem."

21   A feeling of compassion for my creaking boots surged up in me, so well could I imagine the sorrowful long curiosity of regard which he would bend on them.

22   "Zome boods," he said slowly, "are bad from birdt. If I can do noding wid dem, I dake dem off your bill."

23   Once (once only) I went absent-mindedly into his shop in a pair of boots bought in an emergency at some large firm's. He took my order without showing me any leather, and I could feel his eyes penetrating the inferior integument[4] of my foot. At last he said:

24   "Dose are nod by boods."

25   The tone was not one of anger, nor of sorrow, not even of contempt, but there was in it something quiet that froze the blood. He put his hand down and pressed a finger on the place where the left boot, endeavoring to be fashionable, was not quite comfortable.

26   "Id 'urds you dere," he said. "Dose big virms 'ave no self-respect. Drash!" And then, as if something had given way within him, he spoke long and bitterly. It was the only time I ever heard him discuss the conditions and hardships of his trade.

27   "Dey get id all," he said, "dey get id by adverdisement, nod by work. Dey dake it away from us, who lofe our boods. Id gomes to this—bresently I haf no work. Every year id gets less—you will see." And looking at his lined face I saw things I had never noticed before, bitter things and bitter struggle—and what a lot of gray hairs there seemed suddenly in his red beard!

---

4   **integument:** covering such as shell, rind, or skin.

28   As best I could, I explained the circumstances of the purchase of those ill-omened boots. But his face and voice made so deep impression that during the next few minutes I ordered many pairs. Nemesis fell![5] They lasted more terribly than ever. And I was not able conscientiously to go to him for nearly two years.

29   When at last I went I was surprised to find that outside one of the two little windows of his shop another name was painted, also that of a boot-maker—making, of course, for the Royal Family. The old familiar boots, no longer in dignified isolation, were huddled in the single window. Inside, the now contracted well of the one little shop was more scented and dark-er than ever. And it was longer than usual, too, before a face peered down, and the tip-tap of the bast slippers began. At last he stood before me, and, gazing through those rusty iron spectacles, said:

30   "Mr.———, isn'd it?"

31   "Ah! Mr. Gessler," I stammered, "but your boots are really *too* good, you know! See, these are quite decent still!" And I stretched out to him my foot. He looked at it.

32   "Yes," he said, "beople do nod wand good boods, id seems."

33   To get away from his reproachful eyes and voice I hastily remarked: "What have you done to your shop?"

34   He answered quietly: "Id was too exbensif. Do you wand some boods?"

35   I ordered three pairs, though I had only wanted two, and quickly left. I had, I do not know quite what feeling of being part, in his mind, of a con-spiracy against him; or not perhaps so much against him as against his idea of boot. One does not, I suppose, care to feel like that; for it was again many months before my next visit to his shop, paid, I remember, with the feeling: "Oh! well, I can't leave the old boy—so here goes! Perhaps it'll be his elder brother!"

36   For his elder brother, I knew, had not character enough to reproach me, even dumbly.

37   And, to my relief, in the shop there did appear to be his elder brother, handling a piece of leather.

38   "Well, Mr. Gessler," I said, "how are you?"

39   He came close, and peered at me.

40   "I am breddy well," he said slowly; "but my elder brudder is dead."

---

5 **Nemesis fell:** Nemesis was the goddess of retribution. The meaning is that the narrator was thwarted in his attempt to atone for owning factory-made boots.

41   And I saw that it was indeed himself—but how aged and wan! And never before had I heard him mention his brother. Much shocked, I murmured: "Oh! I am sorry!"

42   "Yes," he answered, "he was a good man, he made a good bood; but he is dead." And he touched the top of his head, where the hair had suddenly gone as thin as it had been on that of his poor brother, to indicate, I suppose, the cause of death. "He could nod ged over losing de oder shop. Do you wand any boods?" And he held up the leather in his hand: "Id's a beaudiful biece."

43   I ordered several pairs. It was very long before they came—but they were better than ever. One simply could not wear them out. And soon after that I went abroad.

44   It was over a year before I was again in London. And the first shop I went to was my old friend's. I had left a man of sixty, I came back to one of seventy-five, pinched and worn and tremulous, who genuinely, this time, did not at first know me.

45   "Oh! Mr. Gessler," I said, sick at heart; "how splendid your boots are! See, I've been wearing this pair nearly all the time I've been abroad; and they're not half worn out, are they?"

46   He looked long at my boots—a pair of Russia leather, and his face seemed to regain steadiness. Putting his hand on my instep, he said:

47   "Do dey vid you here? I 'ad drouble wid dat bair, I remember."

48   I assured him that they had fitted beautifully.

49   "Do you wand any boods?" he said. "I can make dem quickly; id is a slack dime."

50   I answered: "Please, please! I want boots all round—every kind!"

51   "I will make a vresh model. Your food must be bigger." And with utter slowness, he traced round my foot, and felt my toes, only once looking up to say:

52   "Did I dell you my brudder was dead?"

53   To watch him was painful, so feeble had he grown; I was glad to get away.

54   I had given those boots up, when one evening they came. Opening the parcel, I set the four pairs in a row. Then one by one I tried them on. There was no doubt about it. In shape and fit, in finish and quality of leather, they were the best he had ever made me. And in the mouth of one of the Town walking-boots I found his bill. The amount was the same as usual, but it gave me quite a shock. He had never before sent it in till quarter day.[6] I flew down-stairs, and wrote a cheque, and posted it at once with my own hand.

---

6   **quarter day:** in England, one of the four days that mark off the quarters of the year and on which, traditionally, quarterly payments are made.

55   A week later, passing the little street, I thought I would go in and tell him how splendidly the new boots fitted. But when I came to where his shop had been, his name was gone. Still there, in the window, were the slim pumps, the patent leathers with cloth tops, the sooty riding boots.

56   I went in, very much disturbed. In the two little shops—again made into one—was a young man with an English face.

57   "Mr. Gessler in?" I said.

58   He gave me a strange, ingratiating look.

59   "No, sir," he said, "no. But we can attend to anything with pleasure. We've taken the shop over. You've seen our name, no doubt, next door. We make for some very good people."

60   "Yes, yes," I said; "but Mr. Gessler?"

61   "Oh!" he answered; "dead."

62   "Dead! But I only received these boots from him last Wednesday week."

63   "Ah!" he said; "a shockin' go. Poor old man starved 'imself."

64   "Good God!"

65   "Slow starvation, the doctor called it! You see he went to work in such a way! Would keep the shop on; wouldn't have a soul touch his boots except himself. When he got an order, it took him such a time. People won't wait. He lost everybody. And there he'd sit, goin' on and on—I will say that for him—not a man in London made a better boot! But look at the competition! He never advertised! Would 'ave the best leather, too, and do it all 'imself. Well, there it is. What could you expect with his ideas?"

66   "But starvation——-!"

67   "That may be a bit flowery, as the sayin' is—but I know myself he was sittin' over his boots day and night, to the very last. You see I used to watch him. Never gave 'imself time to eat; never had a penny in the house. All went in rent and leather. How he lived so long I don't know. He regular let his fire go out. He was a character. But he made good boots."

68   "Yes," I said, "he made good boots."

69   And I turned and went out quickly, for I did not want that youth to know that I could hardly see.

Looking Back

1. What were the reasons for the failure of the Gessler Brothers' business?

2. Why do businesses fail today? Are any of the reasons the same as they were for the Gesslers?

3. What is the connection between quality of goods produced and business success?

4. In a small group, discuss and then list as many reasons as you can for why someone today would choose a custom-made article of clothing over a machine-made article.

5. Is it possible today to find satisfaction in your work? What sorts of jobs do you think would be most likely to bring fulfillment?

Looking Into

1. Think about a job you have now or have had in the past and your attitude toward that job. Describe the job and how you felt about it in a short paper.

2. Imagine that you owned a business that specialized in custom-made goods. What would you choose to make and offer to customers—clothes, shoes, motorcycles? Write an advertising brochure in which you describe your business and the reasons why customers will want your products.

3. Make a list of jobs that interest you. Then for each job give its possible advantages and disadvantages.

La Causa

JESSIE LOPEZ DE LA CRUZ

Jessie Lopez de la Cruz was born in California in 1919. Her father left the family when she was nine, and her mother and grandfather died when she was ten. Her maternal grandmother was left to care for her own six children, Jessie, and Jessie's sister. It was then that the family began the life of migrant workers in California.

De la Cruz left school in the sixth grade and married Arnold de la Cruz in 1938. They had four sons and two daughters, one of whom died as an infant. Jessie was a delegate to the Democratic National Convention in 1972, and in 1977 received an award from the League of Mexican American Women for her contribution to the farm labor movement.

Looking Ahead

Jessie de la Cruz was a union organizer for the United Farmworkers, a union begun in California, not only to improve working conditions of people who were poor and often migrants, but to improve other aspects of their lives as well. In this selection, she tells of her involvement in the union movement, which became known as *La Causa*, the Cause.

¹ Late one night in 1962, there was a knock at the door and there were three men. One of them was Cesar Chavez.[1] And the next thing I knew, they were sitting around our table talking about a union. I made coffee. Arnold had already told me about a union for the farmworkers. He was attending their meetings in Fresno,[2] but I didn't. I'd either stay home or stay outside in the car. But then Cesar said, "The women have to be involved. They're

---

1 **Cesar Chavez:** founder, along with Delores Huerta, of the United Farmworkers of America in 1962, which merged with the United Farmworkers' Organizing Committee in 1965 and became the United Farm Workers (UFW).
2 **Fresno:** city in the San Joaquin Valley in California.

the ones working out in the fields with their husbands. If you can take the women out to the fields, you can certainly take them to meetings." So I sat up straight and said to myself, "*That's* what I want!"

2 When I became involved with the union, I felt I had to get other women involved. Women have been behind men all the time, always. Just waiting to see what the men decide to do, and tell us what to do. In my sister-in-law and brother-in-law's families, the women do a lot of shouting and cussing and they get slapped around. But that's not standing up for what you believe in. It's just trying to boss and not knowing how. I'd hear them scolding their kids and fighting their husbands and I'd say, "Gosh! Why don't you go after the people that have you living like this? Why don't you go after the growers that have you tired from working out in the fields at low wages and keep us poor all the time? Let's go after them! *They're* the cause of our misery! Then I would say we had to take a part in the things going on around us. "Women can no longer be taken for granted—that we're just going to stay home and do the cooking and cleaning. It's way past the time when our husbands could say, 'You stay home! You have to take care of the children! You have to do as I say!"

3 Then some women I spoke to started attending the union meetings, and later they were out on the picket lines.

4 I think I was made an organizer because in the first place I could relate to the farmworkers, being a lifelong farmworker. I was well-known in the small towns around Fresno. Wherever I went to speak to them, they listened. I told them about how we were excluded from the NLRB[3] in 1935, how we had no benefits, no minimum wage, nothing out in the fields—no restrooms, nothing. I would talk about how we were paid what the grower wanted to pay us, and how we couldn't set a price on our work. I explained that we could do something about these things by joining a union, by working together. I'd ask people how they felt about these many years they had been working out in the fields, how they had been treated. And then we'd all talk about it. They would say, "I was working for so-and-so, and when I complained about something that happened there, I was fired." I said, "Well! Do you think we should be putting up with this in this modern age? You know, we're not back in the twenties. We can stand up! We

---

3 **NLRB:** National Labor Relations Board. The board was created in 1933 as a result of the National Labor Relations Act which protected employees' right to organize and made negotiations between employees and employers legal for the first time. Domestic workers and farmworkers were excluded by the act, however.

can talk back! It's not like when I was a little kid and my grandmother used to say, 'You have to especially respect the Anglos,' 'Yessir,' 'Yes, Ma'am!' That's over. This country is very rich, and we want a share of the money these growers make of our sweat and our work by exploiting us and our children!" I'd have my sign-up book and I'd say, "If anyone wants to become a member of the union, I can make you a member right now." And they'd agree!

5   So I found out that I could organize them and make members of them. Then I offered to help them, like taking them to the doctor's and translating for them, filling out papers that they needed to fill out, writing their letters for those that couldn't write. A lot of people confided in me. Through the letter-writing, I knew a lot of the problems they were having back home, and they knew they could trust me, that I wouldn't tell anyone else about what I had written or read. So that's why they came to me.

6   There was a migrant camp in Parlier.[4] And these people, the migrants, were being used as strikebreakers. I had something to do with building that camp. By that time, I had been put on the board of the Fresno County Economic Opportunity Commission, and I was supporting migrant housing for farmworkers. But I had no idea it was going to be turned almost into a concentration camp or prison. The houses were just like matchboxes—square, a room for living, a room for cooking, a bathroom that didn't have a door, just a curtain. The houses are so close together that if one catches fire, the next one does, too, and children have burned in them. It happened in Parlier.

7   So I went to the camp office and said I wanted to go in and visit. By this time, I was well-known as a radical, an educator, and a troublemaker! The man in the office asked what I wanted to talk about. I just wanted to visit, I said.

8   "Well, you have to sign your name here." I said, "I also would like to know when I can use the hall for a meeting."

9   "What kind of meeting?"

10   "An organizing meeting." You see, when it was built, they told us there was supposed to be a hall built for parties and whatever. I felt we could use it for a meeting to talk to the people. But he said, "We can't authorize you to come in here and talk to the people about a union, but you can write Governor Reagan and ask for permission." I left.

11   I met a nurse who had to go to this camp. She said, "Why don't you come with me as my translator?" Even though she spoke perfect Spanish!

---

4   **Parlier:** small town just south of Fresno.

So both of us went in, and she said she was from the Health Department and I was her translator. I got in there and talked to the people and told them about our union meetings, and at our next meeting they were there. I had to do things like that in order to organize.

12   It was very hard being a woman organizer. Many of our people my age and older were raised with the old customs in Mexico: where the husband rules, he is king of his house. The wife obeys, and the children, too. So when we first started it was very, very hard. Men gave us the most trouble—neighbors there in Parlier! They were for the union, but they were not taking orders from women, they said. . . .

13   We'd have a union meeting every week. Men, women, and children would come. Women would ask questions and the men would just stand back. I guess they'd say to themselves, "I'll wait for someone to say something before I do." The women were more aggressive than the men. And I'd get up and say, "Let's go on, let's do it! . . ."

14   The women took the lead for picketing, and we would talk to the people. It got to the point that we would have to find them, because the men just wouldn't go and they wouldn't take their wives. So we would say, "We're having our picket line at the Safeway[5] in Fresno, and those that don't show up are going to have to pay a five-dollar fine." We couldn't have four or five come to a picket line and have the rest stay home and watch TV. In the end, we had everybody out there.

15   One time we were picketing—I think it was the early part of 1972—White River Farms in Delano, for a new contract.[6] To go picket, we had to get up early. See, a lot of these growers were chartering buses, and at four or five o'clock in the morning they'd pick up the scabs.[7] So we would follow these labor bosses who chartered the buses.

16   At White River Farms one morning very early, we were out there by the hundreds by the road, and these people got down and started working out there in the grapes. We were asking them not to work, telling them that there was a strike going on. The grower had two guards at the entrance, and there was a helicopter above us. At other White River Farm ranches they had the sheriff, the county police, *everybody*. But there were

---

5 **Safeway:** one of the groceries in the Safeway chain of stores. The picket lines were formed to keep customers from shopping at a store that sold grapes picked by nonunion workers.

6 **new contract:** The old contract had been negotiated with Schenley Industries, who then sold the property. The new owners were uncooperative, and the UFW struck.

7 **scabs:** workers who replace striking union workers.

pickets at three different ranches, and where we were picketing there wasn't anybody except these two guards. So I said, "Hey! What about the women getting together and let's rush 'em!" And they said, "Do you think we could do that?" And I said, "Of course we can! Let's go in there. Let's get 'em out of there any way we can." So about fifty of us rushed. We went under the vines. We had our banners, and you could see them bobbing up and down, up and down, and we'd go under those rows on our knees and roll over. When the scabs saw us coming they took off. All of them went and they got on the bus. The guards had guns that they would shoot, and something black like smoke or teargas would come out. That scared us, but we still kept on. After we saw all those workers get back on the buses, we went back. Instead of running this time, we rolled over and over all the way out. The vines are about four feet tall, and they have wire where you string up the vines. So you can't walk or run across one of these fences. You have to keep going under these wires. So I tripped, and rolled down about three or four rows before I got up. I rolled so they wouldn't get at me when they were shooting. When I got out there on the road they were getting these big, hard dirty clods and throwing them at us. And then the pickets started doing the same thing. When the first police car came, somebody broke the windshield. We don't know if it was the scabs or someone on the picket lines, but the picketers were blamed.

17   When we women ran into the fields, we knew we'd be arrested if they caught us. But we went in and we told the scabs, "If you're not coming out we're gonna pull you out!" Later I told Arnold, "See? See what women can do? We got all those men out there to come out!"

18   At another place, in Kern County,[8] we were sprayed with pesticides. They would come out there with their sprayers and spray us on the picket lines. They have these big tanks that are pulled by a tractor with hoses attached, and they spray the trees with this. They are strong like a water hose, but wider. They get it started and spray the vines and the trees. When we were picketing, they came out there to spray the pickets. What could we do? We tried to get as far away as we could, and then we would come back. They had goons[9] with these big police dogs on leashes. I think they were trying to scare us by letting them loose on us. . . .

19   When the growers realized how strong we were getting and how we had so many members, when our contracts were up for renewal they called

---

8 **Kern County:** California county northeast of Santa Barbara and at the south end of the San Joaquin Valley.

9 **goons:** men hired to frighten opponents, in this case the strikers.

the Teamsters in. And even before we bargained for our new contract, the growers signed up with the Teamsters. Then they claimed they already had a union and couldn't recognize ours. That was another way they had of not signing with UFW. They were signing hundreds of what we called "sweetheart contracts."

20   Another thing the growers did to break our strikes was to bring in "illegal aliens." I would get a list of names of the scabs and give them to the border patrol. At that time, you see, we were pitted against each other, us and the people from Mexico, so it was either us or them. When I went to the border patrol office, I'd go in and say, "Can I come in?" They'd say, "You can't come in. This is a very small office." They kept telling us they were short of men. But every time I went there, there were all of them with their feet up on the desks in their air-conditioned office. They told me they were under orders not to interfere with labor disputes. So I called Bernie Sisk's office and talked to them about it.[10] Then I came home and called a lot of students who'd been helping us, and other people, and the next morning, there we were at the border patrol. I said, "We're paying our tax money, but not for you to sit here while the illegal aliens are being used to break our strike. . . ."

21   In '68, while we were in Parlier, I was put in charge of the hiring hall. My house was right next to the office, and I had an extension to the office phone in my house. I could do the housework and take care of the children, but I could take care of the office, too. Before the contract, the hiring hall was just a union office, where people came to learn about the union. When they got the first contracts, we began dispatching people out to work.

22   It was up to me to get all the membership cards in order alphabetically. When the grower came to us to ask for workers, I'd look for the ones who were in the union longest, and also working under the Christian Brothers contract. I'd call them: "Can you be ready Monday or Wednesday morning? Be there on time, because you're going to start working for Christian Brothers." One of the things we had to explain over and over to people who had been working for a ranch many years was that no one was going to take their jobs away. The growers told them, "If you sign up for Chavez's union we'll fire you." But the union contract guarantees that the people working here have the right to stay here, so we always made a list of names of people who were working at the ranch. And when the union organizes them, they have the highest seniority, they're the first ones hired.

---

10   **Bernie Sisk:** a Democratic congressman who, at the time, was sympathetic to farmworkers.

23   The hiring hall was also a place where people could meet and talk. A lot of people were migrants who needed to get to know each other. The people who were there all the time were against the migrants. I said, "We have to get these people together. We can't be divided." I was at the hall all day. People would drop by and I'd introduce them.

24 The second year we had a contract I started working for Christian Brothers. The men were doing the pruning on the grape vines. After they did the pruning, the women's crew would come and tie the vines—that was something we got changed. We made them give pruning jobs to women.

25   I was made a steward on the women's crew.[11] If there were any grievances, it was up to me to listen and then enforce the contract. For example, the first time we were paid when I started working, during the break the supervisor would come out there with our checks. It was our fifteen-minute break, which the contract gave us the right to. He always came then! We had to walk to the other end of the row, it took us about five minutes to get there, the rest of the fifteen to get our checks, and walk back, and we'd start working. This happened twice. The third time I said, "We're not going to go after our checks this time. They always come during our break and we don't get to rest." So when we saw the pickup coming with the men who had the checks I said, "Nobody move. You just sit here." I walked over to the pickup. I said to the man inside, "Mr. Rager, these women refuse to come out here on their break time. It's their time to rest. So we're asking you, if you must come during our rest period, you take the checks to these ladies." From that day on, every payday he would come to us. That was the sort of thing you had to do to enforce the contract.

26 I became involved in many of the activities in the community—school board meetings, city council meetings, everything that I could get into. For example, I began fighting for bilingual education in Parlier, went to a lot of meetings about it and spoke about it. . . .

27   Parlier is over eighty-five percent Chicano, yet during that time there were no Chicanos on the school board, on the police force, nowhere. Now it's changed; we fought to get a Chicano mayor and officials. But then I was asking people, "Why are we always asked to go to the public school for our meetings? Why can't they come over to our side of town in Parli-

---

11   **steward:** usually called a shop steward, a union person elected by the workers to represent them in any dealings with management.

er?" So we began having meetings in *la colonia* at the Headstart Center, and there we pushed for bilingual education.

[28] Fresno County didn't give food stamps to the people—only surplus food. There were no vegetables, no meat, just staples like whole powdered milk, cheese, butter. At the migrant camp in Parlier, the people were there a month and a half before work started, and since they'd borrowed money to get to California, they didn't have any food. I'd drive them into Fresno to the welfare department and translate for them, and they'd get food, but half of it they didn't eat. We heard about other counties where they had food stamps to go to the store and buy meat and milk and fresh vegetables for the children. So we began talking about getting that in Fresno. Finally, we had Senate hearings at the Convention Center in Fresno. There were hundreds of people listening. A man I know comes to me and says, "Jessie, you're next." He'd been going to speak, but he said he wanted me to speak in his place. I started in Spanish, and the senators were looking at each other, you know, saying, "What's going on?" So then I said, "Now, for the benefit of those who can't speak Spanish, I'll translate. They tell us there's no money for food stamps for poor people. But if there is money enough to fight a war in Vietnam, and if there is money enough for Governor Reagan's wife to buy a three-thousand-dollar dress for the Inauguration Ball, there should be money enough to feed these people. The nutrition experts say surplus food is full of vitamins. I've taken a look at that food, this cornmeal, and I've seen them come up and down. But you know, we don't call them vitamins, we call them weevils!" Everybody began laughing and whistling and shouting. In the end, we finally got food stamps for the people in Fresno County.

Looking Back

1. Why did de la Cruz want to organize the women farmworkers and why hadn't the women been union members before her efforts?

2. What personal qualities contributed to de la Cruz's success in your opinion?

3. Why is organized effort sometimes necessary to overcome oppression?

4. What are some causes today that might require organized action to remedy?

Looking Into

1. Attempts to unionize workers and workers' insistence on their rights have frequently resulted in violence. In a paper, analyze one such incident in history. You may want to research the lives of some well-known union leaders such as Samuel Gompers, John L. Lewis, or Cesar Chavez. Alternatively, you might focus your research on one group of workers such as farmworkers, garment workers, packing house workers, or mine workers.

2. Imagine that you are a migrant farm worker. Write a journal entry in which you describe either a typical work day, or an instance of injustice and oppression that you have encountered. If you are a migrant farm worker, write a journal entry describing your actual experiences.

Maintenance

NAOMI SHIHAB NYE

Naomi Shihab Nye has published three major collections of poems: *Different Ways to Pray* (1980), *Hugging the Jukebox* (1982), and *Yellow Glove* (1986). She has also selected poems from around the world for *This Same Sky* (1992), a poetry anthology, and has published short stories and essays.

Nye was born in St. Louis in 1952, and she spent her high school years in Ramallah, Jordan, Old City Jerusalem, and San Antonio. In 1974 she received a B.A. in English and world religions from Trinity University. She has been a writer in residence at schools in several states and has taught at the University of California in Berkeley and in San Antonio at the University of Texas and Our Lady of the Lake. She has also been on speaking tours in the Middle East and Asia for the United States Information Agency. In 1988 she received the Academy of American Poets' I.B. Lavan Award.

Looking Ahead

In this wide-ranging essay, Nye describes various philosophies about living, explores her own ideas about cleaning, and comments on Henry David Thoreau.

1   *T*he only maid I ever had left messages throughout our house: *Lady as I was cleaning your room I heard a mouse and all the clothes in your closet fell down to the floor there is too many dresses in there take a few off. Your friend Marta Alejandro.* Sometimes I'd find notes stuck into the couch with straight pins. *I cannot do this room today bec. St. Jude came to me in a dream and say it is not safe.* Our darkroom was never safe because the devil liked dark places and also the enlarger had an eye that picked up light and threw it on Marta. She got sick and had to go to a doctor who gave her green medicine that tasted like leaves.

2   Sometimes I'd come home to find her lounging in the bamboo chair on the back porch, eating melon, or lying on the couch with a bowl of half-

melted ice cream balanced on her chest. She seemed depressed by my house. She didn't like the noise the vacuum made. Once she waxed the bathtub with floor wax. I think she was experimenting.

3   Each Wednesday I paid Marta ten dollars—that's what she asked for. When I raised it to eleven, then thirteen, she held the single dollars away from the ten as if they might contaminate it. She did not seem happy to get raises, and my friends (who paid her ten dollars each for the other days of the week) were clearly unhappy to hear about it. After a while I had less work of my own and less need for help, so I found her a position with two gay men who lived in the neighborhood. She called once to say she liked them very much because mostly what they wanted her to do was shine. Shine?

4   "You know, silver. They have a lot of bowls. They have real beautiful spoons not like your spoons. They have a big circle tray that shines like the moon."

5 My friend Kathy had no maid and wanted none. She ran ten miles a day and lived an organized life. Once I brought her a gift—a blue weaving from Guatemala, diagonal patterns of thread on sticks—and she looked at it dubiously. "Give it to someone else," she said. "I really appreciate your thinking of me, but I try not to keep things around here." Then I realized how bare her mantel was. Who among us would fail to place *something* on a mantel? A few shelves in her kitchen also stood empty, and not the highest ones either.

6   Kathy had very definite methods of housekeeping. When we'd eat dinner with her she'd rise quickly, before dessert, to scrape each plate and place it in one side of her sink to soak. She had Tupperware containers already lined up for leftovers and a soup pan with suds ready for the silverware. If I tried to help she'd slap at my hand. "Take care of your own kitchen," she'd say, not at all harshly. After dessert she'd fold up the card table we'd just eaten on and place it against the wall. Dining rooms needed to be swept after meals, and a stationary table just made sweeping more difficult.

7   Kathy could listen to any conversation and ask meaningful questions. She always seemed to remember what anybody said—maybe because she'd left space for it. One day she described having grown up in west Texas in a house of twelve children, the air jammed with voices, crosscurrents, the floors piled with grocery bags, mountains of tossed-off clothes, toys, blankets, the clutter of her sisters' shoes. That's when she decided to have only one pair of shoes at any time, running shoes, though she later revised this to include a pair of sandals.

8   Somehow I understood her better then, her tank tops and wiry arms
. . . She ran to shake off dust. She ran to leave it all behind.

9 Another friend, Barbara, lived in an apartment but wanted to live in a
house. Secretly I loved her spacious domain, perched high above the city
with a wide sweep of view, but I could understand the wish to plant one's
feet more firmly on the ground. Barbara has the best taste of any person
I've ever known—the best khaki-colored linen clothing, the best books,
the name of the best masseuse. When I'm with her I feel uplifted, excited by
life; there's so much to know about that I haven't heard of yet, and Barbara
probably has. So I agreed to help her look.

10   We saw one house where walls and windows had been sheathed in
various patterns of gloomy brocade. We visited another where the kitchen
had been removed because the owners only ate in restaurants. They had a
tiny office refrigerator next to their bed which I peeked into after they'd left
the room: orange juice in a carton, coffee beans. A Krups coffee maker on
the sink in their bathroom. They seemed unashamed, shrugging, "You
could put a new kitchen wherever you like."

11   Then we entered a house that felt unusually vivid, airy, and hard-to-
define until the realtor mentioned, "Have you noticed there's not a stick of
wood anywhere in this place? No wood furniture, not even a wooden salad
bowl, I'd bet. These people, very hip, you'd like them, want wood to stay
in forests. The man says wood makes him feel heavy."

12   Barbara and her husband bought that house—complete with pear-
shaped swimming pool, terraces of pansies, plum trees, white limestone
rock gardens lush with succulents—but they brought wood into it. Never
before had I been so conscious of things like wooden cutting boards. I helped
them unpack and stroked the sanded ebony backs of African animals.

13   Then, after about a year and a half, Barbara called to tell me they were
selling the house. "You won't believe this," she said, "but we've decided.
It's the maintenance—the yardmen, little things always breaking—I'm so
busy assigning chores I hardly have time for my own work anymore. A
house really seems ridiculous to me now. If I want earth I can go walk in a
park."

14   I had a new baby at the time and everything surprised me. My mouth
dropped open, oh yes. I was living between a mound of fresh cloth diapers
and a bucket of soiled ones, but I agreed to participate in the huge garage
sale Barbara was having.

15   "That day," Barbara said later, "humanity sank to a new lowest level."
We had made signs declaring the sale would start at 9 A.M., but by 8,
middle-aged women and men were already ripping our boxes open, lung-

ing into the back of my loaded pickup truck to see what I had. Two women argued in front of me over my stained dish drainer. I sold a kerosene heater which we'd never lit and a stack of my great-uncle's rumpled tablecloths, so large they completely engulfed an ironing board. One women flashed a charm with my initial on it under my nose, saying, "I'd think twice about selling this, sweetheart—don't you realize it's ten carat?"

16 Afterwards we counted our wads of small bills and felt drained, diluted. We had spent the whole day bartering in a driveway, releasing ourselves from the burden of things we did not need. We even felt disgusted by the thought of eating—yet another means of accumulation—and would derive no pleasure from shopping, or catalogues, for at least a month.

17 While their new apartment was being refurbished, Barbara and her husband lived in a grand hotel downtown. She said it felt marvelous to use all the towels and have fresh ones appear on the racks within hours. Life seemed to regain its old recklessness. Soon they moved back to the same windswept apartment building they'd left, but to a higher floor. Sometimes I stood in their living room staring out at the horizon, which always seemed flawlessly clean.

18 My mother liked to sing along to records while she did housework—Mahalia Jackson, the Hallelujah Chorus. Sometimes we would sing duets, "Tell Me Why" and "Nobody Knows the Trouble I've Seen." I felt lucky my mother was such a clear soprano. We also sang while preparing for the big dinners my parents often gave, while folding the napkins or decorating little plates of hummus with olives and radishes.

19 I hungrily savored the tales told by the guests, the wild immigrant fables and metaphysical links. My mother's favorite friend, a rail-thin vegetarian who had once been secretary to Aldous Huxley,[1] conversed passionately with a Syrian who was translating the Bible from Aramaic, then scolded me for leaving a mound of carrots on my plate.

20 "I'm not going to waste them!" I said. "I always save carrots for last because I love them best."

21 I thought this would please her, but she frowned. "Never save what you love, dear. You know what might happen? You may lose it while you are waiting."

22 It was difficult to imagine losing the carrots—what were they going to do, leap off my plate?—but she continued.

---

1 **Aldous Huxley** (1894–1963): English writer, perhaps best known for *Brave New World*. He lived in California for much of his life.

23   "Long ago I loved a man very much. He had gone on a far journey—our relationship had been delicate—and I waited anxiously for word from him. Finally a letter arrived and I stuffed it into my bag, trembling, thinking I would read it later on the train. Would rejoice in every word, was what I thought, but you know what happened? My purse was snatched away from me—stolen!—before I boarded the train. Things like that didn't even happen much in those days. I never saw the letter again—and I never saw my friend again either."

24   A pause swallowed the room. My mother rose to clear the dishes. Meaningful glances passed. I knew this woman had never married. When I asked why she hadn't written to him to say she lost the letter, she said, "Don't you see, I also lost the only address I had for him."

25   I thought about this for days. Couldn't she have tracked him down? Didn't she know anyone else who might have known him and forwarded a message? I asked my mother, who replied that love was not easy.

26   Later my mother told me about a man who had carried a briefcase of important papers on a hike because he was afraid they might get stolen from the car. The trail wove high up the side of a mountain, between stands of majestic piñon. As he leaned over a rocky gorge to breathe the fragrant air, his fingers slipped and the briefcase dropped down into a narrow crevasse. They heard it far below, clunking into a deep underground pool. My mother said the man fell to the ground and sobbed.

27   The forest ranger whistled when they brought him up to the spot. "Hell of an aim!" He said there were some lost things you just had to say goodbye to, "like a wedding ring down a commode." My parents took the man to Western Union so he could telegraph about the lost papers, and the clerk said, "Don't feel bad, every woman drops an earring down a drain once in her life." The man glared. "This was not an earring—*I am not a woman!*"

28   I thought of the carrots, and the letter, when I heard his story. And of my American grandmother's vintage furniture, sold to indifferent buyers when I was still a child, too young even to think of antique wardrobes or bed frames. And I also thought of another friend of my parents, Peace Pilgrim, who walked across America for years, lecturing about inner peace and world peace. A single, broad pocket in her tunic contained all her worldly possessions: a toothbrush, a few postage stamps, a ballpoint pen. She had no bank account behind her and nothing in storage. Her motto was, "I walk till given shelter, I fast till given food." My father used to call her a freeloader behind her back, but my mother recognized a prophet when she saw one. I grappled with the details. How would it help humanity if I slept in a cardboard box under a bridge?

[29]   Peace Pilgrim told a story about a woman who worked hard so she could afford a certain style of furniture—French provincial, I think. She struggled to pay for insurance to protect it and rooms large enough to house it. She worked so much she hardly ever got to sit on it. "Then her life was over. And what kind of a life was that?"

[30] Peace Pilgrim lived so deliberately she didn't even have colds. Shortly before her death in a car accident—for years she hadn't even ridden in cars—she sat on the fold-out bed in our living room, hugging her knees. I was grown by then, but all our furniture was still from thrift stores. She invited me to play the piano and sing for her, which I did, as she stared calmly around the room. "I loved to sing as a child," she said. "It is nice to have a piano."

[31] In my grandmother's Palestinian village, the family has accumulated vast mounds and heaps of woolly comforters, stacking them in great wooden cupboards along the walls. The blankets smell pleasantly like sheep and wear coverings of cheerful gingham, but no family—not even our huge one on the coldest night—could possibly use that many blankets. My grandmother smiled when I asked her about them. She said people should have many blankets and head scarves to feel secure.

[32]   I took a photograph of her modern refrigerator, bought by one of the emigrant sons on a visit home from America, unplugged in a corner and stuffed with extra yardages of cloth and old magazines. I felt like one of those governmental watchdogs who asks how do you feel knowing your money is being used this way? My grandmother seemed nervous whenever we sat near the refrigerator, as if a stranger who refused to say his name had entered the room.

[33] I never felt women were more doomed to housework than men; I thought women were lucky. Men had to maintain questionably pleasurable associations with less tangible elements—mortgage payments, fan belts and alternators, the IRS. I preferred sinks, and the way people who washed dishes immediately became exempt from after-dinner conversation. I loved to plunge my hands into tubs of scalding bubbles. Once my father reached in to retrieve something and reeled back, yelling, "Do you always make it this hot?" My parents got a dishwasher as soon as they could, but luckily I was out of college by then and never had to touch it. To me it only seemed to extend the task. You rinse, you bend and arrange, you measure soap—and it hasn't even started yet. How many other gratifications were as instant as the old method of washing dishes?

34   But it's hard to determine how much pleasure someone else gets from an addiction to a task. The neighbor woman who spends hours pinching off dead roses and browned lilies, wearing her housecoat and dragging a hose, may be as close as she comes to bliss, or she may be feeling utterly miserable. I weigh her sighs, her monosyllables about weather. Endlessly I compliment her yard. She shakes her head—"It's a lot of work." For more than a year she tries to get her husband to dig out an old stump at one corner but finally gives up and plants bougainvillea in it. The vibrant splash of pink seems to make her happier than anything else has in a long time.

35 Certain bylaws: If you have it, you will have to clean it. Nothing stays clean long. No one else notices your messy house as much as you do; they don't know where things are supposed to go anyway. It takes much longer to clean a house than to mess it up. Be suspicious of any cleaning agent (often designated with a single alphabetical letter, like C or M) that claims to clean everything from floors to dogs. Never install white floor tiles in the bathroom if your family members have brown hair. Cloth diapers eventually make the best rags—another reason beyond ecology. Other people's homes have charisma, charm, because you don't have to know them inside out. If you want high ceilings you may have to give up closets. (Still, as a neighbor once insisted to me, "high ceilings make you a better person.") Be wary of vacuums with headlights; they burn out in a month. A broom, as one of my starry-eyed newlywed sisters-in-law once said, *does a lot*. So does a dustpan. Whatever you haven't touched, worn, or eaten off of in a year should be passed on; something will pop up immediately to take its place.

36   I can't help thinking about these things—I live in the same town where Heloise lives.[2] And down the street, in a shed behind his house, a man produces orange-scented wood moisturizer containing beeswax. You rub it on three times, let it sit, then buff it off. Your house smells like a hive in an orchard for twenty-four hours.

37   I'd like to say a word, just a short one, for the background hum of lesser, unexpected maintenances that can devour a day or days—or a life, if one is not careful. The scrubbing of the little ledge above the doorway belongs in this category, along with the thin lines of dust that quietly gather on bookshelves in front of the books. It took me an hour working with a bent wire to unplug the bird feeder, which had become clogged with fuzzy

---

2 **Heloise**: columnist and author of various types of household hints, having chiefly to do with cleaning.

damp seed—no dove could get a beak in. And who would ever notice? The doves would notice. I am reminded of Buddhism whenever I undertake one of these invisible tasks: one acts, without any thought of reward or foolish notion of glory.

[38] Perhaps all cleaning products should be labeled with additional warnings, as some natural-soap companies have taken to philosophizing right above the price tag. Bottles of guitar polish might read: "If you polish your guitar, it will not play any better. People who close their eyes to listen to your song will not see the gleaming wood. But you may feel more intimate with the instrument you are holding."

[39] Sometimes I like the preparation for maintenance, the motions of preface, better than the developed story. I like to move all the chairs off the back porch many hours before I sweep it. I drag the mop and bucket into the house in the morning even if I don't intend to mop until dusk. This is related to addressing envelopes months before I write the letters to go inside.

[40] Such extended prefacing drives my husband wild. He comes home and can read the house like a mystery story—small half-baked clues in every room. I get out the bowl for the birthday cake two days early. I like the sense of house as still life, on the road to becoming. Why rush to finish? You will only have to do it over again, sooner. I keep a proverb from Thailand above my towel rack: "Life is so short / we must move very slowly." I believe what it says.

[41] My Palestinian father was furious with me when, as a teenager, I impulsively answered a newspaper ad and took a job as a maid. A woman, bedfast with a difficult pregnancy, ordered me to scrub, rearrange, and cook—for a dollar an hour. She sat propped on pillows, clicking her remote control, glaring suspiciously whenever I passed her doorway. She said her husband liked green Jell-O with fresh fruit. I was slicing peaches when the oven next to me exploded, filling the house with heavy black smoke. My meat loaf was only half baked. She shrieked and cried, blaming it on me, but how was I responsible for her oven?

[42] It took me a long time to get over my negative feelings about pregnant women. I found a job scooping ice cream and had to wrap my swollen wrists in heavy elastic bands because they hurt so much. I had never considered what ice cream servers went through.

[43] These days I wake up with good intentions. I pretend to be my own maid. I know the secret of travelers: each time you leave your home with a few suitcases, books, and note pads, your maintenance shrinks to a lovely

tiny size. All you need to take care of is your own body and a few changes of clothes. Now and then, if you're driving, you brush the pistachio shells off the seat. I love ice chests and miniature bottles of shampoo. Note the expansive breath veteran travelers take when they feel the road spinning open beneath them again.

44 Somewhere close behind me the outline of Thoreau's small cabin plods along, a ghost set on haunting. It even has the same rueful eyes Henry David had in the portrait in his book. A wealthy woman with a floral breakfast nook once told me I would "get over him" but I have not—documented here, I have not.

45 Marta Alejandro, my former maid, now lives in a green outbuilding at the corner of Beauregard and Madison. I saw her recently, walking a skinny wisp of a dog and wearing a bandanna twisted and tied around her waist. I called to her from my car. Maybe I only imagined she approached me reluctantly. Maybe she couldn't see who I was.

46 But then she started talking as if we had paused only a second ago. "Oh hi I was very sick were you? The doctor said it has to come to everybody. Don't think you can escape! Is your house still as big as it used to be?"

Looking Back

1. Is maintenance work or pleasure, according to the author? (Recall her comments about housework on pages 78 and 79 and the stories of people who owned little.)

2. One of the author's bylaws is, "If you have it, you will have to clean it." Can you think of any exceptions? Explain.

3. How would you describe the organization of this essay?

4. Do women and men have different ideas about maintenance? What evidence do you have to support your views? Discuss in a small group.

5. Peace Pilgrim leads a very simple life. Do you think it would be worth it to live such a stripped-down, plain life in order to reduce or eliminate the chores of maintenance? Explain.

Looking Into

1. Analyze your own living space and the things in it. In your journal, tell what your private environment would reveal to someone who did not know you.

2. Summarize the main idea of this essay in one or two sentences.

3. Write two paragraphs. In the first paragraph, describe those household chores that you dislike. In a second paragraph, describe those tasks that you enjoy doing.

Imelda

RICHARD SELZER

In his autobiography *Down from Troy: a Doctor Comes of Age* (1992), Richard Selzer describes his boyhood in Troy, New York, where he was born in 1928. His father was Julius Louis Selzer, also a doctor, and his mother was Gertrude Schneider Selzer. He fulfilled both their ambitions for him by becoming a doctor and a writer.

Selzer received his B.S. degree in 1948 from Union College in Schenectady and his M.D. from Albany Medical College in 1953. He did postdoctoral study at Yale University Medical School from which he recently retired as professor of surgery. His books include *Rituals of Surgery* (1974), *Mortal Lessons* (1977), *Confessions of a Knife* (1979), *Letters to a Young Dr.* (1982), from which "Imelda" is taken, and *Raising the Dead* (1994).

Selzer has been a resident scholar at the Rockefeller Foundation's Bellagio Study Center and has won a National Magazine Award, an American Medical Writer's Award, and a Guggenheim Award.

Looking Ahead

Here Selzer recalls his professor of surgery, a remarkably dedicated man who performed an unusual act.

¹ *I* heard the other day that Hugh Franciscus had died. I knew him once. He was the Chief of Plastic Surgery when I was a medical student at Albany Medical College. Dr. Franciscus was the archetype of the professor of surgery—tall, vigorous, muscular, as precise in his technique as he was impeccable in his dress. Each day a clean lab coat monkishly starched, that sort of thing. I doubt that he ever read books. One book only, that of the human body, took the place of all others. He never raised his eyes from it. He read it like a printed page as though he knew that in the calligraphy there just beneath the skin were all the secrets of the world. Long before it

became visible to anyone else, he could detect the first sign of granulation[1] at the end of the base of a wound, the first blue line of new epithelium[2] at the periphery that would tell him that a wound would heal, or the barest hint of necrosis[3] that presaged failure. This gave him the appearance of a prophet. "This skin graft will take," he would say, and you must believe beyond all cyanosis, exudation and inflammation that it would.[4]

2   He had enemies, of course, who said he was arrogant, that he exalted activity for its own sake. Perhaps. But perhaps it was no more than the honesty of one who knows his own worth. Just look at a scalpel, after all. What a feeling of sovereignty, megalomania even, when you know that it is you and you alone who will make certain of it. It was said, too, that he was a ladies' man. I don't know about that. It was all rumor. Besides, I think he had other things in mind than mere living. Hugh Franciscus was a zealous hunter. Every fall during the season he drove upstate to hunt deer. There was a glass-front case in his office where he showed his guns. How could he shoot a deer? we asked. But he knew better. To us medical students he was heroic, someone made up of several gods, beheld at a distance, and always from lesser height. If he had grown accustomed to his miracles, we had not. He had no close friends on the staff. There was something a little sad in that. As though once long ago he had been flayed by friendship and now the slightest breeze would hurt. Confidences resulted in dishonor. Perhaps the person in whom one confided would scorn him, betray. Even though he spent his days among those less fortunate, weaker than he—the sick, after all—Franciscus seemed aware of an air of personal harshness in his environment to which he reacted by keeping his own counsel, by a certain remoteness. It was what gave him the appearance of being haughty. With the patients he was forthright. All the facts laid out, every question anticipated and answered with specific information. He delivered good news and bad with the same dispassion.

3   I was a third-year student, just turned onto the wards for the first time, and clerking on Surgery. Everything—the operating room, the morgue, the emergency room, the patients, professors, even the nurses—was terrifying. One picked one's way among the mines and booby traps of the hospital, hoping only to avoid the hemorrhage and perforation of disgrace. The opportunity for humiliation was everywhere.

---

1 **granulation:** the formation of new tissue around a wound as it heals.
2 **epithelium:** protective tissue such as the epidermis.
3 **necrosis:** death of a tissue or organ.
4 **cyanosis, exudation, and inflammation:** blueness of the skin, a discharge from an infected area, and redness or swelling.

4   It all began on Ward Rounds. Dr. Franciscus was demonstrating a cross-leg flap graft he had constructed to cover a large fleshy defect in the leg of a merchant seaman who had injured himself in a fall. The man was from Spain and spoke no English. There had been a comminuted fracture of the femur, much soft tissue damage, necrosis. After weeks of débridement[5] and dressings, the wound had been ready for grafting. Now the patient was in his fifth postoperative day. What we saw was a thick web of pale blue flesh arising from the man's left thigh, and which had been sutured to the open wound on the right thigh. When the surgeon pressed the pedicle with his finger, it blanched; when he let up, there was a slow return of the violaceous color.

5   "The circulation is good," Franciscus announced. "It will get better." In several weeks, we were told, he would divide the tube of flesh at its site of origin, and tailor it to fit the defect to which, by then, it would have grown more solidly. All at once, the webbed man in the bed reached out, and gripping Franciscus by the arm, began to speak rapidly, pointing to groin and hip. Franciscus stepped back at once to disengage his arm from the patient's grasp.

6   "Anyone here know Spanish? I didn't get a word of that."

7   "The cast is digging into him up above," I said. "The edges of the plaster are rough. When he moves, they hurt."

8   Without acknowledging my assistance, Dr. Franciscus took a plaster shears from the dressing cart and with several large snips cut away the rough edges of the cast.

9   "*Gracias, gracias.*" The man in the bed smiled. But Franciscus had already moved to the next bed. He seemed to me a man of immense strength and ability, yet without affection for the patients. He did not want to be touched by them. It was less kindness that he showed them than a reassurance that he would never give up, that he would bend every effort. If anyone could, he would solve the problems of their flesh.

10   Ward Rounds had disbanded and I was halfway down the corridor when I heard Dr. Franciscus' voice behind me.

11   "You speak Spanish." It seemed a command.

12   "I lived in Spain for two years," I told him.

13   "I'm taking a surgical team to Honduras[6] next week to operate on the natives down there. I do it every year for three weeks, somewhere. This year, Honduras. I can arrange the time away from your duties here if you'd

---

5 **débridement:** removal of dead tissue and foreign matter from a wound.
6 **Honduras:** a republic in Central America.

like to come along. You will act as interpreter. I'll show you how to use the clinical camera. What you'd see would make it worthwhile."

14 So it was that, a week later, the envy of my classmates, I joined the mobile surgical unit—surgeons, anesthetists, nurses and equipment— aboard a Military Air Transport plane to spend three weeks performing plastic surgery on people who had been previously selected by an advance team. Honduras. I don't suppose I shall ever see it again. Nor do I especially want to. From the plane it seemed a country made of clay—burnt umber, raw sienna, dry. It had a deadweight quality, as though the ground had no buoyancy, no air sacs through which a breeze might wander. Our destination was Comayagua, a town in the Central Highlands. The town itself was situated on the edge of one of the flatlands that were linked in a network between the granite mountains. Above, all was brown, with only an occasional Spanish cedar tree; below, patches of luxuriant tropical growth. It was a day's bus ride from the airport. For hours, the town kept appearing and disappearing with the convolutions of the road. At last, there it lay before us, panting and exhausted at the bottom of the mountain.

15 That was all I was to see of the countryside. From then on, there was only the derelict hospital of Comayagua, with the smell of spoiling bananas and the accumulated odors of everyone who had been sick there for the last hundred years. Of the two, I much preferred the frank smell of the sick. The heat of the place was incendiary. So hot that, as we stepped from the bus, our own words did not carry through the air, but hung limply at our lips and chins. Just in front of the hospital was a thirsty courtyard where mobs of waiting people squatted or lay in the meager shade, and where, on dry days, a fine dust rose through which untethered goats shouldered. Against the walls of this courtyard, gaunt, dejected men stood, their faces, like their country, preternaturally solemn, leaden. Here no one looked up at the sky. Every head was bent beneath a wide-brimmed straw hat. In the days that followed, from the doorway of the dispensary, I would watch the brown mountains sliding about, drinking the hospital into their shadow as the afternoon grew later and later, flattening us by their very altitude.

16 The people were mestizos, of mixed Spanish and Indian blood. They had flat, broad, dumb museum feet. At first they seemed to me indistinguishable the one from the other, without animation. All the vitality, the hidden sexuality, was in their black hair. Soon I was to know them by the fissures[7] with which each face was graven. But, even so, compared to us, they were masked, shut away. My job was to follow Dr. Franciscus around,

---

7 **fissures:** narrow openings; clefts.

photograph the patients before and after surgery, interpret and generally act as aide-de-camp.[8] It was exhilarating. Within days I had decided that I was not just useful, but essential. Despite that we spent all day in each other's company, there were no overtures of friendship from Dr. Franciscus. He knew my place, and I knew it, too. In the afternoon he examined the patients scheduled for the next day's surgery. I would call out a name from the doorway to the examining room. In the courtyard someone would rise. I would usher the patient in, and nudge him to the examining table where Dr. Franciscus stood, always, I thought, on the verge of irritability. I would read about the case history, then wait while he carried out his examination. While I took the "before" photographs, Dr. Franciscus would dictate into a tape recorder:

17   "Ulcerating basal cell carcinoma of the right orbit—six by eight centimeters—involving the right eye and extending into the floor of the orbit. Operative plan: wide excision with enucleation of the eye.[9] Later, bone and skin grafting." The next morning we would be in the operating room where the procedure would be carried out.

18   We were more than two weeks into our tour of duty—a few days to go—when it happened. Earlier in the day I had caught sight of her through the window of the dispensary. A thin, dark Indian girl about fourteen years old. A figurine, orange-brown, terra-cotta, and still attached to the unshaped clay from which she had been carved. An older, sun-weathered woman stood behind and somewhat to the left of the girl. The mother was short and dumpy. She wore a broad-brimmed hat with a high crown, and a shapeless dress like a cassock. The girl had long, loose black hair. There were tiny gold hoops in her ears. The dress she wore could have been her mother's. Far too big, it hung from her thin shoulders at some risk of slipping down her arms. Even with her in it, the dress was empty, something hanging on the back of a door. Her breasts made only the smallest imprint in the cloth, her hips none at all. All the while, she pressed to her mouth a filthy, pink, balled-up rag as though to stanch a flow or buttress against pain. I knew that what she had come to show us, what we were there to see, was hidden beneath that pink cloth. As I watched, the woman handed down to her a gourd from which the girl drank, lapping like a dog. She was the last patient of the day. They had been waiting in the courtyard for hours.

---

8   **aide-de-camp:** assistant to a superior.
9   **ulcerating . . . eye:** skin cancer requiring removal of the eye.

19   "Imelda Valdez," I called out. Slowly she rose to her feet, the cloth never leaving her mouth, and followed her mother to the examining-room door. I shooed them in.

20   "You sit up there on the table," I told her. "Mother, you stand over there, please." I read from the chart:

21   "This is a fourteen-year-old girl with a complete, unilateral, left-sided cleft lip and cleft palate.[10] No other diseases or congenital defects. Laboratory tests, chest Xray—negative."

22   "Tell her to take the rag away," said Dr. Franciscus. I did, and the girl shrank back, pressing the cloth all the more firmly.

23   "Listen, this is silly," said Franciscus. "Tell her I've got to see it. Either she behaves, or send her away."

24   "Please give me the cloth," I said to the girl as gently as possible. She did not. She could not. Just then, Franciscus reached up and, taking the hand that held the rag, pulled it away with a hard jerk. For an instant the girl's head followed the cloth as it left her face, one arm still upflung against showing. Against all hope, she would hide herself. A moment later, she relaxed and sat still. She seemed to me then like an animal that looks outward at the infinite, at death, without fear, with recognition only.

25   Set as it was in the center of the girl's face, the defect was utterly hideous—a nude rubbery insect that had fastened there. The upper lip was widely split all the way to the nose. One white tooth perched upon the protruding upper jaw projected through the hole. Some of the bone seemed to have been gnawed away as well. Above the thing, clear almond eyes and long black hair reflected the light. Below, a slender neck where the pulse trilled visibly. Under our gaze the girl's eyes fell to her lap where her hands lay palms upward, half open. She was a beautiful bird with a crushed beak. And tense with the expectation of more shame.

26   "Open your mouth," said the surgeon. I translated. She did so, and the surgeon tipped back her head to see inside.

27   "The palate, too. Complete," he said. There was a long silence. At last he spoke.

28   "What is your name?" The margins of the wound melted until she herself was being sucked into it.

29   "Imelda." The syllables leaked through the hole with a slosh and a whistle.

30   "Tomorrow," said the surgeon, "I will fix your lip. *Mañana.*"

---

10   **cleft lip and cleft palate:** a split in the upper lip; defect of the palate in which there is an opening in the roof of the mouth.

31   It seemed to me that Hugh Franciscus, in spite of his years of experience, in spite of all the dreadful things he had seen, must have been awed by the sight of this girl. I could see it flit across his face for an instant. Perhaps it was her small act of concealment, that he had had to demand that she show him the lip, that he had had to force her to show it to him. Perhaps it was her resistance that intensified the disfigurement. Had she brought her mouth to him willingly, without shame, she would have been for him neither more nor less than any other patient.

32   He measured the defect with calipers, studied it from different angles, turning her head with a finger at her chin.

33   "How can it ever be put back together?" I asked.

34   "Take her picture," he said. And to her, "Look straight ahead." Through the eye of the camera she seemed more pitiful than ever, her humiliation more complete.

35   "Wait!" The surgeon stopped me. I lowered the camera. A strand of her hair had fallen across her face and found its way to her mouth, becoming stuck there by saliva. He removed her hair and secured it behind her ear.

36   "Go ahead," he ordered. There was the click of the camera. The girl winced.

37   "Take three more, just in case."

38   When the girl and her mother had left, he took paper and pen and with a few lines drew a remarkable likeness of the girl's face.

39   "Look," he said. "If this dot is A, and this one B, this, C and this, D, the incisions are made A to B, then C to D. CD must equal AB. It is all equilateral triangles." All well and good, but then came X and Y and rotation flaps and the rest.

40   "Do you see?" he asked.

41   "It is confusing," I told him.

42   "It is simply a matter of dropping the upper lip into a normal position, then crossing the gap with two triangular flaps. It is geometry," he said.

43   "Yes," I said. "Geometry." And relinquished all hope of becoming a plastic surgeon.

44 In the operating room the next morning the anesthesia had already been administered when we arrived from Ward Rounds. The tube emerging from the girl's mouth was pressed against her lower lip to be kept out of the field of surgery. Already, a nurse was scrubbing the face which swam in a reddish-brown lather. The tiny gold earrings were included in the scrub. Now and then, one of them gave a brave flash. The face washed for the last

time, and dried. Green towels were placed over the face to hide everything but the mouth and nose. The drapes were applied.

45   "Calipers!" The surgeon measured, locating the peak of the distorted Cupid's bow.

46   "Marking pen!" He placed the first blue dot at the apex of the bow. The nasal sills were dotted: next, the inferior philtral dimple,[11] the vermilion line. The *A* flap and the *B* flap were outlined. On he worked, peppering the lip and nose, making sense of chaos, realizing the lip that lay waiting in that deep essential pink, that only he could see. The last dot and line were placed. He was ready.

47   "Scalpel!" He held the knife above the girl's mouth.

48   "O.K. to go ahead?" he asked the anesthetist.

49   "Yes."

50   He lowered the knife.

51   "No! Wait!" The anesthetist's voice was tense, staccato. "Hold it!"

52   The surgeon's hand was motionless.

53   "What's the matter?"

54   "Something's wrong. I'm not sure. God, she's hot as a pistol. Blood pressure is way up. Pulse one eighty. Get a rectal temperature." A nurse fumbled beneath the drapes. We waited. The nurse retrieved the thermometer.

55   "One hundred seven . . . no . . . eight." There was disbelief in her voice.

56   "Malignant hyperthermia,"[12] said the anesthetist. "Ice! Ice! Get lots of ice!" I raced out the door, accosted the first nurse I saw.

57   "Ice!" I shouted. "*Hielo!*[13] Quickly! *Hielo!*" The woman's expression was blank. I ran to another. "*Hielo! Hielo!* For the love of God, ice!"

58   "*Hielo?*" she shrugged. "*Nada.*" I ran back to the operating room.

59   "There isn't any ice," I reported. Dr. Franciscus had ripped off his rubber gloves and was feeling the skin of the girl's abdomen. Above the mask his eyes were the eyes of a horse in battle.

60   "The EKG is wild . . ."

61   "I can't get a pulse . . ."

62   "What the hell . . ."

63   The surgeon reached for the girl's groin. No femoral pulse.

64   "EKG flat. My God! She's dead!"

65   "She can't be."

66   "She is."

---

11 **philtral dimple:** the groove on the upper lip below the nose.
12 **malignant hyperthermia:** deadly and abnormally high fever.
13 **Hielo:** Spanish for "ice."

67   The surgeon's fingers pressed the groin where there was no pulse to be felt, only his own pulse hammering at the girl's flesh to be let in.

68   It was noon, four hours later, when we left the operating room. It was a day so hot and humid I felt steamed open like an envelope. The woman was sitting on a bench in the courtyard in her dress like a cassock. In one hand she held a piece of cloth the girl had used to conceal her mouth. As we watched, she folded it once neatly, and then again, smoothing it, cleaning the cloth which might have been the head of the girl in her lap that she stroked and consoled.

69   "I'll do the talking here," he said. He would tell her himself, in whatever Spanish he could find. Only if she did not understand was I to speak for him. I watched him brace himself, set his shoulders. How could he tell her? I wondered. What? But I knew he would tell her everything, exactly as it had happened. As much for himself as for her, he needed to explain. But suppose she screamed, fell to the ground, attacked him, even? All that hope of love . . . gone. Even in his discomfort I knew that he was teaching me. The way to do it was professionally. Now he was standing above her. When the woman saw that he did not speak, she lifted her eyes and saw what he held crammed in his mouth to tell her. She knew, and rose to her feet.

70   "*Señora*," he began, "I am sorry." All at once he seemed to me shorter than he was, scarcely taller than she. There was a place at the crown of his head where the hair had grown thin. His lips were stones. He could hardly move them. The voice dry, dusty.

71   "No one could have known. Some bad reaction to the medicine for sleeping. It poisoned her. High fever. She did not wake up." The last, a whisper. The woman studied his lips as though she were deaf. He tried, but could not control a twitching at the corner of his mouth. He raised a thumb and forefinger to press something back into his eyes.

72   "*Muerte*,"[14] the woman announced to herself. Her eyes were human, deadly.

73   "*Si, muerte.*" At that moment he was like someone cast, still alive, as an effigy for his own tomb. He closed his eyes. Nor did he open them until he felt the touch of the woman's hand on his arm, a touch from which he did not withdraw. Then he looked and saw the grief corroding her face, breaking it down, melting the features so that eyes, nose, mouth ran together in

---

14   **muerte:** Spanish for "dead."

a distortion, like the girl's. For a long time they stood in silence. It seemed to me that minutes passed. At last her face cleared, the features rearranged themselves. She spoke, the words coming slowly to make certain he understood her. She would go home now. The next day her sons would come for the girl, to take her home for burial. The doctor must not be sad. God decided. And she was happy now that the harelip had been fixed so that her daughter might go to Heaven without it. Her bare feet retreating were the felted pads of a great bereft animal.

[74] The next morning I did not go to the wards, but stood at the gate leading from the courtyard to the road outside. Two young men in striped ponchos lifted the girl's body wrapped in a straw mat onto the back of a wooden cart. A donkey waited. I had been drawn to this place as one is drawn, inexplicably, to certain scenes of desolation—executions, battlefields. All at once, the woman looked up and saw me. She had taken off her hat. The heavy-hanging coil of her hair made her head seem larger, darker, noble. I pressed some money into her hand.

[75] "For flowers," I said. "A priest." Her cheeks shook as though minutes ago a stone had been dropped into her navel and the ripples were just now reaching her head. I regretted having come to that place.

[76] "*Si, si,*" the woman said. Her own face was stitched with flies. "The doctor is one of the angels. He finished the work of God. My daughter is beautiful."

[77] What could she mean! The lip had not been fixed. The girl had died before he would have done it.

[78] "Only a fine line that God will erase in time," she said.

[79] I reached into the cart and lifted a corner of the mat in which the girl had been rolled. Where the cleft had been there was now a fresh line of tiny sutures. The Cupid's bow was delicately shaped, the vermilion border aligned. The flattened nostril had now the same rounded shape as the other one. I let the mat fall over the face of the dead girl, but not before I had seen the touching place where the finest black hairs sprang from the temple.

[80] "*Adiós, adiós . . .*" And the cart creaked away to the sound of hooves, a tinkling bell.

[81] There are events in a doctor's life that seem to mark the boundary between youth and age, seeing and perceiving. Like certain dreams, they illuminate a whole lifetime of past behavior. After such an event, a doctor is not the same as he was before. It had seemed to me then to have been the act of someone demented, or at least insanely arrogant. An attempt to reorder events. Her death had come to him out of order. It should have come after

the lip had been repaired, not before. He could have told the mother that, no, the lip had not been fixed. But he did not. He said nothing. It had been an act of omission, one of those strange lapses to which all of us are subject and which we live to regret. It must have been then, at that moment, that the knowledge of what we would do appeared to him. The words of the mother had not consoled him; they had hunted him down. He had not done it for her. The dire necessity was his. He would not accept that Imelda had died before he could repair her lip. People who do such things break free from society. They follow their own lonely path. They have a secret which they can never reveal. I must never let on that I knew.

[82] How often I have imagined it. Ten o'clock at night. The hospital of Comayagua is all but dark. Here and there lanterns tilt and skitter up and down the corridors. One of these lamps breaks free from the others and descends the stone steps to the underground room that is the morgue of the hospital. This room wears the expression as if it had waited all night for someone to come. No silence so deep as this place with its cargo of newly dead. Only the slow drip of water over stone. The door closes gassily and clicks shut. The lock is turned. There are four tables, each with a body encased in a paper shroud. There is no mistaking her. She is the smallest. The surgeon takes a knife from his pocket and slits open the paper shroud, that part in which the girl's head is enclosed. The wound seems to be living on long after she has died. Waves of heat emanate from it, blurring his vision. All at once, he turns to peer over his shoulder. He sees nothing, only a wooden crucifix on the wall.

[83]   He removes a package of instruments from a satchel and arranges them on a tray. Scalpel, scissors, forceps, needle holder. Sutures and gauze sponges are produced. Stealthy, hunched, engaged, he begins. The dots of blue dye are still there upon her mouth. He raises the scalpel, pauses. A second glance into the darkness. From the wall a small lizard watches and accepts. The first cut is made. A sluggish flow of dark blood appears. He wipes it away with a sponge. No new blood comes to take its place. Again and again he cuts, connecting each of the blue dots until the whole of the zigzag slice is made, first on one side of the cleft, then on the other. Now the edges of the cleft are lined with fresh tissue. He sets down the scalpel and takes up scissors and forceps, undermining the little flaps until each triangle is attached only at one side. He rotates each flap into its new position. He must be certain that they can be swung without tension. They can. He is ready to suture. He fits the tiny curved needle into the jaws of the needle holder. Each suture is placed precisely the same number of millimeters from the cut edge, and the same distance apart. He ties each knot down

until the edges are apposed. Not too tightly. These are the most meticulous sutures of his life. He cuts each thread close to the knot. It goes well. The vermilion border with its white skin roll is exactly aligned. One more stitch and the Cupid's bow appears as if by magic. The man's face shines with moisture. Now the nostril is incised around the margin, released, and sutured into a round shape to match its mate. He wipes the blood from the face of the girl with gauze that he has dipped in water. Crumbs of light are scattered on the girl's face. The shroud is folded once more about her. The instruments are handed into the satchel. In a moment the morgue is dark and a lone lantern ascends the stairs and is extinguished.

[84] Six weeks later I was in the darkened amphitheater of the Medical School. Tiers of seats rose in a semicircle above the small stage where Hugh Franciscus stood presenting the case material he had encountered in Honduras. It was the highlight of the year. The hall was filled. The night before he had arranged the slides in the order in which they were to be shown. I was at the controls of the slide projector.

[85]   "Next slide!" he would order from time to time in that military voice which had called forth blind obedience from generations of medical students, interns, residents and patients.

[86]   "This is a fifty-seven-year-old man with a severe burn contracture of the neck. You will notice the rigid webbing that has fused the chin to the presternal tissues.[15] No motion of the head on the torso is possible. . . . Next slide!"

[87]   "Click," went the projector.

[88]   "Here is after the excision of the scar tissue and with the head in full extension for the first time. The defect was then covered. . . . Next slide!"

[89]   "Click."

[90]   ". . . with full-thickness drums of skin taken from the abdomen with the Padgett dermatome.[16] Next slide!"

[91]   "Click."

[92]   And suddenly there she was, extracted from the shadows, suspended above and beyond all of us like a resurrection. There was the oval face, the long black hair unbraided, the tiny gold hoops in her ears. And that luminous gnawed mouth. The whole of her life seemed to have been summed up in this photograph. A long silence followed that was the surgeon's alone

---

15   **presternal tissues:** tissues surrounding the breastbone.
16   **dermatone:** instrument for cutting thin sections of skin for grafting.

to break. Almost at once, like the anesthetist in the operating room in Co-mayagua, I knew that something was wrong. It was not that the man would not speak as that he could not. The audience of doctors, nurses and students seemed to have been infected by the black, limitless silence. My own pulse doubled. It was hard to breathe. Why did he not call out for the next slide? Why did he not save himself? Why had he not removed this slide from the ones to be shown? All at once I knew that he had used his camera on her again. I could see the long black shadows of her hair flowing into the darker shadows of the morgue. The sudden blinding flash . . . The next slide would be the one taken in the morgue. He would be exposed.

93   In the dim light reflected from the slide, I saw him gazing up at her, seeing not the colored photograph, I thought, but the negative of where the ghost of the girl was. For me, the amphitheater had become Honduras. I saw again that courtyard littered with patients. I could see the dust in the beam of light from the projector. It was then that I knew that she was his measure of perfection and pain—the one lost, the other gained. He, too, had heard the click of the camera, had seen her wince and felt his mercy enlarge. At last he spoke.

94   "Imelda." It was the one word he had heard her say. At the sound of his voice I removed the next slide from the projector. "Click" . . . and she was gone. "Click" again, and in her place the man with the orbital cancer. For a long moment Franciscus looked up in my direction, on his face an expression that I have given up trying to interpret. Gratitude? Sorrow? It made me think of the gaze of the girl when at last she understood that she must hand over to him the evidence of her body.

95   "This is a sixty-two-year-old man with a basal cell carcinoma of the temple eroding into the bony orbit . . ." he began as though nothing had happened.

96   At the end of the hour, even before the lights went on, there was loud applause. I hurried to find him among the departing crowd. I could not. Some weeks went by before I caught sight of him. He seemed vaguely convalescent, as though a fever had taken its toll before burning out.

97   Hugh Franciscus continued to teach for fifteen years, although he operated a good deal less, then gave it up entirely. It was as though he had grown tired of blood, of always having to be involved in blood, of having to draw it, spill it, wipe it away, stanch it. He was a quieter, softer man, I heard, the ferocity diminished. There were no more expeditions to Honduras or anywhere else.

98   I, too, have not been entirely free of her. Now and then, in the years that have passed, I see that donkey-cart cortège, or his face bent over hers

in the morgue. I would like to have told him what I now know, that his un-realistic act was one of goodness, one of those small, persevering acts done, perhaps, to ward off madness. Like lighting a lamp, boiling water for tea, washing a shirt. But, of course, it's too late now.

Looking Back

1. In a few words, state what Selzer's feelings were about Hugh Franciscus.

2. Selzer says that Franciscus had no close friends on the [medical] staff and that he reacted to his environment by "keeping his own counsel, by a certain remoteness." He also reports what others said about Franciscus and speculates himself about the man. Are speculations a legitimate part of a biographical essay, or should a writer stick to statements of fact? Discuss in a small group.

3. How would the effect of this essay have changed if the author had not included the imagined scene in the morgue after Imelda's death?

4. What was Franciscus's apparent reaction to Imelda's death, and how can you explain this reaction, especially since, as a doctor, he must have encountered death on other occasions?

5. Discuss some of the problems surrounding the altruistic impulse. Dr. Franciscus means to help Imelda, and yet because of him, she dies. Should we not attempt to help others because sometimes our assistance causes larger problems than it solves? Explain.

Looking Into

1. Selzer describes scenes so vividly that reading about them is almost like seeing them on stage. Describe a scene that you find particularly strik-ing. If possible, write while you are looking at the scene, but narrow your focus so that you can concentrate on a few details. Include details of shape, texture, color, sound, and motion in your description.

2. What would inspire someone to want to become a surgeon? Analyze the possible reasons in a short paper.

from Strikes Have Followed Me All My Life

EMMA MASHININI

Emma Mashinini once wrote, "My experience of being a woman is the experience of being always a victim." She was born in Johannesburg, South Africa, in 1929 and left school early to go to work. She eventually became a supervisor at the Henochsberg garment factory from 1970 to 1975. Increasingly drawn to the union movement, she was a founder of the Catering & Commercial Allied Workers' Union of South Africa, a black trade union. During the time she was secretary of CCAWUSA, from 1975 to 1986, she was harassed by police and arrested and held without charge for six months in solitary confinement, an experience that resulted in both physical and psychological problems.

In 1986, she became Director of the Division of Justice and Reconciliation for the [Anglican] Church of the Province of Southern Africa, working with Bishop Desmond Tutu.

She is one of three editors and a contributor to *Women Hold Up Half the Sky: Women in the Church in Southern Africa* (1991), as well as the author of *Strikes Have Followed Me All My Life* (1989), from which the following excerpt is taken.

Looking Ahead

Here Mashinini writes of her life in the days before apartheid was abolished in South Africa.

[1] *I* left my husband in 1959. In 1956, when I was twenty-six, I had started work in Johannesburg, at a clothing factory called Henochsberg's which provided uniforms for the government forces. It was my first job, apart from working as a nanny to white children when I left school, and I had not begun to develop any political awareness. But I was already angry. The hours my father had been forced to work had contributed to the break-up of my family, and my own need to earn money had put paid to my schooling. And now, when my three children were still young and I could have

done with being at home to look after them, I was having to go out to work to earn a tiny wage, which we needed in order to survive.

2   I found the job through the Garment Workers' Union. Lucy Mvubelo, a woman I admire so much for all she did in those years for her union, was the General Secretary, and she said to me, "Go to number one, Charles Street, they are looking for people there." I went, and within three days they had taken me on as a trainee machinist.

3   The factory was just opening then. I think it was about the second or third week that it had started running. I started off in a branch factory and then, after about a year, moved on into the central factory, in Commissioner Street. In the branch factory there were no white machinists. It was only when I got to the central factory that there was a mix of black and white on the shop floor.

4   I remember my first day very clearly. It was November, and when I walked into the building it seemed to me that there were hundreds of people rushing this way and that, and a terrible volume of noise, with a lot of shouting—"Come on, do your job!"—and that kind of thing. It was completely bewildering. Immediately I got there, on my first day as a worker, I was started on the machines, working very close to people who had already worked as machinists at other factories, so I was a struggler from the start. I remember most of all how they cursed us when we couldn't keep up. I was in a department headed first by an Afrikaner[1] called Mrs. Smit and then by a German-speaking man, Mr. Becker. He used to shout and scream at us, sometimes for no reason at all, and it wasn't unusual for ten people to be dismissed a day. They were always saying you had to push. They would say, *"Roer jou gat,"* which means, "Push your arse"— "Come on, push your arse and be productive." You would be on the machine sweating, but they would tell you, *"Roer jou, roer jou"*—"Push, push, push," and you would push and push. No one would ever say, "Okay, that's enough. Good." You were working for a target. You'd know there was a target you had to meet, and at the back of your mind you were concerned about the welfare of your children. You would be torn in two, because you were at work and in your mind you were at home. This is the problem of the working mother: you are divided. You are only working because you have to.

5   Penny was almost three when I moved to the central factory, and she'd started going to a crèche[2] nearby, so I didn't have a baby that I had to carry

---

1 **Afrikaner:** person of European descent born in South Africa.
2 **crèche:** day nursery.

from one place to another, because even though I stopped work much later than the crèche closed, and after my other two children came home from school, I had a neighbour who wasn't working, and she looked after them. But still at work you were thinking of the children, and at home you were thinking about the job, and then you had this extra person to bother about—a husband.

6   I'd start factory work at seven-thirty in the morning, after travelling about thirty kilometres to get there. Other workers came from double that distance. People think Soweto is the only township in South Africa, but there are many others, like Tembisa and Alexandra, and all of us would be flocking to the centre of Johannesburg for our jobs. People would be sleeping on the trains. Some would have been travelling for a long time, and even before the train there would be some distance to go for a bus stop, and the bus would already have been travelling and picking up more people. So if you had to be at your machine at seven-thirty you would have to be at your work-place by seven, and you would have to be ready to take the train at five. For some it could be about four.

7   I would leave my children sleeping, and the night before I would have made my preparations for the coming day, because I had to leave everything—bread, uniform, everything—lined up for my neighbour, who would come and wake my children for school. There would be nothing for you at the factory—no tea, no coffee. The tea-break was at a certain time, and if you brought something from home that would be when you would eat, in that ten-minute tea-break later in the day. And if you had brought nothing, your tea-break would be exhausted while you were walking to the canteen and queuing there. By the time you got your coffee and sat down, five minutes had gone, and you would have to swallow everything and then run to be back on time.

8   I would get home about seven—and in winter, you know, that was pretty dark. When I got home I'd start making a fire on my coal stove. I used to try to prepare for that the night before, but if not I would have to start chopping wood, getting the coal, getting the ashes out and all that. And there was no one to follow my children when they were getting up, and the basin would be full of dirty water, and I would start emptying that as well, picking up the dirty clothes, and the school clothes they took off when they got home from school, and all that before I actually started cooking.

9   My husband would not be rushing to come home. What would he rush to come home for? When he got out from his job he would go wherever he wanted to, and because he was a man it had to be so. I couldn't question him, or ask him, and anyway when he got home my time was

interfered with because I had to have water to give him to wash his hands—not just ordinary cold water, but warm water. While my fire was still burning I would pump the Primus stove[3] quickly to get the warm water for my dear husband to wash his hands, and then with the remaining water I would make tea. I would so enjoy that, but standing, because my fire would be burning for me to cook our main meal. My husband would sit and read the newspaper—and sometimes I would wonder if he really understood what he read, or if he just knew that the white boss sits when he comes home, and reads his newspaper.

10   I never thought to compare. I never thought that while the white boss was doing that, sitting and reading, there was a black man or woman doing everything for them. It was just the order of the day that I had to do everything. And if, after he washed, he emptied the water instead of just leaving it standing, I would be so grateful. I would feel that was so nice of him.

11   So then I'd cook and give them their food and everything, and if he was tired he would maybe want more water to wash his feet, because he had been standing and maybe he reckoned I'd been sitting at the machine. And then they would go to sleep, and there was the tidying up to do, and the dishes, because that was the only time I had to clean my house, at night, after everyone had gone to bed. I would do the washing as well, at night, and in the morning I would get up and before I left I would hang my washing on the line. We none of us had so many clothes that we could last the week, so I couldn't do all the washing at the weekend. Then, on alternate days, I would do the ironing, with those heavy irons you put on the stove, and my table would be my ironing board.

12   My children would do their homework by candle-light. Our only other means of light was a paraffin lamp, which smelled very strong, so to me a candle was an improvement. There was never any time for me to help them—all I could do was make sure they got on with it. I could never open a book to see. My children say they cannot work for longer hours because they must oversee their children's homework. This is all foreign to me. I could never do it with my children, even though I had been educated to a good standard, because there simply was not time.

13   There was no time to sit and laugh and talk. No time and no energy. Even going to church, trying to cope with catching them, getting them to wash, finding their socks, always shouting. Only on the way there, walking out of that house holding their hands—I think that was the only loving

---

3   **Primus stove:** portable oil stove.

time I had with my children. Just holding their hands and walking with them to church.

14   That was the happiest time. They would be sitting there, and going off to Sunday School or whatever, and you could sit down and relax, and listen to someone. Even today I love to go to church, only now my company is my grandchildren instead of my children.

15   The church was my only pleasure, until we working women got together and had what we called *stokvels*. A *stokvel* is a neighborhood group that is very supportive, socially and financially. Many black women earn meagre wages and cannot afford to buy the necessary comforts of home, so we set up these *stokvels*, where we could pool our resources. You have to be a member to enjoy the benefits of a *stokvel*, and they are properly run. The members decide what is the greatest need. It could be a ceiling, a refrigerator, or pots, or anything that you could not pay for yourself. The members collect money in proportion to their wages, and put it into a pool for one person in the group to purchase what has been decided. After that they pass on to the next person, and the group identifies another pressing need, and so it goes until you find that each person in the group has managed to buy some household gadgets without getting into a hire-purchase contract, which has been disastrous to many a housewife.

16   Another important aspect of *stokvels* is social. Women in the townships are very lonely because their husbands tend to leave them at home when they go to soccer matches, or to the movies, or to taverns to have a drink with the boys. The *stokvel* meetings change from one member's house to another, and you are obliged to serve tea or drinks. After the money has been collected the women start conversing about current affairs, sharing their problems, which leads them to politics. And that is why African women are often much more politically aware than their Coloured[4] and Indian counterparts, who do not have the opportunity of meeting in such a way.

17   That was the way my neighbourhood was. My house was the second from the corner, and there were no fences dividing the house from each other. The woman in the first house from the corner worked in a white kindergarten, and she would be able to bring home leftovers of sandwiches from rich children, and as she had no young children of her own she would pass those leftovers to me. And so we sustained each other, woman to woman—a woman-to-woman sustaining.

---

4   **coloured:** person of mixed race.

[18] On Sunday afternoons, after church, I would start preparing for the coming week. It would be our first time to have a hot meal, perhaps. And there would be more cleaning. We believed in cleaning those houses. They were our pride. What else did we have to show pride in? Only our little rooms were our pride.

[19] I struggled from the first day I got into the factory. After I had learned the machine better I thought that perhaps the most important thing was to do whatever I had to do perfectly, but because I wanted to do this I couldn't produce the number of garments I was supposed to. It was not possible to chase perfection along with production. They made the choice for you, and they wanted production.

[20] As a result of my attempt to work in this way I was screamed at more than anyone else, but I still couldn't get myself to work as fast as all those other people. Every morning when I walked into that factory I really thought, "Today it will be my turn to be dismissed." But then I was elected a shop steward, and soon after, to my surprise (though looking back it does not seem so unexpected), I was promoted. It was after about three or four years, and I was promoted first to be a set leader and then a supervisor, which was unheard of—a black supervisor in that factory. Instead of dismissing me, they were trying to make me one of them.

[21] We were members of the Garment Workers' Union Number 3. There were three garment workers' trade unions at that time. The Garment Workers' Union Number 1 was for whites, headed by Johanna Cornelius, and Number 2 was for Coloureds and Indians. Number 3 was for blacks, headed by Lucy Mvubelo, who had sent me to Henochsberg's in the first place. The union for Africans wasn't registered, of course, but the employers accepted it. Our subscriptions at that time were deducted from our pay and went to the Number 1 and 2 unions, who would negotiate for working conditions and wages for garment workers. We had an agreement which served for all three branches—whites, Indians and Coloureds, and Africans—and we would benefit from their negotiations in that whatever minimum wage was set we would be paid that amount. The other workers would get over and above that wage, but they would be sure to set a minimum wage for the African workers. In my factory we black women workers made up about 70 percent of the work force, all earning that basic flat wage. There was no machinery to challenge that wage. It was for the employer to decide to pay over the minimum wage. It was purely voluntary, and that is in fact what it was called, a "voluntary increase." So our union just had to sit and wait for what came out of the negotiations with the Industrial

Council. Any action we took over their decision was illegal. For us to strike was illegal.

22 None the less, on occasion we did strike, or go on a "go slow." I think the strikes that meant the most to me were in the early 1970s, when we fought to earn an extra cent, and also to narrow our hours. When I first started work the day would be from seven-thirty to four-thirty, and we fought, all of us, for the narrowing down of the time, and succeeded in bringing it down to five minutes past four for leaving the factory. We were fighting for a forty-hour week, and in the course of the fight we did go out on strike.

23 But even more important than the narrowing of hours was that extra cent. By then we were all earning 10 rand[5] 50 cents a week, and only workers earning more than 10 rand 50 cents could contribute to the Unemployment Insurance Fund.

24 Unemployment insurance was a key issue for me, and I was very glad to have been elected a shop steward and that it was part of my duty to go about and influence people. It's strange, really, that I didn't expect to be elected, but when it came I was more than ready to accept the job. I'd say that has been true of my entire career in that I have never sought to be elected to positions of such responsibility, but when they have been offered to me I have found great fulfillment in the work they entail. You have to work hard, and learn and learn, and work even harder, because you don't have the experience, but despite this, and despite the strain, at the end of the day I can say I have enjoyed my work. Often I can't believe how any particular success or achievement has come about, and I say to myself there is no way I could have managed it, except maybe with God's grace.

25 On the occasion when we fought for our extra cent, I remember what a struggle we had, and how hostile the employers were. We went on a go slow strike, and they were so angry, being used to dismissing us for the least mistake, for being late or whatever. It took months for us to win—but when we did, we felt joy, great joy.

26 I had a dual role in the factory, but I was very clear where my first loyalty lay. I was appointed a supervisor, but I was *elected* to be a shop steward[6] by my fellow workers.

---

5 **rand:** monetary unit of South Africa.
6 **shop steward:** union representative of a shop or department who deals with management.

27   As a supervisor I had some access to Mr. Becker, who was held in very high esteem by senior management. He was very much feared by the workers, since he had a way of goading, pushing, and bullying them to produce more garments than any of his white colleagues who headed other departments. He was a slave-driver. But as a shop steward I was able to intervene and reduce the numerous dismissals which were taking place.

28   Circumstances forced me to protect my colleagues. I pointed out to Mr. Becker how counter-productive it was constantly to be dismissing people after I had trained them, and that while it was very easy for him to throw people out, it meant a heavy load of work descended on me, to start training new people all over again. Apart from the inhuman way he dismissed people, I tried to make him see that if he had constantly to train new women to be machinists or table-hands there was no way we could then achieve our work quota.

29   It was very unusual for a black woman to be a supervisor, and because of the superior attitudes of whites towards blacks I had to be doubly determined to demonstrate that I could do the job very well. I remember that when I first confronted Mr. Becker he was quite taken aback, because he did not expect me to speak out. But with time I saw that he came to respect my views.

30   Henochsberg's was one of the largest factories in the clothing industry, with almost a thousand workers. We were producing uniforms for the navy, the air force, police, and traffic cops. At a later stage we started production of a type of uniform totally unknown to us, which I came to realise was a camouflage uniform. These particular garments I saw on people for the first time in 1976, when June 16 we had the uprising of the youth in Soweto, and then their massacre. At the onset of the peaceful protest there arrived in Soweto unusual types of army vehicles, from which hundreds of troops flowed out and littered the streets, all dressed in those camouflage uniforms, uniforms used for the slaughter of my people, and which I personally had helped to make. I felt horrified. There was only one non-governmental uniform we made at Henochsberg's, and that was for the Zionist Christian Church, the largest independent church, led by Bishop Lekganyane.

31   Evilly entwined in all the work at our factory was apartheid and all the disabilities which were imposed on us, the black workers. Job Reservation was one of those punitive decrees. Many jobs—in the cutting room, and stitching around men's jacket sleeves, for example—were reserved by statute for whites only. As a supervisor I was only permitted to supervise blacks, and forbidden by law to supervise our "superior" whites, even though some of the jobs reserved for whites were so simple that we

laughed to ourselves to see how superior they felt in performing them. The assumptions and arrogance of white South Africans never ceases to amaze and astound me, even up to this present day.

32	In the commercial distributive trade even the operating of lifts was reserved for whites, who were usually elderly retired people, or disabled people. Can you imagine what this means, that a tired and often retarded white person was considered more valuable and productive than a young and competent black?

33	In such a society as this, whites developed into very lazy people, because all the menial and hard tasks were landed on the backs of black people, and black women in particular gained from this and learned to develop resourcefulness, and talents and skills, and trained themselves to become truly competent.

34	Of course, we had separate facilities. Canteen, toilets, changing rooms—all these were separated according to sex and according to colour. We had to address the whites as "sir" and "madam," while they always called us by our first names, or, if we were being shouted at, we were called "*meid*" and "*Kaffir*." Yet as black women, we were in the majority—perhaps 70 per cent of the workforce.

35	The Industrial Conciliation Act of 1956 banned employers from deducting union subscriptions from our pay packets, so we shop stewards would have to collect all the subscriptions ourselves. We would ask to be first in the queue when we were paid, so that we could then go and stand at the gate and collect.

36	It was not easy to act for the workers at that time. A lot of awareness has been created over the last years, but then they were often frightened to say aloud that they were not happy with their salaries. Also, they didn't always tell their plans to me, as shop steward. They would always be surprising me. They would say to each other, without my knowledge, "Tomorrow we are not going to start work until a certain demand is met." I would always be early at work, because I would arrange things before the workers came in, and when I got there I would see people were not coming to start work, and I would stand there like a fool. I, a black person and a worker, would be inside with all these whites standing around with me and saying, "Why aren't they coming in to work?" And when the whites would address the workers and say, "What is your problem?" perhaps somebody would answer, "We do have a problem." So they would say, "Who are your spokespeople? Let your spokespeople come in and talk to us." And they would say their spokesperson was Emma, meaning me. So the whites would think I had instigated the stoppage, that I was playing a double role, making the workers stand outside and pretending I didn't know.

[37] They could have sacked me if they had wanted. I was a shop steward, but if they wanted to sack you they could still sack you. Instead, they would try and use me to stop the trouble. They would use me like a fire extinguisher, always there to stop trouble. I would have to go to meet with the workers and ask, "Now what is actually going on?" And they would tell me they wanted money, or they wanted that person who had been shouting and yelling at us to behave him or herself. I would listen to all that, and then I would convey it to the employers. They would be adamant, and so the workers would stay outside and not come in. Often the police would arrive with dogs and surround the workers. Many times with the help of the union we would eventually receive assistance, and perhaps the people would achieve a part of what they wanted and go back to work. But during those days, in the factory I worked in, there was one strike after another. And this has followed me all my life. Wherever I am it seems there must always be trouble.

Looking Back

1. List the many causes of Emma Mashinini's hard life. Could she have done anything to make her life easier?

2. What are the parallels between the lives of Jessie Lopez de la Cruz and Emma Mashinini?

3. Mashinini, in an echo of the Gessler Brothers' plight, says that "it was not possible to chase perfection along with production." Is it natural for people to want to achieve perfection in their work or are only a few people bothered by the rush to produce? Discuss in a small group.

4. Discuss the effect of adversity and struggle on people such as Emma Mashinini and Jessie Lopez de la Cruz.

Looking Into

1. Write a dialogue between Naomi Shihab Nye, Jessie Lopez de la Cruz, and Emma Mashinini about women's work.

2. Mashinini's husband did not do his share of the chores around the house. Imagine that you are she and write out a proposal for an equal division of the daily tasks involved in running the house.

Memorandum

E. B. WHITE

E. B. White was born in Mount Vernon, New York, in 1899. He graduated from Cornell in 1921 and went to work as a reporter with United Press the same year. After working for the *Seattle Times* in 1922–1923, he became a copywriter in New York City and in 1926 began his long association with the *New Yorker* as a writer and contributing editor. He wrote "Talk of the Town" for the magazine for eleven years and contributed poems and essays as well. Fellow writer James Thurber called him "the most valuable person on the magazine." White collaborated with Thurber on a satire of sex manuals in 1929 titled *Is Sex Necessary? or, Why You Feel the Way You Do*. From 1938 to 1943 he wrote a column for Harper's called "One Man's Meat." These pieces were collected in a volume of the same name from which "Memorandum" is taken.

White is known to millions of readers as the author of *Stuart Little* (1945) and *Charlotte's Web* (1952), two children's books beloved by adults as well. *Charlotte's Web* was a Newberry Honor Book and the recipient of many other awards. In 1960 White received a gold medal from the National Institute of Arts and Letters for his contribution to literature, and in 1978 received a Pulitzer Prize special citation for the body of his work.

The collections of his work include *The Second Tree from the Corner* (1954), *The Points of My Compass* (1962), *An E. B. White Reader* (1976), *Essays of E. B. White* (1977), and *Poems and Sketches of E. B. White* (1981). He also contributed to the second edition of *The Elements of Style* by William Strunk, Jr., and collaborated with his wife, Katharine Sergeant White, on *A Subtreasury of American Humor*.

He died on his farm in Maine in 1985 after suffering from Alzheimer's disease.

Looking Ahead

White and his wife, a *New Yorker* editor, bought a farm in North Brooklin, Maine, in 1934 and moved there permanently in 1938. Here they raised sheep, chickens, and geese. White frequently wrote about his farm which, if the following essay is any indication, was a lot of work.

—ᴍ—

[1]   *T*oday I should carry the pumpkins and squash from the back porch to the attic. The nights are too frosty to leave them outdoors any longer. And as long as I am making some trips to the attic I should also take up the boat cushions and the charts and the stuff from the galley and also a fishing rod that belongs up in the attic. Today I should finish filling the trench we dug for the water pipe and should haul two loads of beach gravel from the Naskeag bar[1] to spread on top of the clay fill. And I should stop in and pay the Reverend Mr. Smith for the gravel I got a month or two ago and ask him if he has seen a bear.

[2]   I ought to finish husking the corn and wheel the old stalks out and dump them on the compost pile, and while I am out there I should take a fork and pitch over the weeds that were thrown at the edge of the field last August and rake the little windfalls[2] from under the apple tree and pitch them on to the heap too. I ought to go down to the shore at dead low water[3] and hook on to the mooring with a chain and make the chain fast to the float, so that the tide will pick up the mooring rock and I can tow the whole thing ashore six hours later. I ought to knock the wedges out from the frames of the pier, put a line on the frames, and tow them in on the high water. First, though, I would have to find a line long enough to tie every frame. If I'm to do any work at the shore I ought first put a cement patch on the leak in my right boot. After the frames are on the beach another fellow and myself ought to carry them up and stack them. And there is probably enough rockweed on the beach now, so that I ought to bring up a load or two for the sheep shed. I ought to find out who it is that is shooting coot down in the cove today, just to satisfy my own curiosity. He was out before daybreak with his decoys, but I do not think he has got any birds.

[3]   I ought to take up the wire fence round the chicken range today, roll it up in bundles, tie them with six-thread, and store them at the edge of the woods. Then I ought to move the range houses off the field and into the corner of the woods and set them up on blocks for the winter, but I ought to sweep them out first and clean the roosts with a wire brush. It would be a good idea to have a putty knife in my pocket, for scraping. I ought to

---

1 **bar:** long ridge of sand or gravel near or slightly above the surface of the water.
2 **windfalls:** apples blown down by the wind.
3 **dead low water:** that is, when the tide is at its lowest.

add a bag of phosphate to the piles of hen dressing[4] that have accumulated under the range houses and spread the mixture on the field, to get it ready for plowing. And I ought to decide whether to plow just the range itself or to turn over a little more on the eastern end. On my way in from the range I ought to stop at the henhouse long enough to climb up and saw off an overhanging branch from the apple tree—it might tear the paper roof in the first big wind storm. I shall have to get a ladder of course and a saw.

Today I certainly ought to go over to the mill and get four twelve-inch boards, twelve feet long and half an inch thick, to use in building three new hoppers[5] for dry mash feeding to my pullets,[6] which are now laying seventy-eight per cent and giving me about eighty dozen eggs a week. I should also need one board which would be an inch thick, for the end pieces and for making the ends of the reels. I shouldn't need anything for the stands because I have enough stuff round the place to build the stands—which I had better make twenty-three inches high from floor to perch. If I were to make them less than that, the birds on the floor would pick at the vents of the birds feeding.

I ought to get some shingle nails and some spikes while I am at it, as we are out of those things. And I ought to sharpen the blade of my plane if I am going to build some hoppers. I ought to take the cutting-off saw and have it filed, as long as I am going over to the mill anyway. On the way back I ought to stop in at Frank Hamilton's house and put in my application for government lime and super, because I shall be passing his house and might just as well take advantage of it. Frank will ask me to sit down and talk a while, I imagine.

It is high time I raked up the bayberry brush which has been lying in the pasture since the August mowing. This would be a good chance to burn it today because we have had a rain and it is safe to burn. But before burning it I ought to find out whether it is really better for the pasture to burn stuff like that or to let it rot for dressing. I suppose there is so much wood in it it wouldn't rot up quickly and should be burned. Besides, I was once told in high-school chemistry that no energy is ever lost to the world, and presumably the ashes from the fires will strengthen my pasture in their own way.

---

4 **dressing:** manure.
5 **hoppers:** funnel shaped bins filled from the top with food for the chickens and dispensed from the bottom.
6 **pullets:** young hens.

7   I ought to take the buck lamb out of the flock of lambs today, before he gets to work on the ewe lambs, because I don't want them to get bred. I don't know just where to put him, but I ought to decide that today, and put him there. I should send away today for some phenothiazine[7] so that I can drench[8] my sheep next week. It would probably be a good idea to try phenothiazine this time, instead of copper sulphate, which just gets the stomach worms and doesn't touch the nodular worms or the large-mouth bowel worms. And I ought to close the big doors on the north side of the barn cellar and board them up and bank them, so that the place won't be draughty down there at night when the sheep come in, as they are beginning to do. I have been thinking I ought to enlarge the south door so that I won't lose any lambs next spring from the ewes jamming through the narrow single opening, and this would be the time to do that.

8   Today I ought to start rebuilding the racks in the sheep shed, to fix them so the sheep can't pull hay out and waste it. There is a way to do this, and I know the way. So I am all set. Also I ought to fix up the pigpen down there in the barn cellar too and sweeten it up with a coat of whitening, so that I can get the pig indoors, because the nights are pretty cold now. The trough will probably not have to be rebuilt this year because last year I put a zinc binding all around the edges of it. (But if I *shouldn't* get round to fixing up the pen I should at least carry a forkful of straw down to the house where the pig now is—I should at least do that.)

9   This would be a good day to put in a new light[9] in the window in the woodshed, and also there is one broken in the shop and one in the henhouse, so the sensible thing would be to do them all at once, as long as I have the putty all worked up and the glass cutter out. I ought to hook up the stove in the shop today, and get it ready for winter use. And I ought to run up the road and see Bert and find out why he hasn't delivered the cord of slabwood he said he was going to bring me. At any rate, I ought to make a place in the cellar for it today, which will mean cleaning house down there a little and neating up, and finding a better place to keep my flats and fillers for my egg cases. Incidentally, I ought to collect eggs right now, so there won't be any breakage in the nests.

10   It just occurred to me that if I'm going to the mill today I ought to measure the truck and figure out what I shall need in the way of hardwood boards to build a set of sideboards and a headboard and a tailboard for

---

7   **phenothiazine:** chemical used to expel worms from animal intestines.
8   **drench:** to administer medicine to animals.
9   **light:** pane of glass.

my stakes. I ought to bring these boards back with me along with the pine for the hoppers. I shall need two bolts for the ends of each sideboard, and one bolt for the cleat in the middle, and two bolts for the ends of each of the head- and tailboards, and there will be three each of them, so that makes fifty-four bolts I shall need, and the stakes are about an inch and a half through and the boards will be three-quarters, so that makes two inches and a quarter, and allow another half inch for washer and nut. About a three-inch bolt would do it. I better get them today.

[11]   Another thing I ought to do is take that grass seed that the mice have been getting into in the barn and store it in a wash boiler or some pails or something. I ought to set some mousetraps tonight, I mustn't forget. I ought to set one upstairs, I guess, in the little northeast chamber where the pipe comes through from the set tubs in the back kitchen, because this is the Mouse Fifth Avenue, and it would be a good chance for a kill. I ought to gather together some old clothes and stuff for the rummage sale to raise money to buy books for the town library, and I ought to rake the barnyard and wheel the dressing down into the barn cellar where it will be out of the weather, because there is a lot of good dressing there right now. I ought to note down on the calendar in my room that I saw the ewe named Galbreath go to buck day before yesterday, so I can have her lambing date. Hers will be the first lamb next spring, and it will be twins because she is a twinner. Which reminds me I ought to write Mike Galbreath a letter. I have been owing him one since before Roosevelt was elected for the third time. I certainly should do that, it has been such a long time. I should do it today while it is in my mind.

[12]   One thing I ought to do today is to take a small Stillson wrench and go down cellar and tighten the packing nut on the water pump so it won't drip. I could do that when I am down there making a place for the slab-wood—it would save steps to combine the two things. I also ought to stir the litter in the hen-pen in the barn where the Barred Rocks[10] are, and in the henhouse where the crossbred birds are; and then fill some bushel baskets with shavings and add them to the litter in the places where it needs deepening. The dropping boards under the broody coops need cleaning and I should do that at the same time, since I will be out there anyway. As far as litter is concerned, a man could take and rake the lawn under the maples where there is such an accumulation of leaves and add these dry leaves to the litter in the houses for the birds to scratch around in. Anything to keep their minds occupied in healthy channels.

---

10   **Barred Rocks:** a breed of chickens.

13   Today I intend to pull the young alders in the field on the north side, as they are beginning to get ahead of me. I must do that today, probably later on this afternoon. A bush hook would be a good tool for that. I should also clean up the remaining garden trash and add it to the compost, saving out whatever the sheep might eat, and should remove the pipe from the well under the apple tree and store it down below in the barn.

14   I also think I had better call up a buyer and get rid of my ten old hens, since we have canned all we are going to need. After the hens are gone I shall no longer need the borrowed range house that they are living in and I can get two long poles, lash them on behind the truck, and load the house on and drag it up to Kenneth's house. But it will be necessary to take an ax and flatten the ends of the poles so they won't dig into the highway, although the tar is so cold now they probably wouldn't dig in much anyway. Still, the thing to do is do it right.

15   Another thing I should try to manage to do today is to earmark the two pure-bred lambs. That will be easy enough—it just means finding the ear tags that I put away in a drawer or some place last spring and finding the special pliers that you have to use in squeezing a tag into a sheep's ear. I think I know where those pliers are, I think they are right in my cabinet next to that jar of rubber cement. I shall have to get the lambs up, but they will come without much trouble now because they are hungry. I *could* take the buck away at the same time if I could think of a place to put him.

16   Today I want to get word to Walter about the plowing of the garden pieces, and I had also better arrange down cellar about a bin for the roots, because on account of the extra amount of potatoes we have it will mean a little rearranging down there in order to get everything in. But I can do that when I am down tightening the nut on the pump. I ought to take the car into the village today to get an inspection sticker put on it; however, on second thought if I am going to the mill I guess it would be better to go in the truck and have a sticker put on *that* while I am seeing about the lumber, and then I can bring the boards back with me. But I mustn't be away at low water otherwise I won't be able to hook on to the mooring.

17   Tomorrow is Tuesday and the egg truck will be coming through in the morning to pick up my cases, so I must finish grading and packing the eggs today—I have about fifty dozen packed and only ten to go to make up the two cases. Then I must nail up the cases and make out the tags and tack them on, and lug the cases over to the cellar door, ready to be taken out in the morning, as the expressman is apt to get here early. I've also got to write a letter today to a publisher who wrote me asking what happened to the book manuscript I was supposed to turn in a year ago last spring, and I also should take the green chair in the living room to Eliot Sweet so that

he can put in some little buttons that keep coming out all the time. I can throw the chair into the truck and drop it by his shop on my way to town. If I am going to take the squashes and pumpkins up to the attic I had better take the old blankets which we have been covering them with nights, and hang them on the line to dry. I also ought to nail a pole up somewhere in the barn to hang grain sacks on so the rats won't be able to get at them and gnaw holes in them; empty sacks are worth ten cents for the heavy ones and five cents for the cotton ones, and they mount up quite fast and run into money. I mustn't forget to do that today—it won't take but a minute.

[18]   I've got to see about getting a birthday present for my wife today, but I can't think of anything. Her birthday is past anyway. There were things going on here at the time and I didn't get around to getting her a present but I haven't forgotten about it. Possibly when I am in the village I can find something.

[19]   If I'm going to rebuild the racks for the sheep it would be a good idea to have the mill rip out a lot of two-inch slats for me while I am there, as I shall need some stuff like that. I ought to make a list, I guess. And I mustn't forget shingle nails and the spikes. There is a place on the bottom step of the stairs going down into the woodshed where the crocus sack which I nailed on to the step as a foot-wiper is torn off, and somebody might catch his foot in that and take a fall. I certainly should fix that today before someone has a nasty fall. The best thing would be to rip the old sack off and tack a new one on. A man should have some roofing nails if he is going to make a neat job of tacking a sack on to a step. I think I may have some but I'd better look. I can look when I go out to get the Stillson wrench that I shall need when I go down to tighten the packing nut on the pump, and if I haven't any I can get some when I go to town.

[20]   I've been spending a lot of time here typing, and I see it is four o'clock already and almost dark, so I had better get going. Specially since I ought to get a haircut while I am at it.

Looking Back

1. What have you learned about the author from this personal essay?

2. Picture White writing this essay. Explain why you think it was easy or difficult to write.

3. Farm life involves an almost endless number of chores to be done. Are there other jobs that are as demanding of one's time? What might they be? Do you think the rewards of farm life would compensate for the difficulties?

Looking Into

1. Compare and contrast the style of this essay with "Maintenance" by Naomi Shihab Nye or "Quality" by John Galsworthy. Consider sentence length, vocabulary, tone, and point of view.

2. White's essay is about a world he knew well, and his use of specific detail marks him as an astute observer. Try writing a similar essay about your world and the things you *should* get accomplished.

3. Write an essay in which you detail the pleasures and rewards of farm life that help to balance all the hard work detailed by White.

Looking Around

1. In the quotation introducing this section, Thoreau says that as he valued his freedom, he did not want to spend his time in "earning rich carpets or other fine furniture, or delicate cookery, or a house in the Grecian or Gothic style." Write a paper in which you explain what you think of his idea. (Consider that Thoreau had no dependents.)

2. Clive Bell, a moderately well-to-do British writer of the 1920s, wrote that "almost all kinds of money-making are detrimental to the subtler and more intense states of mind, because almost all tire the body and blunt the intellect." What did he mean? Discuss in a short paper whether you agree and whether any of the writers in this section would agree with him.

3. Of all the jobs described in this section, what kinds of work appeal to you most and why? Give your reasons in a brief essay.

4. What relation do you think your job will have to your life's work and what is the difference between the two? Give your answer in a short paper.

5. Work has sometimes been regarded as a curse imposed on humanity for its sin in the garden of Eden. At other times, work has been regarded as a blessing that helps people fulfill themselves. Discuss in a paper how the writers in this section seem to view work—as a curse or a blessing.

PART 3
Sports

—◊—

*P*rofessional sport, whether carried out for
large wages by carefully selected teams, or (as in
the Olympic Games) engaged in by "amateurs"
representing their national groups, is utterly false
to the ideal of play. The true player enjoys the
game for its own sake, and its own sake alone. If
the game is intended to subserve some other purpose, it is ruined. The play spirit has gone. In the
next Olympic Games we shall no doubt admire
the skill of some of the athletes, but we shall also
know that they are not really playing games, not
indulging in sport. They are making war. They
will not take the half-mile run and the long jump
as a combination of fun and exercise, something
from which they can return with relief and satisfaction to their normal pursuits outside the sphere
of play, as mechanics or librarians or truckdrivers.
On the contrary, they will feel that running faster
or jumping further than anyone else in the world
is the ultimate aim of their existence, and proves
something, not only about them personally, but
also about millions of their countrymen who are
not even present. . . .

Gilbert Highet from "Play and Life"

—⋘—

For whatever reason—the pleasure of companionship, the craving for recognition, an inherent drive to excel, the availability of leisure time, or a desire for entertainment—twentieth century America has seen the rise of a near-obsession with games. Magazine stands burgeon with periodicals such as *Sports Illustrated, Golf Digest, Tennis World,* and *Skiing.* Attendance at such spectator sports as professional hockey, baseball, soccer, basketball, and football expands almost as rapidly as do the various leagues. Individual participation continues to increase in personal fitness programs such as walking, jogging, swimming, and aerobics.

With one exception, the essays in this section are neither by nor about professional athletes. Instead, and in the spirit of the quotation from Gilbert Highet, their focus is on the significance of sports to individuals or families. In "Reasons of the Body," Scott Russell Sanders reflects, as both a son and a father, on the important tie that sports offers to fathers and sons but not, at least yet, to fathers and daughters. In sports, Sanders points out, are lessons in both mortality and immortality. In "A Winter Grouse," Sydney Lea and his dog Annie head out on the last day of hunting season, intent on bagging one last bird. What he finds, however, is far more satisfying.

Not all sports enthusiasts are participants. In "Basketball Season," a memoir about her experiences as a 9th-grade cheerleader, novelist Donna Tartt suggests that conflict is not limited to those who actually play the game; often, the competitiveness between players is mirrored in the lives of those who cheer them on. Frank Conroy, in "Running the Table," writes about a personal victory—his adolescent drive to perfect his skill as a pool player—and the lifelong pleasure his prowess has brought him.

Columnist Anna Quindlen considers the dark side of professional sports in "The $port$ Report" and poses, implicitly and explicitly, some important questions about the lengths to which some athletes go in order to reach questionable goals. In "Sports for the Over-40 Person (or, God had a *Reason* for Creating the Barcalounger)," Pulitzer Prize-winning humorist Dave Barry considers such diverse humiliations as cheering Little League teams, becoming a coach, walking, golf, fishing, and skiing. Barry's is definitely the last word in this section.

—⋘—

Reasons of the Body

SCOTT RUSSELL SANDERS

Scott Russell Sanders, a professor of English at Indiana University, was born in 1945, in Memphis, Tennessee. After receiving his undergraduate degree from Brown University in 1967, he won a Marshall scholarship to Cambridge University where he earned his Ph.D. in 1971. From 1977–1983 he was the author of "One Man's Faction," a column for the *Chicago Sun-Times*. Throughout his career he has contributed to many literary magazines and popular magazines and has been the recipient of various fellowships and awards for writing.

Sanders' literary career has been quite diverse: a scholarly study, *D.H. Lawrence: The World of the Major Novels* (1974); children's books such as *Warm as Wool* (1992) and *Here Comes the Mystery Man* (1993); folktales, as in *Wilderness Plots: Tales about the Settlement of the American Land* (1983) and *Hear the Wind Blow: American Folksongs Retold* (1985). He has also written both science fiction as well as historical novels. In *Secrets of the Universe: Scenes from the Journey Home* (1991), Sanders focuses on personal and nature essays. In an essay in that book, "The Singular First Person," Sanders asks, and answers, why in the late twentieth century so many writers have "[taken] up this risky form": "In this era of prepackaged thought, the essay is the closest thing we have, on paper, to a record of the individual mind at work and play. It is an amateur's raid in a world of specialists. Feeling overwhelmed by data, random information, the flotsam and jetsam of mass culture, we relish the spectacle of a single consciousness making sense of a portion of the chaos."

Looking Ahead

In this personal essay, Scott Russell Sanders speculates that sports provide not only a connection between generations but an area which, eventually and inevitably, separates the generations. His affectionate portrayal of his experiences as both a son and a father, his wistful examination of his wife's and daughter's indifference to sports, and his realization of the metaphoric power of sports—all suggest the complex contribution that sports can make to all our lives.

1    $\mathcal{M}$y son has never met a sport he did not like. I have met a few that left an ugly tingle—boxing and rodeo and pistol shooting, among others—but, then, I have been meeting them for forty-four years, Jesse only for twelve. Our ages are relevant to the discussion, because, on the hill of the sporting life, Jesse is midway up the slope and climbing rapidly, while I am over the crest and digging in my heels as I slip down.

2   "You still get around pretty well for an old guy," he told me last night after we had played catch in the park.

3   The catch we play has changed subtly in recent months, a change that dramatizes a shift in the force field binding father and son. Early on, when I was a decade younger and Jesse a toddler, I was the agile one, leaping to snare his wild throws. The ball we tossed in those days was rubbery and light, a bubble of air as big around as a soup bowl, easy for small hands to grab. By the time he started school, we were using a tennis ball, then we graduated to a softball, then to gloves and a baseball. His repertoire of catches and throws increased along with his vocabulary.

4   Over the years, as Jesse put on inches and pounds and grace, I still had to be careful how far and hard I threw, to avoid bruising his ribs or his pride. But this spring, when we began limbering up our arms, his throws came whistling at me with a force that hurt my hand, and he caught effortlessly anything I could hurl back at him. It was as though the food he wolfed down all winter had turned into spring steel. I no longer needed to hold back. Now Jesse is the one, when he is feeling charitable, who pulls his pitches.

5   Yesterday in the park, he was feeling frisky rather than charitable. We looped the ball lazily back and forth awhile. Then he started backing away, backing away, until my shoulder twinged from the length of throws. Unsatisfied, he yelled, "Make me run for it!" So I flung the ball high and deep, low and wide, driving him over the grass, yet he loped easily wherever it flew, gathered it in, then whipped it back to me with stinging speed.

6   "Come on," he yelled, "put it where I can't reach it." I tried, ignoring the ache in my arm, and still he ran under the ball. He might have been gliding on a cushion of air, he moved so lightly. I was feeling heavy, and felt heavier by the minute as his return throws, grown suddenly and unaccountably wild, forced me to hustle back and forth, jump and dive.

7   "Hey," I yelled, waving my glove at him, "look where I'm standing!"

8   "Standing is right," he yelled back. "Let's see those legs move!" His next throw sailed over my head, and the ones after that sailed farther still, now left now right, out of my range, until I gave up even trying for them, and the ball thudded accusingly to the ground. By the time we quit, I was sucking air, my knees were stiffening, and a fire was blazing in my arm.

REASONS OF THE BODY

Jesse trotted up, his T-shirt dry, his breathing casual. This was the moment he chose to clap me on the back and say, "You still get around pretty well for an old guy."

9   It was a line I might have delivered, as a cocky teenager, to my own father. He would have laughed, and then challenged me to a round of golf or a bout of arm-wrestling, contests he could still easily have won.

10   Whatever else these games may be, they are always contests. For many a boy, a playing field, court, or gym is the first arena in which he can outstrip his old man. For me, the arena was a concrete driveway, where I played basketball against my father, shooting at a rusty hoop that was mounted over the garage. He had taught me how to dribble, how to time my jump, how to follow through on my shots. To begin with, I could barely heave the ball to the basket, and he would applaud if I so much as banged the rim. I banged away, year by year, my bones lengthening, muscles thickening. I shuffled over the concrete to the jazz of birdsong and the opera of thunderstorms. I practiced fervently, as though my life depended on putting the ball through the hoop, practiced when the driveway was dusted with pollen and when it was drifted with snow. From first light to twilight, while the chimney swifts[1] spiraled out to feed on mosquitoes and the mosquitoes fed on me, I kept shooting, hour after hour. Many of those hours, Father was tinkering in the garage, which reverberated with the slap of my feet and the slam of the ball. There came a day when I realized that I could outleap him, outhustle and outshoot him. I began to notice his terrible breathing—terrible because I had not realized he could run short of air. I had not realized he could run short of anything. When he bent over and grabbed his knees, huffing, "You're too much for me," I felt at once triumphant and dismayed.

11   I still have to hold back when playing basketball with Jesse. But the day will come, and soon, when he'll grow taller and stronger, and he will be the one to show mercy. The only dessert I will be able to eat, if I am to avoid growing fat, will be humble pie.[2] Even now my shots appear old-fashioned to him, as my father's arching two-handed heaves seemed antique to me. "Show me some of those Neanderthal moves," Jesse cries, as we shoot around at a basket in the park, "show me how they did it in the Stone Age!" I do show him, clowning and hot-dogging, wishing by turns to

---

1   **swifts:** small, dark-colored birds that nest in or near chimneys.
2   **humble pie:** The expression "to eat humble pie" means that one is forced to apologize, usually publicly, as a form of humiliation.

amuse and impress him. As I fake and spin, I am simultaneously father and son, playing games forward and backward in time.

[12] The game of catch, like other sports where body faces body, is a dialogue carried on with muscle and bone. One body speaks by throwing a ball or a punch, by lunging with a foil,[3] smashing a backhand, sinking a putt, rolling a strike, kicking a shot toward the corner of the net; the other replies by swinging, leaping, dodging, tackling, parrying, balancing. As in lovemaking, this exchange may be a struggle for power or a sharing of pleasure. The call and response may be in the spirit of antiphonal[4] singing, a making of music that neither person could have achieved alone, or it may be in the spirit of insults bellowed across a table.

[13] When a father and son play sports, especially a game the son has learned from the father, every motive from bitter rivalry to mutual delight may enter in. At first eagerly, then grudgingly, and at last unconsciously, the son watches how his father grips the ball, handles the glove, swings the bat. In just the same way, the son has watched how the father swings a hammer, how the father walks, jokes, digs, starts a car, gentles a horse, pays a bill, shakes hands, shaves. There is a season in one's growing up, beginning at about the age Jesse is now, when a son comes to feel his old man's example as a smothering weight. You must shrug free of it, or die. And so, if your father carries himself soldier straight, you begin to slouch; if he strides along with a swagger, you slink; if he talks in joshing Mississippi accents to anybody with ears, you shun strangers and swallow your drawl. With luck and time, you may come to accept that you bear in your own voice overtones of your father's. You may come to rejoice that your own least motion—kissing a baby or opening a jar—is informed by memories of how your father would have done it. Between the early delight and the late reconciliation, however, you must pass through that season of rivalry, the son striving to undo or outdo his father's example, the father chewing on the bitter rind of rejection.

[14] Why do I speak only of boys and men? Because, while there are females aplenty who relish any sport you can name, I have never shared a roof with one. In her seventies, my mother still dances and swims, even leads classes in aerobics, but she's never had much use for games played with

---

3 **foil:** a fencing sword with an extremely thin blade.
4 **antiphonal:** a form of musical composition, chiefly religious, in which two choirs sing alternately or responsively.

balls, and neither has my wife Ruth or our daughter. When Ruth was a child, a bout of rheumatic fever confined her to bed and then to a wheelchair for several years. Until she was old enough for university, a heart rendered tricky by the illness kept her from doing anything that would raise her pulse, and by then she had invested her energies elsewhere, in music and science. To this day, Ruth sees no point in moving faster than a walk, or in defying gravity with exuberant leaps, or in puzzling over the trajectory of a ball.

[15]   And what of our firstborn, sprightly Eva? Surely I could have brought her up to become a partner for catch? Let me assure you that I tried. I put a sponge ball in her crib, as Father had put a baseball in mine. (I was going to follow tradition exactly and teethe her on a baseball, but Ruth, sensible of a baby's delicacy, said nothing doing.) From the moment in the hospital when the nurse handed me Eva, a quivering bundle, ours to keep, I coached my spunky girl, I coaxed and exhorted her, but she would not be persuaded that throwing or shooting or kicking a ball was a sensible way to spend an hour or an afternoon. After seventeen years of all the encouragement that love can buy, the one sport she will deign to play with me is volleyball, in which she hurtles over the grass, leaping and cavorting, as only a dancer could.

[16]   A gymnast and ballerina, Eva has always been on good terms with her body, and yet, along with her mother and my mother, she rolls her eyes when Jesse and I begin rummaging in the battered box on the porch for a baseball, basketball, or soccer ball. "So Dad," she calls, "it's off to recover past glories, is it? You show 'em, tiger. But don't break any bones."

[17]   Eva's amusement has made the opinion of the women in my life unanimous. Their baffled indulgence, bordering at times on mockery, has given to sports a tang of the mildly illicit.

[18]   Like many other women (not all, not all), those in my family take even less interest in talking about sports than in playing them. They pride themselves on being above such idle gab. They shake their heads when my son and I check the scores in the newspaper. They are astounded that we can spend longer rehashing a game than we spent in playing it. When Jesse and I compare aches after a session on field or court, the women observe mildly that it sounds as though we had been mugged. Surely we would not inflict such damage on ourselves? Perhaps we have gotten banged up from wrestling bears? We kid along and say, "Yes, we ran into the Chicago Bears," and my daughter or mother or wife will reply, "You mean the hockey team?"

[19]   In many households and offices, gossip about games and athletes breaks down along gender lines, the men indulging in it and the women

scoffing. Those on each side of the line may exaggerate their feelings, the men pumping up their enthusiasm, the women their indifference, until sport becomes a male mystery. No locker room, no sweat lodge is needed to shut women out; mere talk will do it. Men are capable of muttering about wins and losses, batting averages and slam dunks, until the flowers on the wallpaper begin to wilt and every woman in the vicinity begins to yearn for a supply of gags. A woman friend of mine, an executive in a computing firm, has been driven in self-defense to scan the headlines of the sports pages before going to work, so that she can toss out references to the day's contests and stars, like chunks of meat, to feed the appetites of her male colleagues. After gnawing on this bait, the men may consent to speak with her of things more in keeping with her taste, such as books, birds, and the human condition.

[20] My daughter has never allowed me to buy her a single item of sports paraphernalia. My son, on the other hand, has never declined such an offer. Day and night, visions of athletic gear dance in his head. With religious zeal, he pores over magazine ads for sneakers, examining the stripes and insignia as if they were hieroglyphs of ultimate truth. Between us, Jesse and I are responsible for the hoard of equipment on our back porch, which contains at present the following items: one bicycle helmet and two bicycles; a volleyball set, badminton set, and a bag of golf clubs; three racquets for tennis, two for squash, one for paddle ball; roller skates and ice skates, together with a pair of hockey sticks; goalie gloves, batting gloves, three baseball gloves and one catcher's mitt; numerous yo-yos; ten pairs of cleaned or waffle-soled shoes; a drying rack festooned with shorts and socks and shirts and sweatsuits; and a cardboard box heaped with (I counted) forty-nine balls, including those for all the sports implicated above, as well as for ping-pong, lacrosse, juggling, and jacks.

[21]   Excavated by some future archaeologist, this porch full of gear would tell as much about how we passed our lives as would the shells and seeds and bones of a kitchen midden.[5] An excavation of the word *sport* also yields evidence of breaks, bruises, and ambiguities. A sport is a game, an orderly zone marked off from the prevailing disorder, but it can also be a mutation, a violation of rules. To be good at sports is to be a winner, and yet a good sport is one who loses amiably, a bad sport one who kicks and screams at every setback. A flashy dresser might be called a sport, and so might a

---

5   **kitchen midden:** a refuse heap containing various artifacts, shells, and often animal bones.

gambler, an idler, an easygoing companion, one who dines high on the hog of pleasure. But the same label may be attached to one who is the butt of jokes, a laughingstock, a goat. As a verb, to sport can mean to wear jewelry or clothes in a showy manner, to poke fun, to trifle, to roll promiscuously in the hay. It is a word spiced with unsavory meanings, rather tacky and cheap, with hints of brothels, speakeasies, and malodorous dives. And yet it bears also the wholesome flavor of fairness, vigor, and ease.

[22] The lore of sports may be all that some fathers have to pass down to their sons in place of lore about hunting animals, planting seeds, killing enemies, or placating the gods. Instead of telling him how to shoot a buffalo, the father whispers in the son's ear how to shoot a lay-up. Instead of consulting the stars of the entrails of birds, father and son consult the smudged print of newspapers to see how their chosen spirits are faring. They fiddle with the dials of radios, hoping to catch the oracular murmur of a distant game. The father recounts heroic deeds, not from the field of battle, but from the field of play. The seasons about which he speaks lead not to harvests but to championships. No longer intimate with the wilderness, no longer familiar even with the tamed land of farms, we create artificial landscapes bounded by lines of paint or lime. Within those boundaries, as within the frame of a chessboard or painting, life achieves a memorable, seductive clarity. The lore of sports is a step down from that of nature, perhaps even a tragic step, but it is lore nonetheless, with its own demigods and demons, magic and myths.

[23] The sporting legends I carry from my father are private rather than public. I am haunted by scenes that no journalist recorded, no camera filmed. Father is playing a solo round of golf, for example, early one morning in April. The fairways glisten with dew. Crows rasp and fluster in the pines that border the course. Father lofts a shot toward a par-three hole, and the white ball arcs over the pond, over the sand trap, over the shaggy apron of grass onto the green, where it bounces, settles down, then rolls toward the flag, rolls unerringly, inevitably, until it falls with a scarcely audible click into the hole. The only eyes within sight besides his own are the crows'. For once, the ball has obeyed him perfectly, harmonizing wind and gravity and the revolution of the spheres, one shot has gone where all are meant to go, and there is nobody else to watch. He stands on the tee, gazing at the distant hole, knowing what he has done and that he will never do it again. The privacy of this moment appeals to me more than all the clamor and fame of a shot heard round the world.

[24] Here is another story I live by: The man who will become my father is twenty-two, a catcher for a bush-league baseball team in Tennessee. He

will never make it to the majors, but on weekends he earns a few dollars for squatting behind the plate and nailing runners foolish enough to try steal- ing second base. From all those bus rides, all those red-dirt diamonds, the event he will describe for his son with deepest emotion is an exhibition game. Father's team of whites, most of them fresh from two-mule farms, is playing a touring black team, a rare event for that day and place. To make it even rarer, and the sides fairer, the coaches agree to mix the teams. And so my father, son of a Mississippi cotton farmer, bruised with racial no- tions that will take a lifetime to heal, crouches behind the plate and for nine innings catches fastballs and curves, change-ups and screwballs from a whirling, muttering wizard of the Negro Baseball League, one Leroy Robert Paige,[6] known to the world as Satchel. Afterward, Satchel Paige tells the farm boy, "You catch a good game," and the farm boy answers, "You've got the stuff, mister." And for the rest of my father's life, this man's pitching serves as a measure of mastery.

25   And here is a third myth I carry: One evening when the boy who will become my father is eighteen, he walks into the Black Cat Saloon in Tupelo, Mississippi. He is looking for a fight. Weary of plowing, sick of red dirt, baffled by his own turbulent energy, he often picks fights. This evening the man he picks on is a stranger who occupies a nearby stool at the bar, a husky man in his thirties, wearing a snap-brim hat,[7] dark suit with wide lapels, narrow tie, and infuriatingly white shirt. The stranger is slow to anger. The red-headed Sanders boy keeps at him, keeps at him, mocking the Yankee accent, the hat worn indoors, the monkey suit, the starched shirt, until at last the man stands up and backs away from the bar, fists raised. The Sanders boy lands three punches, he remembers that much, but the next thing he remembers is waking up on the sidewalk, the stranger bending over him to ask if he is all right, and to ask, besides, if he would like a boxing scholarship to Mississippi State. The man is headed there to become the new coach. The boy who will become my father goes to Mis- sissippi State for two years, loses some bouts and wins more, then quits to pursue a Golden Gloves title, and when he fails at that he keeps on fighting in bars and streets, and at last he quits boxing, his nose broken so many

---

6   **Leroy Robert Paige:** Known as "Satchel," Paige (1906–1982) was one of the old Negro Baseball League's most famed pitchers; in 1948, shortly after Jackie Robinson was hired by the Brooklyn Dodgers, Paige was hired by the Cleveland Indians. He subsequently played for the St. Louis Browns (1951–53) and pitched his last three innings in Kansas City in 1965. He was inducted into the Baseball Hall of Fame in 1972.
7   **snap-brim hat:** a hat, primarily a man's, with a flexible brim.

times there is no bone left in it, only a bulb of flesh which a boy sitting in his lap will later squeeze and mash like dough. From all those bouts, the one he will describe to his son with the greatest passion is that brawl from the Black Cat Saloon, when the stranger in the white shirt, a good judge of fighters, found him worthy.

[26] Father tried, with scant success, to make a boxer of me. Not for a career in the ring, he explained, but for defense against the roughs and rowdies who would cross my path in life. If I ran into a mean customer, I told him, I could always get off the path. No, Father said, a man never backs away. A man stands his ground and fights. This advice ran against my grain, which inclined toward quickness of wits rather than fists, yet for years I strove to become the tough guy he envisioned. Without looking for fights, I stumbled into them at every turn, in schoolyard and backyard and in the shadows of barns. Even at my most belligerent, I still tried cajolery and oratory first. Only when that failed did I dig in my heels and start swinging. I gave bruises and received them, gave and received bloody noses, leading with my left, as Father had taught me, protecting my head with forearms, keeping my thumbs outside my balled fists to avoid breaking them when I landed a punch.

[27] Some bullies saw my feistiness as a red flag. One boy who kept hounding me was Olaf Magnuson, a neighbor whose surname I would later translate with my primitive Latin as Son of Big. The name was appropriate, for Olaf was two years older and a foot taller and forty pounds heavier than I was. He pestered me, cursed me, irked and insulted me. When I stood my ground, he pounded me into it. One evening in my twelfth summer, after I had staggered home several times from these frays bloodied and bowed, Father decided it was time for serious boxing lessons. We would train for two months, he told me, then challenge Olaf Magnuson to a fight, complete with gloves and ropes and bell. This did not sound like a healthy idea to me; but Father insisted. "Do you want to keep getting pushed around," he demanded, "or are you going to lick the tar out of him?"

[28] Every day for two months I ran, skipped rope, did chin-ups and push-ups. Father hung his old punching bag from a rafter in the basement, and I flailed at it until my arms filled with sand. He wrapped an old mattress around a tree and told me to imagine Olaf Magnuson's belly as I pounded the cotton ticking. I sparred with my grizzly old man, who showed me how to jab and hook, duck and weave, how to keep my balance and work out of corners. Even though his feet had slowed, his hands were still so quick that I sometimes dropped my own gloves to watch him, dazzled.

"Keep up those dukes,[8]" he warned. "Never lower your guard." For two months I trained as though I had a boxer's heart.

29   Father issued our challenge by way of Olaf Magnuson's father, a strapping man with a voice like a roar in a barrel. "Hell yes, my boy'll fight," the elder Magnuson boomed.

30   On the morning appointed for our bout, Father strung rope from tree to tree in the yard, fashioning a ring that was shaped like a lozenge. My mother, who had been kept in the dark about the grudge match until that morning, raised Cain for a while; failing to make us see what fools we were, disgusted with the ways of men, she drove off to buy groceries. My sister carried word through the neighborhood, and within minutes a gaggle of kids and a scattering of bemused adults pressed against the ropes.

31   "You're going to make that lunkhead bawl in front of the whole world," Father told me in the kitchen while lacing my gloves, "You're going to make him call for his mama. Before you're done with him, he's going to swallow so many teeth that he'll never mess with you again."

32   So long as Father was talking, I believed him. I was a mean hombre. I was bad news, one fist of iron and the other one steel. When he finished his pep talk, however, and we stepped out into the sunshine, and I saw the crowd buzzing against the ropes, and I spied enormous Olaf slouching from his own kitchen door, my confidence hissed away like water on a hot griddle. In the seconds it took me to reach the ring, I ceased to feel like the bringer of bad news and began to feel like the imminent victim. I danced in my corner, eyeing Olaf. His torso, hulking above jeans and clodhopper boots, made my own scrawny frame look like a preliminary sketch for a body. I glanced down at my ropy arms, at my twiggy legs exposed below red gym shorts, at my hightopped basketball shoes, at the grass.

33   "He'll be slow," Father growled in my ear, "slow and clumsy. Keep moving. Bob and weave. Give him that left jab, watch for an opening, and then *bam*, unload with the right."

34   Not trusting my voice, I nodded, and kept shuffling my sneakers to hide the shivers.

35   Father put his palms to my cheeks and drew my face close to his and looked hard at me. Above that smushed, boneless nose, his brown eyes were as dark and shiny as those of a deer. "You okay, big guy?" he asked. "You ready for this?" I nodded again. "Then go get him," he said, turning me around and giving me a light shove toward the center of the ring.

---

8 **dukes:** an old-fashioned term for bare fists.

[36] I met Olaf there for instructions from the referee, a welder who lived down the road from us, a wiry man with scorched forearms who had just fixed our trailer hitch. I lifted my eyes reluctantly from Olaf's boots, along the trunks of his jean-clad legs, over the expanse of brawny chest and palooka jaw to his ice-blue eyes. They seemed less angry than amused.

[37] A cowbell clattered. Olaf and I touched gloves, backed apart and lifted our mitts. The crowd sizzled against the ropes. Blood banged in my ears, yet I could hear Father yelling. I hear him still. And in memory I follow his advice, I bob, I weave, I guard my face with curled gloves. I feint and jab within the roped diamond. I begin to believe in myself, I circle my lummoxy rival and pepper him with punches, I feel a grin rising to my lips, and then Olaf tires of the game and rears back and knocks me flat. He also knocks me out. He also breaks my nose, which will remain crooked forever after.

[38] That ended my boxing career. Olaf quit bullying me, perhaps because my blackout had given him a scare, perhaps because he had proved whatever he needed to prove. What I had shown my father was less clear. He may have seen weakness, may have seen a doomed and reckless bravery, may have seen a clown's pratfall.[9] In any case, he never again urged me to clear the path with my fists.

[39] And I have not offered boxing lessons to my son. Instead, I offered him the story of my defeat. When Jesse would still fit in my lap, I cuddled him there and told of my fight with Olaf, and he ran his delicate finger against the crook in my nose, as I had fingered the boneless pulp of Father's nose. I told Jesse about learning to play catch, the ball passing back and forth like a thread between my father and me, stitching us together. I told him about the time one of my pitches sailed over Father's head and shattered the windshield of our 1956 Ford, a car just three days old, and Father only shook his head and said, "Shoot, boy, you get that fastball down, and the batters won't see a thing but smoke." And I told Jesse about sitting on a feather tick[10] in a Mississippi farmhouse, wedged between my father and grandfather, shaking with their excitement while before us on a tiny black-and-white television two boxers slammed and hugged each other.

---

9 **pratfall:** a purposeful, comic fall originated by clowns and most recently perfected by Chevy Chase, chiefly on the TV program "Saturday Night Live."

10 **feather tick:** a comforter filled with feathers and enclosed in a narrow striped cotton fabric called "ticking."

Cradling my boy, I felt how difficult it is for men to embrace without the liquor of violence, the tonic of pain.

[40] Why do we play these games so avidly? All sports, viewed dispassionately, are dumb. The rules are arbitrary, the behaviors absurd. For boxing and running, perhaps, you could figure out evolutionary advantages. But what earthly use is it to become expert at swatting a ball with a length of wood or at lugging an inflated pigskin through a mob? Freudians might say that in playing with balls we men are simply toying with the prize portion of our anatomies. Darwinians might claim that we are competing for the attention of females, like so many preening peacocks or head-butting rams. Physicians might attribute the sporting frenzy to testosterone, economists might point to our dreams of professional paychecks, feminists might appeal to our machismo, philosophers to our fear of death.

[41] No doubt all of those explanations, like buckets put out in the rain, catch some of the truth. But none of them catches all of the truth. None of them explains, for example, what moves a boy to bang a rubber ball against a wall for hours, for entire summers, as my father did in his youth, as I did in mine, as Jesse still does. That boy, throwing and catching in the lee of garage or barn, dwells for a time wholly in his body, and that is reward enough. He aims the ball at a knothole, at a crack, then leaps to snag the rebound, mastering a skill, working himself into a trance. How different is his rapture from the dancing and drumming of a young brave? How different is his solitude from that of any boy seeking visions?

[42] The less use we have for our bodies, the more we need reminding that the body possesses its own way of knowing. To steal a line from Pascal: The body has its reasons that reason knows nothing of. Although we struggle lifelong to dwell in the flesh without rancor, without division between act and desire, we succeed only for moments at a time. We treasure whatever brings us those moments, whether it be playing cello or playing pool, making love or making baskets, kneading bread or nursing a baby or kicking a ball. Whoever teaches us an art or skill, whoever shows us a path to momentary wholeness, deserves our love.

[43] I am conscious of my father's example whenever I teach a game to my son. Demonstrating a stroke in tennis or golf, I amplify my gestures, like a ham actor playing to the balcony. My pleasure in the part is increased by the knowledge that others, and especially Father, have played it before me. What I know about hitting a curve or shooting a hook shot or throwing a left jab, I know less by words than by feel. When I take Jesse's hand and curl his fingers over the baseball's red stitches, explaining how to make it deviously spin, I feel my father's hands slip over mine like gloves. Move

like so, like so. I feel the same ghostly guidance when I hammer nails or fix a faucet or pluck a banjo. Working on the house or garden or car, I find myself wearing more than my father's hands, find myself clad entirely in his skin.

44   One blistering afternoon when I was a year younger than Jesse is now, a flyball arched toward me in center field. I ran under it, lifted my face and glove, and lost the ball in the sun. The ball found me, however, crashing into my eye. In the split second before blacking out I saw nothing but light. We need not go hunting pain, for pain will find us. It hurts me more to see Jesse ache than to break one of my own bones. I cry out as the ground ball bangs into his throat. I wince as he comes down crookedly with a rebound and turns his ankle. I wish to spare him injury as I wish to spare him defeat, but I could not do so even if I had never lobbed him that first fat pitch.

45   As Jesse nears thirteen, his estimate of my knowledge and my power declines rapidly. If I were a potter, say, or a carpenter, my skills would outreach his for decades to come. But where speed and stamina are the essence, a father in his forties will be overtaken by a son in his teens. Training for soccer, Jesse carries a stopwatch as he jogs around the park. I am not training for anything, only knocking rust from my joints and beguiling my heart, but I run along with him, puffing to keep up. I know that his times will keep going down, while I will never run faster than I do now. This is as it should be, for his turn has come. Slow as I am, and doomed to be slower, I relish his company.

46   In the game of catch, this dialogue of throw and grab we have been carrying on since he was old enough to crawl, Jesse has finally begun to put questions that I cannot answer. I know the answers; I can see how my back should twist, my legs should pump; but legs and back will no longer match my vision. This faltering is the condition of our lives, of course, a condition that will grow more acute with each passing year. I mean to live the present year before rushing off to any future ones. I mean to keep playing games with my son, so long as flesh will permit, as my father played games with me well past his own physical prime. Now that sports have begun to give me lessons in mortality, I realize they have also been giving me, all the while, lessons in immortality. These games, these contests, these grunting conversations of body to body, father to son, are not substitutes for some other way of being alive. They are the sweet and sweaty thing itself.

Looking Back

1. Sanders divides his essay into seven sections. What is the focus of each section?

2. What important motifs does Sanders emphasize throughout his essay?

3. What is the significance of the title?

4. In a small group, discuss the meaning of the Pascal quotation: "The body has its reasons that reason knows nothing of." How might you rephrase this statement? What examples from your own experiences prove or disprove Pascal's observation?

5. What other activities besides sports might provide opportunities for parent and child to get to know each other better?

6. How do sports serve as a link connecting generations?

Looking Into

1. With what three statements in the essay do you most agree? disagree? Explain why.

2. What sports myth or legend involving yourself or a member of your family will you pass down to your own children? Follow Sanders's model in paragraph 5 and write a well-developed paragraph about a specific incident.

3. Write a short paper in which you describe your favorite childhood memory of playing a sport.

A Winter Grouse

Sydney Lea

Born in Philadelphia, Pennsylvania, in 1942, Sydney Lea attended Yale University for both his undergraduate and his two graduate degrees. He began his teaching career at Dartmouth University in 1970, but became an adjunct professor when, in 1978, he took over the editorship of *New England Review*, a periodical dedicated to publishing the best contemporary poetry, essays, fiction, reviews, interviews, and translations, and one of two periodicals which he founded. Since 1980, he has been an adjunct professor at both Yale University and Middlebury College. He is the author of a critical study *Gothic to Fantastic; Readings in Supernatural Fiction* (1981), but most of his published works are collections of poetry: *Searching the Drowned Man* (1980), *The Floating Candles* (1982), and *No Sign* (1987). Lea has also been a contributor to *New Republic, New Yorker,* and *Nation*. Lea's chief interests "are in the out of doors and in 'outdoorsy' people, especially oldtimers whose ilk is vanishing."

Looking Ahead

Not all sports require elaborate equipment, teams, or points flashed onto towering electronic scoreboards. A successful hunter, for example, needs only an adequate weapon, a talented dog whose keen nose "points" to any available game, an unposted area in which to hunt, and a modicum of luck. In the following account of a wintry day of hunting, Lea not only chronicles his experiences on the last November day of grouse season, but meditates on life, death, and the "power and glory" of God.

1   As forecast, last night brought this slight layer of snow. Today will be my final one to hunt grouse: the need is vanished, the game cover skinny, the scent worse and worse.

2   I have, of course, the flu.

3   In recent years the first storm, the last day of my season and this sickness have so perfectly coincided that I've come to believe more than ever in the body's power of recall. My chest tightens, my eyes burn—they know how to mark an anniversary. I should lie in bed and recover, but there are other things to recover. To cover again. The covers . . .

4   "Colder than a frog's mouth," a neighbor says as we stamp by the general store's gas pumps. Across the common, Old Glory, blown straight as a plank. "Take two men to hold on one man's hat today," the neighbor adds; I've heard it before, but am happy to hear it again. Habit becomes me. Yes, it'll be bad scent in such a gale, and bad hearing; after all the explosive years, my ears aren't much even in a still woods.

5   Yet I'm happy, the world so crisp and hard-edged I might be in some museum of the Beautiful, a commemorative place. Death of a season, but I am like a person who, at the term of a bountiful life, may recognize death as the imperative that kept him keen to the bounty itself.

6   I know. All over the globe, desperate or despicable people unsheathe the billy, unfurl the electric lead, approach the cell.[1] Others somewhere contemplate throw weight.[2] Still others—the last of the bottle sucked down—turn on wife or child in a rage that's incomprehensible, even to themselves. Not logical, exactly, this dream of available bliss that I vaguely pursue as I set off along Route 113, yet there it is. It's there even as through my truck window I read the late history of nearby woods where I used to shoot, where new "country estates" dot the hills. I must range farther each year, so much closing down around me.

7   Still, my mood is affirmative—never mind the No Hunting posters on every tree; never mind that this will likely be my last hunt in the Gore, which has been bought by the ski industry; never mind that soon the winter sports enthusiasts will put up even more posters, hoping to save the wildlife they'll never see. (*Two thousand* condos planned in the Gore, each owner a friend to game . . .)

8   I bump my rig out of sight on the creamery lane. Just a cellar hole here now. I remember the proprietor's name: Hazen Flye. I remember the year he died—how trim he left the place, how soon it moldered, how soon the game flocked back to reclaim it. Instant ruin, full of romance.

---

1   **unsheathe the billy, unfurl the electric lead, approach the cell:** take out a billy club, straighten the lead, presumably to an electric prod. Lea's images suggest torturers approaching a prisoner's cell.

2   **throw weight:** Lea continues the images of horror by referring to a hangman's need to know the weight of a body so that it can be counterweighted by a sufficient amount of bagged sand or dirt to ensure the instant breaking of the neck.

9   Annie shrinks and moans as I slip on the bell collar, her usual charade of suffering; then she races across the rough ghost of a meadow to loose her bowels. I step into the cover[3] a few feet to wait. A woodcock, diehard loiterer, whistles up and hovers above me. I stare at him there along my barrels, then watch his long flight over the road. When Annie comes back, she locks on the little bird's scent. *Gone*, I call to her.

10   This is a three-hour cover if you work it all. I have small faith that I'll move many partridge, smaller still that I'll get decent points,[4] almost none that I'll hear wings. But somehow I mean to cover every inch.

11   Behind the creamery, land plummets down a steep lane of haw and blasted apple. I follow. A blaze flares from a trunk where a buck has hooked,[5] and here and there his cuff marks and the orange dribble of his rut show as I wobble downhill. Jesus, I'm weak. It's going to be a real struggle coming out, but I'll worry about that then.

12   The only sign of feed is a solitary thorn apple in a clump of untracked snow—perfectly red, perfectly shaped and displayed. I behold it a moment.

13   I move on, pausing frequently in fealty to my sickness and in order to pick up the sound of the bell. What a wind! More than once, I blow my lungs out on the whistle, so that the dog (close by after all) skulks, confused. What is bothering me?

14   Nothing, really. The sky is that near purple I'd sooner associate with February than November. No cloud softens the prospect, but that seems part of the general rightness this morning—rude as barbed wire, lovely.

15   Was that a grouse's flush? I don't know. I think so, but it may have been merely the hurtle of air. When I come on Annie, I think she has that slightly offended look she wears when a partridge has flown and no shot been fired. Has she been pointing all this time?

16   I toot her on, losing the sound of her in an instant, noisy as I am, crunching past the abandoned hunter's shack, tripping once on a downed alder and crashing. I smile to recall the rage such accidents used to induce, how once I stood throwing forearm shivers at a hornbeam, as if that would

---

3   **cover:** the area which the hunter will systematically walk in hopes of disturbing any game birds hiding in the brush or trees.

4   **decent points:** adequate warnings as given by the hunting dog, or pointer, who stands quietly when it senses game and, thus, alerts the hunter.

5   **blaze...hooked:** A male deer will mark its territory, and indicate its interest in a female deer, by marking, or "blazing," a tree by hooking its horns around the trunk and cutting the bark.

avenge the indignity of my pratfall. You're a grown-up now at least, I think. For better or worse . . .

17   No grouse among the grapevines below the shack. Why would there be, the grapes burst or bitten or buried long since?

18   I should take my usual route west through the remaining cover, but I'm beset by odd curiosity to explore new ground, the likelihood of killing anything remote as it is. Younger, I'd have scoffed at the notion of exploring on the last day, especially in a zone the skiers had doomed. Maybe this morning I seek a farewell that's inclusive. I don't know, I don't know.

19   I push on to a wide brook. Now where does *it* come from, go to? Bizarre territory: high grass waves tawny in the wind. I squint hotly at a small patch around me, watching the near stalks riffle, ignoring the snowy ridges to north and south. *This might be Africa, a lion crouched in that stuff, big tail flickering, dark stare on his face.*

20   A hallucination of wonder, however, not terror.

21   Water leaving me no choice, I do turn west and follow the brook along its ice-beaded ledges. Annie rushes past—I can hear the bell for once, and can just make out her color in the lioncover. She stops dead forty yards on. What the hell? I scrooch to the ground; it would be soft in a softer season, and I can believe that some maverick woodcock might drop to it for a brief, disenchanting spell; but surely I saw the autumn's last woodcock up where I came in, wished him well, willed him southward.

22   Thus it's carelessly that I amble to the point, and in complete surprise that I behold the flush. The bird crosses the brook in the frank light, scales into larches whose last needles tumble in cascades. I have not thought to raise my gun.

23   I know that this winter I'll see the grouse again in mind, almost black against that drift of gold. It's true what they say about fish, I think, by sudden association—you remember The One That Got Away. I have not fired at this partridge, but somehow I've also had *him* on a line. I think just now I pray, if wordlessly, that the snow stay fluffy, that no fox paw through an overnight crust, that till melt the bird keep busy on high limbs decked in fat, nourishing buds . . .

24   *Perfect, perfect, perfect,* I whisper as I swish through the wavy stuff beside this pristine stream. Once I stop at water's edge to watch a wild brook trout dart under the cutback. Perfect, that deep green jacket, those vermilion dots, that shearwater shape.

25 I don't comprehend my sudden electric expectation, but it has nothing to do with grouse. I can't yet know that within the hour I will see God, or more accurately, will understand that I've been in His presence right along.

Indeed, my thoughts as I break out of the strange savannah are not epical but domestic: of my tall wife, chuckling over some piece of humor we shared last night; of the children too, each a treasure. Have you had such moments, when the clutter and strife that befall the happiest of families seem never to have been? If not, I wish them on you.

26 I turn north again, into the blow, against the swell of that hill I tripped so dreamily down at the start. The dog begins to make game—straight up, of course. I must labor to follow, the flu like a flatiron in my chest, each breath a bubble of phlegm, my legs no firmer than jam.

27   No. I must stop and sit, and I do, facing downhill, and to hell with a bird! I'll find another; if not today, then . . .

28   My tracks in the snow dust retreat into jackfirs. I follow them there with my eyes. I could rise and retrace them, seeing much on the way of what I've already seen this morning. But not all. To see it all, I must do what I'm doing, close down my burning lids and recreate it. An impulse as of tears, not unpleasant, stirs at the back of my throat. If I sat long enough, letting go, the mind's backtrack would take me through that strange yellow grass, across the frozen bottom by the dead hunter's camp, back up the hawthorn lane to the creamery's cellar cavity where I flushed the wood-cock; but it would also lead me back through a thousand other thickets, up and down a thousand sidehills, around slough and slough, over the knob-by apples that a thousand grouse have pecked at. I'd come on the points of five beloved dogs. I'd come on myself, maybe flailing my wrath against that ironwood or casting down the empty shotgun, having missed an easy straightway. And I'd come on men (especially my father and three others) who are ever my age in vision, but who are gone now, all but one. Gone, or as that one puts it, "used up."

29   Behind me, in wind's momentary lull, a grouse rattles away; I'm sure of it this time. Annie has been pointing, not twenty yards distant. Now she takes two steps, the bell barely clinking, and pauses. I whistle her ahead; she starts her hunt again, never daunted. I get up and puff to the knoll's top, my gun shouldered, melancholy settled on me like a huge affirmation . . . which of course it is; after all, is it not signs of life that make us mourn their pass-ing, that joy and fullness to which we now and then have had access?

30   I can't know that my dog, who's so busy, so much in her prime, will be eaten up with cancer four months from now, that she'll die in my arms on a table at the clinic, that the vet—a good man, but stiff—will fumble for words to console this weeping fool, and will fail to find them.

31   I pause in the creamery meadow. The dung that Annie left as I waited under that hovering woodcock has already hardened. It marks where she

started, and now, so soon after, she paces back and forth by the pickup, wanting me to take her someplace where the action's livelier. She's just a dog, after all, and a young one at that.

32   Not that I'm so old myself. I'm in good shape, ordinarily in perfect health, and this side of fifty. Not young and not old, then, but between. This is not a physical matter alone, I'm thinking, as at the wheel I ponder which dirt road to follow. The easterly one, which my doctor would recommend, takes me directly home. The westerly will take me to the Gore's far side and another big cover. But there's a third road that runs north for fifteen miles and then winds homeward. At twenty, flu be damned, I'd have ordered myself through that other big patch. In a different mood, I might still be dismayed or angry at myself for not doing so not, for not *being* twenty anymore. At sixty (if there are still places to hunt), I may in a similar circumstance choose the home road. But just now I'm in middle way, as they say, and that seems—in accord with the day's judgments—a good place.

33 This little middle-road tangle is almost square and sits in the center of a timber yard, ancient and vast. The loggers cut all the surrounding highland pine and oak, and there was nothing but ledge under the topsoil: the whole ridge is turned to bone, its only growth a few maple whips. Why they left this square down below I don't know. Was there no market for the cedars that loom now over the sumac, witch hazel and barberry I'll stagger through? At the northwest corner of the square they also left a hedge that juts uphill like the handle on a pot. A freshet runs through it in spring, but in fall you can hike up its bed, as I always do, because of a certain day in 1976.

34   There were three of us. We knew, we know, one another's moves by heart: I handle the dog, Joey to my right and Terry to my left. I was running Gus then, a real ranger, and he had spilled out of the usual cover and come on point in the hedgerow. Joe crossed the brook bed, Terry staying on the east edge, and I walked up the middle. The grouse had nowhere to go. There were six of them, and we got them all.

35   We have religiously tramped the row's full length ever since, though we've never found another partridge there, for whatever his conservation ethic—and ours is acute—each hunter wants just one time to see the dream of annihilation come true. If he stays at it, it will come true—just that once and never again. Yet the urge to retrace such a path of dream and memory won't be resisted.

36   I am nothing but aching joints and hot gasps by now, but I walk the path to its difficult uphill end. Of course I flush nothing. Annie obligingly works the strip, then breaks from it downhill toward the "real" cover. She is a rocket over the granite, with its spare adornments of cane maple, lichen,

ground pine. Head high, she cuts across the rough, unseeable wind. I watch her grow smaller, and somehow whiter, as she approaches the thicket below. At the last moment, I blast the whistle and she wheels without breaking stride. I regard her in the frame of the larger landscape: black softwood at cover's edge, two knolls behind it with their stark poplar fringes. And in this instant, the air is invisible no longer, but possesses a shine, like paint in the halos of quattrocento saints.[6]

37   It is a blasphemy, even to those of us whose faith is uncanonical, to have said that I would this morning see God. But it is in any case not God I claim now to see so much as what Paul calls His power and glory, evident "in the things that have been made."

38   I pass in this fever of mine through what's left of the cover, slowly, and ever more so as I near the road. There will be no game in these last hundred or so feet—there never is—but I mean to protract the sense of a perfect end. The winter will be long, and what may be beyond it?

39   Annie already stands by the truck's door, anxious again to try the birds somewhere else. She doesn't know that the hunt and season are done for. I hear her whine excitement, mouth gaped in a yawn whose climax is a vibrato squeal. The wind's still broad and urgent, second growth around me tossing, clicking.

40   I look up, as we have been taught to do in such moods, and there in a deal elm, for no reason at all, unless it be the one I surmise, sits the last grouse I'll see this year with a scattergun in my hand. I begin to raise the Winchester, speculating on which direction the bird will take when it flies. But it continues to sit, chiseled, stationary.

41   How long do I behold that grouse? I don't know. But the gun comes down and I break it, momentarily feeling the shapeliness of shotshells before I slip them into my vest.

42   If this were a true vision, I'd report that from that limb a voice thunders, demanding, *What manner of man art thou?* Indeed, though it makes no sound that an outer ear could hear, I imagine I do hear that voice. Perhaps to that exact extent this is—all of it—as true a vision as I believe, my gun cased, my dog crated, my truck following the snow-smeared lane back eastward.

43   Back to where I've come from today—home and heat and family, and the young year's white coming months.

---

6   **quattrocento saints:** saints in Renaissance pictures painted in the fifteenth century, one of the greatest periods of Italian painting and sculpture.

Looking Back

1. As he prepares to go hunting, the author ignores a number of bad omens. What are they? Why do you think the author chooses to ignore them?

2. How many birds does the author actually see? Why does he fail to shoot each of them?

3. How has middle age changed the author?

4. Lea's essay title may contain a pun. What is it and why might it be appropriate to his topic?

5. The author claims to have an acute conservation ethic (paragraph 35). Discuss how hunting might lead one to an increased awareness of the need to conserve resources.

Looking Into

1. What qualities does hunting demand that seem transferable to life? Make a list of the two or three most significant to you. Then, in a small group, defend your choices.

2. Choose one of the qualities you listed for the question above and write a short narrative about a situation in which you found that quality indispensable.

3. What is your opinion of hunting? Write a short paper in which you state your objections to or support of hunters and hunting. Give reasons to support your position.

Basketball Season

Donna Tartt

Born in Grenada, Mississippi, in the mid-1960s, Donna Tartt wrote her first poem at the age of five, had a sonnet published in a Mississippi literary review at the age of thirteen, and had won various essay contests before entering "Ole Miss," the University of Mississippi, at Oxford, Mississippi, in 1981. Encouraged by classmates and teachers who had read some of her short stories, Tartt transferred to Bennington College in her sophomore year, the same year she began her first novel, *The Secret History* (1992). After graduating from college, she worked at a bookstore in Boston and for a painting teacher in New York City while finishing her novel.

Looking Ahead

In that long era before Title IX became law and allowed high school girls to achieve equal sports rights with boys, high school inter-scholastic competitions occurred solely between males. In those unenlightened times, a high school girl's "official" association with an inter-scholastic sports event was limited to being a member of the cheerleading squad. Those lucky and popular few who could get past the try-outs and onto the squad usually thought of themselves as socially elite. Just as sports had its hierarchy of freshman, junior varsity and varsity teams, the cheerleaders, too, had a pecking order. In the following essay, Donna Tartt recounts her thoughts and feelings during the long drives to and from the away games, the humiliations of being a decidedly junior member of the squad, and the ominous parallels she eventually discerns between the frivolous world of cheerleading and the frightening worlds of George Orwell's novels *Animal Farm* and *1984*.

[1] The year I was a freshman cheerleader, I was reading *1984*. I was fourteen years old then and failing algebra and the fact that I was failing it worried me as I would worry now if the Mafia was after me, or if I had shot

somebody and the police were coming to get me. But I did not have an awful lot of time to brood about this. It was basketball season then, and there was a game nearly every night. In Mississippi the schools are far apart, and sometimes we would have to drive two hundred miles to get to Panola Academy, Sharkey-Issaquena, funny how those old names come back to me; we'd leave sometimes before school was out, not get home till twelve or one in the morning. I was not an energetic teenager and this was hard on me. Too much exposure to the high-decibel world of teen sports—shrieking buzzers; roaring stomping mobs; thunderous feet of players charging up the court—kept me in a kind of perpetual stunned condition; the tin roof echo of rural gymnasiums rang through all my silences, and frequently at night I woke in a panic, because I thought a player was crashing through my bedroom window or a basketball was flying at me and about to knock my teeth out.

2   I read *1984* in the back seats of Cadillacs, Buicks, Lincoln Town Cars, riding through the flat wintry Delta[1] with my saddle oxfords off and my schoolbooks piled beneath my feet. Our fathers—professional men, mostly, lawyers and optometrists, prosperous local plumbers—took turns driving us back and forth from the games; the other cheerleaders griped about this but though I griped along with them, I was secretly appalled at the rowdy team bus, full of boys who shouted things when you walked by their table in the cafeteria and always wanted to copy your homework. The cars, on the other hand, were wide, spacious, quiet. Somebody's mother would usually have made cookies; there were always potato chips and old issues of *Seventeen*. The girls punched listlessly at the radio; applied Bonne Bell lip gloss; did their homework or their hair. Sometimes a paperback book would make the rounds. I remember reading one book[2] about a girl whose orphaned cousin came to live with her, gradually usurping the girl's own position in the household and becoming homecoming queen and family favorite. ("'Why can't *you* be more like Stephanie?' yelled Mom, exasperated.") It turned out that Stephanie was not the girl's real cousin at all, but a witch: a total surprise to the nincompoop parents, who had not noticed such key signs as Stephanie failing to show up in photographs, or the family dog ("Lady") and the girl's horse ("Wildfire") going crazy every time Stephanie came within fifty feet.

---

1 **Delta**: the rich farming area in southern Mississippi formed by the Pearl, Yazoo, and Mississippi rivers as they empty into the Gulf of Mexico.

2 **one book**: *Summer of Fear* by Lois Duncan.

³   Now that I think about it, I believe I read *Animal Farm*³ before *1984*. I read it in the car, too, riding through monotonous cottonfields in the weak winter afternoon, on the way to a tournament at Yalobusha Academy. It upset me a little, especially the end, but the statement "All Animals are Equal, but Some Animals are more Equal than Others" echoed sentiments which I recognized as prevalent in the upper echelons of the cheerleading squad. Our captain was a mean senior girl named Cindy Clark. She talked a lot about spirit and pep, and how important it was we work as a team, but she and her cronies ostracized the younger girls and were horrible to us off the court. Cindy was approximately my height and was forced to be my partner in some of the cheers, a circumstance which displeased her as much as it did myself. I remember a song that was popular around that time—it had lyrics that went:

> We are family
> I've got all my sisters with me

⁴   This had for some reason been incorporated into one of the chants and Cindy and I were frequently forced to sing together: arms around each other, leaning on each other like drunks, beaming with joy and behaving in every way like the sisters which we, in fact, were most certainly not.

⁵   Though there was a sharp distinction between the older girls and the younger ones, we were also divided, throughout our ranks and regardless of age, into two distinct categories: those of snob and slut. The snobs had flat chests, pretty clothes, and were skittish and shrill. Though they were always sugary-sweet to one's face, in reality they were a nasty, back-biting lot, always doing things like stealing each other's boyfriends and trying to rig the elections for the Beauty Revue. The sluts were from poorer families, and much better liked in general. They drank beer, made out with boys in the hallways, and had horrible black hickeys all over their necks. Our squad was divided pretty much half and half. Physically and economically, I fell into the category of snob, but I did poorly in school and was not gung-ho or clubbish enough to fit in very well with the rest of them. (To be a proper snob, one had always to be making floats for some damn parade or other, or organizing pot-luck dinners for the Booster Club.) The sluts, I

---

3   *Animal Farm:* a famed novella by the English writer George Orwell (1903-1950); its characters are all barnyard animals.

thought, took a more sensible view of such foolishness; they smoked and drank; I found them, as a rule, much nicer. Being big girls generally, they were the backbones of the stances, the foundations from which the pyramids rose and, occasionally, fell; I, being the smallest on the squad, had to work with them rather closely, in special sessions after the regular cheerleading practices, since they were the ones who lifted me into the air, who spotted me in gymnastics, upon whose shoulders I had to stand to form the obligatory pyramid. They all had pet names for me, and—though vigorously heterosexual—babied me in what I am sure none of them realized was a faintly lecherous way: tickles and pinches, slaps on the rump, pulling me into their laps in crowded cars and crooning stupid songs from the radio into my ear. Most of this went on in the afterschool practices. At the games they completely ignored me, as every fiber of their attention was devoted to flirting with—and contriving to make out with—various boys. As I was both too young to be much interested in boys, and lacking the fullness of bosom and broadness of beam which would have made them much interested in me, I was excluded from this activity. But still they felt sorry for me, and gave me tips on how to make myself attractive (pierced ears, longer hair, tissue paper in the bra)—and, when we were loitering around after practices, often regaled me with worldly tales of various sexual, obstetric, and gynecological horrors, some of which still make my eyes pop to think about.

6   The gymnasiums were high-ceilinged, barnlike, drafty, usually in the middle of some desolate field. We were always freezing in our skimpy plaid skirts, our legs all goose pimples as we clapped and stamped on the yellowed wooden floor. (Our legs, being so much exposed, were frequently chapped from cold, yet we were forbidden to put lotion on them, Cindy and the older girls having derived a pathological horror of "grease" from—as best as I could figure—the Clearasil ads in *Tiger Beat* and *Seventeen*—this despite the fact that grease was the primary element of all our diets.) Referee's whistle, sneakers squeaking on the varnish. "Knees together," Cindy would hiss down the line, or "Spit out that gum," before she hollered "Ready!" and we clapped our hands down to our sides in unison and yelled the response: "O-Kay!" At halftime there were the detested stances, out in the middle of the court, which involved perilous leaps, and complex timing, and—more likely than not—tears and remonstrations in the changing rooms. These were a source of unremitting dread, and as soon as they were over and the buzzer went off for third quarter the younger girls rushed in a greedy flock to the snack bar for Cokes and French fries, Hershey bars, scattering to devour them in privacy while Cindy and her crew slunk out to the parking lot to rendezvous with their

boyfriends. We were all of us, all the time, constantly sick—coughing, blowing our noses, faces flushed with fever—a combination of cold, bad food, cramped conditions, and yelling ourselves hoarse every night. Hoarseness was, in fact, a matter of pride: we were accused of shirking if our voices weren't cracked by the end of the evening, the state to which we aspired being a rasping, laryngitic croak. I remember the only time the basketball coach—a gigantic, stone-faced, terrifying man who was also the principal of the school and who, to my way of thinking, held powers virtually of life or death (there were stories of his punching kids out, beating them till they had bruises, stories which perhaps were not apocryphal in a private school like my own, which prided itself on what it called "old-fashioned discipline" and where corporal punishment was a matter of routine); the only time this coach ever spoke to me was to compliment me on my burnt-out voice, which he overheard in the hall the morning after a game. "Good job," he said. My companions and I were struck speechless with terror. After he was gone they stared at me with awestruck apprehension and then, one by one, drifted gently away, not wishing to be seen in the company of anyone who had attracted the attention—even momentarily—of this dangerous lunatic.

7   There were pep squads, of a sort, in George Orwell's Oceania.[4] I read about them with interest. Banners, processions, slogans, games, were as popular there as they were at Kirk Academy. Realizing that there were certain correspondences between this totalitarian nightmare and my own high school gave me at first a feeling of smug superiority, but after a time I began to have an acute sense of the meaninglessness of my words and gestures. Did I really care if we won or lost? No matter how enthusiastically I jumped and shouted, the answer to this was unquestionably No. This epiphany both confused and depressed me. And yet I continued—outwardly at least—to display as much pep as ever. "I always look cheerful and I never shirk anything," says Winston Smith's girlfriend, Julia.[5] Always yell with the crowd, that's what I say. It's the only way to be safe." Our rival team was called the Patriots. I remember one rally, the night before a big game, when a dummy Patriot was hanged from the gymnasium rafters, then taken outside and burned amid the frenzied screams and stomps of the mob. I yelled as loud as anybody even though I was suf-

---

4   **Oceania**: the setting of George Orwell's dystopian novel *1984*.
5   **Julia**: one of the major characters in Orwell's *1984* and the lover of the protagonist, Winston Smith.

fused by an airy, perilous sense of unreality, a conviction that—despite the apparently desperate nature of this occasion—that none of it meant anything at all. In my diary that night—a document which was as secretive and, to my mind at least, as subversive as Winston's own—I noted tersely: "Hell's own Pep Rally. Freshmen won the spirit stick. Rah, rah."

8   It was on the rides home—especially on the nights we'd won—that the inequity of not being allowed on the team bus was most keenly felt by the cheerleaders. Moodily, they stared out the windows, dreaming of back seats, and letter jackets, and smooching with their repulsive boyfriends. The cars smelled like talcum powder and tickle deodorant and—if we were with one of the nicer dads, who had allowed us to stop at a drive-in—cheeseburgers and french fries. It was too dark to read. Everyone was tired, but for some reason we were all too paranoid to go to sleep in front of each other; afraid we might drool, perhaps, or inadvertently scratch an armpit.

9   Whispers, giggles, sighs. We rode four to a car and all four of us would be crammed in the back seat; bare arms touching, goosebumped knees pressed together, our silences punctuated by long ardent slurps of Tab. The console lights of the Cadillac dashboards were phosphorescent, eerie. The radio was mostly static that time of night but sometimes you could get a late-night station coming out of Greenwood or Memphis; slow songs, that's what everyone wanted, sloppy stuff by Olivia Newton-John or Dan Fogelberg.[6] (The cheerleaders had a virtual cult of Olivia Newton-John; they tried to do their hair like her, emulate her in every possible way, and were fond of speculating what Olivia would or would not do in certain situations. She was like the ninth, ghost member of the squad. I was secretly gratified when she plummeted—with alarming swiftness—from favor because someone heard a rumor that she was gay.)

10   Olivia or not, the favorite song that winter hands down was "You Light Up My Life" by Debbie Boone. It must have been number one for months; at least, it seemed to come on the radio just about every other song, which was fine with everybody. When it came on the girls would all start singing it quietly to themselves, staring out the window, each in their own little world; touching the fogged window-glass gently with their fingertips and

---

6 **Olivia Newton-John and Dan Fogelberg**: two popular 1970s pop musicians.

each thinking no one could hear them, but all their voices combined in a kind of low, humming harmony that blended with the radio:

> So many nights
> I sit by my window
> Waiting for someone
> To sing me his song . . .

[11]   Full moon; hard frost on the stubbled cottonfields. They opened up on either side of the car in long, gray spokes, like a fan.

Looking Back

1. Why does Tartt begin by establishing the fact that she was reading Orwell's futuristic novel *1984*? Is that an irrelevant detail in the total essay, or does she tie that book to some event or thought in the essay?

2. How does Tartt differentiate between the snobs and sluts? What details in this memoir explain why Tartt classifies herself as a snob rather than as a slut?

3. What changes in the author occur during the season? Working in small groups, discuss which of the following is primarily responsible for those changes: George Orwell? the other cheerleaders? the boys on the team? the author's family? the author herself?

4. What positive benefits are supposed to derive from being a member of a group—whether as a team member or as a member of the cheerleading squad? Does the author, in fact, get such benefits? Why or why not? Do you think it likely that Tartt became a sophomore cheerleader?

5. Which of the following defines Tartt's style: extensive use of figures of speech? sensory description? precise details? an emphasis on her feelings? a tone of nostalgia for these bygone days? something else?

Looking Into

1. Often, an otherwise excellent piece of writing becomes obsolete because readers no longer recognize the author's various references. Tartt's essay contains a number of proper nouns denoting people, places, or products. In a small group, locate any proper nouns not already footnoted and write an identifying footnote. Follow the form of the footnotes in this book.

2. A memoir is defined as a brief autobiographical note. In "Basketball Season," Tartt limits her memoir to a single sports season, and then telescopes various experiences into this brief, unified piece. Choose an experience that recurred in your life over a three- to four-month period. Make a list of everything you can recall—people, places, events, reactions. Then in a three- or four-page paper, convey both a limited number of memorable events and your emotions toward them. The topic need not be related to sports.

Running The Table

FRANK CONROY

Born in Washington, D.C., in 1936, Frank Conroy graduated from Haverford College in 1958. In 1967, he published his first book, *Stoptime*, a work that reviewer Charles Bronze enthusiastically described as part autobiography, part novel, part nonfiction chronicle. Conroy's second book was *Midair*, a collection of short stories published in 1985. His most recent publication is *Body and Soul (1993)*, a novel about a musical prodigy who discovers himself through music; Conroy himself has worked as a jazz pianist. In addition to writing articles and short stories for such periodicals as *New Yorker*, *Harper's*, the *New York Times* magazine section, *GQ*, and the *Chicago Tribune*, Conroy has taught at George Mason University, MIT, and Brandeis University. Since 1987, he has been a professor of English at the University of Iowa where he is currently the director of its famed Writers' Workshop.

Looking Ahead

In some types of sports, physical strength is imperative; in others, skill and finesse are more essential. If boxing stands as an example of the first type, the various games played on a pool table surely exemplify the second. A steady head, an agile body, the ability to calculate speeds and angles, the skill of putting "English," or spin, on the cue ball—these involve dexterities and mathematical calculations that have little to do with sheer strength. In "Running the Table," Conroy writes about his introduction to the game of pool at the age of fifteen and the game's lasting effect on him.

1   When I was fifteen and living in New York City, I was supposed to be going to Stuyvesant High School and in fact I did actually show up three or four times a week, full of gloom, anger and adolescent narcissism. The world was a dark place for me in those days. I lived in a kind of tunnel of melancholy, constantly in trouble at home, in school and occasionally with the police. (Pitching pennies, sneaking into movies, jumping the turnstile in

the subway, stealing paperback books—fairly serious stuff in that earlier, more innocent time.) I was haunted by a sense of chaos, chaos within and chaos without. Which is perhaps why the orderliness of pool, the Euclidean cleanness[1] of it, so appealed to me. The formality of pool struck me as soothing and reassuring, a sort of oasis of coolness, utterly rational and yet not without its elegant little mysteries. But I'm getting ahead of myself.

2   One day, meandering around 14th Street, I stepped through the open doors on an impulse and mounted the long, broad stairway. Halfway up I heard the click of balls. What a marvelous sound! Precise, sharp, crisp, and yet somehow mellow. There was an intimacy to the sound that thrilled me. At the top of the stairs I pushed through the saloon-style swinging doors and entered a vast, hushed, dim hall. Rows of pool tables stretched away in every direction, almost all of them empty at this early hour, but here and there in the distance, a pool of light, figures in silhouette circling, bending, taking shots. Nearby, two old men were playing a game I would later learn to be billiards on a large table without pockets. The click of three balls, two white, one red, was what I had heard on the stairs. The men played unhurriedly, pausing now and then with their cues held like walking sticks to stare down at the street below. Cigar smoke swirled in the air.

3   I had walked into Julian's, little knowing that it was one of the most important pool halls on the East Coast. I was impressed by the stark functionality of the place—the absence of decoration of any kind. It seemed almost institutional in its atmosphere, right down to the large poster hung on the cashier's cage setting out the rules and regulations. No drinking, no eating, no sitting on the edges of the tables, no spitting except in the cuspidors, no massé shots[2], etc. Tables were twenty-five cents an hour. Cue sticks were to be found on racks against the walls. Balls available from the cashier as he clocked you in.

4   "How do you play," I asked.

5   The cashier was bald and overweight. He wore, for some reason, a green eyeshade. "You from Stuyvesant?"

6   I nodded, and he grunted, reached down to some hidden shelf and gave me a small paper pamphlet, pushing it forward across the worn wooden counter. I scanned it quickly. Basic information about straight pool, eight ball, nine ball, billiards, snooker and a few other games. "Start with

---

1 **Euclidean cleanliness**: Since pool is a game involving precise angles, Conroy refers to Euclid, the father of geometry.
2 **massé shot**: a shot that involves spinning the cue ball in such a way that it circles around without touching the sides of the table.

straight pool," he said. "Go over there and watch those guys on twenty-two for a while. Sit still, don't talk, and don't move around."

7 I did as I was told, sitting on a kind of mini-bleachers against the wall, my chin in my hands. The two men playing were in their twenties, an Abbott-and-Costello duo, thin Bud wearing a vest and smoking constantly, pudgy Lou moving delicately around the table, using the bridge[3] now and then because of his short arms. They paid no attention to me and played with concentration, silent except for calling combinations.

8 "Six off the thirteen," Lou said.

9 Bud nodded. They only called combinations. All straight shots, no matter how difficult, were presumably obvious. After a while, with a few discreet glances at my pamphlet, I began to get the hang of it. All the balls, striped and solid, were fair game. You simply kept shooting until you missed, and then it was the other guy's turn. After each run, you moved some beads on a wire overhead with the tip of your cue, marking up the number of balls you'd sunk. So much for the rules. What was amazing was the shooting.

10 Object balls[4] clipped so fine they moved sideways. Bank shots off the cushion into a pocket. Long combinations. Breakout shots[5] in which a whole cluster of balls would explode in all directions while one from the middle would limp into a nearby pocket. And it didn't take long to realize that making a given shot was only part of what was going on. Controlling the position of the cue ball after the shot was equally important, so as to have a makable next shot. I could see that strategy was involved, although how they made the cue ball behave so differently in similar situations seemed nothing short of magical. Lou completed a run of nine or ten balls and reached fifty on the wire overhead. He had won, apparently.

11 "Double or nothing?"

12 Bud shook his head. Money changed hands. Lou put the balls in a tray, turned out the light over the table, and both men checked out at the cashier's. I sat for a while, thinking over what I had seen, reading the pamphlet again. I didn't have enough money to play that day, but I knew I was coming back.

---

3 **bridge**: a small wooden or metal holder at the end of a stick which can be placed on the table and used by a player to extend his reach.

4 **object balls**: the balls which the shooter is attempting to sink into one of six pockets at the corners or the sides of the table.

5 **breakout shots**: the shot that begins the game; the player, using the white ball, shoots from one end of the table at the fifteen balls arranged in a triangle at the other end.

[13] Sometime in the late sixties, as an adult, I went to the Botanic Garden in Brooklyn to visit the recently completed Zen rock garden. It was a meticulous re-creation of a particular installation from a particular Japanese monastery. No one else was there. I sat on the bench gazing at the spiral patterns in the sand, looking at the black rocks set like volcanic islands in a white sea. Peace. Tranquility. Absurd as it may sound, I was reminded of my childhood experience of Julian's on a quiet afternoon—a sense of harmony, of an entirely disinterested material world entirely unaffected by one's perception of it.

[14] For me, at fifteen, Julian's was a sort of retreat, a withdrawal from the world. I would shoot for hours at a time, racking up[6], breaking, shooting, racking, breaking, shooting, in a solitary trance. Or I would surrender to the ritual of practice—setting up long shots over the length of the table again and again, trying to sink a shot with the same configuration ten times in a row, and then twenty, and then a more difficult configuration to a different pocket three times in a row, then five, etc. I did not get bored with the repetition. Every time a ball went in the pocket I felt satisfaction. When I missed I simply ignored the fact, reset the shot and tried again. This went on for several weeks at a remote table in a far corner of the hall—table nineteen—which nobody else ever seemed to want. Once in a while I'd play with another kid, usually also from Stuyvesant, and split the time. After a couple of months I would sometimes play for the time—loser pays—against opponents who looked even weaker than myself. But most of the time I played alone.

[15] Late one afternoon, racking up on table nineteen for perhaps the tenth time, I noticed a man sitting in the gloom up against the wall. He was extremely thin, with a narrow face and a protruding brow. He wore a double-breasted suit and two-tone shoes, one leg dangling languidly over the other. He gave me an almost imperceptible nod. I chalked the tip of my cue, went to the head of the table and stroked a clean break. Aware that I was being watched, I studied the lie of the balls for a moment and proceeded to sink seven in a row, everything going according to plan, until I scratched[7]. I pulled up the cue ball and the object ball, recreated the shot and scratched again.

---

6   **racking up**: arranging the balls by placing them in a triangular wooden rack prior to the start of a game.

7   **scratched**: a pool term that can mean any one of the following: failing to hit a ball; or hitting a ball so that it goes into a pocket or touches the side wall; or sinking the cue ball into one of the pockets.

16   "Why don't you use English," he asked quietly.

17   I stared at the table. "What's English?"

18   A moment's pause. "Set it up again," he said.

19   I did so.

20   "Aim, but don't hit. Pretend you're going to shoot."

21   I made a bridge with my left hand, aimed at the object ball and held the tip of my stick right behind the center of the cue ball.

22   "All right. All lined up?"

23   "Yes," I said, almost flat on the table.

24   "Do not change the line. Are you aiming at the center of the cue ball?"

25   "Yes."

26   "Aim a quarter of an inch higher."

27   "You mean I should . . ." For some reason what he was suggesting seemed almost sacrilegious.

28   "Yes, yes. Don't hit the cue ball in the center. Strike a quarter of an inch above. Now go ahead. Shoot."

29   I made my stroke, watched the object ball go in, and watched the cue ball take a different path after impact than it had before. It didn't scratch this time, but missed the pocket, bounced smartly off the cushion and rolled to a stop near the center of the table for an easy next shot.

30   "Hey. That's terrific!" I said.

31   "That's English." He unfolded his legs and stood up. He came over and took the pool cue from my hands. "If a person pays attention," he said, "a person can learn about ninety-five percent of what he needs to know in about ten minutes. Ten minutes for the principles, then who knows how many years for the practice." His dark, deep-set eyes gave his face a vaguely ominous cast. "You want to learn?"

32   "Absolutely," I said without hesitation. "Yes."

33   As it turned out, it took about half an hour. The man teaching me was called Smilin' Jack, after the comic-strip character and presumably because of his glum demeanor. He was a Julian's regular, and it was my good luck to have caught him when somebody had stood him up for what was to have been a money game. I could sense that he enjoyed going through the drill—articulate, methodical, explicating on cause and effect with quiet relish, moving the balls around the table with no wasted motion whatsoever, executing the demo shots with a stroke as smooth as powdered silk— it was an elegant dance, with commentary. A sort of offering to the gods of pool.

34   I cannot possibly recount here what I learned. Follow, draw, left and right English and how they affect the movement of the cue ball after impact. The object ball picking up opposite English from the cue ball. The ef-

fectiveness of different kinds of English as a function of distance (between cue ball and object ball) and of speed. *Sliding* the cue ball. Playing the diamond points. Shooting a ball frozen on the cushion. How to read combinations, and on and on. I paid very close attention and jotted down what notes I could. (*Over*shoot bank shots to the side pockets. *Under*shoot bank shots to the corner pockets.) At the end of the half hour my head ached. In addition to trying to grasp the principles, I'd been trying to film the whole thing, to superimpose an eidetic memory on the cells of my brain, so I could retrieve what I'd seen at will. I was exhausted.

35   He handed me the stick, shot his cuffs[8] and adjusted the front of his jacket with a slight forward movement of his shoulders. "That should keep you busy for a while." Then he simply walked away.

36   "Thanks," I called after him.

37   Without looking back, he raised his hand and gave a laconic little wave.

38 Practice, practice. Months of practice. It was a delicate business, English, affected by things like the relative roughness of the cue tip and its ability to hold chalk, or the condition of the felt, or infinitesimal degrees of table lean. But it worked. There was no doubt about it, when you got the feel of it you greatly increased your power over the all-important position of the cue ball. There was a word for it—the "leave," as in "good shot, but a tough leave." And of course the more you could control the leave, the more deeply involved was the strategy—planning out how to sink twelve balls in a row, rather than just five or six. Progress was slow, but it was tangible, and very, very satisfying. I began to beat people. I moved off table nineteen up toward the middle of the hall and began to beat almost everybody from Stuyvesant.

39   The most important hurdle for a straight-pool player involves being able to run into the second rack. You have to sink fourteen balls and leave the fifteenth ball and the cue ball positioned in such a way as to be able to sink the last ball (breaking open the new rack at the same time) and have a good enough leave to start all over again. I achieved this shortly before my sixteenth birthday, with a run of twenty-three.

40   The owners of Julian's recognized the accomplishment as a significant rite of passage and awarded certain privileges to those who had achieved

---

8 **shot his cuffs**: to throw the arms out, or down, in order to make the shirt cuffs extend beyond the suit coat.

it. During my last year of high school a cue of my own selection, with my name taped to the handle, was kept in a special rack behind the cashier's cage. No one else could use that particular cue stick. It was reserved, along with thirty or forty others for young players who had distinguished themselves.

41   I was a nonentity at school, but I could walk up to the cage at Julian's and the cashier would reach back for my stick and say, "Hey, Frank. How's it going?"

42   What a splendid place it was.

43   There's a lot to feel in pool, a physical aspect to the game, which means you have to play all the time to stay good. I've lost most of my chops (to borrow a word from jazz), but I still drop down to my local bar, the Foxhead, every now and then to play on the undersize table. It's a challenge arrangement. Put your name on the chalkboard, slip two quarters in the slot when it's your turn, and try to win.

44   There's a good deal more chance in eight ball, your basic bar game, than in straight pool, but it's fun. We've got some regulars. Jerry, a middle-aged man with a gorgeous stroke (a nationally ranked player in his youth), can beat anybody who walks into the place if he isn't furious at having to play doubles, at kids slopping beer onto the felt, or some other infraction of civilized behavior. There's Doug, a graduate student who always looked as if he'd spent the previous night in a cardboard box in an alley and who hits every shot as hard as he can, leaving the question of where the cue ball is going to end up more or less to the gods, in the hope that they will thus tangibly express the favor in which they hold him. (He is a poet.) We have George, an engineer, who exhausts our patience by approaching each situation with extreme care, circling the table several times, leaning over to stare down at a cluster of balls in what appears to be a hypnotic trance, chalking up with the care of Vermeer[9] at the easel and running through a complicated series of various facial and physical tics before committing himself. There's Henry, who programs the jukebox to play "Brown Sugar" ten times in a row before he racks up. We've got students, working people, teachers, nurses (Yes. Women! Smilin' Jack would be scandalized) and barflies. We've got everybody at the Foxhead.

45   There are nights when I can hold the table for a couple of hours, but not very often. My touch is mostly gone, and bifocals make things difficult.

---

9   **Vermeer**: a famous seventeenth-century Dutch painter, known for the realism of his

Still, a bit of Julian's is still with me and, at the very least, I talk a good game.

Looking Back

1. What pun makes the title of Conroy's essay doubly meaningful?

2. What four stages does Conroy pass through in his attempt to master the game?

3. Working with one or two other people, discuss and record your answers to the following questions. Why might mastering the game of pool have been so important to the young Conroy? What reasons does he state? What reasons does he imply?

4. Why, even after losing his "touch," would Conroy still enjoy playing eightball?

Looking Into

1. In one or two paragraphs, discuss a skill that you have mastered which has given you a real sense of accomplishment?

2. After his visit to the Zen garden, Conroy mentions the "sense of harmony" that both it and his experiences at Julian's brought to him. Think about such a place in your own life and in two or three paragraphs describe that place.

3. Conroy writes that in his youth he was "haunted by a sense of chaos, chaos within and chaos without." Write about how the game of pool helped him achieve a sense of order.

The $port$ Report

ANNA QUINDLEN

Anna Quindlen was born in Philadelphia, Pennsylvania, in 1952. After attending parochial schools, she applied to Barnard College in New York City, writing in her college application essay that her goal in life was "to write the great American novel." Her first fiction success occurred when she was a senior and *Seventeen* magazine accepted a story she had submitted; her first professional writing was as a part-time reporter for the *New York Post*, a position she secured as a freshman at Barnard. After graduating from Barnard in 1974, she worked full-time for the *Post* for three years and then took a job with the *New York Times* as a general assignment reporter. She covered city hall for four years before being given a feature column to write: "About New York." In this column, she notes, "I developed a voice of my own without using the first person, and I developed the ability to come up with column ideas."

In 1983, Quindlen became deputy metropolitan editor, one of the few women to become a *Times* editor. In 1985, while writing a free-lance column on issues affecting women, she began work on the novel *Object Lessons*, eventually published in 1991. In 1988, she began writing a new column, "Life in the 30's," one devoted to personal and domestic matters. These columns, syndicated to more than thirty newspapers, were eventually collected and published as the book *Living Out Loud* (1988). In January, 1990, Quindlen initiated her third *Times* column: "Public & Private." Here she addressed such issues as abortion, AIDS, drug use, wife-beating, and numerous other topics. A second collection of Quindlen's essays, *Thinking Out Loud: On the Personal, the Political, the Public and the Private* (1993), was followed by her second novel *One True Thing* (1994). Quindlen was honored in 1992 with the Pulitzer Prize for commentary.

Looking Ahead

Anna Quindlen was only the third woman to write a regular column for the *New York Times*. Her topics ranged, as the subtitle of a recent collection suggests, from the personal to the political, the public and the private. In the following essay, written for her January 22, 1994, column, Quindlen reacts to an incident that, like most people, she found deeply troubling. You may wish to compare her comments with those of Gilbert Highet on the part-opening page.

[1] *F*igure skating is like a dream, grace and beauty in slow motion, what the body could be if released from everyday burdens of gravity. "Everything was beautiful at the ballet," three dancers with fractured childhoods sing in "A Chorus Line" of their refuge in toe shoes and tutus. That's what skating evokes, when the ice is silver-bright, the blades swift, the skater accomplished—a beautiful momentary release from the tatters of real life.

[2] That is somewhat illusory, as any girl-child who has risen before dawn to practice her compulsory figures day after day, year after year, can testify. Behind the glorious line of leg and upraised arm, behind the double axels and the triple-toe combinations, lie sweat and tears and pain. And behind it all, at the highest levels, lies that golden thing that has become all that glitters in much professional sport today.

[3] In the words of another musical number, this one from "Cabaret," money, money, money.

[4] So why so shocked, sports fans, to find how far and how low the love of lucre can take competitive athletics? Why so shocked to discover that those allied with Tonya Harding's brilliant, bumpy skating career—and, some say, Tonya herself—were allegedly willing to do violence[1] to her rival, Nancy Kerrigan, for a pot of gold at the end of the Olympic rainbow?

[5] Get real. The statistics about top football, basketball and baseball players today are as often the sum total of their commercial endorsements and contract negotiations as they are batting averages or pass completions. Watch Wimbledon and it is like watching a collection of tiny moving billboards, the corporate logos of juice companies and shoe manufacturers plastered on sleeves, wristbands, shorts.

[6] It has gotten so bad that Chris Evert, the champ who always knew the difference between competitive and cutthroat, said this week that she was glad she was not playing tennis professionally today. "Wherever there's more money, there's going to be more downfall," she told the *Times* reporter Robin Finn.

[7] Jennifer Capriati, tennis whiz and teen-ager, didn't sell her adolescence for the thrill of that percussive sound of ball meeting racket. She spent the years between 13 and 17 in child labor on the pro circuit, earning more

---

1 **do violence to**: Six weeks before the 1994 Winter Olympics, associates of Portland figure skater Tonya Harding attacked Nancy Kerrigan, Harding's chief rival, hitting the knee of her landing leg in an attempt to take her out of competition.

than $1 million. No one should be surprised that bad things are done for that amount of cash, or that Jennifer is now burned out and wants nothing more than to finish high school.

8   For a time figure skating held itself above all this, with little of the rough-and-tumble—or dirty laundry—of contact sports. But Peggy Fleming and Dorothy Hamill proved that a gold medal could lead to brighter rewards, and in recent years it has sometimes seemed that officials might as well simply hang a calculator around the neck of the winner.

9   And it also became clear how much athletes were willing to do to win. Featherlight gymnasts, their rib cages aflutter as they stood with arms raised to the crowd, threw up their low-cal meals or didn't eat in the first place. Steroids became the breakfast of champions for the bulk-up sports. Is it really that great a leap from hurting yourself to hurting the competition?

10   There may have been a time, light years ago, when the feeling of the earth moving so effortlessly beneath the blades of her skates was Tonya Harding's great reward. And maybe there are moments when those blades still mute the sound of coins clinking, when she forgets that she is famous and just about broke and cares only that she is superb at the sport.

11   Tonya, like so many others, was in it for the money. Now, with all the bad publicity, it will never come. Perhaps it never would have. Tonya is a hard case, tough and smart-mouthed and enormously talented. As a young man in baseball, she might have made a mint. But figure skating's still a dream, and Nancy Kerrigan, not Tonya Harding, is a dream girl, sweet, beautiful, graceful and suited to chiffons.

12   No bad childhood, no financial woes, no competition or rewards, could ever excuse the moment when someone acting on Tonya Harding's behalf, if not her behest, whacked Nancy Kerrigan in the leg. But why so shocked? The motto of professional athletics has been clear for some time—it isn't how you play the game, its whether you win. Twist a biblical caution, and recent events seem almost inevitable. When money is the root of all, evil follows. What shattered the reverie of figure skating was despicable. But not surprising.

Looking Back

1. In the introductory paragraphs to her essay, Quindlen quotes lines from the songs of two Broadway musicals: *A Chorus Line* and *Cabaret*. What

implicit connection do you think Quindlen might be making between musicals and figure skating?

2. Quindlen accuses professional athletes of betraying the spirit that initially impelled them to achieve. What specific details does she provide in support of "how far and how low the love of lucre can take competitive athletics" (paragraph 4)?

3. In many of her nonfiction pieces, Quindlen has vigorously argued the feminist position on a variety of issues. To what extent is that position evident in this essay?

4. In both paragraph 2 and in the final paragraph, Quindlen alludes to two quotations, but with a twist. Consult a reference book such as *The Oxford Dictionary of Quotations* or Bartlett's *Familiar Quotations* to determine the original quotations. Then discuss in class Quindlen's "twist"? Are there any other direct quotations or allusions to quotations in the piece?

Looking Into

1. Why might Quindlen have included the quotations or allusions referred to in Question 4 above? In a well-developed paragraph, justify an author's use of quotations by providing at least two explanations for their use.

2. In your opinion which of the following has most corrupted the ideal of sports: the goal of winning at all costs? commercial endorsements? high salaries? Write a three- or four-page persuasive paper in which you state your opinion as the thesis; then provide at least three supporting examples.

Sports for the Over-40 Person (Or, God had a REASON for Creating the Barcalounger)

DAVE BARRY

Dave Barry, born in the late 1940s, grew up in New York state, the son of a clergyman with a decided social conscience and a mother whom he has described as "the funniest person" he has ever known. He majored in English literature at Haverford College in Philadelphia, graduating in 1969. Following graduation, he worked for the Episcopal church for two years before becoming a reporter and, later, an editor for the *Daily Local News* in West Chester, Pennsylvania. After working briefly for the Associated Press, he accepted a neighbor's offer to teach business seminars. While teaching, he began contributing to the *Daily Local News* a humor column that soon was being syndicated throughout the country.

In 1983, he accepted an offer from the *Miami Herald*; his column is now syndicated in more than three hundred American newspapers. According to reporter Peter Richmond, who interviewed Barry for the *New York Times*, "it is Barry's special talent that he can take that back-of-the-classroom irreverence and layer it onto the mundane ingredients of his generation's everyday experience." Barry has published numerous collections of his columns, including *Babies and Other Hazards of Sex: How to Make A Tiny Person in Only Nine Months, with Tools You Probably Have around the House* (1984), *Stay Fit and Healthy Until You're Dead* (1985), *Dave Barry's Greatest Hits* (1988), *Dave Barry Slept Here: A Sort Of History of the United States* (1989), and *Dave Barry Talks Back* (1991).

Looking Ahead

By definition, a columnist is a writer who, unlike other journalists, is allowed to express his or her opinions on matters of interest or significance. Some columnists specialize in politics; others, in international affairs; still others, in gardening, sports, women's issues. Dave Barry, Pulitzer Prize-winning columnist for the *Miami Herald*, writes—as the title of this essay suggests—humorously about virtually everything: home-owning, a trip to Japan, American history, parenting, and a myriad of other topics. In the following essay, Barry examines the indignities of supporting and coaching Little League teams, walking, fishing, golfing, and skiing.

[1] *I*n the Pantheon of Sports Heroes (which is located next to the Skeet-Shooting Hall of Fame), you'll find the names of many legendary athletes who remained active in sports well after they turned 40—Babe Ruth, Jack Dempsey, Picasso, Secretariat—the list goes on and on.

[2] What do these great competitors have in common? Right. They're all dead. So you see how important it is for you to slow down as you get older, to abandon the active sports you enjoyed so much in your youth—basketball, tennis, racquetball, drinking a quart of Jim Beam and leaping naked into the motel pool from the eighth-floor balcony, etc. It's time for you to start "acting your age" by getting involved in the kinds of sports activities that are more appropriate for mature, responsible adults, such as:

SHRIEKING AT LITTLE LEAGUERS

[3] To participate in this highly popular sport, all you need to do is get a small child who would be infinitely happier just staying home and playing in the dirt, and put a uniform on this child and make him stand for hours out on a field with other reluctant children who are no more capable of hitting or catching or accurately throwing a baseball than they are of performing neurosurgery. Then you and the other grownups stand around the perimeter and leap up and down and shriek at these children as though the fate of the human race depended on their actions.

[4] The object of the game is to activate your child if the ball goes near him, similar to the way you use levers to activate the little men in table-hockey games. Your child will be standing out in right field, picking his nose, staring into space, totally oblivious to the game, and the ball will come rolling his way, and your job is to leap violently up and down and shriek, "GET THE BALL! GET THE *BALL!!*" repeatedly for several minutes until your child finally is aroused from his reverie long enough to glance down and discover, to his amazement, the ball. The ball! Of all things! Right here in the middle of a Little League game! While your child is staring at the ball curiously, as if examining a large and unusual tropical insect, you switch to yelling: "THROW THE BALL! THROW THE BALL! THROWTHEBALL THROWTHEBALL THROWTHEBALL THROWTHEBALL THROWTHE-BALL THROWTHEBALL! *THROWTHEBALL, DAMMIT!!*" After several minutes of this an idea will start to form somewhere deep inside your child's brain: *Perhaps I should throw the ball.* Yes! It's crazy, but it just might work!

5   And so, seconds before you go into cardiac arrest on the sidelines, your child will pick up the ball and hurl it, Little League-style, in a totally random direction, then resume picking his nose and staring off into space. As you collapse, exhausted, the ball will roll in the general direction of some *other* child, whose poor unfortunate parent must then try to activate *him*. Meanwhile, the *other* team's parents will be shrieking at *their* children to run around the bases in the correct direction. It is not uncommon for 150 runs to score on one Little League play. A single game can go on for weeks.

6   I get to engage in a lot of sideline-shrieking, because tragically we have very nice weather down here in South Florida, which means that while most of the nation enjoys the luxury of being paralyzed by slush, we subtropical parents are trapped in Year-Round Youth Sports Hell. The reason we have a high crime rate is that many parents are so busy providing transportation that they have to quit their jobs and support their families by robbing convenience stores on their way to practices, games, lessons, etc.

7   But at least our children are becoming well rounded. That's what I tell myself while I shriek at my son, who is out there in left field, watching commercial air craft fly overhead while the ball rolls cheerfully past him and seven runners score. I tell myself that if my son were not out there participating in sports, he would not be learning one of life's most important lessons, namely: "It doesn't matter whether you win or lose, because you are definitely going to lose."

8   My son's teams lose a lot. This is because he is a Barry. We Barrys have a tradition of terrible sports luck dating back to my father, whose entire high-school football career—this is true—consisted of a single play, which was blocking a punt with his nose. As a child, I played on an unbroken succession of losing baseball teams, although "played" is probably too strong a term. My primary role was to sit on the bench, emitting invisible but potent Loser Rays and joining with the other zero-motor-control bench-sitters in thinking up hilarious and highly creative insults to hurl at members of the other team. Let's say the opposing batter was named Frank. We'd yell: "Hey, FRANK! What's your last name? *FURTER?*" Then we'd laugh so hard that we'd fall backward off the bench while Frank hit a triple, scoring twelve runs.

9   My son is a much better player than I was, but he's still a Barry, and consequently his teams generally lose. He was on one Little League team, the Red Sox, that lost at least 45,000 games in a span of maybe four months. Teams were coming from as far away as Guam to play the Red Sox. All of these teams complied with the First Law of Little League Physics, which states: "The other team always has much larger kids." You parents may have noticed that your child's team always consists of normal-sized, even

puny, children, while the other team is always sponsored by Earl's House of Steroids.

10   So the Red Sox were consistently playing against huge, mutant 9-year-olds who had more bodily hair than I do and drove themselves to the game, and we were getting creamed. I served as a part-time first-base coach, and I spent a lot of time analyzing our technique, trying to pinpoint exactly what it was that we were doing wrong, and as best as I could figure it, our problem was that—follow me closely here—*we never scored any runs.* Ever.

11   There was a good reason for this: The boys were not idiots. They did not wish to be struck by the ball. When they were batting, they looked perfect—good stance, fierce glare at the pitcher, professional-style batting glove, etc.—until the pitcher would actually pitch, at which point, no matter where the ball was going, the Red Sox batters would twitch their bodies violently backward like startled squids, the difference being that a squid would have a better chance of hitting the baseball because it keeps its eyes open.

12   Frankly, I didn't blame the boys. This was exactly the hitting technique that I used in Little League on those rare occasions when I got to play. But as a first-base coach I had a whole new perspective on the game, namely the perspective of a person who never had to get up to bat. So my job was to yell foolish advice to the batters. "Don't back up!" I'd yell. "He's not gonna hit you!" Every now and then a Red Sock, ignoring his common sense, would take me seriously and fail to leap backward, and of course when this happened the hormonally unbalanced, 275-pound pitcher always fired the ball directly into the batter's body. Then my job was to rush up and console the batter by telling him, "Legally, you cannot be forced to play organized baseball."

13   I'm just kidding, of course. Far be it from me to bring down the republic. What I'd say was, "Rub it off! Attaboy! Okay!" And the boy, having learned the important life lesson that adults frequently spout gibberish, would sniffle his way down to first base, while our next batter was silently resolving to be in a different area code by the time the ball reached home plate.

14   Speaking of coaching, this is an excellent way for the sports-oriented person to avoid the physical risks of actually participating physically in the sport, and yet still have the opportunity to experience the emotion and excitement of sudden heart failure. I coached my son's soccer team, the Phantoms, for one game. This was pretty ridiculous, because the only soccer rules I remembered, from junior high school, were:

1. You're allowed to hit the ball with your head.

2. But it hurts.

[15] The way I was selected as coach was that the regular coach, Rick, was on vacation for two weeks, and the other parents decided that I was best qualified to be the substitute coach on account of I wasn't there when they decided.

[16] The Phantoms, needless to say, were a struggling team. In addition to being cursed by the Barry luck, they had been decimated by birthday parties, and they were not having a banner year in the sense of winning games or even necessarily getting the ball down the field far enough so the opposing goalkeeper had to stop picking his ear.

[17] So I was concerned about being the coach. I had, of course, attended many soccer games over the years, but all I ever did was stand around with the other parents, randomly yelling, "KICK IT!" After I was elected substitute coach, I did attend a team practice in hopes of learning some strategy, but unfortunately this was the practice at which the Official Team Photograph was taken, which was very time-consuming because every time the photographer got the team posed, several players would be attacked by ants. Down here in South Florida we have highly aggressive ants, ants that draw no distinction between a cashew nut and a human being. You turn your back on them, and next thing you know, you hear this rhythmic ant work chant and your child is being dragged underground.

[18] So the Phantoms spent most of the practice swatting at their legs and moving, gypsy-like, around the field, looking for an ant-free location, and the only thing they really practiced was getting into team-photograph formation. I did speak briefly with Rick, who gave me the following coaching pointers:

1. The game starts at 1:30.

He also gave me a coach-style clipboard and some official league literature on Soccer Theory, which I attempted to read about an hour before game time. Unfortunately, it was not designed to be read by desperate, unprepared fathers. It was designed to be read by unusually smart nuclear physicists. It starts out with these handy definitions:

a. Principles of Play: the rules of action (guidelines) that support the basic objectives of soccer.

b. Tactics: the means by which the principles or rules are executed.

c. Strategy: which tactics are to be used, the arrangement of . . .

[19] And so on. I read these words several times, gradually becoming convinced that they'd make equal sense to me in any order. They could say: "Strategy: the tactics by which the rules (principles) support the execution." Or, "Principles: the strategic (tactical) arrangement of executives wearing supporters."

[20] So you can imagine how well prepared I felt when I arrived at the soccer field. The Phantoms gathered around me, awaiting leadership. Nearby, our opponents, looking like the Brazilian national team, only larger, were running through some snappy pre-game drills. The Phantoms looked at them, then looked at me expectantly. My brain, working feverishly under pressure, began to form a shrewd coaching concept, a tactic by which we might be able to execute the guidelines of our strategy.

[21] "Okay!" I announced. "Let's run some pre-game drills!"

[22] The Phantoms, showing rare unity of purpose, responded immediately. "We don't have a ball," they pointed out. There was nothing about this in the coaching materials.

[23] Next it was time for the Pre-game Talk. "Okay, Phantoms!" I shouted. "Gather 'round! Listen up!"

[24] The Phantoms gathered 'round. They listened up. Suddenly it occurred to me that I had nothing whatsoever to tell them.

[25] "Okay!" I said. "Let's go!"

[26] The game itself is a blur in my memory. My strategy—yelling "KICK IT!"—did not seem to be effective. The other team, which at times appeared to be playing with as many as four balls, was scoring on us regularly. We were not scoring at all. We were having trouble just executing the play where you run without falling down. As the situation deteriorated, I approached some of the other fathers on the sidelines. "What do you think we should do?" I asked. They did not hesitate.

[27] "We should go to a bar," they said.

[28] In the third quarter I changed my strategy from yelling "KICK IT!" to yelling "WAY TO GO!" This had no effect on anything, but I felt better. Finally the game ended, and I attempted to console the Phantoms over their heartbreaking loss. But they were beyond consolation. They were already

into racing around, pouring Gatorade on each other. I'm sure they'll eventually overcome the trauma of this loss. Whereas I will probably never again be able to look at a clipboard without whimpering.

[29] Probably the fastest-growing sport for the over-40 person is one that combines the advantages of a good cardiovascular workout with the advantages of looking like you have a bizarre disorder of the central nervous system. I refer to:

Walking Like a Dork

[30] Walking like a dork has become very popular among older people who used to jog for their health but could no longer afford the orthopedic surgery. The object of dork-walking is to make a simple, everyday act performed by millions of people every day, namely walking, look as complex and strenuous as Olympic pole-vaulting. To do this, you need to wear a special outfit, including high-tech, color-coordinated shorts and sweatclothes and headbands and wristbands and a visor and a Sony Walkperson tape player and little useless weights for your hands and special dork-walking shoes that cost as much per pair as round-trip airfare to London.

[31] But the most important thing is your walking technique. You have to make your arms and legs as stiff as possible and swing them violently forward and back in an awkward, vaguely Richard Nixon-like manner. It helps a lot to have an enormous butt, waving around back there like the Fiji blimp in a tornado. You'll know you're doing it right when passing motorists laugh so hard that they drive into trees.

[32] But as you age, you may find that even dork-walking is too strenuous for you. In this case, you'll want to look into the ultimate aging-person activity, a "sport" that requires so little physical activity that major tournaments are routinely won by coma victims. I refer, of course, to:

Golf

[33] Nobody knows exactly how golf got started. Probably what happened was, thousands of years ago, a couple of primitive guys were standing around, holding some odd-shaped sticks, and they noticed a golf ball lying on the grass, and they said, "Hey! Let's see if we can hit this into a hole!"

And then they said, "Nah, let's just tell long, boring anecdotes about it instead."

34 Which is basically the object, in golf. You put on the most unattractive pants that money can buy, pants so ugly that they have to be manufactured by blind people in dark rooms, and you get together in the clubhouse with other golfers and drone away for hours about how you "bogeyed" your three-iron on the par six, or your six-iron on the par three, or whatever. Also you watch endless televised professional golf tournaments with names like the Buick Merrill Lynch Manufacturers Hanover Frito-Lay Ti-D-Bol Preparation H Classic, which consist entirely of moderately overweight men holding clubs and frowning into the distance while, in the background, two announcers hold interminable whispered conversations like this:

> FIRST ANNOUNCER: Bob, he's lying about eighteen yards from the green with a fourteen-mile-per-hour wind out of the northeast, a relative humidity of seventy-two percent, and a chance of afternoon or evening thundershowers. He might use a nine-iron here.
>
> SECOND ANNOUNCER: Or possibly an eight, Bill. Or even—this makes me so excited that I almost want to speak in a normal tone of voice—a seven.
>
> FIRST ANNOUNCER: Or he could just keep on frowning into space. Remember that one time we had a professional golfer frown for five solid hours, never once hitting a ball, us whispering the whole time in between Buick commercials, and it turned out he'd had some kind of seizure and died, standing up, gripping his sand wedge?
>
> SECOND ANNOUNCER: In that situation, Bill, I'd have used a putter.

35 If you *really* get into golf, you can actually try to play it some time, although this is not a requirement. I did it once, with a friend of mine named Paul, who is an avid golfer in the sense that if he had to choose between playing golf and ensuring permanent world peace, he'd want to know how many holes.

36 So we got out on the golf course in one of those little electric carts that golfers ride around in to avoid the danger that they might actually have to contract some muscle tissue. Also, we had an enormous collection of random clubs and at least 3,000 balls, which turned out to be not nearly enough.

37 The way we played was, first Paul would hit his ball directly toward the hole. This is basic golfing strategy: You want to hit the ball the least

possible number of times so you can get back to the clubhouse to tell boring anecdotes and drink. When it was my turn, we'd drive the cart to wherever my ball was, which sometimes meant taking the interstate highway. When we finally arrived at our destination, Paul would examine the situation and suggest a club.

38   "Try a five-iron here," he'd say, as if he honestly believed it would make a difference.

39   Then, with a straight face, he'd give me very specific directions as to where I should hit the ball. "You want to aim it about two and a half yards to the right of that fourth palm tree," he'd say, pointing at a palm tree that I could not hit with a Strategic Defense Initiative laser. I'd frown, pro-golfer-style, at this tree, then I'd haul off and take a violent swing at the ball, taking care to keep my head down, which is an important part of your golf stroke because it gives you a legal excuse if the ball winds up lodged in somebody's brain.

40   Sometimes, after my swing, the ball would still be there, surrounded by a miniature scene of devastation, similar to the view that airborne politicians have of federal disaster areas. Sometimes the ball would be gone, which was the signal to look up and see how hard Paul was trying not to laugh. Usually he was trying very hard, which meant the ball had gone about as far as you would hide an Easter egg from a small child with impaired vision. But sometimes the ball had completely disappeared, and we'd look for it, but we'd never see it again. I think it went into another dimension, a parallel universe where people are still talking about the strange day when these golf balls started materializing out of thin air, right in the middle of dinner parties, concerts, etc.

41   So anyway, by following this golfing procedure, Paul and I were able to complete nine entire holes in less time than it would have taken us to memorize *Moby Dick* in Korean. We agreed that nine holes was plenty for a person with my particular level of liability insurance, so we headed back to the clubhouse for a beer, which, despite being a novice at golf, I was able to swallow with absolutely no trouble. The trick is to keep your head up.

42   Speaking of drinking beer, another sport that you'll want to get into as you get older is:

FISHING

43 Fishing is very similar to golf because in both sports you hold a long skinny thing in your hand while nothing happens for days at a time. The major

advantage of fishing is that you are somewhat less likely to be killed by a golf ball; the disadvantage is that you have to become involved with bait, which consists of disgusting little creatures with a substance known to biologists as "bait glop" constantly oozing out of various orifices. The function of the bait is to be repulsive and thereby reduce the chances that a fish will bite it and wind up in your boat thrashing and gasping piteously and occasionally whispering, in a quiet but clear voice, "Please help me!" If you were to put a nice roast-beef sandwich on your hook, or an egg roll, you'd have fish coming from entirely different time zones to get caught. But not so with bait. "He's so dumb, he'd eat bait," is a common fish expression, which means that the only fish you're in any danger of catching are the total morons of the marine community, which is why, when you see them mounted on people's walls, they always have a vaguely vice-presidential expression[1]. Not that I am naming names.

SKIING

[44] If you're bored by slower activities such as fishing and golf, and you're looking for the kind of youth-recapturing, action-packed sport that offers you the opportunity to potentially knock down a tree with your face, you can't do better than skiing.

[45]   The key to a successful ski trip, of course, is planning, by which I mean *money*. For openers, you have to buy a special outfit that meets the strict requirements of the Ski Fashion Institute, namely:

1.   It must cost as much as a medium wedding reception.

2.   It must make you look like the Giant Radioactive Easter Bunny From Space.

3.   It must be made of a mutant fiber with a name that sounds like the villain on a Saturday-morning cartoon show, such as "Gore-Tex," so as to provide the necessary resistance to moisture—

---

1   **vaguely vice-presidential expression**: Barry's dedication in the book from which this essay was taken reads: "For Dan Quayle, who proved to my generation that, frankly, *anybody* can make it."

which, trust me, will be gushing violently from all of your major armpits once you start lunging down the mountain.

[46]   You also have to buy ski goggles costing upwards of fifty dollars per eyeball that are specially designed not to fog up under any circumstances except when you put them on, at which time they become approximately as transparent as the Los Angeles telephone directory, which is why veteran skiers recommend that you do not pull them down over your eyes until just before you make contact with the tree. And you'll need ski boots, which are made from melted bowling balls and which protect your feet by preventing your blood, which could contain dangerous germs, from traveling below your shins.

[47]   As for the actual skis, you should rent them, because of the feeling of confidence you get from reading the fine print on the lengthy legal document that the rental personnel make you sign, which is worded as follows: "The undersigned agrees that skiing is an INSANELY DANGEROUS ACTIVITY, and that the rental personnel were just sitting around minding their OWN BUSINESS when the undersigned, who agrees that he or she is a RAVING LOON, came BARGING IN UNINVITED, waving a LOADED REVOLVER and demanding that he or she be given some rental skis for the express purpose of suffering SERIOUS INJURY OR DEATH, leaving the rental personnel with NO CHOICE but to . . ." etc.

[48]   Okay! Now you're ready to "hit the slopes." Ski experts recommend that you start by taking a group lesson, because otherwise they would have to get real jobs. To start the lesson, your instructor, who is always a smiling 19-year-old named Chip, will take you to the top of the mountain and explain basic ski safety procedures until he feels that the cold has killed enough of your brain cells that you will cheerfully follow whatever lunatic command he gives you. Then he'll ski a short distance down the mountain, just to the point where it gets very steep, and swoosh to a graceful stop, making it look absurdly easy. It *is* absurdly easy for Chip, because underneath his outfit he's wearing an antigravity device. All the expert skiers wear them. You don't actually believe that "ski jumpers" can go off those ridiculously high ramps and just float to the ground unassisted without breaking into walnut-sized pieces, do you? Like Tinkerbell or something? Don't be a cretin.

[49]   After Chip stops, he turns to the group, his skis hovering as much as three inches above the snow, and orders the first student to copy what he did. This is the fun part. Woodland creatures often wake up from hibernation just to watch this part, because even they understand that the laws of

physics, which are strictly enforced on ski slopes, do not permit a person to simply stop on the side of a snow-covered mountain if his feet are encased in bowling balls attached to what are essentially large pieces of Teflon. Nevertheless, the first student, obeying Chip's command, cautiously pushes himself forward, and then, making an unusual throat sound, passes Chip at Warp Speed and proceeds on into the woods, flailing his arms like a volunteer in a highly questionable nerve-gas experiment.

50 "That was good!" shouts Chip, grateful that he is wearing waterproof fibers inasmuch as he will be wetting his pants repeatedly during the course of the lesson. Then he turns to the rest of the group and says, "Next!"

51 The group's only rational response, of course, would be to lie down in the snow and demand a rescue helicopter. But these are not rational beings; these are ski students. And so, one by one, they, too, ski into the woods, then stagger out, sometimes with branches sticking out, antler-like, from their foreheads, and do it *again*. "Bend your knees this time!" Chip advises, knowing that this will actually make them go *faster*. He loves his work.

52 Eventually, of course, you get better at it. If you stick with your lessons, you'll become an "intermediate" skier, meaning you'll learn to fall *before* you reach the woods. That's where I am now, in stark contrast to my 9-year-old son, who has not yet studied gravity in school and therefore became an expert in a matter of hours. Watching him flash effortlessly down the slope, I experience, as a parent, feelings of both pride and hope: pride in his accomplishment, and hope that someday, somehow, he'll ski near enough to where I'm lying that I'll be able to trip him with my poles.

Important Final Word of Advice

53 Whatever sport you decide to become involved in, you should not plunge into it without first consulting your physician. You can reach him on his cellular phone, in a dense group of trees, somewhere in the vicinity of the fourteenth hole.

Looking Back

1. In the section "Shrieking At Little Leaguers," which of the following techniques for achieving humor does Barry employ: understatement? hyperbole? overstatement? irony?

2. In "Shrieking At Little Leaguers," what picture does Barry paint of himself as a father? Is that picture ironic?

3. Why does Barry include the imaginary conversation between the two golf announcers?

4. This essay was taken from the book *Dave Barry Turns 40*. Discuss the extent to which the author's age explains the major topics of his essay?

Looking Into

1. In a small group, make a list of the words and/or phrases in paragraph 1 that establish Barry's humorous tone.

2. Choose a sport with which you have some familiarity and write a humorous description of your involvement in it.

Looking Around

1. American newspaperman and cynic H. L. Mencken once said: "I hate all sports as rabidly as a person who likes sports hates common sense." Using any of the authors in this section, how would you refute the last part of this observation? How would you support it? Express your opinions in a brief paper.

2. To what extent would the authors in this section agree with Highet's observation: "The true player enjoys the game for its own sake, and its own sake alone"? Write a paper in which you sum up the opinions of the authors.

3. According to several of the authors, sports are one way of understanding yourself and life. What understanding of yourself have you gained through participation in sports? Describe your understanding in an essay.

4. Catalogue the sports that you enjoy watching. What qualities do they share? Describe the qualities in a short paper.

5. Unlike most alumni groups, professors in many colleges regularly question the appropriateness of interscholastic athletics. They contend that the function of a college is academic, not athletic. Do you agree or disagree with the professors? Defend your position in a brief paper.

6. List some of the advantages and disadvantages of participating in sports. Then write a short paper in which you weigh both sides of the issue and reach a conclusion. Focus on either team sports or individual sports.

PART 4
Nature

—∿—

*T*he history of life on earth has been a history of interaction between living things and their surroundings. To a large extent, the physical form and the habits of the earth's vegetation and its animal life have been molded by the environment. Considering the whole space of earthly time, the opposite effect, in which life actually modifies its surroundings, has been relatively slight. Only within the moment of time represented by the present century has one species—man—acquired significant power to alter the nature of his world.

Rachel Carson from *Silent Spring*

The authors in this section write of different environments and from different perspectives, but all of them are keen observers of the natural world, and they record their observations and speculations in distinctive styles.

Rachel Carson writes from a biologist's point of view and as one who has an intimate acquaintance with the creatures of the sea and shore "where the drama of life played its first scene on earth" in "The Marginal World."

Annie Dillard is not a scientist but a trained observer who sees the life of a wild creature almost as a metaphor as she reflects on the necessity of choosing to live as one should in "Living Like Weasels."

In a letter now titled "The Gall of the Wild," James Sheridan writes of his struggle with the beavers with whom he shares a habitat and his efforts to effect some sort of compromise with these ambitious builders.

With "Here Be Chickens," the scene shifts from relatively tame environments to the island of Komodo, the home of the Komodo dragons. Douglas Adams, an amused onlooker of both animal and human oddities, emerges from his experiences there somewhat shaken and considerably wiser.

How much of the natural world exists in a city? In "My Empty Lot," Joseph Kastner analyzes the life cycle of a Manhattan lot and tells of the amazing ability of nature, by working hard and fast, to populate an urban wasteland.

The only writer in this section who actually makes her living from the land, Sue Hubbell tells of her life in the Missouri Ozarks as a beekeeper in three short chapters from *A Country Year*.

An impassioned environmentalist, Edward Abbey reveals himself in "Serpents of Paradise" as a man at ease with and fascinated by the wildlife of the West, if not with some members of the human species.

The Marginal World

RACHEL CARSON

As a marine biologist, Rachel Carson wrote often about the sea, including the books *Under the Sea Wind*, (1941), *The Sea Around Us* (1951), and *The Edge of the Sea* (1955).

A *Time* Magazine critic wrote of *The Edge of the Sea*: "Again author Carson has shown her remarkable talent for catching the breath of science on the still glass of poetry." A *Saturday Review* critic wrote that "it appeals both to the mind's eye and to the physical eye."

She was born in Springfield, Pennsylvania, in 1907, received her A.B. degree from the Pennsylvania College for Women, and her A.M. degree from Johns Hopkins. She did additional graduate study at the Marine Biological Laboratory in Woods Hole, Massachusetts, and went on to receive four honorary degrees. She was a member of the zoological staff at the University of Maryland from 1931 to 1936. In 1936 she began work at the U.S. Bureau of Fisheries (now the Fish and Wildlife Service) in Washington, D.C., as an aquatic biologist. She became a full-time writer in 1952.

She won many awards, including a National Book Award for *The Sea Around Us* and a Guggenheim fellowship in 1951. She also received the Schweitzer Medal from the Animal Welfare Institute and a Conservationist of the Year Award from the National Wildlife Federation.

Her other writings include *Silent Spring* (1962) and *The Sense of Wonder* (1965). *Silent Spring* was, perhaps, her most influential book. It warned of the dangers of pesticides to human and animal life and was largely responsible for the banning of the use of DDT in the United States. The book sold over 500,000 copies in the hardback edition.

Rachel Carson died of cancer in Silver Spring, Maryland, in 1964.

Looking Ahead

In this essay from *The Edge of the Sea*, she evokes a sense of wonder at the sea shore. Note also how she evokes a sense of the age of the earth.

—◆—

1   *T*he edge of the sea is a strange and beautiful place. All through the long history of Earth it has been an area of unrest where waves have broken heavily against the land, where the tides have pressed forward over the continents, receded, and then returned. For no two successive days is the shore line precisely the same. Not only do the tides advance and retreat in their eternal rhythms, but the level of the sea itself is never at rest. It rises or falls as the glaciers melt or grow, as the floor of the deep ocean basins shifts under its increasing load of sediments, or as the earth's crust along the continental margins warps up or down in adjustment to strain and tension. Today a little more land may belong to the sea, tomorrow a little less. Always the edge of the sea remains an elusive and indefinable boundary.

2   The shore has a dual nature, changing with the swing of the tides, belonging now to the land, now to the sea. On the ebb tide it knows the harsh extremes of the land world, being exposed to heat and cold, to wind, to rain and drying sun. On the flood tide it is a water world, returning briefly to the relative stability of the open sea.

3   Only the most hardy and adaptable can survive in a region so mutable, yet the area between the tide lines is crowded with plants and animals. In this difficult world of the shore, life displays its enormous toughness and vitality by occupying almost every conceivable niche. Visibly, it carpets the intertidal rocks; or half hidden, it descends into fissures and crevices, or hides under boulders, or lurks in the wet gloom of sea caves. Invisibly, where the casual observer would say there is no life, it lies deep in the sand, in burrows and tubes and passageways. It tunnels into solid rock and bores into peat and clay. It encrusts weeds or drifting spars or the hard, chitinous shell of a lobster. It exists minutely, as the film of bacteria that spreads over a rock surface or a wharf piling; as spheres of protozoa, small as pinpricks, sparkling at the surface of the sea; and as Lilliputian beings swimming through dark pools that lie between the grains of sand.

4   The shore is an ancient world, for as long as there has been an earth and sea there has been this place of the meeting of land and water. Yet it is a world that keeps alive the sense of continuing creation and of the relentless drive of life. Each time that I enter it, I gain some new awareness of its beauty and its deeper meanings, sensing that intricate fabric of life by which one creature is linked with another, and each with its surroundings.

5   In my thoughts of the shore, one place stands apart for its revelation of exquisite beauty. It is a pool hidden within a cave that one can visit only rarely and briefly when the lowest of the year's low tides fall below it, and perhaps from that very fact it acquires some of its special beauty. Choosing such a tide, I hoped for a glimpse of the pool. The ebb was to fall early in

the morning. I knew that if the wind held from the northwest and no interfering swell ran in from a distant storm the level of the sea should drop below the entrance to the pool. There had been sudden ominous showers in the night, with rain like handfuls of gravel flung on the roof. When I looked out into the early morning the sky was full of a gray dawn light but the sun had not yet risen. Water and air were pallid. Across the bay the moon was a luminous disc in the western sky, suspended above the dim line of distant shore—the full August moon, drawing the tide to the low, low levels of the threshold of the alien sea world. As I watched, a gull flew by, above the spruces. Its breast was rosy with the light of the unrisen sun. The day was, after all, to be fair.

6 Later, as I stood above the tide near the entrance to the pool, the promise of that rosy light was sustained. From the base of the steep wall of rock on which I stood, a moss-covered ledge jutted seaward into deep water. In the surge at the rim of the ledge the dark fronds of oarweeds swayed, smooth and gleaming as leather. The projecting ledge was the path to the small hidden cave and its pool. Occasionally a swell, stronger than the rest, rolled smoothly over the rim and broke in foam against the cliff. But the intervals between such swells were long enough to admit me to the ledge and long enough for a glimpse of that fairy pool, so seldom and so briefly exposed.

7 And so I knelt on the wet carpet of sea moss and looked back into the dark cavern that held the pool in a shallow basin. The floor of the cave was only a few inches below the roof, and a mirror had been created in which all that grew on the ceiling was reflected in the still water below.

8 Under water that was clear as glass the pool was carpeted with green sponge. Gray patches of sea squirts glistened on the ceiling and colonies of soft coral were a pale apricot color. In the moment when I looked into the cave a little elfin starfish hung down, suspended by the merest thread, perhaps by only a single tube foot. It reached down to touch its own reflection, so perfectly delineated that there might have been, not one starfish, but two. The beauty of the reflected images and of the limpid pool itself was the poignant beauty of things that are ephemeral, existing only until the sea should return to fill the little cave.

9 Whenever I go down into this magical zone of the low water of the spring tides, I look for the most delicately beautiful of all the shore's inhabitants—flowers that are not plant but animal, blooming on the threshold of the deeper sea. In that fairy cave I was not disappointed. Hanging from its roof were the pendent flowers of the hydroid Tubularia, pale pink, fringed and delicate as the wind flower. Here were creatures so exquisitely fashioned that they seemed unreal, their beauty too fragile to exist in a

world of crushing force. Yet every detail was functionally useful, every stalk and hydranth and petal-like tentacle fashioned for dealing with the realities of existence. I knew that they were merely waiting, in that moment of the tide's ebbing, for the return of the sea. Then in the rush of water, in the surge of surf and the pressure of the incoming tide, the delicate flower heads would stir with life. They would sway on their slender stalks, and their long tentacles would sweep the returning water, finding in it all that they needed for life.

10   And so in that enchanted place on the threshold of the sea the realities that possessed my mind were far from those of the land world I had left an hour before. In a different way the same sense of remoteness and of a world apart came to me in a twilight hour on a great beach on the coast of Georgia. I had come down after sunset and walked far out over sands that lay wet and gleaming, to the very edge of the retreating sea. Looking back across that immense flat, crossed by winding, water-filled gullies and here and there holding shallow pools left by the tide, I was filled with awareness that this intertidal area, although abandoned briefly and rhythmically by the sea, is always reclaimed by the rising tide. There at the edge of low water the beach with its reminders of the land seemed far away. The only sounds were those of the wind and the sea and the birds. There was one sound of wind moving over water, and another of water sliding over the sand and tumbling down the faces of its own wave forms. The flats were astir with birds, and the voice of the willet rang insistently. One of them stood at the edge of the water and gave its loud, urgent cry; an answer came from far up the beach and the two birds flew to join each other.

11   The flats took on a mysterious quality as dusk approached and the last evening light was reflected from the scattered pools and creeks. Then birds became only dark shadows, with no color discernible. Sanderlings scurried across the beach like little ghosts, and here and there the darker forms of the willets stood out. Often I could come very close to them before they would start up in alarm—the sanderlings running, the willets flying up, crying. Black skimmers flew along the ocean's edge silhouetted against the dull, metallic gleam, or they went flitting above the sand like large, dimly seen moths. Sometimes they "skimmed" the winding creeks of tidal water, where little spreading surface ripples marked the presence of small fish.

12   The shore at night is a different world, in which the very darkness that hides the distractions of daylight brings into sharper focus the elemental realities. Once, exploring the night beach, I surprised a small ghost crab in the searching beam of my torch. He was lying in a pit he had dug just above the surf, as though watching the sea and waiting. The blackness of the

night possessed water, air, and beach. It was the darkness of an older world, before Man. There was no sound but the all-enveloping, primeval sounds of wind blowing over water and sand, and of waves crashing on the beach. There was no other visible life—just one small crab near the sea. I have seen hundreds of ghost crabs in other settings, but suddenly I was filled with the odd sensation that for the first time I knew the creature in its own world—that I understood, as never before, the essence of its being. In that moment time was suspended; the world to which I belonged did not exist and I might have been an onlooker from outer space. The little crab alone with the sea became a symbol that stood for life itself—for the delicate, destructible, yet incredibly vital force that somehow holds its place amid the harsh realities of the inorganic world.

13   The sense of creation comes with memories of a southern coast, where the sea and the mangroves, working together, are building a wilderness of thousands of small islands off the southwestern coast of Florida, separated from each other by a tortuous pattern of bays, lagoons, and narrow waterways. I remember a winter day when the sky was blue and drenched with sunlight; though there was no wind one was conscious of flowing air like cold clear crystal. I had landed on the surf-washed tip of one of those islands, and then worked my way around to the sheltered bay side. There I found the tide far out, exposing the broad mud flat of a cove bordered by the mangroves with their twisted branches, their glossy leaves, and their long prop roots reaching down, grasping and holding the mud, building the land out a little more, then again a little more.

14   The mud flats were strewn with the shells of that small, exquisitely colored mollusk, the rose tellin, looking like scattered petals of pink roses. There must have been a colony nearby, living buried just under the surface of the mud. At first the only creature visible was a small heron in gray and rusty plumage—a reddish egret that waded across the flat with the stealthy, hesitant moves of its kind. But other land creatures had been there, for a line of fresh tracks wound in and out among the mangrove roots, marking the path of a raccoon feeding on the oysters that gripped the supporting roots with projections from their shells. Soon I found the tracks of a shore bird, probably a sanderling, and followed them a little; then they turned toward the water and were lost, for the tide had erased them and made them as though they had never been.

15   Looking out over the cove I felt a strong sense of the interchangeability of land and sea in this marginal world of the shore, and of the links between the life of the two. There was also an awareness of the past and of the continuing flow of time, obliterating much that had gone before, as the sea had that morning washed away the tracks of the bird.

16   The sequence and meaning of the drift of time were quietly summarized in the existence of hundreds of small snails—the mangrove periwinkles—browsing on the branches and roots of the trees. Once their ancestors had been sea dwellers, bound to the salt waters by every tie of their life processes. Little by little over the thousands and millions of years the ties had been broken, the snails had adjusted themselves to life out of water, and now today they were living many feet above the tide to which they only occasionally returned. And perhaps, who could say how many ages hence, there would be in their descendants not even this gesture of remembrance for the sea.

17   The spiral shells of other snails—these quite minute—left winding tracks on the mud as they moved about in search of food. They were horn shells, and when I saw them I had a nostalgic moment when I wished I might see what Audubon[1] saw, a century and more ago. For such little horn shells were the food of the flamingo, once so numerous on this coast, and when I half closed my eyes I could almost imagine a flock of these magnificent flame birds feeding in that cove, filling it with their color. It was a mere yesterday in the life of the earth that they were there; in nature, time and space are relative matters, perhaps most truly perceived subjectively in occasional flashes of insight, sparked by such a magical hour and place.

18   There is a common thread that links these scenes and memories—the spectacle of life in all its varied manifestations as it has appeared, evolved, and sometimes died out. Underlying the beauty of the spectacle there is meaning and significance. It is the elusiveness of that meaning that haunts us, that sends us again and again into the natural world where the key to the riddle is hidden. It sends us back to the edge of the sea, where the drama of life played its first scene on earth and perhaps even its prelude; where the forces of evolution are at work today, as they have been since the appearance of what we know as life; and where the spectacle of living creatures faced by the cosmic realities of their world is crystal clear.

---

1   **Audubon**: John James (1785-1881), American artist and naturalist. He was born in Haiti, educated in France, and came to the U.S. in 1803. He is best known for *The Birds of America*, a monumental work containing detailed drawings of birds in their habitat.

Looking Back

1. What seems to be the author's purpose in writing this essay? How does the organization of the essay help to fulfill that purpose?

2. What can you infer about Carson from reading this essay?

3. To what does the title refer?

4. Why is this selection an appropriate starting point for a section on nature?

5. According to the author, what makes the little crab described in paragraph 12 a symbol of life itself?

Looking Into

1. Choose a place that you know well and have seen in various seasons and times of day and describe it in a paper or in a poem.

2. Although DDT is now banned, many pesticides are still in use all over the world. Why do people pollute the natural world, and what are at least three measures that could effectively prevent such pollution? Discuss these questions in a small group and present your findings in a well-organized paper.

3. Write a description of a body of water near you, even if it is only a creek or small pond. Describe some aspect of any life that exists in or near the water. In a city landscape, even a small pond of rain water will serve for this purpose.

Living Like Weasels

ANNIE DILLARD

Annie Dillard has the somewhat unusual distinction of winning a Pulitzer Prize for her first prose book, *Pilgrim at Tinker Creek*. A *Commentary* critic said of her work: "One of the most pleasing traits of this book is the graceful harmony between scrutiny of real phenomena and the reflections to which that gives rise."

Dillard was born in Pittsburgh in 1945 and received her B.A. and M.A. degrees from Hollins College. She has been a teacher of poetry and creative writing at Western Washington University at Bellingham and at Wesleyan University where she was a writer in residence beginning in 1987. She received grants from the National Endowment for the Arts (1980–1981) and the Guggenheim Foundation (1985–1986). In 1982, she was a member of the U.S. Cultural Delegation to China.

Her books include a book of poetry, *Tickets for a Prayer Wheel* (1974), *Pilgrim at Tinker Creek* (1974), *Holy the Firm* (1977), *Encounters with Chinese Writers* (1984), *The Writing Life* (1989), and *The Living* (1992). *Teaching a Stone to Talk*, from which the essay in this book was taken, appeared in 1982.

Looking Ahead

In this essay, Dillard writes of encountering a weasel, a small carnivorous mammal, near Tinker Creek, the setting for her first book of narrative prose. What is it about the weasel that sparks the thoughts in this essay?

1   *A* weasel is wild. Who knows what he thinks? He sleeps in his underground den, his tail draped over his nose. Sometimes he lives in his den for two days without leaving. Outside, he stalks rabbits, mice, muskrats, and birds, killing more bodies than he can eat warm, and often dragging the carcasses home. Obedient to instinct, he bites his prey at the neck, either splitting the jugular vein at the throat or crunching the brain at the base of the skull, and he does not let go. One naturalist refused to kill a weasel who was socketed into his hand deeply as a rattlesnake. The man

could in no way pry the tiny weasel off, and he had to walk half a mile to water, the weasel dangling from his palm, and soak him off like a stubborn label.

2   And once, says Ernest Thompson Seton[1]—once, a man shot an eagle out of the sky. He examined the eagle and found the dry skull of a weasel fixed by the jaws to his throat. The supposition is that the eagle had pounced on the weasel and the weasel swiveled and bit as instinct taught him, tooth to neck, and nearly won. I would like to have seen that eagle from the air a few weeks or months before he was shot: was the whole weasel still attached to his feathered throat, a fur pendant? Or did the eagle eat what he could reach, gutting the living weasel with his talons before his breast, bending his beak, cleaning the beautiful airborne bones?

3 I have been reading about weasels because I saw one last week. I startled a weasel who startled me, and we exchanged a long glance.

4   Twenty minutes from my house, through the woods by the quarry and across the highway, is Hollins Pond, a remarkable piece of shallowness, where I like to go at sunset and sit on a tree trunk. Hollins Pond is also called Murray's Pond; it covers two acres of bottomland near Tinker Creek with six inches of water and six thousand lily pads. In winter, brown-and-white steers stand in the middle of it, merely dampening their hooves; from the distant shore they look like miracle itself, complete with miracle's nonchalance. Now, in summer, the steers are gone. The water lilies have blossomed and spread to a green horizontal plane that is terra firma to plodding blackbirds, and tremulous ceiling to black leeches, crayfish, and carp.

5   This is, mind you, suburbia. It is a five-minute walk in three directions to rows of houses, though none is visible here. There's a 55 mph highway at one end of the pond, and a nesting pair of wood ducks at the other. Under every bush is a muskrat hole or a beer can. The far end is an alternating series of fields and woods, fields and woods, threaded everywhere with motorcycle tracks—in whose bare clay wild turtles lay eggs.

6   So. I had crossed the highway, stepped over two low barbed-wire fences, and traced the motorcycle path in all gratitude through the wild rose and poison ivy of the pond's shoreline up into high grassy fields. Then I cut down through the woods to the mossy fallen tree where I sit. This

---

1 **Ernest Thompson Seton** (1860-1946): American naturalist and artist. Born in England, his most famous work was *Wild Animals I Have Known* (1898), a book familiar to every school child at one time.

tree is excellent. It makes a dry, upholstered bench at the upper, marshy end of the pond, a plush jetty raised from the thorny shore between a shallow blue body of water and a deep blue body of sky.

7   The sun had just set. I was relaxed on the tree trunk, ensconced in the lap of lichen, watching the lily pads at my feet tremble and part dreamily over the thrusting path of a carp. A yellow bird appeared to my right and flew behind me. It caught my eye; I swiveled around—and the next instant, inexplicably, I was looking down at a weasel, who was looking up at me.

8 Weasel! I'd never seen one wild before. He was ten inches long, thin as a curve, a muscled ribbon, brown as fruitwood, soft-furred, alert. His face was fierce, small and pointed as a lizard's; he would have made a good arrowhead. There was just a dot of chin, maybe two brown hairs' worth, and then the pure white fur began that spread down his underside. He had two black eyes I didn't see, any more than you see a window.

9   The weasel was stunned into stillness as he was emerging from beneath an enormous shaggy wild rose bush four feet away. I was stunned into stillness twisted backward on the tree trunk. Our eyes locked, and someone threw away the key.

10   Our look was as if two lovers, or deadly enemies, met unexpectedly on an overgrown path when each had been thinking of something else: a clearing blow to the gut. It was also a bright blow to the brain, or a sudden beating of brains, with all the charge and intimate grate of rubbed balloons. It emptied our lungs. It felled the forest, moved the fields, and drained the pond; the world dismantled and tumbled into that black hole of eyes. If you and I looked at each other that way, our skulls would split and drop to our shoulders. But we don't. We keep our skulls. So.

11   He disappeared. This was only last week, and already I don't remember what shattered the enchantment. I think I blinked, I think I retrieved my brain from the weasel's brain, and tried to memorize what I was seeing, and the weasel felt the yank of separation, the careening splashdown into real life and the urgent current of instinct. He vanished under the wild rose. I waited motionless, my mind suddenly full of data and my spirit with pleadings, but he didn't return.

12   Please do not tell me about "approach-avoidance conflicts." I tell you I've been in that weasel's brain for sixty seconds, and he was in mine. Brains are private places, muttering through unique and secret tapes—but the weasel and I both plugged into another tape simultaneously, for a sweet and shocking time. Can I help it if it was a blank?

13   What goes on in his brain the rest of the time? What does a weasel think about? He won't say. His journal is tracks in clay, a spray of feath-

ers, mouse blood and bone: uncollected, unconnected, loose-leaf, and blown.

14 I would like to learn, or remember, how to live. I come to Hollins Pond not so much to learn how to live as, frankly, to forget about it. That is, I don't think I can learn from a wild animal how to live in particular—shall I suck warm blood, hold my tail high, walk with my footprints precisely over the prints of my hands?—but I might learn something of mindlessness, something of the purity of living in the physical senses and the dignity of living without bias or motive. The weasel lives in necessity and we live in choice, hating necessity and dying at the last ignobly in its talons. I would like to live as I should, as the weasel lives as he should. And I suspect that for me the way is like the weasel's: open to time and death painlessly, noticing everything, remembering nothing, choosing the given with a fierce and pointed will.

15 I missed my chance. I should have gone for the throat. I should have lunged for that streak of white under the weasel's chin and held on, held on through mud and into the wild rose, held on for a dearer life. We could live under the wild rose wild as weasels, mute and uncomprehending. I could very calmly go wild. I could live two days in the den, curled, leaning on mouse fur, sniffing bird bones, blinking, licking, breathing musk, my hair tangled in the roots of grasses. Down is a good place to go, where the mind is single. Down is out, out of your ever-loving mind and back to your careless senses. I remember muteness as a prolonged and giddy fast, where every moment is a feast of utterance received. Time and events are merely poured, unremarked, and ingested directly, like blood pulsed into my guts through a jugular vein. Could two live that way? Could two live under the wild rose, and explore by the pond, so that the smooth mind of each is as everywhere present to the other, and as received and as unchallenged, as falling snow?

16 We could, you know. We can live any way we want. People take vows of poverty, chastity, and obedience—even of silence—by choice. The thing is to stalk your calling in a certain skilled and supple way, to locate the most tender and live spot and plug into that pulse. This is yielding, not fighting. A weasel doesn't "attack" anything; a weasel lives as he's meant to, yielding at every moment to the perfect freedom of single necessity.

17 I think it would be well, and proper, and obedient, and pure, to grasp your one necessity and not let it go, to dangle from it limp wherever it takes you. Then even death, where you're going no matter how you live, cannot

you part. Seize it and let it seize you up aloft even, till your eyes burn out and drop; let your musky flesh fall off in shreds, and let your very bones unhinge and scatter, loosened over fields, over fields and woods, lightly, thoughtlessly, from any height at all, from as high as eagles.

Looking Back

1. What was your first reaction to this essay?

2. What are some of the things that weasels come to symbolize for Dillard in this selection?

3. What is it about "living like weasels" that appeals to Dillard?

4. Dillard writes: "I would like to live as I should." How can nature be an inspiration for living as you should?

5. Dillard writes of grasping "your one necessity" and not letting it go. It is obvious that she is not referring to material things. In a small group, discuss what you think she means.

Looking Into

1. In your journal, write what you think your "one necessity" might be and whether you think this will change.

2. Dillard describes a moment of heightened awareness (sometimes called an epiphany) that occurred as a result of her meeting with the weasel. Have you had such a moment? If so, write about it in a journal entry.

3. Describe some creature that you encountered unexpectedly. What were the circumstances of the encounter? Were you frightened? Write about it in a paper.

Gall of the Wild

JAMES E. SHERIDAN

Born in Wilmington, Delaware, in 1922, James E. Sheridan received his B.S. degree in 1949 and his M.A. degree in 1950 from the University of Illinois and his Ph.D. from the University of California at Berkeley in 1961.

He was a lecturer in modern Chinese history at Stanford in 1960 and continued his teaching career at Northwestern University where he became Chairman of the History Department in 1969, a position he held until 1974. He was professor of Far Eastern history from 1968 until his retirement.

He has received a Fulbright fellowship to France and several Ford Foundation fellowships and has traveled in Taiwan, Japan, and Hong Kong. His writings include *Chinese Warlord: the Career of Feng Yu-hsiang* and *China in Disintegration: the Republican Era in Chinese History, 1912–1949.*

Looking Ahead

Sheridan has perhaps not looked a beaver in the eye, as Annie Dillard did her weasel, but he knows the habits of beavers quite well. When he retired from teaching history at Northwestern, he went to live in the northern Wisconsin woods. In a letter to a former colleague, he recounts his battles with the beavers, a battle whose outcome is not at all clear.

Dear Steve,

[1] You can't imagine the havoc that the beaver creates on the land. My creek today is an utterly different creek from what it was only a few years ago. In some areas, where beavers have carved out clumps of grass and earth for their dams, it is twice as wide as it once was. The land on either side is marked by canals and well-worn paths created by beavers on their way to harvest trees—*my* trees—and everywhere there are little pointed stumps left by beavers where they felled and carried trees away. When you see what three or four beavers can do to a landscape in a few days, and then

you think of the millions of beavers in this country for centuries before Europeans came, you come to realize that the beaver is substantially responsible for the shape of America.

2 If you have ever seen areas where all the trees have been transformed into dead gray sticks, you have probably been looking at areas where beavers have flooded the trees. The configuration of my land is such that even a low beaver dam will spread water over many acres; in only a few days that water can kill all the tamaracks, black spruce, pine, and various other trees there. So when the beavers build a dam I have to tear it up, and I can't wait too long before doing so. But to tear up a beaver dam is surprisingly difficult to do.

3 The construction of a beaver dam is devilishly clever; you have to dismantle a dam to fully appreciate the genius of its construction. The beavers weave sticks and branches and logs together and deposit clumps of mud and vegetation against the structure so that the flow of the stream presses the muck in place and keeps it there. It is not unusual to find waterlogged logs six to eight feet long and four to six inches in diameter. More common are branches or small tree trunks about three inches thick and sometimes eight or more feet in length.

4 To dismantle a dam, I have to stand on it or next to it, then start pulling out branches and tossing them on the creek bank. The branches do not come out easily; all are entangled with the one being pulled as well as with attached globs of water-soaked foliage and mud. For a branch to come out, I must strain and tug and pull with all the power my back and shoulders can generate. When I do, and am well into a mighty effort, the branch suddenly gives way, and I am thrown violently off balance and go hurtling backwards into the creek. On other occasions, as I am grimacing with effort and opening my mouth to pant and grunt, the end of the branch, laden with muck and foliage and water, springs out of the dam to slap me across the mouth and drive the muck down my throat.

5 I used to wear breast-high waders for the work, but it was slightly awkward to move in the waders on the irregular top of the dam and the uncertain mud at the bottom. Moreover, each time I rocketed backwards into the creek the waders filled with a couple of hundred pounds of water and threatened to carry me bouncing along the bottom of the creek like a bloated walrus. So now I go out in old trousers and shirt and tennis shoes. It is messier and less comfortable but easier to work and also safer.

6 All the time I am engaged in dismantling the dam, black flies, no-see-ums, and assorted other carnivorous insects, realizing that it is difficult for me to brush them off with hands that are coated with muck, have their

way with me. (No-see-ums, as you probably know, are very tiny insects, virtually invisible—hence the name—who bite like Siberian tigers.)

[7] It is not enough simply to put a hole in the dam large enough to allow the backed up water to get through. The beavers will repair such a hole in short order and go on to build the dam higher. So I try to clean out the dam down to the very bottom of the creek. I persist in thinking that the beavers will return to the dam site, see that all their work has been destroyed, and become discouraged and move elsewhere. But all the evidence shows that is not going to happen.

[8] No matter how thoroughly I remove the dam, the beavers quickly rebuild, usually that very night. So I must tear it down the following day. The whole thing becomes a matter of perseverance, of determination; who will outlast the other?

[9] But I am a human being, an intelligent, reasoning creature, and he is little more than a mouse with a glandular problem. It should be no difficult matter, I reason, to outsmart the dumb animal. One of the first things I tried, some years ago, was to string a rope about six or eight inches over the water at the dam site and hang cans and pieces of metal from it. Well, the beavers paid no attention to it, ultimately building right over it. I am not really surprised; it was a poor idea, hardly worthy of a reasoning human being.

[10] Then I acquired a large jug of deer repellent, a fluid that looks like molasses and smells ineffably bad. I spread it around the dam site, but it had no perceptible effect. Next I obtained a dried castor gland, the beaver's sexual gland that contains an oily substance and has a strong smell. I soaked it in water and poured the fluid on several spots around the dam. In theory, the beavers would smell it, think the territory had been claimed by another beaver, and leave. (You see how subtle and intelligent that plan was; I am a human being, not a dumb animal.) The rebuilt dam the following morning suggested that the smell simply turned them on and made them work harder.

[11] Next, I purchased 50 feet of plastic drain pipe: flexible pipe about 10 inches in diameter with dime-sized holes all along its length. I ran the pipe through the dam, at right angles to it, so that one end of the pipe was 25 feet upstream and the other was 25 feet downstream, each end secured to a sturdy post anchored in the creek bed.

[12] I reasoned that since the water would continue to flow through the pipe and thus through the dam, the beavers could go on building indefinitely but the water level would never rise high enough to threaten my trees. Even if the beavers stuffed the end of the inlet pipe with grass

or mud, water could still flow through the dime-sized holes along the pipe's length. If ever there was subtle human intelligence at work, that was the time. I went home that day chuckling with satisfaction at this triumph of human reason over dumb animal instinct. But the next morning I found that the beavers had incorporated the entire pipe, together with the posts that held it in place, into the dam; they had used my pipe as building material!

13   I had to become more subtle and clever still. Beavers, like all sensible animals, fear human beings; they normally flee as soon as a human approaches. All I had to do was to introduce a human presence at the dam site, and the beaver would be afraid to work there. So I bought a cheap plastic radio, battery powered, and after having torn up the dam, hung the radio—tuned to an all-night station—from a tree near the dam site. Next to it I hung a flashing light. (You see the difference between a human being and a dumb animal?)

14   The next morning, I found I could not get my canoe close to the radio and light until I cleared away the dam that had been created during the night. It was unusually large for a single night's work; I suspect the music refreshed the beavers and increased their productivity, just as it does for assembly line workers.

15   Of course, I could shoot the beavers (an increasingly attractive notion), but I can't help feeling that there is something profoundly selfish and a bit stupid about coming to a region because I like the natural surroundings and the wildlife, and then killing any wildlife that inconveniences me. Some conservationists in Colorado (the problem of beavers is now nationwide) arranged to trap beavers, pick out the females, and fit them with a birth control device, so the population will inexorably decline. I like that idea, but since I can't distinguish between male and female beavers, I am afraid that if I were to take that approach I might only create a lot of constipated male beavers.

16   It would also be possible to catch them in live traps and then deal with them. (What marvelous possibilities for revenge leap to mind! I could put flaming aspen slivers into the beaver's gums. Or nail his tail to the hubcap of my truck and then drive rapidly over a rough road. Or defrost him in the microwave.) In fact, I tried live traps some years ago but did not catch a single beaver. In any event, if I catch one, I have to take him miles away to release him. And, while en route, I will probably pass somebody from that place bringing his beavers to my area.

[17]   Oh well, I am confident that I will win out in the end. After all, I am a human being, and the beaver is a dumb animal. Ultimately there can be no contest.

With warm regards,
Jim

Looking Back

1. Why does the author want to get rid of the beavers?

2. Contrast the tone (author's attitude toward the subject) of this letter with the tone of the essay "Living Like Weasels."

3. If you faced Sheridan's difficulties, would you too refuse to shoot the beavers? Why or why not?

4. Sheridan says that "the beaver is substantially responsible for the shape of America." How could this be true?

5. The title of this letter was added by an editor. To what famous novel is it an allusion? Is the title appropriate here?

Looking Into

1. Have you had an unpleasant, annoying, or amusing encounter with the natural world? If so, write about it in a letter that could be published in a magazine for outdoor sports enthusiasts.

2. Do a little research on beaver dams and write a brief essay in which you describe them. Include as much factual information as you can find about such dams and share your findings with the class.

3. What other solutions might Sheridan have tried for dealing with the beavers? Write a short paper in which you list some possible solutions.

Here Be Chickens

DOUGLAS ADAMS AND MARK CARWARDINE

Douglas Adams is perhaps best known for "The Hitchhiker's Guide to the Galaxy," a radio and television series he produced and wrote, and for "Dr. Who," a television series for which he was script editor. Both series were produced by the BBC in London.

Based on the BBC series, *The Hitchhiker's Guide to the Galaxy* became a book and the title of an eight-book series that was listed among the best books for young adults by the American Library Association in 1980.

Adams was born in Cambridge in 1952 and educated at St. John's College, Cambridge. He graduated with a B.A. with honors in 1974.

His other novels include *Dirk Gently's Holistic Detective Agency* (1987), which tells of Gently, a psychic, Richard MacDuff, and Reg, a time-traveler and Cambridge professor so aged he can't remember where he came from; *The Long Dark Tea-Time of the Soul* (1988); and *Mostly Harmless* (1992). He is also co-author of an interactive computer program, "Bureaucracy," and a BBC radio series, "Last Chance to See."

A *Washington Post Book World* critic called *The Hitchhiker's Guide to the Galaxy* series "inspired lunacy that leaves hardly a science fictional cliché alive." Adams himself claims to be a comedy writer.

Looking Ahead

Adams and zoologist Mark Carwardine have traveled the world in search of endangered species. On one such expedition, described in the book *Last Chance to See,* they decided to head for Komodo Island, home of the Komodo dragons (really lizards) and several species of poisonous snakes as well. How do you feel about allowing groups of tourists to view endangered species?

¹ The first animal we went to look for, three years later, was the Komodo dragon lizard. This was an animal, like most of the animals we were going to see, about which I knew very little. What little I did know was hard to like.

2   They are man-eaters. That is not so bad in itself. Lions and tigers are man-eaters, and though we may be intensely wary of them and treat them with respectful fear, we nevertheless have an instinctive admiration for them. We don't actually like to be eaten by them, but we don't resent the very idea. The reason, probably, is that we are mammals and so are they. There's a kind of unreconstructed species prejudice at work: a lion is one of us but a lizard is not. And neither, for that matter, is a fish, which is why we have such an unholy terror of sharks.

3   The Komodo lizards are also big. Very big. There's one on Komodo at the moment which is over twelve feet long and stands about a yard high, which you can't help but feel is entirely the wrong size for a lizard to be, particularly if it's a man-eater and you're about to go and share an island with it.

4   Though they are man-eaters, they don't get to eat man very often, and more generally their diet consists of goats, pigs, deer, and such like, but they will only kill these animals if they can't find something that's dead already, because they are, at heart, scavengers. They like their meat bad and smelly. We don't like our meat like that and tend to be leery of things that do. I was definitely leery of these lizards. . . .

5   We met up in a hotel room in Melbourne and examined our array of expeditionary equipment. "We" were Mark, myself, and Gaynor Shutte, a BBC producer who was going to be recording our exploits for a radio documentary series. Our equipment was a vast array of cameras, tape recorders, tents, sleeping bags, medical supplies, mosquito coils, unidentifiable things made of canvas and nylon with metal eyelets and plastic hooks, windbreakers, boots, penknives, torches, and a cricket bat.

6   None of us would admit to having brought the cricket bat. We couldn't understand what it was doing there. We phoned room service to bring us up some beers and also to take the cricket bat away, but they didn't want it. The guy from room service said that if we were really going to look for man-eating lizards, maybe the cricket bat would be a handy thing to have.

7   "If you find you've got a dragon charging toward you at thirty miles an hour snapping its teeth, you can always drive it defensively through the covers," he said, deposited the beers and left.

8   We hid the cricket bat under the bed, opened the beers, and let Mark explain something of what we were in for.

9   "For centuries," he said, "the Chinese told stories of great scaly man-eating monsters with fiery breath, but they were thought to be nothing more than myths and fanciful imaginings. Old sailors would tell of them, and would write 'Here be dragons' on their maps when they saw a land they didn't at all like the look of.

10 "And then, at the beginning of this century, a pioneering Dutch visitor was attempting to island-hop his way along the Indonesian archipelago to Australia when he had engine trouble and had to crash-land his plane on the tiny island of Komodo. He survived the crash but his plane didn't.

11 "He went to search for water. As he was searching, he found a strange wide track on the sandy shore, followed the track, and suddenly found himself confronted with something that he, also, didn't at all like the look of. It appeared to be a great scaly man-eating monster, fully ten feet long. What he was looking at was the thing we are going to look for—the Komodo dragon lizard."

12 "Did he survive?" I asked, going straight for the point.

13 "Yes, he did, though his reputation didn't. He stayed alive for three months, and then was rescued. But when he went home, everyone thought he was mad and nobody believed a word of it."

14 "So were the Komodo dragons the origin of the Chinese dragon myths?"

15 "Well, nobody really knows, of course. At least I don't. But it certainly seems like a possibility. It's a large creature with scales, it's a man-eater, and though it doesn't actually breathe fire, it does have the worst breath of any creature known to man. But there's something else you should know about the island as well."

16 "What?"

17 "Have another beer first."

18 I did.

19 "There are," said Mark, "more poisonous snakes per square meter of ground on Komodo than on any equivalent area on earth. . . ."

[After a series of misadventures, they finally set sail on a fishing vessel from Labuan Bajo on the island of Flores in the Indonesian Archipelago, the nearest port to Komodo. Komodo is a protected national park. Aboard are Kiri, who is their local guide, the boat captain's father (the boat captain seems to be missing), "two small boys aged about twelve who ran the boat, and four [live] chickens." As they approach the island, it appears to have "great serrated heaps of rocks . . . , behind them, heavy undulating hills," and a few palm trees.]

20 We moored at a long, rickety, wooden jetty that stuck out from the middle of a wide pale beach. At the landward end the jetty was surmounted by an archway, nailed to the top of which was a wooden board which welcomed us to Komodo, and therefore served slightly to diminish our sense of intrepidness.

21 The moment we passed under the archway there was suddenly a strong smell. You had to go through it to get the smell. Until you'd been

through the archway you hadn't arrived and you didn't get the strong, thick, musty, smell of Komodo.

22 The next blow to our sense of intrepidness was the rather neatly laid-out path. This led from the end of the jetty parallel to the shore toward the next and major blow to our sense of intrepidness, which was a visitors' village.

23 This was a group of fairly ramshackle wooden buildings: an administration centre from which the island (which is a wildlife reserve) is run, a cafeteria terrace, and a small museum. Behind these, ranged around the inside of a steep semicircular slope, were about half a dozen visitors' huts—on stilts.

24 It was about lunchtime, and there were nearly a dozen people sitting in the cafeteria eating noodles and drinking 7-Up; Americans, Dutch, you name it. Where had they come from? How had they got here? What was going on?

25 Outside the administration hut was a wooden sign with regulations all over it, such as "Report to National Park office," "Travel outside visitors' center only with guards," "Wear pants and shoes," and "Watch for snakes."

26 Lying on the ground underneath this was a small stuffed dragon. I say small because it was only about four feet long. It had been modeled in completely spread-eagled posture, lying flat on the ground with its fore-limbs stretched out in front and its back limbs lying alongside its long tapering tail. I was a little startled to see it for a moment, but then went up to have a look at it.

27 It opened its eyes and had a look at me.

28 I rocketed backward with a yell of astonishment, which provoked barks of derisive laughter from the terrace.

29 "It's just a dragon!" called out an American girl.

30 I went over.

31 "Have you all been here long?" I asked.

32 "Oh, hours," she said. "We came over on the ferry from Labuan Bajo. Done the dragons. Bored with them. The food's terrible."

33 "What ferry?" I asked.

34 "Comes over most days."

35 "Oh. Oh, I see. From Labuan Bajo?"

36 "You have to go and sign the visitors' book in the office," she said, pointing at it.

37 Rather ruffled, I went and joined Mark and Gaynor.

38 "This isn't at all what I expected," said Mark, standing there in the middle of our pile of intrepid baggage, holding the four chickens. "Did we need to bring these?" he asked Kiri.

39   Kiri said that it was always a good idea to bring chickens for the kitchen. Otherwise we'd just have to eat fish and noodles.

40   "I think I prefer fish," said Gaynor.

41   Kiri explained that she was wrong and that she preferred chicken to fish. Westerners, he explained, preferred chicken. It was well known. Fish was only cheap food for peasants. We would be eating chicken, which was sexy and which we preferred.

42   He took the chickens, which were tethered together with a long piece of string, put them down by our baggage, and ushered us up the steps to the park office, where one of the park guards gave us forms and a pencil. Just as we were starting to fill them in, giving details of our passport numbers, date, country, and town of birth, and so on, there was a sudden commotion outside.

43   At first we paid it no mind, wrestling as we were to remember our mothers' maiden names,[1] and trying to work out who to elect as next of kin, but the racket outside increased, and we suddenly realized that it was the sound of distressed chickens. Our chickens.

44   We rushed outside. The stuffed dragon was attacking our chickens. It had one of them in its mouth and was shaking it, but as soon as it saw us and others closing in, it scurried rapidly around the corner of the building and off across the clearing behind in a cloud of dust, dragging the other distraught chickens tumbling along in the dust behind it, still tethered together with the string and screeching.

45   After the dragon put about thirty yards between it and us, it paused, and with a vicious jerk of its head bit through the string, releasing the other three chickens, which scrambled off toward the trees, shrieking and screaming and running in ever-decreasing circles as park guards careered after them trying to round them up. The dragon, relieved of its excess chickens, galloped off into thick undergrowth.

46   With a lot of "After you," "No, after you," we ran carefully toward where it had disappeared and arrived breathless and a little nervous. We peered in.

47   The undergrowth covered a large bank, and the dragon had crawled up the bank and stopped. The thick vegetation prevented us from getting closer than a yard to the thing, but then, we weren't trying terribly hard.

---

1   **mother's maiden names:** information evidently required, the theory being that only the person providing that information would be likely to know the name and thus is not pretending to be somebody else.

48   It lay there quite still. Protruding from between its jaws was the back end of the chicken, its scrawny legs quietly working the air. The dragon lizard watched us unconcernedly with the one eye that was turned toward us, a round, dark brown eye.

49   There is something profoundly disturbing about watching an eye that is watching you, particularly when the eye that is watching you is almost the same size as your eye, and the thing it is watching you out of is a lizard. The lizard's blink was also disturbing. It wasn't the normal rapid reflex movement that you expect from a lizard, but a slow, considered blink which made you feel that it was thinking about what it was doing.

50   The back end of the chicken struggled feebly for a moment, and the dragon chomped its jaw a little to let the chicken's struggles push it farther down its throat. This happened a couple more times, until there was only one scrawny chicken foot still sticking ridiculously out of the creature's mouth. Otherwise it did not move. It simply watched us. In the end it was us who slunk away trembling with an inexplicable cold horror.

51   Why? we wondered as we sat in the terrace cafeteria and tried to calm ourselves with 7-Up. The three of us were sitting ashen-faced as if we had just witnessed a foul and malignant murder. At least if we had been watching a murder, the murderer wouldn't have been looking us impassively in the eye as he did it. Maybe it was the feeling of cold, unflinching arrogance that so disturbed us. But whatever malign emotions we tried to pin on to the lizard, we knew that they weren't the lizard's emotions at all, only ours. The lizard was simply going about its lizardly business in a simple, straightforward lizardly way. It didn't know anything about the horror, the guilt, the shame, the ugliness that we, uniquely guilty and ashamed animals, were trying to foist on it. So we got it all straight back at us, as if reflected in the mirror of its single unwavering and disinterested eye.

52   Subdued with the thought that we had somehow been horrified by our own reflection, we sat quietly and waited for lunch.

53   Lunch.

54   In view of all the events of the day so far, lunch suddenly seemed to be a very complicated thing to contemplate. . . .

[While the three are having lunch (plain noodles), Carwardine explains that being bitten by a Komodo dragon is serious because the bacteria in a dragon's saliva is so potent that the wound may not heal. Nevertheless, the three are scheduled to see the dragons the next day. Unable to sleep in the hut assigned for sleeping on account of unpleasant smells and the noise of rats and snakes fighting, they take their sleeping bags to the deck of the boat.]

55   We awoke early, cold and damp with the dew, but feeling safe. We rolled up our bags and made our way back along the rickety jetty and under the arch. Once again, as soon as we had passed through the arch, the smell of the place assailed us and we were in that malign other world, Komodo.

56   This morning, we had been told, we would definitely see dragons. Big dragons. We didn't know precisely what it was we were in for, but clearly it was not what we had originally expected. It didn't look as if we would be pegging a dead goat out on the ground[2] and then hiding up a tree all day.

57   The day was to consist almost entirely of things we had not been expecting, starting with the arrival of a group of about two dozen American tourists on a specially chartered boat. They were mostly of early retirement age, festooned with cameras, polyester leisure suits, gold-rimmed glasses and Midwestern accents, and I didn't think that they would all be sitting up a tree all day either.

58   We were severely put out by their arrival and felt that the last vestige of any sense of intrepidness we were still trying to hold on to was finally slipping away.

59   We found a guard and asked what was going on. He said we could go on ahead now if we wanted to avoid the large party, so we set off with him immediately. We had a walk of about three or four miles through the forest along a path that was obviously well prepared and well trodden. The air was hot and dusty, and we walked with a sense of queasy uncertainty about how the day was going to go. After a while we became aware of the faint sound of a bell moving along ahead of us, and quickened our footsteps to find out what it was. We rounded a corner, and were confronted with some stomach-turning reality.

60   Up till now there had been something dreamlike about the whole experience. It was as if the action of walking through the archway and ingesting the musty odor of the island spirited you into an illusory world, in which words like *dragon* and *snake* and *goat* acquired fantastical meanings that had no analogue in the real world, and no consequence in it either. Now I had the feeling that the dream was slithering down the slope into nightmare, and that it was the sort of nightmare from which you would wake to discover that you had indeed wet the bed, that someone was indeed shaking you and shouting, and that the acrid smell of smoke was indeed your house incinerating itself.

---

2 **pegging a dead goat out on the ground:** The author had originally been told that a goat was needed to lure dragons out of the underbrush, which turns out to be true.

[61] Ahead of us on the path was a goat. It had a bell and a rope around its neck and was being led unwillingly along the pathway by another guard. We followed it numbly. Occasionally it would trot along hesitantly for a few paces, and then an appalling dread would seem suddenly to seize it and it would push its forelegs into the ground, put its head down, and struggle desperately against the tugging of the rope, bleating and crying. The guard would pull roughly on the rope and swipe at the goat's hindquarters with a bunch of leafy twigs he was carrying in his other hand, and the goat would at last tumble forward and trot along a few more paces, light-headed with fear. There was nothing for the goat to see to make it so afraid, and nothing, so far as we could tell, to hear; but who knows what the goat could smell in that place toward which we all were moving.

[62] Our deeply sinking spirits were next clouded sideways from a totally unexpected direction. We came across a circle of concrete set in the middle of a clearing. The circle was about twenty feet across, and had two parallel black stripes painted on it, with another black stripe at right angles to them, connecting their centres. It took us a few moments to work out what the symbol was and what it meant. Then we got it. It was just an "H." The circle was a helicopter pad. Whatever it was that was going to happen to this goat was something people came by helicopter to see.

[63] We trotted on, numb and light-headed, suddenly finding meaningless things to laugh wildly and hysterically at, as if we were walking willfully toward something that would destroy us as well.

[64] Leading from the helipad was a yet more formal pathway. It was a couple of yards wide with a stout wooden fence about two feet high along either side. We followed this along for a couple of hundred yards until we came at last to a wide gully, about ten feet deep, and here there were a number of things to see.

[65] To our left was a kind of bandstand. Several rows of bench seats were banked up behind one another, with a sloping wooden roof to protect them from the sun and other inclemencies in the weather. Tied to the front rail of the bandstand were both ends of a long piece of blue nylon rope, which ran out and down into the gully, where it was slung over a pulley wheel which hung from the branches of a small bent tree. A small iron hook hung from the rope.

[66] Stationed around the tree, basking in the dull light of a hot but overcast day, and in the stench of rotten death, were six large, muddy grey dragon lizards.

[67] The largest of them was probably about ten feet long.

[68] It was at first quite difficult to gauge their size. We were not that close as yet, the light was too blear and grey to model them clearly to the eye,

and the eye was simply not accustomed to equating something with the shape of a lizard with something of that size.

69   I stared at them awhile, aghast, until I realized that Mark was tapping me on the arm. I turned to look. On the other side of the short fence, a large dragon was approaching us.

70   It had emerged from the undergrowth, attracted, no doubt, by the knowledge that the arrival of human beings meant that it was feeding time. We learned later that the group of dragons that hang out in the gully rarely go very far from it and now do very little at all other than lie and wait to be fed.

71   The dragon lizard padded toward us, slapping its feet down aggressively, first its front left and back right, then vice versa, carrying its great weight easily and springily, with the swinging, purposeful gait of a bully. Its long, narrow, pale, forked tongue flickered in and out, testing the air for the smell of dead things.

72   It reached the far side of the fence, and then began to range back and forth tetchily, waiting for action, swinging and scraping its heavy tail across the dusty earth. Its rough, scaly skin hung a little loosely over its body, like chain mail, gathering to a series of cowl-like folds just behind its long death's head of a face. Its legs are thick and muscular, and end in claws such as you'd expect to find at the bottom of a brass table leg.

73   The thing is just a monitor lizard, and yet it is massive to a degree that is unreal. As it rears its head up over the fence and around as it turns, you wonder how it's done, what trickery is involved.

74   At that moment the party of tourists began to straggle toward us along the path, cheery and unimpressed, wanting to know what was up, what was happening. Look, there's one of those dragons! Ooh, it's a big one. Nasty-looking feller!

75   And now the worst of it was about to happen.

76   At a discreet distance behind the bandstand, the goat was being slaughtered. Two park guards held the struggling, bleating creature down on the ground with its neck across a log and hacked its head off with a machete, holding the bunch of leafy twigs against it to staunch the eruption of blood. The goat took several minutes to die.

77   Once it was dead, they cut off one of its back legs for the dragon behind the fence, then took the rest of the body and fastened it on to the hook on the blue nylon rope. It rocked and swayed in the breeze as they winched it down to the dragons lying in the gully.

78   The dragons took only a lethargic interest in it for a while. They were very well-fed and sleepy dragons. At last one reared itself up, approached the hanging carcass, and ripped slowly at its soft underbelly. A great mud-

dle of intestines slipped out of the goat and flopped over the dragon's head. They lay there for a while, steaming gently. The dragon seemed, for the moment, not to take any further interest.

79   Another dragon then heaved itself into motion and approached. It sniffed and licked at the air, and then started to eat the intestines of the goat from off the head of the first dragon, until the first dragon rounded on it and started to claim part of its meal for itself. At first nip, a thick green liquid flooded out of the glistening gray coils, and as the meal proceeded, the head of each dragon in turn became wet with the green liquid.

80   "Boy, this makes it big, Pauline," said a man standing near me, watching through his binoculars. "It makes it bigger than it is. You know, with these it's the size I really thought we'd be seeing." He handed the binoculars to his wife.

81   "Oh, that really does magnify it!" she said.

82   "It really is a superb pair of binoculars, Pauline. And they're not heavy either."

83   Others of the group clustered around.

84   "May I take a look? Whose are they?"

85   "My gosh, Howard would adore these!"

86   "Al? Al, take a look at these binoculars—see how heavy they are!"

87   Just as I was making the charitable assumption that the binoculars were just a diversion from having actually to watch the hellish floor show in the pit, the woman who now had possession of them suddenly exclaimed delightedly, "Gulp, gulp gulp! All gone! What a digestive system! Now he's smelling us!"

88   "He probably wants fresher meat," growled her husband. "Live, on the hoof!"

89   It was in fact at least an hour or so before all of the goat was gone, by which time the party had drifted, chatting, back to the village. As they did so, a lone Englishwoman in the party confided to us that she didn't actually care much about the dragons. "I like the landscape," she said airily. "The dragons are just thrown in. And of course, with all the strings and the goats and the tourists, well, it's just comedy really. If you were walking by yourself and you came across one, that might be different, but it's kind of like a puppet show."

90   When the last of them had left, a park guard told us that if we wished to we could climb down into the gully and see the dragons close up, and with swimming heads we did so. Two guards came with us, armed with long sticks, which branched into a "Y" at the end. They used these to push the dragons' necks away when they came too close or began to look aggressive.

91   We clambered and slithered down the slope, almost too scared to know or care what we were doing, and within a few minutes I found myself standing just two feet from the largest of the dragons. It regarded me without much interest, having plenty already to feed on. A length of dripping intestine was hanging from its open jaws, and its face was glistening with blood and saliva. The inside of its mouth was a pale, hard pink, and its fetid breath, together with the hot foul air of the gully, produced a stench so overpowering that our eyes were stinging and streaming and we were half faint with nausea.

92   All that remained by now of the goat which we had followed as it struggled bleating down the pathway ahead of us was one bloody and dismembered leg hanging by its ankle from the hook on the blue nylon rope. One dragon alone was still interested in it, and was gnawing moodily at the thigh muscles. Then it got a proper grip on the whole leg and tried with vicious twists of its head to pull it off the hook, but the leg was held fast at the ankle bone. Then, astoundingly, the dragon began instead very slowly to swallow the leg whole. It pulled and tugged, and maneuvered itself, so that more and more of the leg was pushed down its throat, until all that protruded was the hoof and the hook. After a while the dragon gave up struggling with it and simply squatted there, frozen in this posture for at least ten minutes until at last a guard did it the favor of hacking the hook away with his machete. The very last piece of the goat slithered away into the lizard's maw, where bones, hooves, horns, and all would now slowly be dissolved by the corrosive power of the enzymes that live in a Komodo dragon's digestive system.

93   We made our excuses and left.

94 The first of our three remaining chickens made its appearance at lunch, but our mood wasn't right for it. We pushed the scrawny bits of it listlessly around our plates and could find little to say.

95   In the afternoon we took the boat to Komodo village, where we met a woman who was the only known survivor of a dragon attack. A giant lizard had gone for her while she was out working in the fields, and by the time her screams had brought her neighbors and their dogs to rescue her and beat the creature away, her leg was in tatters. Intensive surgery in Bali saved her from having it amputated and, miraculously, she fought off the infection and lived, though her leg was still a mangled ruin. On the neighboring island of Rinca, we were told, a four-year-old boy had been snatched by a dragon as he lay playing on the steps of his home. The living build their houses on stilts, but on these islands not even the dead are safe, and they are buried with sharp rocks piled high on their graves. . . .

96   I went and sat on the beach by a mangrove tree and gazed out at the quiet ripples of the sea. Some fish were jumping up the beach and into the tree, which struck me as an odd thing for a fish to do, but I tried not to be judgmental about it. I was feeling pretty raw about my own species, and not much inclined to raise a quizzical eyebrow at others. The fish could play about in trees as much as they liked if it gave them pleasure, so long as they didn't try to justify themselves or tell one another it was a malign god who made them want to play in trees.

97   I was feeling pretty raw about my own species because we presume to draw a distinction between what we call good and what we call evil. We find our images of what we call evil in things outside ourselves, in creatures that know nothing of such matters, so that we can feel revolted by them, and, by contrast, good about ourselves. And if they won't be revolting enough of their own accord, we stoke them up with a goat. They don't want the goat, they don't need it. If they wanted one, they'd find it themselves. The only truly revolting thing that happens to the goat is in fact done by us.

98   So why didn't we say something? Like "Don't kill the goat"?

99   Well, there are a number of possible reasons:

—If the goat hadn't been killed for us, it would have been killed for someone else—for the party of American tourists, for instance.

—We didn't really realize what was going to happen till it was too late to stop it.

—The goat didn't lead a particularly nice life, anyway. Particularly not today.

—Another dragon would probably have got it later.

—If it hadn't been the goat, the dragons would have got something else, like a deer or something.

—We were reporting the incident for this book and for the BBC. It was important that we went through the whole experience so that people would know about it in detail. That's well worth a goat.

—We felt too polite to say, "Please don't kill the goat on our account."

—We were a bunch of lily-livered rationalizing turds.

100   The great thing about being the only species that makes a distinction between right and wrong is that we can make up the rules for ourselves as we go along.

101 The fish were still hopping harmlessly up and down the tree. They were about three inches long, brown and black, with little bobble eyes set very close together on the top of their heads. They hopped along using their fins as crutches.

102   "Mudskippers," said Mark, who happened along at that moment. He squatted down to look at them.

103   "What are they doing in the tree?' I asked.

104   "You could say they were experimenting." said Mark. "If they find they can make a better living on the land than in the water, then in the course of time and evolution they may come to stay on the land. They absorb a certain amount of oxygen through their skin at the moment, but they have to rush back into the sea from time to time for a mouthful of water, which they process through their gills. But that can change. It's happened before."

105   "What do you mean?"

106   "Well, it's probable that life on this planet started in the oceans, and that marine creatures migrated onto the land in search of new habitats. There's one fish that existed about three hundred and fifty million years ago that was very like a mudskipper. It came up on to the land using its fins as crutches. It's possible that it was the ancestor of all landliving vertebrates."

107   "Really? What was it called?"

108   "I don't think it had a name at the time."

109   "So this fish is what we were like three hundred and fifty million years ago?"

110   "Quite possibly."

111   "So in three hundred and fifty million years' time one of its descendants could be sitting on the beach here with a camera around its neck watching other fish hopping out of the sea?"

112   "No idea. That's for science-fiction novelists to think about. Zoologists can only say what we think has happened so far."

113   I suddenly felt, well, terribly *old* as I watched a mudskipper hopping along with what now seemed to me like a wonderful sense of hopeless, boundless naive optimism. It had such a terribly, terribly, terribly long way to go. I hoped that if its descendant was sitting here on this beach in 350 million years' time with a camera around its neck, it would feel that the journey had been worth it. I hoped that it might have a clearer understanding of itself in relation to the world it lived in. I hoped that it wouldn't

be reduced to turning other creatures into horror circus shows in order to try and ensure them their survival. I hoped that if someone tried to feed the remote descendant of a goat to the remote descendant of a dragon for the sake of little more than a shudder of entertainment, that it would feel it was wrong.

114   I hoped it wouldn't be too chicken to say so.

Looking Back

1. Adams is careful to explain that "whatever malign emotions we tried to pin onto the lizards, we knew that they weren't the lizard's emotions at all, only ours." Later he writes: "We find our images of what we call evil in things outside ourselves, in creatures that know nothing of such matters, so that we can feel revolted by them, and by contrast, good about ourselves." Examine your own feelings about parts of this selection and about anything in nature that you have considered malign or evil. Do Adams' statements make sense to you? Discuss.

2. What purpose is served by describing the American tourists who are watching the lizards eat the goat?

3. Explain why you would or would not venture to Komodo Island to see the lizards.

4. If you could ask Adams one question, what would it be?

Looking Into

1. In one or two paragraphs, write about some place you would like to visit and give your reasons.

2. What are the differences between Adams' encounter and attitudes toward the Komodo dragons and Sheridan's encounter and attitudes toward beavers? Examine the differences in a short paper.

3. Write a short paper in which you speculate on whether or not dragons and other legendary creatures might have had their origins in animals, such as the Komodo dragon, that really exist.

My Empty Lot

Joseph Kastner

Joseph Kastner has been a free-lance writer since 1971. Prior to that, he was a reporter for the *New York World*, a *New Yorker* magazine writer, a staff writer for *Fortune* and *Life*, and a copy editor and consulting editor for *Life*.

Kastner was born in Brooklyn in 1907 and received his Ph. D. from City College (now the City University of New York) in 1930. His writings include *A Species of Eternity* (1977), for which he received a National Book Award nomination in history; *Evergreens* (with James Crockett) (1975); *Hector Berlioz* (1976), a book about the nineteenth-century French composer; *A World of Watchers* (1986); *The Bird Illustrated, 1550–1900* (1988); and *John James Audubon* (1992), a young adult book. He has been a contributor to many magazines, including *Smithsonian* and *Horticulture*.

Looking Ahead

One needn't travel to remote areas of the world or even to a rural area to observe nature. Joseph Kastner, who calls himself an urban explorer, examines a vacant lot in lower Manhattan and finds it full of fascinating artifacts as well as an astonishing variety of plant life. What would you say are at least two qualifications for being an urban explorer?

1   This past spring, while walking along Houston Street in lower Manhattan, I passed a wooden fence too high and tight to see over or squeeze through. Nosy, as all urban explorers should be, I turned the corner and, stepping through a break in the fence, entered an empty lot not much different from any other in New York, except that it seemed particularly littered with the city's leftovers. In the middle of it I stumbled upon a bright yellow flower called coltsfoot.

2   Coltsfoot is usually seen in early spring along rural roads and damp woodland edges. There, it pokes up among last year's brown leaves, fresh patches of onion grass and the first budding violets. Here, though, it had

pushed between shards of soda bottles, pieces of moldy cardboard, rotting plasterboard and a used hypodermic needle. Nearby, a pair of mourning doves were foraging among old potato chip bags, and a starling sat on a leafless ailanthus branch, whistling. Spring was stirring this untidy patch of urban wasteland and so, kicking aside the rubbish, I began my brief and star-crossed[1] study of the natural history of an empty lot.

3   In a few weeks the lot would resemble a field of wildflowers. But on this gray April morning I found only a few hints of that future—a dandelion in bud, an ox-eye daisy plant and the dried seedpods of last year's evening primroses. Cataloging what I could identify, I listed: aster, clover, daisy, goldenrod, locust, mugwort, mullein, sorrel. But the lot was so rich in rubbish, which seemed more natural to it than flora, that I started making a field guide to urban litter: apple juice cans, asphalt slabs, baby carriage, bar stool, bedroom slippers, bicycle wheel, blinds, bottles, a brassiere, bulbs. . . . I seemed to be stuck in the B's so I skipped through cardboard and deep freezer to radiator, an old Singer sewing machine with "Model A97900029" on its base in elegant gold and black lettering and finally to vacuum cleaner and window glass.

4   A man wandered through, poking the debris with a stick.

5   Find anything? I asked.

6   Nothing good, he answered.

7   It seemed odd that in all this wealth of castoffs there was nothing worth picking up. Later, a street-smart friend said I had been naïve: the scavenger was probably looking for some dregs in a bottle left by the two young winos living in a plywood shack up against the fence, or for a few grains of crack in a discarded plastic envelope.

8 The lot is at the northwest corner of Houston and Elizabeth Streets, in a neighborhood where several historic sections of the city meet: the old Jewish East Side, Little Italy, Chinatown, SoHo. The Bowery lies a block to the east, Broadway four blocks to the west. It is an area dense with low houses, apartment buildings, small businesses and truck traffic.

9   The lot, which occupies a quarter of the block, is bounded on the west by old tenements renovated into modern apartments and on the north by the Holy Name Center. The terrain, at least when I first visited, was flat, except for a large hole at the southeast corner where a Texaco gas station once stood and which now was filled with large metal junk and slabs of

---

1   **star-crossed**: not favored by the stars, from the early belief that the stars influence people's destinies.

broken concrete; and four mounds of gravel and clay, which created a miniature hill-and-dale effect in the northeast corner. The fence had been broken in a couple of places, providing access for dumpers, homeless people, night-working prostitutes who aren't afraid of rats, and students of urban natural history.

10   The site is a prime example of what might be called a mature empty lot. As I learned later, the last buildings there—a convent of the Order of St. John the Baptist, a Catholic school and a church—had been torn down in 1988. Normally a piece of land in this crowded part of the city would not stay empty so long. But the recession and (neighbors say) seepage from the gas station hindered development, and so the lot has remained vacant.

11   Ecologically an empty lot is known as a disturbed area, meaning a place that has been, literally or figuratively, dumped on. Land-filled swamps and railroad rights of way are common examples of disturbed areas, as are, in a wilder context, the remains of burnt forests. Plants that grow in disturbed areas are called "ruderal," after the Latin "rudera," referring to ruins, rubbish or broken stone. Having their own Latin category somehow confers a certain dignity on the lot's plants. In view of how hard they work to grow there, they deserve it.

12   Ecologists calculate environmental stress in terms of what they call abiotic factors—temperature, soil quality, amount of light and moisture. The abiotic factors of the empty lot on Houston Street are pretty much negative. Except for one small area, it is an arid place, as most urban lots are. The typical lot is composed primarily of rubble—broken stone, concrete, bricks from the buildings that once stood there—and thus tends to be porous. Rain runs straight down into old cellars, leaving little available moisture for plants. There is, at least initially, almost no decaying plant material to give the soil substance. Earthworms, which feed on decayed plant material and aerate the soil, stay away from empty lots.

13   Whatever life does spring up faces a battery of urban challenges. Wind funneling between buildings dries leaves and dehydrates plants. Exhaust from automobiles clogs the minute leaf openings through which plants breathe, and toxic chemicals fall from the city's air. People walking through the lot compact the soil, keeping out air and killing bacteria necessary for plant growth. Nearby buildings often block direct sunlight, and temperatures are exaggerated by the heat that the buildings and the pavement absorb and reflect. A botanical team from Cornell University that studied a stretch of streets near Central Park one August recorded the temperature on the roofs of parked cars at 127 degrees, some 38 degrees above temperatures in the park.

[14] And yet, when I returned to the lot in early May, the desolate dumping ground had turned, implausibly, into a meadow. I was accompanied by Stuart Lowrie, a botanist and urban ecologist at Eugene Lang College of the New School for Social Research in New York, and deputy director of Operation Greenthumb, a city agency that, among other things, helps turn vacant city land into community vegetable and flower gardens.

[15] As he stepped over the broken fence, Lowrie noted a dead vine. "Hops," he said. Then he glanced at branches coming into leaf ("ailanthus, of course, and a paulownia and cottonwood"), and knelt down to examine several saplings ("Japanese pagoda tree, black cherry, mulberry"), tested a prickly branch with his thumb ("honey locust, and that one over there must be black locust, and that one crab apple") and uncovered several seedlings ("American elm, quaking aspen, plane, Norway maple, silver maple, mulberry, honeysuckle, multiflora rose, and at the bottom of that mound, willow"). That made 19 different trees, shrubs and vines, an astonishing arboretum for so barren a place.

[16] The plant count was even more surprising: alfalfa, annual wormwood, annual bluegrass, aster, bindweed, boneset, burdock, Canada thistle, chicory, coltsfoot, common plantain, curly dock, daisy fleabane, dandelion, deadly nightshade, English plantain, evening primrose, false buckwheat, field garlic, goldenrod, lady's thumb, lamb's quarters, mugwort, mullein, orchard grass, ox-eye daisy, pepper grass, phragmites, pigweed, potentilla, Queen Anne's lace, red clover, smartweed (two kinds), shepherd's purse, sorrel, speedwell, strawberry, Veronica peregrina (which Lowrie had never seen before), white clover and wild lettuce. That came to 41 different plants, plus the 19 trees, shrubs and vines, for a total of 60 plants on a disturbed area in existence for only five years.

[17] The forces of nature must work fast in any lot. Here, the plants were helped by a fair amount of sunlight, by some gravelly soil dumped on it and by the compost created over the five years by decaying paper, cardboard and garbage. The plants themselves were tough and opportunistic, testament to what will grow wild in the city when given half or even a hundredth of a chance. Perhaps the lot should be viewed as a metaphor for the city in general—a tough place where opportunists survive by working fast and bending the odds to their advantage. But the lot is not a metaphor. It's a lot and if there is any philosophizing lying around in its litter, it concerns nature's constant confrontation with the city. Falcons nest on skyscraper ledges and prey on street pigeons. Owls hunt rats in abandoned landfills. Seeds fall into subway gratings and sprout into underground trees. In this lot, nature—an obsessive housekeeper—had moved in to build a meadow from man's mess.

18   And nature was proceeding in a very classy manner. The lot was no mere weed patch, a bunch of plants settling for any home that would take them. The plants are residents of country fields and medieval tapestries, of still lifes and pastoral sonnets.[2] They had a long local lineage. Many were native to Houston Street, flourishing there in 1626 when the Dutch bought their bargain $24 island.[3] To the tidy Dutch farmers, the asters, goldenrods, evening primroses and daisy fleabanes were weedy nuisances, but the land itself was verdant and well watered. A stream evidently ran north from what is now Rivington Street and, as it came to Houston Street, turned east and emptied into a large marsh. The lot may have been part of the extensive holdings of Peter Stuyvesant, the cranky governor of New Amsterdam who, after surrendering the colony to the British in 1664, spent his last days on the island.

19   By the mid-19th century, Houston Street had settled into a pattern of small, mostly brick houses on 20-foot-wide lots, each with a backyard containing small outbuildings and a privy. Tenements[4] sprang up later and for years a large coal yard conducted business across from the present lot. Nearby Broadway became very fashionable, with town houses selling for an unheard-of $30,000. Elizabeth Street, huddled between Broadway's grand hotels and shops and the Bowery's bawdy music halls, became a backwater, as it remains today—modestly gentrified,[5] a desirable but not fancy place to live.

20   After the Civil War "the block probably looked pretty much as it does now," remarked Marta Gutman, architect and urban historian, walking along Elizabeth Street one morning in mid-May. "The buildings across from the lot are old tenements dating back 130 years or so. The buildings on Bleecker Street at the head of Elizabeth date from the same period—three stories, with dormer windows on the top floor and shops on the bottom. Standard working- or middle-class homes. But earlier there must have been some money on the block. That wooden doorway," she said, pointing at 310 Elizabeth, "is hand-carved and very elegant; the brickwork looks expensive. The tall building on the corner was put up 100 years ago for business and light manufacturing." It is an apartment house now and the only business on the block is Parisi's Bakery.

---

2   **still lifes and pastoral sonnets**: A still life is a painting of inanimate objects such as flowers in a vase; a pastoral sonnet is a poem extolling the rural life.

3   **bargain $24 island**: a reference to the purchase of Manhattan Island from the Man-a-hat-a Indians in 1626 by Peter Minuit, supposedly for trinkets worth $24.

4   **tenements**: apartment houses; the term often refers to buildings that are run-down.

5   **gentrified**: renewed or upgraded by or for middle- and upper middle-class residents.

[21]   Like the people who came to fill the houses, many of the plants that fill the empty lot were immigrants—grown from seeds stowed away in bags of grain and vegetables, crates and bales and trunks. "Aliens," botanists call them, although it is hard today to think of such familiar plants as dandelion, daisy, chicory and Queen Anne's lace as foreigners. Several dominant plants of the empty lot—plantain, ailanthus, mugwort—are aliens.

[22]   Plantain arrived with the first wave of European settlers; the Indians named it White Man's Footsteps because wherever the settlers went, a plantain sprang up. It may have been the original ruderal plant: its seeds, thousands of years old, have been found at the sites of ancient Middle Eastern settlements where early agriculturists, scratching the earth for their crops, created the first man-made disturbed areas. Plantain is a Uriah Heep[6] kind of plant—plain and humble. Its tough leaves seem impervious to trampling, its flower is easily overlooked, and it survives on whatever nourishment an infertile soil provides.

[23]   Much more aggressive are two other aliens, the ailanthus tree—17 of which I found on the lot—and mugwort. Horticulturally speaking, the ailanthus has seen better days. Brought to the United States from China in the early 19th century, it was chosen as a specimen tree by Frederick Olmsted[7] when he was planting Central Park. It has since escaped respectability to become the quintessential city tree. Weedy-looking, with punky wood[8], it is scorned for its virtues: it grows easily and anywhere, its seeds sprouting in any available spot—a crack in the pavement, crumbling mortar in old brick walls. Investing heavily in basics, the ailanthus pushes its large, spongy roots down to any morsel of soil or any damp spot, settling in before permitting itself the luxury of a trunk.

[24]   The mugwort, cousin to the American wormwood, grows in tight bunches, elbowing out other plants. It is as unappealing as its name—awkwardly tall, with coarse, slightly aromatic leaves and undistinguished greenish flowers. Botanists classify it as a "pioneer" plant because it settles in waste areas early, opening the soil with its long roots, enriching it with its decaying stems and leaves, and giving latecomers a chance to take root. In an empty lot, however, being a pioneer plant is an empty distinction, since a lot rarely stays empty long enough for slow and patient buildup.

---

6   **Uriah Heep**: character in Charles Dickens's *David Copperfield*, who, although professing to be humble, is really malicious.

7   **Frederick Olmsted** (1822–1903): American landscape architect.

8   **punky wood**: decayed wood that is dry and crumbly.

25 Sidney Horenstein grumped when I asked him in late May to come down and look over the empty lot. "No such thing as an *empty* lot," he exclaimed. Horenstein works at the American Museum of Natural History, where he lectures on the urban environment and creates exhibits of it.

26   Horenstein rummaged the lot, with a particular eye toward his interest, geology. He found less evidence of earthly cataclysm than of man's disruptions. Picking through the brick and cement, he arranged odds and ends of stone on the ground. "Black limestone probably comes from upstate New York," he began. "These pebbles and sandstone come from New Jersey. This is diabase, what the Palisades[9] is made of; once it was molten rock. The green slate was the steps of an old apartment house, and the black slate was a rooftop." Underlying all of this, he explained, is Manhattan's durable bedrock, mica schist.

27   He looked up to survey the topography. "Those mounds of debris are little reservoirs, about 10 percent air. When it rains, the water collects in the air spaces and seeps down (instead of running right through) and is stored at the bottom." Growing at the top were patches of parched mugwort and plantain. Around the bottom grew phragmites, a tall plumed marsh reed, and a willow that favors moist places. There was another reason to grow there, it seemed. Msgr. John Ahern, who administers the Holy Name Center next door, recalled that from time to time a nearby fire hydrant would leak water into the lot, serving as a spring until a crew came to fix it.

28   Horenstein took out a soil-testing kit, mixed some gravelly dirt with a chemical in a large glass vial, stopped it with his thumb, shook it and waited. The sludge soon turned purple. Matching the color to his chart, Horenstein said: "Pretty alkaline." He repeated the ritual a few yards away, near a patch of white clover. Even deeper purple. "Very, very alkaline. Probably a big piece of decayed cement buried here."

29   Alkalinity is another characteristic of empty lots. Typical soil in the northeastern United States is acidic, while further west in Ohio and Kentucky, the abundance of natural limestone makes soil more alkaline. Discarded cement, so common to vacant lots, is of course full of lime. The flora[10] varies accordingly. Plants like laurel or heather, which thrive in acidic soils, could not grow here. Clover, alfalfa and locust, all alkaline

---

9   **Palisades:** fifteen-mile-long line of cliffs on the west bank of the Hudson River.
10 **flora:** plant life; Flora was the Roman goddess of flowers. Animal life is referred to as fauna.

lovers, do very well. As it turns out, alkalinity is generally a boon to the lot's plants, since it slows their absorption of toxic lead from the soil.

30   Horenstein was impressed by the lot's variety and lushness. "Empty?" he said, beaming, and I felt a surge of pride in the lot.

31   "My lot," I would call it when describing it to friends. I walked blocks out of the way to admire its progress, and was pleased in mid-June to discover a wild pea winding into a cottonwood and a jimson weed at the fence line. I stood next to a paulownia tree that, when I first encountered it, was barely chin-high, but which now was a foot taller than I. The ailanthus trees, thick with foliage, offered a shady respite from the heat. I kept studying the rubbish to see what new treasures would turn up. (Most interesting was a thick college thesis on Camus,[11] entitled "The Rebel: An Evaluation of Existentialist Courage." I tried to read it but the moldy pages stuck together, and besides, it was too pungent to hold within reading distance.) Whenever I approached the break in the fence, I would grumble at the shiftless dumpers who had dropped everything on the sidewalk outside the entrance instead of taking a few considerate steps and dropping it inside, out of sight. Now that the plants had grown enough to hide the rubbish, I had developed a wary way of walking around the lot, pausing at each step before bringing my foot down, as a horse might when confronted with uncertain terrain.

32   From the far side of Houston Street I could see where some of the trees in the lot had come from. Plane trees, Norway maple and a cherry tree lined the median strip, and in a small space right next door grew a large crab apple. Farther down Elizabeth Street stood a row of Japanese pagoda trees.

33   But most of what grew in the lot had traveled longer distances, borne as seeds by wind and passing birds. The phragmites likely blew across the Hudson River from the New Jersey swamps. Never mind the almost incalculable odds against a seed falling on a spot of soil in the paved city. A single plant produces thousands of seeds every year—for just such exigencies, it seems, as an empty lot.

34   The trees, now grown well above the fence line, gave the lot the aspect of a leafy woodland; the cottonwood near the back was at least 35 feet tall. Earlier this year the city discussed a proposal to spend millions of dollars to plant trees to cool the streets in summer and help cleanse the

---

11   **Camus**: Albert (1913–1960), French philosopher and writer. Existentialism is a philosophic movement.

air, at the cost of at least $200 a tree. A quick tally showed that some $6,000 worth of trees grew on the lot, cooling and cleaning the local air free of charge. I felt even prouder of my lot.

35 So I was deflated when Steven E. Clemants, whom I had asked in June to rate the lot on a scale of 1 to 10, gave it only a 6. Clemants, a taxonomist[12] at the Brooklyn Botanic Garden, is fast becoming a connoisseur of empty lots, as a result of a grand study he is conducting of all the uncultivated flora in New York City. He wanted to show me a lot in Brooklyn near the Gowanus Canal. It was impressive—saponaria, an aromatic wild carrot, a Deptford-pink, bladder campion, brome grass, a woodbine, a patch of moss on a barren stretch of solid concrete. I gave his lot a grudging 8, noting that it was much larger than mine on Houston Street and had been empty for two or three times as long.

36 Clemants views all New York as one disconnected empty lot, encountering flora in any piece of vacant land—railroad rights of way, city landfills, the shores of dirty streams, overgrown backyards. As we walked along the street toward the Botanic Garden he noted carpet weed and pepper grass growing in a little plot around a street tree, and shepherd's purse and spotted spurge in a pavement crack. The sidewalk crack, he said, is among the harshest environments in the city. Its abiotic factors are worse even than those of an empty lot—temperatures are consistently higher, soil is harder to come by, moisture evaporates faster and, of course, people are always stepping on it.

37 Meanwhile, some white butterflies had been flitting around the lot, so I asked Nick Wagerik to come over and check them out. One of the city's most highly regarded amateur lepidopterists, Wagerik works nights as an usher at the Metropolitan Opera so he can spend his days studying butterflies and dragonflies. The white butterflies, he said, are cabbage whites, attracted by the various mustard plants growing there. "They'll lay their eggs on a shepherd's purse or pepper grass. When they hatch, the larvae will feed on the leaves. But the adult butterflies feed on the nectar of the flowers." Different plants would bring other butterflies to the lot—monarchs drawn to milkweed, painted ladies seeking thistles.

38 A honeybee hovered at the clover. A larger bee droned idly by. "Carpenter bee," Wagerik said. "Maybe it's nesting in one of those old fence posts and eating it away." He picked up a brown beetle. "Wharf beetle.

---

12 **taxonomist**: person expert in taxonomy, the branch of science dealing with identification and classification of plants and animals.

Eats dock pilings. Very destructive." Lifting a piece of cardboard, he disturbed a sow bug. He placed it in a glass vial, studied it with his magnifying glass and rhapsodized over the ugly creature: "So precise, look at its legs and joints, how finely manufactured it is."

[39]   Naturalists subdivide habitats into niches—spots where particular plants and animals thrive. Niches can be quite small, and include depressions, tree trunks and the small areas around rocks. Wagerik explores niches unique to empty lots. Here, under an old plant, he uncovered a colony of ants, many of them winged females, ready to fly off and found new colonies; a brown spider had spun a web on a nearby mugwort to catch them. Under some old rags were centipedes, while an old wine carton sheltered some millipedes. A slug oozed around a plastic Clorox container.

[40]   Further exploration revealed a minor drama. On a cottonwood branch, clusters of tiny aphids busily sucked sap and deposited the sticky nectar on their backs. Ants shuttled back and forth along the stem, milking the aphids for the nectar and carrying it back to their nest. Other ants stood by, guarding their aphid herd from a predatory ladybug on a nearby pokeweed. It was a standoff: the aphids fed, the ants kept guard, the ladybug waited—until, at last dissuaded, it flew off.

[41]   Except for the mice and rats, which live in a labyrinth of nests and passageways underneath the rubble, and the bats that flit around the street lamps on summer nights, the lot harbored no indigenous animal life. The resident birds—sparrows, starlings, finches and mourning doves—nested on nearby windowsills, ledges and roofs. In early May I had spotted a yellow rumped warbler in the flowering crab apple next door; Houston Street serves as a flyway for birds migrating to Long Island or New England. On other occasions, a song sparrow, a robin and a mockingbird were heard singing somewhere in the vicinity. Over the years, Monsignor Ahern has heard blue jays squawking at each other in the lot.

[42]   Woodpeckers and cardinals also had been spotted just a block away. Walking down Houston Street to investigate, I entered a whole new world of empty lots: the Liz Christy Bowery-Houston garden created from an eyesore of old cars and ancient garbage by the late Liz Christy, a local artist who rallied a group of residents to clean it up. She then went on to found the Green Guerillas, devoted to redeeming empty lots all around the city.

[43]   This empty lot had been put to spectacular use; it was decked out with poppies and larkspur and bleeding hearts, shaded by flowering pear and cherry trees. In small, weed-free plots, several dozen members of the Green Guerillas grew raspberries, pole beans and herbs. There was a beehive that yielded about 100 pounds of honey a year.

⁴⁴   Amid this elegance I saw no trace of the garden's empty-lot ancestry, nor did I find any in a plainer community garden a few blocks east on Avenue B. A large and lively urban farm, set up under the auspices of Operation Greenthumb, it was very much of the city. Children from the public school across the street visited it as a nature classroom, learning not to pick the marigolds or step on the carrots. In early evening gardeners who have only just shed their office clothes emerged to weed their plots and prune the grapevines.

⁴⁵   The past was much more apparent in community gardens in the Bronx, manifest in worn rubber tires, chipped bathtubs, old bricks, ragged carpets, discarded lumber. But here, the tires had been turned into neat planters and the tubs into pools. Old lumber provided the foundation for raised garden beds and bricks and carpets pave the walkways. The gardens are possessively tended by Bronx Green-Up, a project of the New York Botanical Garden, but a kind of ethnic anarchy nevertheless prevails: delphinium and hybrid lilies grow alongside collards and calabaza pumpkins, dogs lie in the paths and chickens cluck in wire-fronted crates. The police had stopped by to point out that it was illegal to keep poultry in the city, and so the chickens would have to go. Sure, said the director: just as soon as the crack dealers on the corner go, so will the chickens. The chickens remain.

⁴⁶   The tour of community gardens inflated my pride even more. In its stubborn way, with no one to coddle it, my lot on Houston Street had transformed itself into a garden—all on its own. Then, abruptly, I was reminded of what always happened to hubris and the ancient Greeks.¹³

⁴⁷   Stopping by one day in late June, I found the lot in a state of unnatural neatness. Whole sections had been cleared and a cleanup crew was stuffing rubbish into tall paper bags. Vesta Howard, in charge of the operation, explained. Neighbors, it seemed, had complained that rats had been venturing boldly into the streets in the evenings, scaring everyone except the cats that guard Parisi's Bakery. The Board of Health moved in. "And such a pretty place it's become," Howard said admiringly as he walked among the clover and wild peas. After he finished the cleanup, Howard said, a bulldozer would come in and scrape the whole place.

⁴⁸   Suddenly the lot was not a dump but an endangered species. I climbed one of the mounds and, from the six-foot peak, surveyed my sturdy little

---

13 **hubris and the ancient Greeks**: in ancient Greek thought, great pride or overconfidence that often results in a hero's downfall; arrogance.

ecosystem. White cabbage butterflies floated over the blue chickory, the yellow sweet clover, the pink wild pea. The locust trees dappled the mugwort with shadows; the leaves on the top branches of the tall cottonwood fluttered in a breeze drifting over from the Bowery. In its own scruffy way, I decided, the empty lot was as much a feat of nature as a flowered New England roadside or any shaded prairie grove.

[49]   When I next visited the lot, in early July, the only things still standing were some stumps along the north wall. "A neighbor wanted us to leave some trees," the bulldozer operator said. "But we couldn't." The lot was completely scraped—flat, sterile, bare even of rubbish. I found hard consolation in remembering that it is the fate of empty lots to lead brief desperate lives.

[50] I should not have given up so soon.

[51]   The first rubbish over the new chain-link fence that now surrounds the lot appeared a few days later: a Sprite bottle and a nail-studded 2-by-4. Then came some used paint rollers, Moroccan sandals, old bricks, a miraculously intact pane of window glass, a painting of a lobster and a stuffed animal that looked like a bee. Meanwhile, up against the north wall, the stumps that had been spared in the cleanup were sprouting into locust trees, and ailanthus saplings all over the lot had grown a foot high. Jimson weeds were thick with purple flowers, a bindweed crawled across the rubble, some thin blades of phragmites had sprouted in a wet spot and a bunch of Chinese takeout containers had settled on a patch of mugwort. When I last looked, in early autumn, the place was beginning to look like its old self again—plants growing, rubbish piling up, everything going along as it inevitably does in an empty lot.

Looking Back

1. Most people think of vacant city lots as eyesores, possibly unhealthful, and probably magnets for criminal activity. How does Kastner view them?

2. The author writes that the lot on Houston Street contained plants that are "residents of country fields and medieval tapestries, of still lifes and pastoral sonnets." What does he mean?

3. Kastner invited a botanist and urban ecologist, an architect and urban historian, a lecturer on urban environment whose interest is geology, a taxonomist, and an amateur lepidopterist to visit his vacant lot. How does each person prove Sidney Horenstein's statement that there is "no such thing as an *empty* lot"?

Looking Into

1. Urban dwellers who favor parks and trees over concrete and buildings often face stiff opposition. What would you say to convince people that parks and trees are invaluable? Present your views in a persuasive letter that could be sent to a newspaper.

2. With a small group, write a summary of this article for someone who has not read it. Limit your summary to one paragraph.

3. Imagine a vacant city lot that you would like to improve. What things would you like to have in the lot? Write a brief description of your ideal city lot.

from A Country Year

SUE HUBBELL

Sue Hubbell was a bookstore manager and a librarian for twelve years before she became a commercial beekeeper in southwestern Missouri in 1973. She was born in Kalamazoo, Michigan, in 1935 and attended Swarthmore and the University of Michigan before receiving her B.A. degree from the University of Southern California in 1956 and her M.S. degree from Drexel Institute in 1963.

Reviewers had high praise for *A Country Year: Living the Questions* (1986), a collection of essays that was her first published book. Ivan Doig, writing in the *Washington Post Book World*, said that she "watches language as sagaciously as she eyes nature."

Since her second marriage, she divides her time between the Ozarks and Washington, D.C. Her other books include *A Book of Bees* (1988), *On This Hilltop* (1991), and *Broadsides from the Other Orders; A Book of Bugs* (1993), which examines the habits and lifestyles of mites, tree frogs, and other insects that most people encounter but know little about.

Looking Ahead

In this excerpt from *A Country Year*, she writes of cutting firewood for her only source of heat in the winter, her black woodstove, and the work involved in keeping bees and harvesting the honey. She also shows that she is a faithful journal writer.

1   *A*nyone who has kept bees is a pushover for a swarm[1] of them. We always drop whatever we are doing and go off to pick one up when asked to do so. It doesn't make sense, because from a standpoint of serious beekeeping and honey production a swarm isn't much good. Swarms are

---

1   **swarm:** a large number of honeybees leaving a hive with a queen bee to start a new colony.

headed up by old queens with not much vitality or egg-laying potential left, and so a beekeeper should replace her with a new queen from a queen breeder. He will probably have to feed and coddle the swarm through its first year; it will seldom produce any extra honey the first season. And yet we always hive them.

2   There is something really odd about swarms, and I notice that bee-keepers don't talk about it much, probably because it is the sort of thing we don't feel comfortable about trying to put into words, something the other side of rationality.

3   The second year I kept bees, I picked up my first swarm. I was in the middle of the spring beework, putting in ten to twelve hours a day, and very attuned to what the bees were doing out there in their hives. That day had begun with a heavy rainstorm, and so rather than working out in the beeyards, I was in the honey house making new equipment. By afternoon the rain had stopped, but the air was warm and heavy, charged and expectant. I began to feel odd, tense and anticipatory, and when the back of my neck began to prickle I decided to take a walk out to the new hives I had started. Near them, hanging pendulously from the branch of an apple tree, was a swarm of bees. Individual bees were still flying in from all directions, adding their numbers to those clinging around their queen.

4   In the springtime some colonies of bees, for reasons not well understood, obey an impulse to split in two and thus multiply by swarming. The worker bees thoughtfully raise a new queen bee for the parent colony, and then a portion of the bees gather with the old queen, gorge themselves with honey and fly out of the hive, never to return, leaving all memory of their old home behind. They cluster somewhere temporarily, such as on the branch of my apple tree. If a beekeeper doesn't hive them, scout bees fly from the cluster and investigate nearby holes and spaces, and report back to the cluster on the suitability of new quarters.

5   We know about two forms of honeybee communication. One is chemical: information about food sources and the wellbeing of the queen and colony is exchanged as bees continually feed one another with droplets of nectar which they have begun to process and chemically tag. The other form of communication is tactile: bees tell other bees about good things such as food or the location of a new home by patterned motions. These elaborate movements, which amount to a highly stylized map of landmarks, direction and the sun's position, are called the bee dance.

6   Different scout bees may find different locations for the swarm and return to dance about their finds. Eventually, sometimes after several days, an agreement is reached, rather like the arrival of the Sense of the

Meeting among Quakers,[2] and all the bees in the cluster fly off to their new home.

[7] I watched the bees on my apple tree for a while with delight and pleasure, and then returned to the barn to gather up enough equipment to hive them. As I did so, I glanced up at the sky. It was still dark from the receding thunderstorm, but a perfect and dazzling rainbow arched shimmering against the deep blue sky, its curve making a stunning and pleasing contrast with the sharp inverted V of the barn roof. I returned to the apple tree and shook the bees into the new beehive, noticing that I was singing snatches of one of Handel's coronation anthems.[3] It seemed as appropriate music to hive a swarm by as any I knew.

[8] Since then, I have learned to pay attention in the springtime when the air feels electric and full of excitement. It was just so one day last week. I had been working quietly along the row of twelve hives in an outyard when the hair on the back of my neck began to stand on end. I looked up to see the air thick with bees flying in toward me from the north. The swarm was not from any of my hives, but for some reason bees often cluster near existing hives while they scout a new location. I closed up the hive I was working on and stood back to watch. I was near a slender post oak sapling, and the bees began to light on one of its lower limbs right next to my elbow. They came flying in, swirling as they descended, spiraling around me and the post oak until I was enveloped by the swarm, the air moving gently from the beat of their wings. I am not sure how long I stood there. I lost all sense of time and felt only elation, a kind of human emotional counterpart of the springlike, optimistic, burgeoning state that the bees were in. I stood quietly; I was nothing more to the bees than an object to be encircled on their way to the spot where they had decided, in a way I could not know, to cluster. In another sense I was not remote from them at all, but was receiving all sorts of meaningful messages in the strongest way imaginable outside of human mental process and language. My skin was tingling as the bees brushed past and I felt almost a part of the swarm.

[9] Eventually the bees settled down in the cluster. Regaining a more suitable sense of my human condition and responsibilities, I went over to my pickup and got the empty hive that I always carry with me during swarm-

---

2 **Sense of the Meeting among Quakers**: A Quaker or Friend is a member of a Christian group called the Religious Society of Friends. The "sense of the meeting" emerges from the group's deliberations about some matter of concern to all.

3 **Handel's coronation anthems**: George Frederick Handel (1685–1759) was an English composer born in Germany. He composed operas, oratorios, and much other music.

ing season. I propped it up so that its entrance was just under the swarm. A frame of comb[4] from another hive was inside and the bees in the cluster could smell it, so they began to walk up into the entrance. I watched, looking for the queen, for without her the swarm would die. It took perhaps twenty minutes for all of them to file in, and the queen, a long, elegant bee, was one of the last to enter.

10   I screened up the entrance and put the hive in the back of the pickup. After I was finished with my work with the other hives in the beeyard, I drove back home with my new swarm.

11   I should have ordered a new queen bee, killed the old one and replaced her, but in doing that I would have destroyed the identity of the swarm. Every colony of bees takes its essence, character and personality from the queen who is mother to all its members. As a commercial beekeeper, it was certainly my business to kill the old queen and replace her with a vigorous new one so that the colony would become a good honey producer.

12   But I did not.

* * *

13 This week I have started cutting my firewood. It should be cut months ahead of time to let it dry and cure, so that it will burn hot in the winter. It is June now, and almost too late to be cutting firewood, but during the spring I was working with the bees from sunup until sundown and didn't have time. By midday it is stifling back in the woods, so I go out at sunrise and cut wood for a few hours, load it into the pickup and bring it back to stack below the barn.

14   I like being out there early. The spiders have spun webs to catch night-flying insects, and as the rising sun slants through the trees, the dewdrops that line the webs are turned into exquisite, delicate jewels. The woodlot smells of shade, leaf mold and damp soil. Wild turkey have left fresh bare spots where they scratched away the leaves looking for beetles and grubs. My dogs like being there too, and today snuffled excitedly in a hollow at the base of a tree. The beagle shrieked into it, his baying muffled. The squirrel who may have denned in the tree last night temporarily escaped their notice and sat on a low limb eying the two dogs suspiciously, tail twitching. A sunbeam lit up a tall thistle topped with a luxuriant purple blossom

---

4   **comb**: rows of hexagonal wax cells made by bees in their hive to store honey and their eggs.

from which one butterfly and one honeybee sipped nectar. Red-eyed vireos[5] sang high in the treetops where I could not see them.

15   For me their song ended when I started the chain saw. It makes a terrible racket, but I am fond of it. It is one of the first tools I learned to master on my own, and it is also important to me. My woodstove, a simple black cast-iron-and-sheet-metal affair, is the only source of heat for my cabin in the winter, and if I do not have firewood to burn in it, the dogs, cat, the houseplants, the water in my pipes and I will all freeze. It is wonderfully simple and direct: cut wood or die.

16   When Paul[6] was here he cut the firewood and I, like all Ozark wives, carried the cut wood to the pickup. When he left, he left his chain saw, but it was a heavy, vibrating, ill-tempered thing. I weigh a hundred and five pounds, and although I could lift it, once I had it running it shook my hands so much that it became impossibly dangerous to use. One year I hired a man to cut my wood, but I was not pleased with the job he did, and so the next year, although I could not afford it, I bought the finest, lightest, best-made chain saw money could buy. It is a brand that many woodcutters use, and has an antivibration device built into even its smaller models.

17   The best chain saws are formidable and dangerous tools. My brother nearly cut off his arm with one. A neighbor who earns his living in timber just managed to kill the engine on his when he was cutting overhead and a branch snapped the saw back toward him. The chain did not stop running until it had cut through the beak of his cap. He was very solemn when I told him that I had bought my own chain saw, and he gave me a good piece of advice. "The time to worry about a chain saw," he said, "is when you stop being afraid of it."

18   I am cautious. I spend a lot of time sizing up a tree before I fell it. Once it is down, I clear away the surrounding brush before I start cutting it into lengths. That way I will not trip and lose my balance with the saw running. A dull chain and a poorly running saw are dangerous, so I've learned to keep mine in good shape and sharpen the chain each time I use it.

19   This morning I finished sawing up a tree from the place where I had been cutting for the past week. In the process I lost, in the fallen leaves somewhere, my scrench—part screwdriver, part wrench—that I use to make adjustments on the saw. I shouldn't have been carrying it in my

---

5 **red-eyed vireos**: North American birds about six inches long with olive-green wings and a white stripe over the red eye.
6 **Paul**: the author's former husband.

pocket, but the chain on the saw's bar had been loose; I had tightened it and had not walked back to the pickup to put it away. Scolding myself for being so careless, I began looking for another tree to cut, but stopped to watch a fawn that I had frightened from his night's sleeping place. He was young and his coat was still spotted, but he ran so quickly and silently that the two dogs, still sniffing after the squirrel, never saw him.

20   I like to cut the dead trees from my woodlot, leaving the ones still alive to flourish, and I noticed a big one that had recently died. This one was bigger than I feel comfortable about felling. I've been cutting my own firewood for six years now, but I am still awed by the size and weight of a tree as it crashes to the ground, and I have to nerve myself to cut the really big ones.

21   I wanted this tree to fall on a stretch of open ground that was free of other trees and brush, so I cut a wedge-shaped notch on that side of it. The theory is that the tree, thus weakened, will fall slowly in the direction of the notch when the serious cut, slightly above the notch on the other side, is made. The trouble is that trees, particularly dead ones that may have rot on the inside, do not know the theory and may fall in an unexpected direction. That is the way accidents happen. I was aware of this, and scared, besides, to be cutting down such a big tree; as a result, perhaps I cut too timid a wedge. I started sawing through on the other side, keeping an eye on the tree top to detect the characteristic tremble that signals a fall. I did not have time to jam the plastic wedge in my back pocket into the cut to hold it open because the tree began to fall in my direction, exactly opposite where I had intended. I killed the engine on the saw and jumped out of the way.

22   There was no danger, however. Directly in back of where I had been standing were a number of other trees, which was why I had wanted to have the sawed one fall in the opposite direction; as my big tree started to topple, its upper branches snagged in another one, and it fell no further. I had sawed completely through the tree, but now the butt end had trapped my saw against the stump. I had cut what is descriptively called a "widow maker." If I had been cutting with someone else, we could have used a second saw to cut out mine and perhaps brought down the tree, but this is dangerous and I don't like to do it. I could not even free my saw by taking it apart, for I had lost my scrench, so I drove back to the barn and gathered up the tools I needed; a socket wrench, chains and a portable winch known as a come-along. A come-along is a cheery, sensible tool for a woman. It has a big hook at one end and another hook connected to a steel cable at the other. The cable is wound around a ratchet gear operated by a long handle to give leverage. It divides a heavy job up into small manageable bits that

require no more than female strength, and I have used it many times to pull my pickup free from mud and snow.

23   The day was warming up and I was sweating by the time I got back to the woods, but I was determined to repair the botch I had made of the morning's woodcutting. Using the socket wrench, I removed the bar and chain from the saw's body and set it aside. The weight of the saw gone, I worked free the bar and chain pinched under the butt of the tree. Then I sat down on the ground, drank ice water from my thermos and figured out how I was going to pull down the tree.

24   Looking at the widow maker, I decided that if I could wind one of the chains around the butt of it, and another chain around a nearby standing tree, then connect the two with the come-along, I might be able to winch the tree to the ground. I attached the chains and come-along appropriately and began. Slowly, with each pump of the handle against the ratchet gear, the tree sank to the ground.

25   The sun was high in the sky, the heat oppressive and my shirt and jeans were soaked with sweat, so I decided to leave the job of cutting up the tree until tomorrow. I gathered my tools together, and in the process found the scrench, almost hidden in the leaf mold. Then I threw all the tools into the back of the pickup, and sat on the tailgate to finish off the rest of the ice water and listen to the red-eyed vireo singing.

26   It is satisfying, of course, to build up a supply of winter warmth, free except for the labor. But there is also something heady about becoming a part of the forest process. It sounds straightforward enough to say that when I cut firewood I cull and thin my woods, but that puts me in the business of deciding which trees should be encouraged and which should be taken.

27   I like my great tall black walnut, so I have cut the trees around it to give it the space and light it needs to grow generously. Dogwoods don't care. They frost the woods with white blossoms in the spring, and grow extravagantly in close company. If I clear a patch, within a year or two pine seedlings move in, grow up exuberantly, compete and thin themselves to tolerable spacing. If I don't cut a diseased tree, its neighbors may sicken and die. If I cut away one half of a forked white oak, the remaining trunk will grow straight and sturdy. Sap gone, a standing dead tree like the one I cut today will make good firewood, and so invites cutting. But if I leave it, it will make a home for woodpeckers, and later for flying squirrels and screech owls. Where I leave a brush pile of top branches, rabbits make a home. If I leave a fallen tree, others will benefit: ants, spiders, beetles and wood roaches will use it for shelter and food, and lovely delicate fungi

will grow out of it before it mixes with leaf mold to become a part of a new layer of soil.

[28] One person with a chain saw makes a difference in the woods, and by making a difference becomes part of the woodland cycle, a part of the abstraction that is the forest community.

* * *

[29] I keep twenty hives of bees here in my home beeyard, but most of my hives are scattered in outyards across the Ozarks, where I can find the thickest stands of wild blackberries and other good things for bees. I always have a waiting list of farmers who would like the bees on their land, for the clover in their pastures is more abundant when the bees are there to pollinate it.

[30] One of the farmers, a third-generation Ozarker and a dairyman with a lively interest in bees, came over today for a look at what my neighbors call my honey factory. My honey house contains a shiny array of stainless-steel tanks with clear plastic tubing connecting them, a power uncapper for slicing open honeycomb, an extractor for spinning honey out of the comb, and a lot of machinery and equipment that whirs, thumps, hums and looks very special. The dairyman, shrewd in mountain ways, looked it all over carefully and then observed, "Well . . . ll . . . ll, wouldn't say for sure now, but it looks like a still to me."

[31] There have been droughty years and cold wet ones when flowers refused to bloom and I would have been better off with a still back up here on my mountain top, but the weather this past year was perfect from a bee's standpoint, and this August I ran 33,000 pounds of honey through my factory. This was nearly twice the normal crop, and everything was overloaded, starting with me. Neither I nor my equipment is set up to handle this sort of harvest, even with extra help.

[32] I always need to hire someone, a strong young man who is not afraid of being stung, to help me harvest the honey from the hives.

[33] The honey I take is the surplus that the bees will not need for the winter; they store it above their hives in wooden boxes called supers. To take it from them, I stand behind each hive with a gasoline-powered machine called a beeblower and blow the bees out of the supers with a jet of air. Meanwhile, the strong young man carries the supers, which weigh about sixty pounds each, and stacks them on pallets in the truck. There may be thirty to fifty supers in every outyard, and we have only about half an hour to get them off the hives, stacked and covered before the bees get really cross about what we are doing. The season to take the honey in this part of the country is summer's end, when the temperature is often above

ninety-five degrees. The nature of the work and the temper of the bees require that we wear protective clothing while doing the job: a full set of coveralls, a zippered bee veil and leather gloves. Even a very strong young man works up a considerable sweat wrapped in a bee suit in hot weather hustling sixty-pound supers—being harassed by angry bees at the same time.

[34]   This year my helper has been Ky, my nephew, who wanted to learn something about bees and beekeeping. He is a sweet, gentle, cooperative giant of a young man who, because of a series of physical problems, lacks confidence in his own ability to get on in the world.

[35]   As soon as he arrived, I set about to desensitize him to bee stings. The first day, I put a piece of ice on his arm to numb it; then, holding the bee carefully by her head, I placed her abdomen on the numbed spot and let her sting him there. A bee's stinger is barbed and stays in the flesh, pulling loose from her body as she struggles to free herself. Lacking her stinger, the bee will live only a short time. The bulbous poison sac at the top of the stinger continues to pulsate after the bee has left, its muscles pumping the venom and forcing the barbed stinger deeper into the flesh.

[36]   I wanted Ky to have only a partial dose of venom that first day, so after a minute I scraped the stinger out with my fingernail and watched his reaction closely. A few people—about one percent of the population—are seriously sensitive to bee venom. Each sting they receive can cause a more severe reaction than the one before, reactions ranging from hives, difficulty in breathing and accelerated heartbeat, to choking, anaphylactic shock[7] and death. Ky had been stung a few times in his life and didn't think he was seriously allergic, but I wanted to make sure.

[37]   The spot where the stinger went in grew red and began to swell. This was a normal reaction, and so was the itchiness that Ky felt the next day. That time I let a bee sting him again, repeating the procedure, but leaving the stinger in his arm a full ten minutes, until the venom sac was emptied. Again the spot was red, swollen and itchy, but had disappeared the next day. Thereafter Ky decided that he didn't need the ice cube any more, and began holding the bee himself to administer his own stings. I kept him at one sting a day until he had no redness or swelling from the full sting, and then had him increase to two stings daily. Again the greater amount of venom caused redness and swelling, but soon his body could tolerate them

---

7   **anaphylactic shock**: severe and sometimes fatal reaction to something like bee or wasp venom or penicillin after previous sensitization.

without an allergic reaction. I gradually had him build up to ten full stings a day with no reaction.

38   To encourage Ky, I had told him that what he was doing might help protect him from the arthritis that runs in our family. Beekeepers generally believe that getting stung by bees is a healthy thing, and that bee venom alleviates the symptoms of arthritis. When I first began keeping bees, I supposed this to be just another one of the old wives' tales that make beekeeping such an entertaining occupation, but after my hands were stung the pain in my fingers disappeared and I too became a believer. Ky was polite, amused and skeptical of what I told him, but he welcomed my taking a few companionable stings on my knuckles along with him.

39   In desensitizing Ky to bee venom, I had simply been interested in building up his tolerance to stings so that he could be an effective helper when we took the honey from the hives, for I knew that he would be stung frequently. But I discovered that there had been a secondary effect on Ky that was more important: he was enormously pleased with himself for having passed through what he evidently regarded as a rite of initiation. He was proud and delighted in telling other people about the whole process. He was now one tough guy.

40   I hoped he was prepared well enough for our first day of work. I have had enough strong young men work for me to know what would happen the first day: he would be stung royally.

41   Some beekeepers insist that bees know their keeper—that they won't sting that person, but *will* sting a stranger. This is nonsense, for summertime bees live only six weeks and I often open a particular hive less frequently than that, so I am usually a stranger to my bees; yet I am seldom stung. Others say that bees can sense fear or nervousness. I don't know if this is true or not, but I do know that bees' eyes are constructed in such a way that they can detect discontinuities and movement very well and stationary objects less well. This means that a person near their hives who moves with rapid, jerky motions attracts their attention and will more often be blamed by the bees when their hives are being meddled with than will the person whose motions are calm and easy. It has been my experience that the strong young man I hire for the honey harvest is always stung unmercifully for the first few days while he is new to the process and a bit tense. Then he learns to become easier with the bees and settles down to his job. As he gains confidence and assurance, the bees calm down too, and by the end of the harvest he usually is only stung a few times a day.

42   I knew that Ky very much wanted to do a good job with me that initial day working in the outyards. I had explained the procedures we would

follow in taking the honey from the hives, but of course they were new to him and he was anxious. The bees from the first hive I opened flung themselves on him. Most of the stingers could not penetrate his bee suit, but in the act of stinging a bee leaves a chemical trace that marks the person stung as an enemy, a chemical sign other bees can read easily. This sign was read by the bees in each new hive I opened, and soon Ky's bee suit began to look like a pincushion, bristling with stingers. In addition, the temperature was starting to climb and Ky was sweating. Honey oozing from combs broken between the supers was running down the front of his bee suit when he carried them to the truck. Honey and sweat made the suit cling to him, so that the stingers of angry bees could penetrate the suit and he could feel the prick of each one as it entered his skin. Hundreds of bees were assaulting him and finally drove him out of the beeyard, chasing him several hundred yards before they gave up the attack. There was little I could do to help him but try to complete the job quickly, so I took the supers off the next few hives myself, carried them to the truck and loaded them. Bravely, Ky returned to finish the last few hives. We tied down the load and drove away. His face was red with exertion when he unzipped his bee veil. He didn't have much to say as we drove to the next yard, but sat beside me gulping down ice water from the thermos bottle.

At the second yard the bees didn't bother Ky as we set up the equipment. I hoped that much of the chemical marker the bees had left on him had evaporated, but as soon as I began to open the hives they were after him again. Soon a cloud of angry bees enveloped him, accompanying him to the truck and back. Because of the terrain, the truck had to be parked at an odd angle and Ky had to bend from the hips as he loaded it, stretching the fabric of the bee suit taut across the entire length of his back and rear, allowing the bees to sting through it easily. We couldn't talk over the noise of the beeblower's engine, but I was worried about how he was taking hundreds more stings. I was removing the bees from the supers as quickly as I could, but the yard was a good one and there were a lot of supers there.

In about an hour's time Ky carried and stacked what we later weighed in as a load of 2500 pounds. The temperature must have been nearly a hundred degrees. After he had stacked the last super, I drove the truck away from the hives and we tied down the load. Ky's long hair was plastered to his face and I couldn't see the expression on it, but I knew he had been pushed to his limits and I was concerned about him. He tried to brush some of the stingers out of the seat of his bee suit before he sat down next to me in the truck in an uncommonly gingerly way. Unzipping his bee veil, he tossed it aside, pushed the hair back from his sweaty face, reached for the thermos bottle, gave me a sunny and triumphant grin and said, "If I ever get arthritis of the ass, I'll know all that stuff you've been telling me is a lot of baloney."

Looking Back

1. Why do you think Hubbell decides not to kill the old queen to make the swarm more productive?

2. Hubbell expresses a number of feelings and opinions about cutting trees in her woodlot. Which statements indicate that she is an ecologically responsible person?

3. Hubbell says that there have been "droughty years and cold wet ones when flowers refused to bloom." Why would this have affected honey production?

4. Would you have volunteered for Ky's job? Why or why not?

Looking Into

1. Are you an expert or nearly an expert at something? Write directions in narrative form for how to do something that you do very well. Work with a partner to decide on a topic and then read each other's papers to make sure your directions are clear.

2. When Hubbell was living in the Ozarks year round, she supported herself by processing and selling honey, in effect, living off the land. If you decided to live off the land (or the sea), where would you live, and what would you do? Write a journal entry telling how you would support yourself.

3. Hubbell seems occasionally to feel a real sense of unity or oneness with her bees. Have you ever felt carried outside yourself by a sense of communion with the natural world? Write a paper in which you describe your experience.

The Serpents of Paradise

EDWARD ABBEY

Edward Abbey was born in Home, Pennsylvania, in 1927 and spent much of his life in the West and Southwest. He received B.A. and M.A. degrees from the University of New Mexico and served as a park ranger and fire lookout for the National Park Service from 1956 to 1971. He was in the Army in 1945–1946 and was a Fulbright Fellow in 1951–1952.

His first book was published in 1956, the year he received his M.A. degree. *Desert Solitaire*, from which the essay in this book is taken, was his fourth book and was published in 1968. Edwin Way Teale, writing in the *New York Times Book Review*, described *Desert Solitaire*, a collection of essays, as "a voice crying in the wilderness, *for* the wilderness."

Appalachian Wilderness, with text by Abbey and photos by Eliot Porter, was published in 1970. His many other books include *The Monkey Wrench Gang* (1975), a novel that describes an environmentalist group's plans to blow up a dam in Arizona, *The Brave Cowboy*, which was made into the film *Lonely Are the Brave* in 1962 and starred Kirk Douglas, Walter Matthau, and Gena Rowlands, *Abbey's Road* (1979), *The Fool's Progress* (1988), and *Hayduke Lives!* (1990), a sequel to *The Monkey Wrench Gang*. Abbey died in 1989 and was buried in the desert in Arizona.

Looking Ahead

In an essay in the *New York Times Book Review* in 1989 after Abbey's death, Edward Hoagland wrote that Abbey "came to detest" the term "nature writer, a term used to pigeonhole and marginalize some of the more intriguing American writers alive, who are dealing with matters central to us. . . ." In the essay from *Desert Solitaire* that follows, Abbey writes of some of his desert neighbors. To what is Abbey alluding in the title of this essay?

¹ The April mornings are bright, clear and calm. Not until the afternoon does the wind begin to blow, raising dust and sand in funnelshaped

twisters that spin across the desert briefly, like dancers, and then collapse—whirlwinds from which issue no voice or word except the forlorn moan of the elements under stress. After the reconnoitering dust-devils comes the real, the serious wind, the voice of the desert rising to a demented howl and blotting out sky and sun behind yellow clouds of dust, sand, confusion, embattled birds, last year's scrub-oak leaves, pollen, the husks of locusts, bark of juniper. . . .

2   Time of the red eye, the sore and bloody nostril, the sand-pitted windshield, if one is foolish enough to drive his car into such a storm. Time to sit indoors and continue that letter which is never finished—while the fine dust forms neat little windrows under the edge of the door and on the windowsills. Yet the springtime winds are as much a part of the canyon country as the silence and the glamorous distances; you learn, after a number of years, to love them also.

3   The mornings therefore, as I started to say and meant to say, are all the sweeter in the knowledge of what the afternoon is likely to bring. Before beginning the morning chores I like to sit on the sill of my doorway, bare feet planted on the bare ground and a mug of hot coffee in hand, facing the sunrise. The air is gelid, not far above freezing, but the butane heater inside the trailer keeps my back warm, the rising sun warms the front, and the coffee warms the interior.

4   Perhaps this is the loveliest hour of the day, though it's hard to choose. Much depends on the season. In mid-summer the sweetest hour begins at sundown, after the awful heat of the afternoon. But now, in April, we'll take the opposite, that hour beginning with the sunrise. The birds, returning from wherever they go in winter, seem inclined to agree. The pinyon jays[1] are whirling in garrulous, gregarious flocks from one stunted tree to the next and back again, erratic exuberant games without any apparent practical function. A few big ravens hang around and croak harsh clanking statements of smug satisfaction from the rimrock,[2] lifting their greasy wings now and then to probe for lice. I can hear but seldom see the canyon wrens singing their distinctive song from somewhere up on the cliffs: a flutelike descent—never ascent—of the whole-tone scale.[3] Staking out new nesting claims, I understand. Also invisible but invariably present at some indefinable distance are the mourning doves whose plaintive call suggests

---

1 **pinyon jays**: gray-blue jays of the Southwest.
2 **rimrock**: stratum of rock that forms the vertical face of a plateau.
3 **whole-tone scale**: scale progressing by whole tones such as C, D, E, F#, G#, A#, and C.

irresistibly a kind of seeking-out, the attempt by separated souls to restore a lost communion:

5   *Hello . . .* they seem to cry, *who . . . are . . . you?*

6   And the reply from a different quarter. *Hello . . .* (pause) *where . . . are . . . you?*

7   No doubt this line of analogy must be rejected. It's foolish and unfair to impute to the doves, with serious concerns of their own, an interest in questions more appropriate to their human kin. Yet their song, if not a mating call or a warning, must be what it sounds like, a brooding meditation on space, on solitude. The game.

8   Other birds, silent, which I have not yet learned to identify, are also lurking in the vicinity, watching me. What the ornithologist terms l.g.b.'s—little gray birds—they flit about from point to point on noiseless wings, their origins obscure.

9   As mentioned before,[4] I share the housetrailer with a number of mice. I don't know how many but apparently only a few, perhaps a single family. They don't disturb me and are welcome to my crumbs and leavings. Where they came from, how they got into the trailer, how they survived before my arrival (for the trailer had been locked up for six months), these are puzzling matters I am not prepared to resolve. My only reservation concerning the mice is that they do attract rattlesnakes.

10   I'm sitting on my doorstep early one morning, facing the sun as usual, drinking coffee, when I happen to look down and see almost between my bare feet, only a couple of inches to the rear of my heels, the very thing I had in mind. No mistaking that wedgelike head, that tip of horny segmented tail peeping out of the coils. He's under the doorstep and in the shade where the ground and air remain very cold. In his sluggish condition he's not likely to strike unless I rouse him by some careless move of my own.

11   There's a revolver inside the trailer, a huge British Webley .45, loaded, but it's out of reach. Even if I had it in my hands I'd hesitate to blast a fellow creature at such close range, shooting between my own legs at a living target flat on solid rock thirty inches away. It would be like murder; and where would I set my coffee? My cherrywood walking stick leans against the trailerhouse wall only a few feet away but I'm afraid that in leaning over for it I might stir up the rattler or spill some hot coffee on his scales.

12   Other considerations come to mind. Arches National Monument[5] is meant to be among other things a sanctuary for wildlife—for all forms of

---

4   **As mentioned before**: that is, in a previous essay.
5   **Arches National Monument**: now Arches National Park, it contains large red sandstone arches on over seventy thousand acres in Utah.

wildlife. It is my duty as a park ranger to protect, preserve and defend all living things within the park boundaries, making no exceptions. Even if this were not the case I have personal convictions to uphold. Ideals, you might say. I prefer not to kill animals. I'm a humanist; I'd rather kill a *man* than a snake.

¹³ What to do. I drink some more coffee and study the dormant reptile at my heels. It is not after all the mighty diamondback, *Crotalus atrox*, I'm confronted with but a smaller species known locally as the horny rattler or more precisely as the Faded Midget. An insulting name for a rattlesnake, which may explain the Faded Midget's alleged bad temper. But the name is apt: he is small and dusty-looking, with a little knob above each eye—the horns. His bite though temporarily disabling would not likely kill a full-grown man in normal health. Even so I don't really want him around. Am I to be compelled to put on boots or shoes every time I wish to step outside? The scorpions, tarantulas, centipedes, and black widows are nuisance enough.

¹⁴ I finish my coffee, lean back and swing my feet up and inside the doorway of the trailer. At once there is a buzzing sound from below and the rattler lifts his head from his coils, eyes brightening, and extends his narrow black tongue to test the air.

¹⁵ After thawing out my boots over the gas flame I pull them on and come back to the doorway. My visitor is still waiting beneath the doorstep, basking in the sun, fully alert. The trailerhouse has two doors. I leave by the other and get a long-handled spade out of the bed of the government pickup. With this tool I scoop the snake into the open. He strikes; I can hear the click of the fangs against steel, see the strain of venom. He wants to stand and fight, but I am patient; I insist on herding him well away from the trailer. On guard, head aloft—that evil slit-eyed weaving head shaped like the ace of spades—tail whirring, the rattler slithers sideways, retreating slowly before me until he reaches the shelter of a sandstone slab. He backs under it.

¹⁶ You better stay there, cousin, I warn him; if I catch you around the trailer again I'll chop your head off.

¹⁷ A week later he comes back. If not him, his twin brother. I spot him one morning under the trailer near the kitchen drain, waiting for a mouse. I have to keep my promise.

¹⁸ This won't do. If there are midget rattlers in the area there may be diamondbacks too—five, six or seven feet long, thick as a man's wrist, dangerous. I don't want *them* camping under my home. It looks as though I'll have to trap the mice.

¹⁹ However, before being forced to take that step I am lucky enough to capture a gopher snake. Burning garbage one morning at the park dump,

I see a long slender yellow-brown snake emerge from a mound of old tin cans and plastic picnic plates and take off down the sandy bed of a gulch. There is a burlap sack in the cab of the truck which I carry when plucking Kleenex flowers from the brush and cactus along the road; I grab that and my stick, run after the snake and corner it beneath the exposed roots of a bush. Making sure it's a gopher snake and not something less useful, I open the neck of the sack and with a great deal of coaxing and prodding get the snake into it. The gopher snake, *Drymarchon corais couperi*, or bull snake, has a reputation as the enemy of rattlesnakes, destroying or driving them away whenever encountered.

20   Hoping to domesticate this sleek, handsome and docile reptile, I release him inside the trailerhouse and keep him there for several days. Should I attempt to feed him? I decide against it—let him eat mice. What little water he may need can also be extracted from the flesh of his prey.

21   The gopher snake and I get along nicely. During the day he curls up like a cat in the warm corner behind the heater and at night he goes about his business. The mice, singularly quiet for a change, make themselves scarce. The snake is passive, apparently contented, and makes no resistance when I pick him up with my hands and drape him over an arm or around my neck. When I take him outside into the wind and sunshine his favorite place seems to be inside my shirt, where he wraps himself around my waist and rests on my belt. In this position he sometimes sticks his head out between shirt buttons for a survey of the weather, astonishing and delighting any tourists who may happen to be with me at the time. The scales of a snake are dry and smooth, quite pleasant to the touch. Being a cold-blooded creature, of course, he takes his temperature from that of the immediate environment—in this case my body.

22   We are compatible. From my point of view, friends. After a week of close association I turn him loose on the warm sandstone at my doorstep and leave for patrol of the park. At noon when I return he is gone. I search everywhere beneath, nearby and inside the trailerhouse, but my companion has disappeared. Has he left the area entirely or is he hiding somewhere close by? At any rate I am troubled no more by rattlesnakes under the door.

23   The snake story is not yet ended.

24   In the middle of May, about a month after the gopher snake's disappearance, in the evening of a very hot day, with all the rosy desert cooling like a griddle with the fire turned off, he reappears. This time with a mate.

25   I'm in the stifling heat of the trailer opening a can of beer, barefooted, about to go outside and relax after a hard day watching cloud formations. I happen to glance out the little window near the refrigerator and see two

gopher snakes on my verandah engaged in what seems to be a kind of ritual dance. Like a living caduceus[6] they wind and unwind about each other in undulant, graceful, perpetual motion, moving slowly across a dome of sandstone. Invisible but tangible as music is the passion which joins them—sexual? combative? both? A shameless *voyeur*,[7] I stare at the lovers, and then to get a closer view run outside and around the trailer to the back. There I get down on hands and knees and creep toward the dancing snakes, not wanting to frighten or disturb them. I crawl to within six feet of them and stop, flat on my belly, watching from the snake's-eye level. Obsessed with their ballet, the serpents seem unaware of my presence.

26   The two gopher snakes are nearly identical in length and coloring; I cannot be certain that either is actually my former household pet. I cannot even be sure that they are male and female, though their performance resembles so strongly a *pas de deux*[8] by formal lovers. They intertwine and separate, glide side by side in perfect congruence, turn like mirror images of each other and glide back again, wind and unwind again. This is the basic pattern but there is a variation; at regular intervals the snakes elevate their heads, facing one another, as high as they can go, as if each is trying to outreach or overawe the other. Their heads and bodies rise, higher and higher, than topple together and the rite goes on.

27   I crawl after them, determined to see the whole thing. Suddenly and simultaneously they discover me, prone on my belly a few feet away. The dance stops. After a moment's pause the two snakes come straight toward me, still in flawless unison, straight toward my face, the forked tongues flickering, their intense wild yellow eyes staring directly into my eyes. For an instant I am paralyzed by wonder; then, stung by a fear too ancient and powerful to overcome I scramble back, rising to my knees. The snakes veer and turn and race away from me in parallel motion, their lean elegant bodies making a soft hissing noise as they slide over the sand and stone. I follow them for a short distance, still plagued by curiosity, before remembering my place and the requirements of common courtesy. For godsake let them go in peace, I tell myself. Wish them luck and (if lovers) innumerable offspring, a life of happily ever after. Not for their sake alone but for your own.

---

6   **caduceus:** staff with two snakes twined around it. In mythology, the staff of Mercury; now, often used as a symbol of the medical profession.

7   **voyeur:** person who obtains pleasure by watching the private acts of others without being seen by them.

8   **pas de deux:** French dance in ballet for two persons.

28   In the long hot days and cool evenings to come I will not see the gopher snakes again. Nevertheless I will feel their presence watching over me like totemic[9] deities, keeping the rattlesnakes far back in the brush where I like them best, cropping off the surplus mouse population, maintaining useful connections with the primeval. Sympathy, mutual aid, symbiosis, continuity.

29   How can I descend to such anthropomorphism?[10] Easily—but is it, in this case entirely false? Perhaps not. I am not attributing human motives to my snake and bird acquaintances. I recognize that when and where they serve purposes of mine they do so for beautifully selfish reasons of their own. Which is exactly the way it should be. I suggest, however, that it's a foolish, simple-minded rationalism which denies any form of emotion to all animals but man and his dog. This is no more justified than the Moslems are in denying souls to women. It seems to me possible, even probable, that many of the nonhuman undomesticated animals experience emotions unknown to us. What do the coyotes mean when they yodel at the moon? What are the dolphins trying so patiently to tell us? Precisely what did those two enraptured gopher snakes have in mind when they came gliding toward my eyes over the naked sandstone? If I had been as capable of trust as I am susceptible to fear I might have learned something new or some truth so very old we have all forgotten it.

> They do not sweat and whine about their condition,
> They do not lie awake in the dark and weep for their sins. . . .[11]

30   All men are brothers, we like to say, half-wishing sometimes in secret it were not true. But perhaps it is true. And is the evolutionary line from protozoan to Spinoza[12] any less certain? That also may be true. We are obliged, therefore, to spread the news, painful and bitter though it may be for some to hear, that all living things on earth are kindred.

---

9   **totemic:** suggestive of a totem, something that is a revered symbol such as an animal or plant.

10 **anthropomorphism:** the attribution of human qualities to animals or objects.

11 **They . . . sins:** a quotation from Walt Whitman's *Song of Myself.*

12 **protozoan to Spinoza:** Protozoan is a phylum of one-celled animals; Spinoza (1632–1677) was a Dutch philosopher.

Looking Back

1. Edward Abbey seemed reasonably comfortable with mice and nonpoisonous snakes. What would it take for you to feel the same ease?

2. What do you suppose Abbey means when he says, " I prefer not to kill animals. I'm a humanist; I'd rather kill a man than a snake"?

3. With what writers in this section does Abbey seem most akin in his attitudes toward nature?

4. What is your opinion about his suggestion that it may be possible that "many of the nonhuman undomesticated animals experience emotions unknown to us"?

5. Give at least three reasons of your own why it may be "painful and bitter . . . to hear, that all living things on earth are kindred."

Looking Into

1. Observe an animal, wild or domestic, for as long as you can, take notes, and then describe in a paragraph or two how it looks and what it does.

2. Abbey writes that the desert cools "like a griddle with the fire turned off." What is your weather like today? With a partner, think of several similes that describe the temperature, the clouds or sky, and the atmosphere and include them in a descriptive paragraph.

3. Many people feel an aversion to snakes. Write a brief paper in which you speculate about the reasons for this aversion.

Looking Around

1. What would you say are the requirements for being a writer about nature? Write a paper in which you support your answer with examples from this section.

2. Many people have written and spoken eloquently for a more responsible attitude toward our planet. Which of the selections in this section would you most want a major polluter of both air and water to read and why? Explain in a brief paper.

3. Economic and conservationist views are frequently in conflict over use of natural resources. In a short paper, discuss what some of these arguments are about, referring to recent conflicts if possible.

4. With which of the authors in this section would you most like to spend (or most like to have spent) an afternoon out-of-doors? Why? Answer these questions in a paragraph or two.

5. What are your relationships with the natural world? Write a brief article on this topic that would be suitable for publication in a general-interest magazine. Try to emulate the style of one of the writers in this section.

6. John Muir, a nineteenth-century conservationist, wrote: "In God's wildness lies the hope of the world—the great fresh unblighted, unredeemed wilderness." Discuss what you think he meant in a short paper.

7. Which of the writers in this section do you think has the least sympathy with nature? Which writer do you think has to struggle hardest to establish a sense of rapport or empathy with nature? Explain in a paper.

PART 5
Science and Technology

—·w—

$\mathcal{M}$an is a puny, slow, awkward, un-
armed animal—he had to invent a pebble, a flint,
a knife, a spear. But why to these scientific inventions, which were essential to his survival, did he
from an early time add those arts that now aston-
ish us: decorations with animal shapes? Why,
above all, did he come to caves . . . , live in them,
and then make paintings of animals not where he
lived but in places that were dark, secret, remote,
hidden, inaccessible?

For us, the cave paintings re-create the
hunter's way of life as a glimpse of history; we
look through them into the past. But for the
hunter, I suggest, they were a peep-hole into the
future; he looked ahead. In either direction, the
cave paintings act as a kind of telescope tube of
the imagination: they direct the mind from what is
seen to what can be inferred or conjectured.

Art and science are both uniquely human actions, outside the range of anything that an animal can do. And here we see that they derive from
the same human faculty: the ability to visualize
the future, to foresee what may happen and plan
to anticipate it, and to represent it to ourselves in
images that we project and move about inside our
head, or in a square of light on the dark wall of a
cave or a television screen.

Jacob Bronowski from *The Ascent of Man*

The root of the word *science* derives from a Latin verb "scio," meaning "to know." Humanity's quest for knowledge about the world and, indeed, the entire cosmos can be seen as clearly in the creation myths of the ancients as in the careful observations and experiments of modern astronomers, chemists, biologists, or physicists. The root of the word *technology* comes from a Greek word meaning "art, skill." Over several thousand years that combination of knowledge and skill has resulted in an impressive number of discoveries and inventions—the nature and extent of the solar system, the elemental constituents of the world, the varieties of flora and fauna, the mysteries of the atom, the intricacies of the personal computer.

Isaac Asimov, trained as a chemist and one of the twentieth century's most prolific writers, introduces this collection of essays by chronicling the development of science and by probing the essential nature of the scientist in his essay "What Is Science?" Lynn Margulis, a leading research biologist who often writes with her son Dorion Sagan, depicts in "Out of the Cosmos" the evolution of the solar system and the eventual creation of planet Earth.

Historian Daniel Boorstin's essay "Measuring the Dark Hours" focuses on some early technological devices for the measuring of time, especially the "dark hours" of the night. In "Anosmia," poet and traveler Diane Ackerman explores the senses, especially a peculiar condition that deprives its victim of all sense of smell.

Michel de Montaigne, the creator of the essay form, also ruminates about the sense of smell in "On Smells," but from a perception quite different from that of Ackerman. One of the most recent of neuroscientists' discoveries are endorphins, natural opiate receptors in the brain that, as James Gorman drolly discusses in "The Man with No Endorphins," ease pain and produce pleasure.

In "The Scribe," Italian chemist Primo Levi considers the wonders of the word processor, one of modern man's more complex technological creations.

What Is Science?

ISAAC ASIMOV

Issac Asimov was born in Russia in 1920, emigrated to the United States when he was three, and became a citizen when he was eight. He grew up in Brooklyn and earned three degrees in biochemistry from Columbia University. In 1955, he became an associate professor of biochemistry at Boston University, and a full professor in 1979. At the age of nine Asimov discovered science fiction; at the age of nineteen his first science fiction story, "Nightfall," was published.

In addition to his famous Foundation series (1951–1986), a classic of modern science fiction, he published six Robot novels (1950–1986), the last three of which connected the Robot series with his Foundation series. Science fiction, however, was only one aspect of Asimov's writing. He wrote textbooks and scientific histories—*A Short History of Chemistry* (1965); a series of science books for young people—*How Did We Find Out About* _____ (1973–1990); the two-volume *Asimov's Guide to Shakespeare* (1970); *Asimov's Guide to Gilbert and Sullivan* (1988); a two-volume commentary on the Old and New Testament—*Asimov's Guide to the Bible* (1976, 1982); and several volumes of an autobiography—*In Memory Yet Green* (1979) and *In Joy Still Felt* (1980). In fact, as he once noted, he wrote nearly 350 books "distributed through every major division of the Dewey system of library classification." Isaac Asimov died in 1993.

Looking Ahead

This introductory essay to the book *Asimov's New Guide to Science* (1984) focuses first on the critical, initial trait necessary to the advancement of knowledge—curiosity, and its manifestation in the early Greek myths. Asimov then discusses the contributions of the early Greeks to mathematics and science, the historical development of science from the deductions of the early Greek investigators through the experiments of key Renaissance thinkers, the development of modern science's inductive method, and the critical importance of greater scientific knowledge on the part of all human beings.

1   *A*lmost in the beginning was curiosity.

2   Curiosity, the overwhelming desire to know, is not characteristic of dead matter. Nor does it seem to be characteristic of some forms of living organism, which, for that very reason, we can scarcely bring ourselves to consider alive.

3   A tree does not display curiosity about its environment in any way we can recognize; nor does a sponge or an oyster. The wind, the rain, the ocean currents bring them what is needful, and from it they take what they can. If the chance of events is such as to bring them fire, poison, predators, or parasites, they die as stoically and as undemonstratively as they lived.

4   Early in the scheme of life, however, independent motion was developed by some organisms. It meant a tremendous advance in their control of the environment. A moving organism no longer had to wait in stolid rigidity for food to come its way, but went out after it.

5   Thus, adventure entered the world—and curiosity. The individual that hesitated in the competitive hunt for food, that was overly conservative in its investigation, starved. Early on, curiosity concerning the environment was enforced as the price of survival.

6   The one-celled paramecium, moving about in a searching way, cannot have conscious volitions and desires in the sense that we do, but it has a drive, even if only a "simple" physical-chemical one, which causes it to behave as if it were investigating its surroundings for food or safety, or both. And this "act of curiosity" is what we most easily recognize as being inseparable from the kind of life that is most akin to ours.

7   As organisms grew more intricate, their sense organs multiplied and became both more complex and more delicate. More messages of greater variety were received from and about the external environment. At the same time, there developed (whether as cause or effect we cannot tell), an increasing complexity of the nervous system, the living instrument that interprets and stores the data collected by the sense organs.

The Desire to Know

8 There comes a point where the capacity to receive, store, and interpret messages from the outside world may outrun sheer necessity. An organism may be sated with food, and there may, at the moment, be no danger in sight. What does it do then?

9   It might lapse into an oysterlike stupor. But the higher organisms at least still show a strong instinct to explore the environment. Idle curiosity,

we may call it. Yet, though we may sneer at it, we judge intelligence by it. The dog, in moments of leisure, will sniff idly here and there, pricking up its ears at sounds we cannot hear; and so we judge it to be more intelligent than the cat, which in its moments of leisure grooms itself or quietly and luxuriously stretches out and falls asleep. The more advanced the brain, the greater the drive to explore, the greater the "curiosity surplus." The monkey is a byword for curiosity. Its busy little brain must and will be kept going on whatever is handy. And in this respect, as in many others, man is a supermonkey.

10 The human brain is the most magnificently organized lump of matter in the known universe, and its capacity to receive, organize, and store data is far in excess of the ordinary requirements of life. It has been estimated that, in a lifetime, a human being can learn up to 15 trillion items of information.

11 It is to this excess that we owe our ability to be afflicted by that supremely painful disease, boredom. A human being, forced into a situation where one has no opportunity to utilize one's brain except for minimal survival, will gradually experience a variety of unpleasant symptoms, up to and including serious mental disorganization. The fact is that the normal human being has an intense and overwhelming curiosity. If one lacks the opportunity to satisfy it in immediately useful ways, one will satisfy it in other ways—even regrettable ways to which we have attached admonitions such as "Curiosity killed the cat," and "Mind your own business."

12 The overriding power of curiosity, even with harm as the penalty, is reflected in the myths and legends of the human race. The Greeks had the tale of Pandora and her box. Pandora, the first woman, was given a box that she was forbidden to open. Quickly and naturally enough she opened it and found it full of the spirits of disease, famine, hate, and all kinds of evil—which escaped and have plagued the world ever since.

13 In the Biblical story of the temptation of Eve, it seems fairly certain (to me, at any rate) that the serpent had the world's easiest job and might have saved his words: Eve's curiosity would have driven her to taste the forbidden fruit even without external temptation. If you are of a mind to interpret the Bible allegorically, you may think of the serpent as simply the representation of this inner compulsion. In the conventional cartoon picturing Eve standing under the tree with the forbidden fruit in her hand, the serpent coiled around the branch might be labeled "Curiosity."

14 If curiosity can, like any other human drive, be put to ignoble use—the prying invasion of privacy that has given the word its cheap and unpleasant connotation—it nevertheless remains one of the noblest properties of the human mind. For its simplest definition is "the desire to know."

15   This desire finds its first expression in answers to the practical needs of human life: how best to plant and cultivate crops, how best to fashion bows and arrows, how best to weave clothing—in short, the "applied arts." But after these comparatively limited skills have been mastered, or the practical needs fulfilled, what then? Inevitably the desire to know leads on to less limited and more complex activities.

16   It seems clear that the "fine arts" (designed to satisfy inchoate and boundless and spiritual needs) were born in the agony of boredom. To be sure, one can easily find more mundane uses and excuses for the fine arts. Paintings and statuettes were used as fertility charms and as religious symbols, for instance. But one cannot help suspecting that the objects existed first and the use second.

17   To say that the fine arts arose out of a sense of the beautiful may also be putting the cart before the horse. Once the fine arts were developed, their extension and refinement in the direction of beauty would have followed inevitably, but even if this had not happened, the fine arts would have developed nevertheless. Surely the fine arts antedate any possible need or use for them, other than the elementary need to occupy the mind as fully as possible.

18   Not only does the production of a work of fine art occupy the mind satisfactorily; the contemplation or appreciation of the work supplies a similar service to the audience. A great work of art is great precisely because it offers a stimulation that cannot readily be found elsewhere. It contains enough data of sufficient complexity to cajole the brain into exerting itself past the usual needs; and, unless a person is hopelessly ruined by routine or stultification, that exertion is pleasant.

19   But if the practice of the fine arts is a satisfactory solution to the problem of leisure, it has this disadvantage; it requires, in addition to an active and creative mind, physical dexterity. It is just as interesting to pursue mental activities that involve only the mind, without the supplement of manual skill. And, of course, such activity is available. It is the pursuit of knowledge itself, not in order to do something with it but for its own sake.

20   Thus, the desire to know seems to lead into successive realms of greater etherealization and more efficient occupation of the mind—from knowledge of accomplishing the useful, to knowledge of accomplishing the esthetic, to "pure" knowledge.

21   Knowledge for itself alone seeks answers to such questions as How high is the sky? or, Why does a stone fall? This is sheer curiosity—curiosity at its idlest and therefore perhaps at its most peremptory. After all, it serves no apparent purpose to know how high the sky is or why the stone falls. The lofty sky does not interfere with the ordinary business of life; and, as for the stone, knowing why it falls does not help us to dodge it

more skillfully or soften the blow if it happens to hit us. Yet there have always been people who ask such apparently useless questions and try to answer them out of the sheer desire to know—out of the absolute necessity of keeping the brain working.

22   The obvious method of dealing with such questions is to make up an esthetically satisfying answer: one that has sufficient analogies to what is already known to be comprehensible and plausible. The expression "to make up" is rather bald and unromantic. The ancients liked to think of the process of discovery as the inspiration of the muses or as a revelation from heaven. In any case, whether it was inspiration, revelation, or the kind of creative thinking that goes into storytelling, the explanations depended heavily on analogy. The lightning bolt is destructive and terrifying but appears, after all, to be hurled like a weapon and does the damage of a hurled weapon—a fantastically violent one. Such a weapon must have a wielder similarly enlarged in scale, and so the thunderbolt becomes the hammer of Thor or the flashing spear of Zeus. The more-than-normal weapon is wielded by a more-than-normal man.

23   Thus a myth is born. The forces of nature are personified and become gods. The myths react on one another, are built up and improved by generations of mythtellers until the original point may be obscured. Some myths may degenerate into pretty stories (or ribald ones), whereas others may gain an ethical content important enough to make them meaningful within the framework of a major religion.

24   Just as art may be fine or applied, so may mythology. Myths may be maintained for their esthetic charm or bent to the physical uses of human beings. For instance, the earliest farmers were intensely concerned with the phenomenon of rain and why it fell capriciously. The fertilizing rain falling from the heavens on the earth presented an obvious analogy to the sex act; and, by personifying both heaven and earth, human beings found an easy explanation of the release or the withholding of the rains. The earth goddess, or the sky god, was either pleased or offended, as the case might be. Once this myth was accepted, farmers had a plausible basis for the art of bringing rain—namely, appeasing the god by appropriate rites. These rites might well be orgiastic in nature—an attempt to influence heaven and earth by example.

The Greeks

25 The Greek myths are among the prettiest and most sophisticated in our Western literary and cultural heritage. But it was the Greeks also who, in

due course, introduced the opposite way of looking at the universe—that is, as something impersonal and inanimate. To the mythmakers, every aspect of nature was essentially human in its unpredictability. However mighty and majestic the personification, however superhuman the powers of Zeus, or Ishtar or Isis or Marduk or Odin,[1] they were also—like mere humans—frivolous, whimsical, emotional, capable of outrageous behavior for petty reasons, susceptible to childish bribes. As long as the universe was in the control of such arbitrary and unpredictable deities, there was no hope of understanding it, only the shallow hope of appeasing it. But in the new view of the later Greek thinkers, the universe was a machine governed by inflexible laws. The Greek philosophers now devoted themselves to the exciting intellectual exercise of trying to discover just what the laws of nature might be.

26   The first to do so, according to Greek tradition, was Thales of Miletus, about 600 B.C. He was saddled with an almost impossible number of discoveries by later Greek writers, and it may be that he first brought the gathered Babylonian knowledge to the Greek world. His most spectacular achievement is supposed to have been predicting an eclipse for 585 B.C.—which actually occurred.

27   In engaging in this intellectual exercise, the Greek assumed, of course, that nature would play fair; that, if attacked in the proper manner, it would yield its secrets and would not change position or attitude in midplay. (Over two thousand years later, Albert Einstein[2] expressed this feeling when he said, "God may be subtle, but He is not malicious.") There was also the feeling that the natural laws, when found, would be comprehensible. This Greek optimism has never entirely left the human race.

28   With confidence in the fair play of nature, human beings needed to work out an orderly system for learning how to determine the underlying laws from the observed data. To progress from one point to another by established rules or argument is to use "reason." A reasoner may use "intuition" to guide the search for answers, but must rely on sound logic to

---

1   **Zeus, or Ishtar or Isis or Marduk or Odin:** Zeus was the chief Greek God; Ishtar, in Assyrian and Babylonian mythology, the goddess of love, fertility and war; Isis, an ancient Egyptian goddess of fertility; Marduk, the chief god of ancient Babylon; Odin, the supreme god of Norse mythology and the god of wisdom, war, art, culture, and the dead.

2   **Albert Einstein:** Born in Ulm, Germany, in 1879, Einstein became one of the world's greatest physicists with the creation of the special and the general theory of relativity (1905); he also contributed greatly to statistical mechanics and to the quantum theory. He died in Princeton, New Jersey, in 1955.

test particular theories. To take a simple example: if brandy and water, whiskey and water, vodka and water, and rum and water are all intoxicating beverages, one may jump to the conclusion that the intoxicating factor must be the ingredient these drinks hold in common—namely, water. There is something wrong with this reasoning, but the fault in the logic is not immediately obvious; and in more subtle cases, the error may be hard indeed to discover.

[29] The tracking down of errors or fallacies in reasoning has amused thinkers from Greek times to the present. And we owe the earliest foundations of systematic logic to Aristotle of Stagira who in the fourth century B.C. first summarized the rules of rigorous reasoning.

[30] The essentials of the intellectual game of man-against-nature are three. First, you must collect observations about some facet of nature. Second, you must organize these observations into an orderly array. (The organization does not alter them but merely makes them easier to handle. This is plain in the game of bridge, for instance, where arranging the hand in suits and order of value does not change the cards or show the best course of play, but makes it easier to arrive at the logical plays.) Third, you must derive from your orderly array of observations some principle that summarizes the observations.

[31] For instance, we may observe that marble sinks in water, wood floats, iron sinks, a feather floats, mercury sinks, olive oil floats, and so on. If we put all the sinkable objects in one list and all the floatable ones in another and look for a characteristic that differentiates all the objects in one group from all in the other, we will conclude: Objects denser than water sink in water, and objects less dense than water, float.

[32] The Greeks named their new manner of studying the universe *philosophia* ("philosophy"), meaning "love of knowledge" or, in free translation, "the desire to know."

GEOMETRY AND MATHEMATICS

[33] The Greeks achieved their most brilliant successes in geometry. These successes can be attributed mainly to the development of two techniques: abstraction and generalization.

[34] Here is an example. Egyptian land surveyors had found a practical way to form a right angle: they divided a rope into twelve equal parts and made a triangle in which three parts formed one side, four parts another, and five parts the third side—the right angle lay where the three-unit side

joined the four-unit side. There is no record of how the Egyptians discovered this method, and apparently their interest went no further than to make use of it. But the curious Greeks went on to investigate why such a triangle should contain a right angle. In the course of their analysis, they grasped the point that the physical construction itself was only incidental; it did not matter whether the triangle was made of rope or linen or wooden slats. It was simply a property of "straight lines" meeting at angles. In conceiving of ideal straight lines, which are independent of any physical visualization and can exist only in imagination, the Greeks originated the method called abstraction—stripping away nonessentials and considering only those properties necessary to the solution of the problem.

[35] The Greek geometers made another advance by seeking general solutions for classes of problems, instead of treating individual problems separately. For instance, one might have discovered by trial that a right angle appeared in triangles, not only with sides 3, 4, and 5 feet long, but also in triangles of 5, 12, and 13 feet and of 7, 24, and 25 feet. But these were merely numbers without meaning. Could some common property be found that would describe all right triangles? By careful reasoning, the Greeks showed that a triangle is a right triangle if, and only if, the lengths of the sides have the relation $x^2 + y^2 = z^2$, z being the length of the longest side. The right angle lies where the sides of length x and y meet. Thus for the triangle with sides of 3, 4, and 5 feet, squaring the sides gives $9 + 16 = 25$; similarly, squaring the sides of 5, 12, and 13 gives $25 + 144 = 169$; and squaring 7, 24, and 25 gives $49 + 576 = 625$. These are only three cases out of an infinity of possible ones and, as such, trivial. What intrigued the Greeks was the discovery of a proof that the relation must hold in all cases. And they pursued geometry as an elegant means of discovering and formulating such generalizations.

[36] Various Greek mathematicians contributed proofs of relationships existing among the lines and points of geometric figures. The one involving the right triangle was reputedly worked out by Pythagoras of Samos about 525 B.C. and is still called the Pythagorean theorem in his honor.

[37] About 300 B.C., Euclid gathered the mathematical theorems known in his time and arranged them in a reasonable order, such that each theorem could be proved through the use of theorems proved previously. Naturally, this system eventually worked back to something unprovable: if each theorem had to be proved with the help of one already proved, how could one prove theorem no. 1? The solution was to begin with a statement of truths so obvious and acceptable to all as to need no proof. Such a statement is called an "axiom." Euclid managed to reduce the accepted axioms

of the day to a few simple statements. From these axioms alone, he built an intricate and majestic system of "Euclidean geometry." Never before was so much constructed so well from so little, and Euclid's reward is that his textbook has remained in use, with but minor modification, for more than 2,000 years.

THE DEDUCTIVE PROCESS

[38] Working out a body of knowledge as the inevitable consequence of a set of axioms ("deduction") is an attractive game. The Greeks fell in love with it, thanks to the success of their geometry—sufficiently in love with it to commit two serious errors.

[39] First, they came to consider deduction as the only respectable means of attaining knowledge. They were well aware that, for some kinds of knowledge, deduction was inadequate; for instance, the distance from Corinth to Athens could not be deduced from abstract principles but had to be measured. The Greeks were willing to look at nature when necessary; however, they were always ashamed of the necessity and considered that the highest type of knowledge was that arrived at by cerebration. They tended to undervalue knowledge directly involved with everyday life. There is a story that a student of Plato, receiving mathematical instruction from the master, finally asked impatiently, "But what is the use of all this?" Plato, deeply offended, called a slave and, ordering him to give the student a coin, said, "Now you need not feel your instruction has been entirely to no purpose." With that, the student was expelled.

[40] There is a well-worn belief that this lofty view arose from the Greek's slave-based culture, in which all practical matters were relegated to the slaves. Perhaps so, but I incline to the view that the Greeks felt that philosophy was a sport, an intellectual game. Many people regard the amateur in sports as a gentleman socially superior to the professional who makes his living at it. In line with this concept of purity, we take almost ridiculous precautions to make sure that the contestants in the Olympic games are free of any taint of professionalism. The Greek rationalization for the "cult of uselessness" may similarly have been based on a feeling that to allow mundane knowledge (such as the distance from Athens to Corinth) to intrude on abstract thought was to allow imperfection to enter the Eden of true philosophy. Whatever the rationalization, the Greek thinkers were severely limited by their attitude. Greece was not barren of practical contri-

butions to civilization, but even its great engineer, Archimedes of Syracuse,[3] refused to write about his practical inventions and discoveries; to maintain his amateur status, he broadcast only his achievements in pure mathematics. And lack of interest in earthly things—in invention, in experiment, in the study of nature—was but one of the factors that put bounds on Greek thought. The Greeks' emphasis on purely abstract and formal study—indeed, their very success in geometry—led them into a second great error and, eventually, to a dead end.

41   Seduced by the success of the axioms in developing a system of geometry, the Greeks came to think of the axioms as "absolute truths" and to suppose that other branches of knowledge could be developed from similar "absolute truths." Thus in astronomy they eventually took as self-evident axioms the notions that (1) the earth was motionless and the center of the universe, and (2) whereas the earth was corrupt and imperfect, the heavens were eternal, changeless, and perfect. Since the Greeks considered the circle the perfect curve, and since the heavens were perfect, it followed that all the heavenly bodies must move in circles around the earth. In time, their observations (arising from navigation and calendar making) showed that the planets do not move in perfectly simple circles, and so the Greeks were forced to allow planets to move in ever more complicated combinations of circles, which, about 150 A.D., were formulated as an uncomfortably complex system by Claudius Ptolemaeus (Ptolemy) at Alexandria. Similarly, Aristotle worked up fanciful theories of motion from "self-evident" axioms, such as the proposition that the speed of an object's fall was proportional to its weight. (Anyone could see that a stone fell faster than a feather.)

42   Now this worship of deduction from self-evident axioms was bound to wind up at the edge of a precipice, with no place to go. After the Greeks had worked out all the implications of the axioms, further important discoveries in mathematics or astronomy seemed out of the question. Philosophic knowledge appeared complete and perfect; and for nearly 2,000 years after the Golden Age of Greece, when questions involving the material universe arose, there was a tendency to settle matters to the satisfaction of all by saying, "Aristotle says . . . ," or, "Euclid says. . . ."

---

3 **Archimedes of Syracuse:** Greek mathematician and inventor (*c.* 287–212 B.C.) who is probably best remembered for his cry "*Eureka, Eureka*" ("I have found it, I have found it") when he thought of a solution to a problem that was puzzling him.

THE RENAISSANCE AND COPERNICUS

[43] Having solved the problems of mathematics and astronomy, the Greeks turned to more subtle and challenging fields of knowledge. One was the human soul.

[44] Plato was far more interested in such questions as What is justice? or, What is virtue? than in why rain falls or how the planets move. As the supreme moral philosopher of Greece, he superseded Aristotle, the supreme natural philosopher. The Greek thinkers of the Roman period found themselves drawn more and more to the subtle delights of moral philosophy and away from the apparent sterility of natural philosophy. The last development in ancient philosophy was an exceedingly mystical "neo-Platonism" formulated by Plotinus about 250 A.D.

[45] Christianity, with its emphasis on the nature of God and His relation to man, introduced an entirely new dimension into the subject matter of moral philosophy that increased its apparent superiority as an intellectual pursuit over natural philosophy. From 200 A.D. to 1200 A.D., Europeans concerned themselves almost exclusively with moral philosophy, in particular with theology. Natural philosophy was nearly forgotten.

[46] The Arabs, however, managed to preserve Aristotle and Ptolemy through the Middle Ages; and, from them, Greek natural philosophy eventually filtered back to Western Europe. By 1200, Aristotle had been redis-covered. Further infusions came from the dying Byzantine empire, which was the last area in Europe to maintain a continuous cultural tradition from the great days of Greece.

[47] The first and most natural consequence of the rediscovery of Aristotle was the application of his system of logic and reason to theology. About 1250, the Italian theologian Thomas Aquinas established the system called "Thomism," based on Aristotelian principles, which still represents the basic theology of the Roman Catholic Church. But Europeans soon began to apply the revival of Greek thought to secular fields as well.

[48] Because the leaders of the Renaissance shifted emphasis from matters concerning God to the works of humanity, they were called "humanists," and the study of literature, art, and history is still referred to as the "hu-manities."

[49] To the Greek natural philosophy, the Renaissance thinkers brought a fresh outlook, for the old views no longer entirely satisfied. In 1543, the Pol-ish astronomer Nicolaus Copernicus published a book that went so far as to reject a basic axiom of astronomy: he proposed that the sun, not the earth, be considered the center of the universe. (He retained the notion of circular

orbits for the earth and other planets, however.) This new axiom allowed a much simpler explanation of the observed motions of heavenly bodies. Yet the Copernican axiom of a moving earth was far less "self-evident" than the Greek axiom of a motionless earth, and so it is not surprising that it took more than half a century for the Copernican theory to be accepted.

50   In a sense, the Copernican system itself was not a crucial change. Copernicus had merely switched axioms; and Aristarchus of Samos[4] had already anticipated this switch to the sun as the center 2,000 years earlier. I do not mean to say that the changing of an axiom is a minor matter. When mathematicians of the nineteenth century challenged Euclid's axioms and developed "non-Euclidean geometries" based on other assumptions, they influenced thought on many matters in a most profound way: today the very history and form of the universe are thought to conform to a non-Euclidean geometry rather than the "commonsense" geometry of Euclid. But the revolution initiated by Copernicus entailed not just a shift in axioms but eventually involved a whole new approach to nature. This revolution was carried through in the person of the Italian Galileo Galilei[5] toward the end of the sixteenth century.

EXPERIMENTATION AND INDUCTION

51 The Greeks, by and large, had been satisfied to accept the "obvious" facts of nature as starting points for their reasoning. It is not on record that Aristotle ever dropped two stones of different weight to test his assumption that the speed of fall is proportional to an object's weight. To the Greeks, experimentation seemed irrelevant. It interfered with and detracted from the beauty of pure deduction. Besides, if an experiment disagreed with a deduction, could one be certain that the experiment was correct? Was it likely that the imperfect world of reality would agree completely with the perfect world of abstract ideas; and if it did not, ought one to adjust the perfect to the demands of the imperfect? To test a perfect theory with imperfect

---

4 **Aristarchus of Samos:** Greek astronomer who around 270 B.C. anticipated Copernicus's idea that the earth revolves around the sun.
5 **Galileo Galilei:** Italian astronomer and experimental philosopher (1564–1642) who embraced Copernicus's theories, explored the universe with the newly developed telescope, and through applied mathematics extended human knowledge of dynamics and mechanics.

instruments did not impress the Greek philosophers as a valid way to gain knowledge.

52   Experimentation began to become philosophically respectable in Europe with the support of such philosophers as Roger Bacon (a contemporary of Thomas Aquinas) and his later namesake Francis Bacon. But it was Galileo who overthrew the Greek view and effected the revolution. He was a convincing logician and a genius as a publicist. He described his experiments and his point of view so clearly and so dramatically that he won over the European learned community. And they accepted his methods along with his results.

53   According to the best-known story about him, Galileo tested Aristotle's theories of falling bodies by asking the question of nature in such a way that all Europe could hear the answer. He is supposed to have climbed to the top of the Leaning Tower of Pisa and dropped a 10-pound sphere and a 1-pound sphere simultaneously; the thump of the two balls hitting the ground in the same split second killed Aristotelian physics.

54   Actually Galileo probably did not perform this particular experiment, but the story is so typical of his dramatic methods that it is no wonder it has been widely believed through the centuries.

55   Galileo undeniably did roll balls down inclined planes and measured the distance that they traveled in given times. He was the first to conduct time experiments and to use measurement in a systematic way.

56   His revolution consisted in elevating "induction" above deduction as the logical method of science. Instead of building conclusions on an assumed set of generalizations, the inductive method starts with observations and derives generalizations (axioms, if you will) from them. Of course, even the Greeks obtained their axioms from observation; Euclid's axiom that a straight line is the shortest distance between two points was an intuitive judgment based on experience. But whereas the Greek philosopher minimized the role played by induction, the modern scientist looks on induction as the essential process of gaining knowledge, the only way of justifying generalizations. Moreover, the scientist realizes that no generalization can be allowed to stand unless it is repeatedly tested by newer and still newer experiments—the continuing test of further induction.

57   The present general viewpoint is just the reverse of the Greeks. Far from considering the real world an imperfect representation of ideal truth, we consider generalizations to be only imperfect representatives of the real world. No amount of inductive testing can render a generalization completely and absolutely valid. Even though billions of observations tend to bear out a generalization, a single observation that contradicts or is inconsistent with it must force its modification. And no matter how many times

a theory meets its tests successfully, there can be no certainty that it will not be overthrown by the next observation.

58   This, then, is a cornerstone of modern natural philosophy. It makes no claim of attaining ultimate truth. In fact, the phrase "ultimate truth" becomes meaningless, because there is no way in which enough observations can be made to make truth certain and, therefore, "ultimate." The Greek philosophers recognized no such limitation. Moreover, they saw no difficulty in applying exactly the same method of reasoning to the question What is justice? as to the question What is matter? Modern science, on the other hand, makes a sharp distinction between the two types of question. The inductive method cannot make generalizations about what it cannot observe; and, since the nature of the human soul, for example, is not observable by any direct means yet known, this subject lies outside the realm of the inductive method.

59   The victory of modern science did not become complete until it established one more essential principle—namely, free and cooperative communication among all scientists. Although this necessity seems obvious now, it was not obvious to the philosophers of ancient and medieval times. The Pythagoreans of ancient Greece were a secret society who kept their mathematical discoveries to themselves. The alchemists of the Middle Ages deliberately obscured their writings to keep their so-called findings within as small an inner circle as possible. In the sixteenth century, the Italian mathematician Niccolò Tartaglia, who discovered a method of solving cubic equations, saw nothing wrong in attempting to keep it a secret. When Geronimo Cardano, a fellow mathematician, wormed the secret out of Tartaglia on the promise of confidentiality and published it, Tartaglia naturally was outraged; but aside from Cardano's trickery in breaking his promise, he was certainly correct in his reply that such a discovery had to be published.

60   Nowadays no scientific discovery is reckoned a discovery if it is kept secret. The English chemist Robert Boyle, a century after Tartaglia and Cardano, stressed the importance of publishing all scientific observations in full detail. A new observation or discovery, moreover, is no longer considered valid, even after publication, until at least one other investigator has repeated the observation and "confirmed" it. Science is the product not of individuals but of a "scientific community."

61   One of the first groups (and certainly the most famous) to represent such a scientific community was the Royal Society of London for Improving Natural Knowledge, usually called simply the "Royal Society." It grew out of informal meetings, beginning about 1645, of a group of gentlemen interested in the new scientific methods originated by Galileo. In 1660, the society was formally chartered by King Charles II.

[62] The members of the Royal Society met and discussed their findings openly, wrote letters describing them in English rather than Latin, and pursued their experiments with vigor and vivacity. Nevertheless, through most of the seventeenth century, they remained in a defensive position. The attitude of many of their learned contemporaries might be expressed by a cartoon, after the modern fashion, showing the lofty shades of Pythagoras, Euclid, and Aristotle staring down haughtily at children playing with marbles and labeled "Royal Society."

[63] All this was changed by the work of Isaac Newton, who became a member of the society. From the observations and conclusions of Galileo, of the Danish astronomer Tycho Brahe, and of the German astronomer Johannes Kepler, who figured out the elliptical nature of the orbits of the planets, Newton arrived by induction at his three simple laws of motion and his great fundamental generalization—the law of universal gravitation. (Nevertheless, when he published his findings, he used geometry and the Greek method of deductive explanation.) The educated world was so impressed with this discovery that Newton was idolized, almost deified, in his own lifetime. This majestic new universe, built upon a few simple assumptions derived from inductive processes, now made the Greek philosophers look like boys playing with marbles. The revolution that Galileo had initiated at the beginning of the seventeenth century was triumphantly completed by Newton at the century's end.

MODERN SCIENCE

[64] It would be pleasant to be able to say that science and human beings have lived happily ever since. But the truth is that the real difficulties of both were only beginning. As long as science remained deductive, natural philosophy could be part of the general culture of all educated men (women, alas, being rarely educated until recent times). But inductive science became an immense labor—of observation, learning, and analysis. It was no longer a game for amateurs. And the complexity of science grew with each decade. During the century after Newton, it was still possible for a man of unusual attainments to master all fields of scientific knowledge. But, by 1800, this had become entirely impracticable. As time went on, it was increasingly necessary for a scientist to limit himself to a portion of the field with which he was intensively concerned. Specialization was forced on science by its own inexorable growth. And with each generation of scientists, specialization has grown more and more intense.

65   The publications of scientists concerning their individual work have never been so copious—and so unreadable for anyone but their fellow specialists. This has been a great handicap to science itself, for basic advances in scientific knowledge often spring from the cross-fertilization of knowledge from different specialties. Even more ominous, science has increasingly lost touch with nonscientists. Under such circumstances, scientists come to be regarded almost as magicians—feared rather than admired. And the impression that science is incomprehensible magic, to be understood only by a chosen few who are suspiciously different from ordinary mankind, is bound to turn many youngsters away from science.

66   Since the Second World War, strong feelings of outright hostility toward science were to be found among the young—even among the educated young in the colleges. Our industrialized society is based on the scientific discoveries of the last two centuries, and our society finds it is plagued by undesirable side effects of its very success.

67   Improved medical techniques have brought about a runaway increase in population; chemical industries and the internal-combustion engine are fouling our water and our air; the demand for materials and for energy is depleting and destroying the earth's crust. And this is all too easily blamed on "science" and "scientists" by those who do not quite understand that while knowledge can create problems, it is not through ignorance that we can solve them.

68   Yet modern science need not be so complete a mystery to nonscientists. Much could be accomplished toward bridging the gap if scientists accepted the responsibility of communication—explaining their own fields of work as simply and to as many as possible—and if nonscientists, for their part, accepted the responsibility of listening. To gain a satisfactory appreciation of the developments in a field of science, it is not essential to have a total understanding of the science. After all, no one feels that one must be capable of writing a great work of literature in order to appreciate Shakespeare. To listen to a Beethoven symphony with pleasure does not require the listener to be capable of composing an equivalent symphony. By the same token, one can appreciate and take pleasure in the achievements of science even though one does not oneself have a bent for creative work in science.

69   But what, you may ask, would be accomplished? The first answer is that no one can really feel at home in the modern world and judge the nature of its problems—and the possible solutions to those problems—unless one has some intelligent notion of what science is up to. Furthermore, initiation into the magnificent world of science brings great esthetic satisfac-

tion, inspiration to youth, fulfillment of the desire to know, and a deeper appreciation of the wonderful potentialities and achievements of the human mind.

Looking Back

1. Why does Asimov begin an essay entitled "What is Science?" by exploring both the concept of curiosity and early Greek myths?

2. Both Bronowski, the author of the part-opening quotation, and Asimov discuss the place of the "fine arts" in life. In small groups, discuss the following questions: How are the attitudes of the two writers dissimilar? How are they similar?

3. The variety of Asimov's publications show a lively mind and prodigious knowledge. How are those qualities evident in this essay?

4. What devices of approach, organization, and style does Asimov use in order to make his material accessible to a nonscientist?

5. At the end of his essay, Asimov pleads for greater efforts on the part of both scientists and nonscientists: the scientists to be better communicators about their fields of work, the nonscientists to accept the responsibility of listening [or reading]. One scientist who has used the mass media (magazines and television in particular) to communicate effectively about his field is the astronomer Carl Sagan. Find an article by another scientist who bridges the gap between the professional scientist and the layperson and be prepared to discuss what techniques (style, tone, organization, diction, imagery) this scientist uses to make his information accessible. For sources of articles, you might explore such publications as *Discover, Scientific American,* or *Omni.*

Looking Into

1. Write a brief narrative in which you chronicle an instance in which you became curious about a topic and then explored it. Establish how you

became interested in the topic and indicate each step of your pursuit of the topic.

2. Describe a simple scientific truth that you have proven inductively.

3. At the end of his essay, Asimov briefly lists some of the "undesirable side effects of [science's] very success": population increase, water and air pollution, the destruction of the earth's crust. In an argumentative essay focus on a scientific discovery made in the last half of the twentieth century that in your opinion has had similarly undesirable side effects.

Out of the Cosmos

LYNN MARGULIS AND DORION SAGAN

Lynn Margulis, Professor of Biology at the University of Massachusetts, was born in Chicago, Illinois, in 1938. At the age of fifteen, she entered the University of Chicago, graduating in 1957. In 1960, she earned a master's degree in both zoology and genetics from the University of Wisconsin; by 1965, she had her Ph.D. in genetics from the University of California at Berkeley. In the 1960s and 1970s, she began to champion the "symbiotic theory of the origin of the cell," a belief that cells with nuclei—including all the cells in the human body—derived from bacteria that formed symbiotic affiliations in the seas and microbial mats that covered the earth more than two billion years ago. Initially regarded with doubt and even laughter, this theory is now taken seriously by the scientific community. A measure of that seriousness is Margulis's election, in 1983, to the National Academy of Sciences, an institution open only to the most eminent of research scientists. She began writing regularly as a young girl, and is quoted in *Current Biography Yearbook* as saying, "Whether diary entry or essay, jingle or dialogue, if I failed to write on any given day I suffered a sense of deprivation." She has published *Symbiosis in Cell Evolution* (1981, a revision of her 1970 book *The Origin of Eucaryotic Cells*), *Early Life* (1982), and *Diversity of Life: the Five Kingdoms* [with K. V. Schwartz] (1992).

Margulis's son, Dorion Sagan, describes himself as both a "science writer and a sleight-of-hand magician." Born in 1959, he received his B.A. from the University of Massachusetts. Together, he and Margulis have written *The Origins of Sex: Three Billion Years of Genetic Recombination* (1986) and *Microcosmos: Four Billion Years of Evolution from Our Microbial Ancestors* (1991). In addition to articles for many magazines, Sagan has written *Biospheres: Metamorphosis of Planet Earth* (1990) and *Mystery Dance: On the Evolution of Human Sexuality* (1991).

Looking Ahead

In this, the first chapter of their book *Microcosmos*, the authors describe the creation of the cosmos and, more specifically, the planet Earth. Basing their description on the Big Bang theory, they trace the geological evolution of the solar system from the creation of hydrogen, to the creation of the heavier elements as a result of intense heat, to the formation of dust and gas, to the igniting of the sun, to the eventual creation of earth and its various continents. What enlivens this essentially expository essay is the clarity and vividness of the writing.

—m—

[1] *F*rom the moment we consider origins on a cosmic scale, the view of ourselves as a part—a minuscule part—of the universe is thrust upon us. For the very atoms that compose our bodies were created not, of course, when we were conceived, but shortly after the birth of the universe itself.

[2] It is a known astrophysical fact that most stars in the sky are shooting away from each other at tremendous speeds. If we reverse this trend in our minds we come up with the so-called Big Bang, the hypothetical release of all the energy, matter, and antimatter in existence. Like any other look into what Shakespeare called "the dim backward and abysm of time," we must not mistake our best guesses or relatively straight-line extrapolations of present conditions into the past for the literal truth. Slight alterations in the most minor assumptions can lead to major distortions when magnified over the 15,000 million year time span that is the purported age of the present universe. Nonetheless, such extrapolations yield the best picture we have of the cosmos which preceded the evolution of life in the microcosm, as well as of the microcosm and its relentless expansion.

[3] Over the first million years of expansion after the Big Bang, the universe cooled from 100 billion degrees Kelvin, as estimated by physicist Steven Weinberg, to about 3000 degrees K, the point at which a single electron and proton could join to create hydrogen, the simplest and most abundant element in the universe. Hydrogen coalesced into supernovae—enormous clouds that over billions of years contracted from cosmic to submicrocosmic densities. Under the sheer force of gravity, the cores of the supernovae became so hot that thermonuclear reactions were fired, creating from hydrogen and various disparate subatomic particles all the heavier elements in the universe that we know today. The richness of hydrogen is in our bodies still—we contain more hydrogen atoms than any other kind—primarily in water. Our bodies of hydrogen mirror a universe of hydrogen.

[4] The newly created elements spewed off into space as the dust and gas that compose the galactic nebulae. Within the nebulae, more stars and sometimes their satellite planets were born, again as particles of dust and gas gravitated toward each other, falling in and concentrating until nuclear reactions were generated. Before the first matter that could be called

Table 1

GEOLOGICAL TIME SCALE*

(IN MILLIONS OF YEARS AGO)

When aeon began	Aeons	Eras	Periods		Epochs	
4,500	Hadean	Prephanerozoic	beginning and ending dates for periods and epochs (in millions of years ago)			
3,900	Archean					
2,500	Proterozoic					
580	Phanerozoic	Paleozoic 580–245	Cambrian	580–500		
			Ordovician	500–440		
			Silurian	440–400		
			Devonian	400–345		
			Carboniferous	345–290		
			Permian	290–245		
		Mesozoic 245–66	Triassic	245–195		
			Jurassic	195–138		
			Cretaceous	138–66		
		Cenozoic 66–0	Paleogene	66–26	Paleocene	66–54
					Eocene	54–38
					Oligocene	38–26
			Neogene	26–0	Miocene	26–7
					Pleiocene	7–2
					Pleistocene	2–0.1
0					Recent	0.1–Now

*Not to scale and simplified

the earth gathered within our solar nebula at an outer arm of the Milky Way, five to fifteen billion years and billions of coalescing events forming the stars of the universe had already occurred.

5   In the cloud of gases destined to become Earth were hydrogen, helium, carbon, nitrogen, oxygen, iron, aluminum, gold, uranium, sulfur, phosphorus, and silicon. The other planets in our solar system began as similar clumps of gas and dust particles. But all would have cooled and floated

about as the aimless detritus of lifeless space were it not for the huge star that formed from the center of the nebula, pulling the hardening smaller bodies into orbit and igniting into a stable, long-lasting burn that bathed its satellites in continuous emanations of light, gas, and energy.

6   At this point, about 4,600 million years ago, the earth mass was already in circumstances that were to suit it for the emergence of life. First, it was near a source of energy: the sun. Second, of the nine major planets orbiting the sun, the earth mass was not close enough so that its elements were all blown away as gases or all liquefied as molten rock. Nor was it far enough away for its gases to be frozen as ice, ammonia, and methane as they are today on Titan, the largest moon of Saturn. Water is liquid on Earth but not on Mercury where it has all evaporated into space or on Jupiter where it is ice. Finally, the earth was large enough to hold an atmosphere, enabling the fluid cycling of elements, yet not so large that its gravity held an atmosphere too dense to admit light from the sun.

7   When the sun ignited, an explosive blast of radiation swept through the nascent solar system, stirring up the early atmospheres of the earth and other inner planets. Hydrogen, too light a gas to be held by the earth's gravity, either floated into space or combined with other elements, producing ingredients in the recipe for life. Of the hydrogen that was left, some combined with carbon to make methane (CH_4), some with oxygen to make water (H_2O), some with nitrogen to make ammonia (H_3N), and some with sulfur to make hydrogen sulfide (H_2S).

8   These gases, rearranged and recombined into long-chained compounds, make practically every component of our bodies. They are still retained as gases in the atmospheres of the massive outer planets, Jupiter, Saturn, Uranus, and Neptune, or as solids frozen into their icy surfaces. On the smaller, new, and molten Earth, however, phenomena more complex than gravity began to involve these gases in cyclical processes that would keep them here to the present day.

9 The fury and heat in which the early earth was formed was such that during these first years of the Hadean Aeon (4,500–3,900 million years ago) there was no solid ground, no oceans or lakes, perhaps not even the snow and sleet of northern winters. The planet was a molten lava fireball, burning with heat from the decay of radioactive uranium, thorium, and potassium in its core. The water of the earth, shooting in steam geysers from the planet's interior, was so hot that it never fell to the surface as rain but remained high in the atmosphere, an uncondensable vapor. The atmosphere was thick with poisonous cyanide and formaldehyde. There was no breathable oxygen, nor any organisms capable of breathing it.

10   No earth-rocks have survived this hellish primeval chaos. The Hadean Aeon is dated from meteorites and from rocks taken by Apollo astronauts from the airless moon, which began to cool 4,600 million years ago while the earth was still molten. By about 3,900 million years ago, the earth's surface had cooled enough to form a thin crust that lay uneasily on the still-molten mantle, the structure below it. The crust was punctured from below and impacted from above. Volcanoes erupted at cracks and rifts, violently spilling their molten glass. Meteorites—some as huge as mountains and more explosive than the combined nuclear warheads of both superpowers—made violent crash landings. They cratered the chaotic terrain, sending up vast plumes of dust which were rich in extraterrestrial materials. The dark dust clouds, swept by vicious winds, swirled around the globe for months before finally settling down. Meanwhile, tremendous frictional activity caused widespread thunderclaps and electrical lightning storms.

11   Then, 3,900 million years ago, the Archean Aeon began. It was to last for one-and-a-third billion years, and was to see everything from the origin of life to its spread as soft, colorful, purple and green mats and hard, rounded domes of bacteria. The immense amounts of rock that 3,000 million years later would become the American, African, and Eurasian land masses floated about the globe in the unfamiliar shapes of ancient continents. The recognizable continents appeared in their present positions in only the last tenth of a percent of our planetary history.

12   Heat and radioactivity still brewing in the earth's core sent lava boiling up through cracks in the just-cooling crust. Much of the lava contained molten magnetic iron whose molecules oriented themselves to the earth's magnetic pole as it froze into rock. In the early 1960s, studies of these ancient magnetic orientations confirmed what earlier eyes had observed from the shapes of continents and the correspondence of rock layers and fossil wildlife at their edges: the several "plates" into which the earth's crust is split move about on the molten mantle, separating from some and crashing into others as they shift. At the rate of millimeters to centimeters a year, a continental plate can cover hundreds of miles in a million years. Two hundred million years ago, for example, India was attached to Antarctica, far from the rest of Asia. Drifting nearly two inches a year, India moved northward over 4,000 miles, joining the Asian continent only about sixty million years ago.

13   The seams between the plates host violent activity. Where the plates are separating and magma boils up to fill the widening rifts, new land or ocean floor is created. Where they collide, earthquakes and volcanoes abound and the earth is thrown up into mountains. The slow but violent con-

frontation between the Indian and Asian plates thrust Mount Everest and the Himalayas to the peak of the world.

[14]   Today the quakes and tremors along the San Andreas fault in California signal the inexorable progress of the huge Pacific plate, moving northwest as it collides against the northward-moving plate from which the North American continent sticks up. And in North Africa, the Zambezi River in Mozambique traces a split in the earth's armor—the Great African rift—that is cracking the continent of Africa apart. Toward the south, huge amounts of water fill the cracks as soon as they form; great volumes of rock are caving in. Toward the north, at Afar in Ethiopia, water has not yet obscured the view. Molten rock oozes toward the surface and freezes into "pillow basalts" to form the floor of a new Pan-African ocean. The floor of this future ocean is still largely dry. And the panoramic view of the Afar valley is just what you would see if the water of the Atlantic Ocean were drained and you could watch the formation of sea floor along a rift zone.

[15]   The San Andreas fault, the African rift, the Mid-Atlantic rift, the East Pacific rise, and the volcanic islands of Hawaii are rare sites of earth-building activity on a largely placid planet today. But during the Archean Aeon, the earth's surface was riddled by such tectonic activities. Huge quantities of steam shot out of blow holes and splitting seams. The earth lay covered in a darkening fog of carbon gases and sulfurous fumes. Showers of icy comets and carbonaceous meteorites bombarded the planet, burning through the atmosphere to the weak and unstable surface, further rupturing the crust. Carbon and water came with them from space in sufficient quantities to add to the earth's own supplies of what were later to become the staples of life.

[16]   As the earth's surface continued to cool, the clouds of steam filling the atmosphere could finally condense. Torrential rains fell for perhaps a hundred thousand years without cease, creating hot, shallow oceans. Submerged plate boundaries, rich in chemicals and energy, steadily vented hydrogen-rich gases into the seas. Water hitting the boiling lava in rifts and volcanoes evaporated, condensed, and rained down again. The waters began to erode the rocky landscape, smoothing out the pockmarks and wounds made by the constant belching of volcanoes and powerful impacting of meteorites. The waters rounded off the mountains as they were created, washing minerals and salts into the oceans and land pools. Meanwhile, in an event sometimes called the Big Belch, tectonic activity released gases trapped in the earth's interior to form a new atmosphere of water vapor, nitrogen, argon, neon, and carbon dioxide. By this time much of the ammonia, methane, and other hydrogen-rich gases of the primary atmosphere had been lost into space. Lightning struck. The sun continued to

beam heat and ultraviolet light into the earth's thickening atmosphere, as the fast-spinning planet spun in cycles of five-hour days and five-hour nights. The moon too had condensed from the sun's nebula. Our faithful natural satellite, rather large for a puny inner planet like the earth, from the beginning pulled rhythmically on the great bodies of water, creating tides.

17   It is from this Archean Aeon, from 3,900 to 2,500 million years ago, that we have found the first traces of life.

Looking Back

1. Given the traditional assumption that humans are unique, what startling assertion do Margulis and Sagan make in the first paragraph?

2. What do you think the inclusion of the Geological Time Scale contributes to the essay?

3. What explanation do the authors give for the suitability of the planet Earth for the emergence of life?

4. One of Margulis and Sagan's virtues as writers is the liveliness of their verbs and verbals [participles and gerunds]. In what paragraphs do you find their verb choices particularly striking?

Looking Into

1. Review the second section of the essay, starting with paragraph 9. Now imagine that you have still photographs of the series of processes occurring and that your task is to provide for each photo a single word or short phrase caption. List those captions.

2. Of all the evolutionary stages described in the essay, discuss in a brief essay of opinion what you find the most surprising and why.

3. Write a journal entry in which you describe your feelings and thoughts as you contemplate the age of the universe and the huge span of geological time.

Measuring the Dark Hours

DANIEL BOORSTIN

Daniel Boorstin was born in Atlanta, Georgia, in 1914, but grew up in Tulsa, Oklahoma, where his father (a lawyer) moved the family in 1916. He enrolled in Harvard University in 1930, having graduated first in his high school class at the age of fifteen. Following graduation in 1934, he was a Rhodes Scholar at Balliol College, Oxford University, where he studied law and earned two degrees. In 1937, having been admitted to the bar in England, he returned to the United States, studied law at Yale University Law School, received a Doctor of Juridical Science degree in 1940 and, in 1942, was admitted to the Massachusetts bar. Between 1942–1944, he worked briefly for the government as a senior attorney. In 1938, Boorstin began to teach American history and literature at Harvard. He taught briefly at Swarthmore College in Pennsylvania before moving on to the University of Chicago where he stayed for twenty-five years.

In 1969, he left Chicago to become director of the National Museum of History and Technology of the Smithsonian Institution and, later, senior historian of the Smithsonian. In 1975, President Gerald R. Ford appointed him to the position of Librarian of Congress. Boorstin's most notable publication is the three-volume work *The Americans* (1958–1973), a massive work in which he analyzes the distinctive character of American institutions and culture. Boorstin's companion books, *The Discoverers* (1983) and *The Creators* (1992), are wide-ranging histories of the many forms of human discovery and creation. His most recent publication, *Cleopatra's Nose* (1994), is a collection of essays.

Looking Ahead

In this chapter from *The Discoverers*, Boorstin chronicles the devices by which the Egyptians, the Greeks, and the Romans measured time, especially those sunless hours of the night. Their ingenuity is seen in the various instruments they devised, from sundials to water clocks. Boorstin combines scholarship with an easy style which both informs and entertains the reader.

1 So long as mankind lived by raising crops and herding animals there was not much need for measuring small units of time. The seasons were all-important—to know when to expect the rain, the snow, the sun, the cold. Why bother with hours and minutes? Daylight time was the only important time, the only time when men could work. To measure useful time, then, was to measure the hours of the sun.

2 No change in daily experience is more emptying than the loss of the sense of contrast between day and night, light and dark. Our century of artificial light tempts us to forget the meaning of night. Life in a modern city is always a time of mixed light and darkness. But for most of the human centuries night was a synonym for the darkness that brought all the menace of the unknown. "Never greet a stranger in the night," warned the Talmud[1] (c. 200 B.C.), "for he may be a demon." "I must work the works of him that sent me, while it is day," announced Jesus (John 9:4–5), "the night cometh, when no man can work. As long as I am in the world, I am the light of the world." Few subjects have been more enticing to the literary imagination. "In the dead vast and middle of the night" was when Shakespeare and other dramatists placed their crimes.

> O comfort-killing night, image of Hell;
> Dim register and notary of shame;
> Black stage for tragedies and murders fell;
> Vast sin-concealing chaos, nurse of blame.

3 The first step in making night more like day was taken long before people became accustomed to artificial lighting. It came when man, playing with time, began measuring it off into shorter slices.

4 While the ancients measured the year and the month, and set the pattern for our week, the shorter units of time remained vague and played little part in the common human experience until the last few centuries. Our precise uniform hour is a modern invention, while the minute and the second are still more recent. Naturally enough, when the working day was the sunlit day, the first efforts to divide time measured the passing of the sun across the heavens. For this purpose sundials, or shadow clocks, were the

---

1 **Talmud:** a collection of ancient writings that form the basis of religious authority for traditional Judaism.

first measuring devices. The original meaning of our English word "dial," which since has taken on so many other meanings (from the Latin *dies*, or day; medieval Latin *dialis*), was sundial. Primitive societies noticed that the shadow of an upright post (or *gnomon*, from the Greek "to know") became shorter as the sun rose in the heavens, and lengthened again as the sun set. The ancient Egyptians used such a device, and we can still see one that survives from the time of Thutmose III[2] (c. 1500 B.C.). A horizontal bar about a foot long had a small T-shaped structure at one end which would cast a shadow on the calibration on the horizontal bar. In the morning the bar was set with the T facing east; at noon the device was reversed with the T facing west. When the prophet Isaiah[3] promised to cure King Hezekiah by making time go backward, he announced that he would do so by making the sun's shadow recede.

5   For centuries the sun's shadow remained the universal measure of time. And this was a handy measure, since a simple sundial could be made anywhere by anybody without special knowledge or equipment. But the cheery boast "I count only the sunny hours," inscribed on modern sundials, announces the obvious limitation of the sundial for measuring time. A sundial measures the sun's shadow: no sun, no shadow. A shadow clock was useful only in those parts of the world where there was lots of sunlight, and then it served only when the sun was actually shining.

6   Even when the sun shone bright, the movement of the sun's shadow was so slow that it would be small help in marking minutes and useless for signaling seconds. The dial that marked the day's passing in any one place was ill suited to measure a universal standard unit, such as our hour of sixty minutes. For everywhere except on the equator the length of daylight hours varies from one day to the next and around the seasons. To use the sun's shadow in any place to define the hour according to Greenwich Mean Time[4] requires a combined knowledge of astronomy, geography, mathematics, and mechanics. Not until about the sixteenth century could sundials be marked with these true hours. When this "science of dialing" was developed, it became fashionable to carry a pocket sundial. But by then the clock and the watch existed and were more convenient and useful in every way.

---

2 **Thutmose III:** an energetic pharaoh of the New Kingdom who waged numerous campaigns and extended the range of the Egyptian empire.
3 **Isaiah:** an Old Testament prophet.
4 **Greenwich Mean Time:** the mean solar time for the meridian at Greenwich, England; used as the basis for calculating time throughout most of the world.

⁷   The early sundials had other limitations. The horizontal instrument of Thutmose III could not record the earliest hour in the morning or the latest hour of the afternoon because the shadow of the horizontal T-bar would stretch to infinite length and so not register on the scale. The great ancient advance in sundial design, while no help in describing universal time, did make it easier to divide the daylight hours into equal parts. This was a sundial shaped into a hemicycle, the interior of a half-sphere, with the pointer extended from one side to the center and the opening facing upward. The shadow path during any day, then, would be a perfect replica of the sun's path in the hemisphere of the sky above. This arc traced by the sun and marked inside the hemicycle was divided into twelve equal parts. After paths were drawn for different dates, the twelve "hour" divisions for each date were joined with curves, indicating the varying twelfth of the daylight hours.

⁸   The Greeks, adept at geometry, succeeded in making many advances in sundial design. One delightful example survives in the Tower of the Winds in Athens. On this eight-sided tower, each of the eight principal directions is personified in its winds, and each face bears a sundial, so that an Athenian could read the time on at least three faces at once. The sundial became so common a Roman fixture that the architect Vitruvius, in the first century B.C., could list thirteen kinds of sundials. But the many beautiful monumental sundials that the Romans looted abroad to decorate their villas were nearly useless as timepieces in the Roman latitude. If we believe Plautus[5] (d. 184 B.C.), the Romans relied on sundials to fix their mealtimes:

> The gods confound the man who first found out
> How to distinguish hours! Confound him, too,
> Who in this place set up a sun-dial,
> To cut and hack my days so wretchedly
> Into small portions. When I was a boy,
> My belly was my sun-dial; one more sure,
> Truer, and more exact than any of them.
> This dial told me when 'twas proper time
> To go to dinner, when I had aught to eat.
> But now-a-days, why even when I have,
> I can't fall-to, unless the sun give leave.

---

5   **Plautus:** a comic playwright who lived in Rome from c. 254?–184 B.C.

The greater part of its inhabitants,
Shrunk up with hunger, creep along the streets!

9   Even after the sundial was designed to divide the daylight time into
equal segments, it was not much help in comparing times from one season
to another. Summer days were long, so too were summer hours. Roman
soldiers, in the reign of Emperor Valentinian I (364–375), were drilled to
march "at the rate of 20 miles in five *summer* hours." An "hour"—one-
twelfth of the daylight—on a particular day in one place would be quite
different from that on another day or in another place. The sundial was
an elastic yardstick.

10   How was mankind liberated from the sun? How did we conquer the night,
making it part of the intelligible world? Only by escaping the sun's tyranny would we ever learn to measure out our time in universally uniform
spoonfuls. Only then could the recipes for action, for making and doing be
understood anywhere anytime. Time was, in Plato's phrase, "a moving
image of eternity." No wonder that measuring its course tantalized
mankind all over the planet.

11   Anything that would flow, that would be consumed or would consume has been tried somewhere or another as a measure of time. All were
efforts to escape the tyranny of the sun, to grasp time more firmly, more
predictably and bring it into the service of man. The simple universal measure needed every day, the measure of life itself, would have to be something better than the whimsical, fleeting, slow-moving, often obscured
shadow. Man must find something better than the Greeks' "timepiece they
call Hunt-the-Shadow."

12   Water, that wonderful, flowing medium, the luck of the planet—which
would serve humankind in so many ways, and which gives our planet a
special character—made possible man's first small successes in measuring the dark hours. Water, which could be captured in any small bowl, was
more manageable than the sun's shadow. When mankind began to use
water to serve him for a timepiece, he took another small step forward in
making the planet into his household. Man could make the captive water
flow fast or slow, day and night. He could measure out its flow in regular,
constant units, which would be the same at the equator or on the tundra,
winter or summer. But perfecting this device was long and difficult. By
the time the water clock was elaborated into a more or less precision instrument, it had already begun to be supplanted by something far more
convenient, more precise, and more interesting.

[13]   Yet, for most of history, water provided the measure of time when the sun was not shining. And until the perfection of the pendulum clock about 1700, the most accurate timepiece was probably the water clock. During all those centuries, the water clock ruled man's daily—or, rather, his night-ly—experience.

[14]   Man discovered very early that he could measure the passage of time by the amount of water that dripped from a pot. Within five hundred years after their first sundials, the ancient Egyptians were using water clocks. In their sunny country, the sundial well served their needs by day, but they needed the water clock to measure off hours of night. Their god of the night, Thoth, who was also god of learning, of writing, and of measure-ment, presided over both outflow and inflow models of water clocks. The outflow type was an alabaster vessel with a scale marked inside and a sin-gle hole near the bottom from which the water dripped. By noting the drop in the water level inside from one mark to the next mark below on the scale, the passage of time was measured. The later inflow type, which marked the passing time by the rise of water in the vessel, was more com-plicated, as it required a constant source of regulated supply. Even such simple devices were not without their problems. In cold climates the chang-ing viscosity of the water would be troublesome. But, in any climate, to keep the clock at constant speed, the hole through which the water poured must not become clogged or worn larger. The outflow clocks posed an-other minor problem because the speed of flow depended on the water pressure, and that always varied with the amount of water left in the bowl. The Egyptians therefore slanted the walls of the vessel so that, as the amount of water decreased, the pressure remained constant by being con-centrated on a smaller area.

[15]   The problem of designing a useful water clock was simple enough so long as its only purpose was like that of a modern egg timer, which marks the passage of short uniform units of time. But to use the water clock as an instrument for dividing the hours of daylight or of darkness into equal segments posed a difficult problem of calibration. The winter night in Egypt was, of course, longer than the night in summer. The water clock at Thebes required, according to Egyptian measures, that the summer night be measured by only twelve fingers of water, while the winter night re-quired fourteen. These variant "hours"—equal subdivisions of the total hours of daylight or darkness—were not really chronometric hours. They came to be called "temporary hours" or "temporal" hours, for they had meaning that was only temporary and did not equal an hour the next day. It would have been much simpler to make a water clock measure off a fixed, unchanging unit. But centuries passed before abstracted time was

captured by a machine that measured something other than a fragment of daylight or darkness.

16   The Greeks, who had perfected the sundial to measure their daylight, also used the water clock as an everyday timer. Their picturesque name, *klepsydra*, meaning water-thief, would designate the device for centuries to come. They used their water clock to limit the times for pleading in Athenian courts. The surviving court clocks flow for about six minutes. Demosthenes in his legal speeches, referring to the time running out in the water clock, often asked that the flow of the water be stopped while he read from laws or depositions so that his speaking time would not be used up. The elegant Tower of the Winds had attached to it a circular cistern as a reservoir for a water clock. Ctesibius of Alexandria (second century B.C.), the ingenious Greek physicist and inventor, who also devised a hydraulic organ and an air gun, contrived a water clock with a floating indicator to mark the time on a vertical scale set above.

17   Adept though they were at engineering and mechanics, the Romans relied on the water clock as their only mechanical device, apart from the sundial, for measuring time. Latinizing *klepsydra* to *clepsydra*—or the *horologium ex aqua*—they elaborated and popularized it into an everyday convenience. They made miniature sundials measuring only one and a half inches across for carrying about in the pocket. At the same time the Roman feeling for the grandiose was displayed on the Campus Martius in the great obelisk of Montecitorio,[6] serving as gnomon for a giant sundial whose shadow was measured on lines of bronze in the surrounding marble pavement.

18   The Romans showed a similar versatility with their water clocks. Like other practical, commercial people, they were alert to the value of time. But only gradually, and then only crudely, did they divide their day into smaller parts. They never invented a mechanical clock that would conveniently subdivide the hours. Even at the end of the fourth century B.C. they formally divided their day into only two parts: before midday (*ante meridiem*, A.M.) and after midday (*post meridiem*, P.M.). An assistant to the consul was assigned to notice when the sun crossed the meridian, and to announce it in the Forum, since lawyers had to appear in the courts before

---

6   **Campus Martius . . . Montecitorio:** In ancient times the Campus Martius, or "Field of Mars," was a center of Rome; it featured public parks that led to the Tiber River, baths, theaters, and areas for military and gymnastics exercises. A short distance away was the Piazza Montecitorio, a square in whose center the obelisk of Psammaticus forms the center, or gnomen, of an ancient sundial.

noon. Eventually they made finer subdivisions. First by dividing each half of the day into two parts: early morning (*mane*) and forenoon (*ante meridiem*); afternoon (*de meridie*) and evening (*suprema*). Then they took to marking the "temporary" hours according to a sundial that had been brought from Catana in Sicily. Made for a different latitude, it was hardly precise. Finally in 164 B.C. the censor Q. Marcius Philippus[7] earned popularity by setting up a sundial properly oriented for Rome. Beside the sundial a waterclock was installed to tell time on foggy days and at night.

[19]   The Romans used their sundials to calibrate and set the water clocks, which had become the common timepiece in imperial Rome. The water clocks still offered only "temporary" hours, with daylight and darkness measurements for all the days of a month lumped together, though these really varied from day to day. Since no one in Rome could know the exact hour, promptness was an uncertain, and uncelebrated, virtue. It was as impossible to find agreement among the clocks of Rome, the wit Seneca (c. 4 B.C.–A.D. 65) observed, as to find agreement among Roman philosophers.

[20]   The "hours" of their daily lives—their temporary "hour" was one-twelfth the time of daylight or of darkness on that day—were more elastic than we can now imagine. At the winter solstice, even if the sun shone all day there would be, by our modern measures, only 8 hours, 54 minutes of sunlight, leaving a long night of 15 hours, 6 minutes. At the summer solstice the time, by our modern hours, was exactly reversed. But from the Romans' point of view both day and night always had precisely 12 hours year round. In Rome at the winter solstice the *first* hour of their day (*hora prima*) began at what we would call 7:33 A.M. and lasted only till 8:17 A.M., while the *twelfth* hour (*hora duodecima*) began at 3:42 P.M. and expired at 4:27 P.M., when the longer night hours began. What a problem for the clockmakers! We must be amazed not that they did not provide a more precise timepiece, but that under these circumstances they were able to provide an instrument that served daily needs at all.

[21]   By elaborate systems of calibration they made their water clocks indicate the shifting lengths of hours from month to month. It was far too complicated to mark the shifting increments from day to day. This meant, too, that there was no accepted way of subdividing each day's passing hours.

[22]   When daily needs required shorter standard units, a simple water clock served them with all the precision of an egg timer. In the Roman court-

---

7   **censor Q. Marcius Phillippus:** A censor was a Roman public official responsible for supervising the census as well as public behavior and morals.

room, for example, where the lawyers of opposing parties were supposed to have equal time, the simple water clock worked well. For this purpose they followed the Athenian example, using a bowl with a hole near the bottom. This timer emptied in about twenty minutes. A lawyer might ask the judge to grant him an additional "six clepsydrae," or about two of our modern hours, to make his case. A particularly long-winded advocate was once actually granted sixteen water clocks—five hours! While the Romans doubtless shared our view that "time is money," they often equated time with water. In Rome the phrase *aquam dare*, "to grant water," meant to allot time to a lawyer, while *aquam perdere*, "to lose water," meant to waste time. If a speaker in the Senate spoke out of turn or talked too long, his colleagues would shout that his water should be taken away. Under other circumstances they might petition that more water be allowed.

[23]   Lawyers were no less wordy then they are today. One especially tiresome advocate inspired the Roman wit Martial (c. 40–c. 102) to suggest:

> Seven water-clocks' allowance you asked for in loud tones, Caecilianus, and the judge unwillingly granted them. But you speak much and long, and with backtilted head, swill tepid water out of glass flasks. That you may once for all sate your oratory and your thirst, we beg you, Caecilianus, now to drink out of the water-clock!

For every bowlful of water the lawyer drank he would reduce the judge's boredom by twenty minutes.

[24]   The simple water clock challenged the Romans' ingenuity. To prevent the escape hole from wearing away or being clogged, the hole was fashioned from a gem, much as later mechanical clockmakers used "jewels." Some of the Roman water clocks described by the architect Vitruvius were fitted with elaborate floats which announced the Roman "hour" by tossing pebbles—or eggs—into the air, or by blowing a whistle. The water clock, like the piano in middle-class European households in the nineteenth century, became a symbol status. "Has he not got a clock in his dining-room?" observed the admirers of the parvenu Trimalchio in the Age of Nero. "And a uniformed trumpeter to keep telling him how much of his life is lost and gone?"

[25]   In later centuries people everywhere, after their fashion, found ways to use water to mark off the portions of life. The Saxons in the ninth century characteristically used a bowl of strong and rustic elegance. The bowl, with a small hole in the bottom, was floated on water and sank as it filled, al-

ways marking the same period. The Chinese, who had their own simple water clocks from remote antiquity, returned home from Western travels with astonishing tales of complicated striking water clocks. They especially admired a giant water clock that ornamented the east gate of the Great Mosque at Damascus. At each "hour" of the day or night two weights of brightly shining brass fell from the mouths of two brazen falcons into brazen cups, perforated to allow the balls to return into position. Above the falcons was a row of open doors, one for each "hour" of the day, and above each door was an unlighted lamp. At each hour of the day, when the balls fell, a bell was struck and the doorway of the completed hour was closed. Then, at nightfall, the doors all automatically opened. As the balls fell announcing each "hour" of the night, the lamp of that hour was lit, giving off a red glow, so that finally by dawn all the lamps were illuminated. With the coming of daylight the lamps were extinguished and the doors of daytime hours resumed their cycle. It required the full time of eleven men to keep this machine in working order.

[26] Not the flowing waters of time but the falling sands of time have given modern poets their favorite metaphor for the passing hours. In England, sandglasses were frequently placed in coffins as a symbol that life's time had run out. "The sands of time are sinking," went the hymn. "The dawn of heaven breaks."

[27] But the hourglass, measuring time by dripping sand, comes late in our story. Sand was, of course, less fluid than water, and hence less adapted to the subtle calibration required by the variant "hours" of day and night in early times. You could not float an indicator on it. But sand would flow in climates where water would freeze. A practical and precise sandglass required the mastery of the glassmaker's art.

[28] We hear of sand hourglasses in Europe in the eighth century, when legend credits a monk at Chartres[8] with their invention. As glassmaking progressed it became possible to seal the hourglass to keep out the moisture that slowed the fall of the sand. Elaborate processes dried the sand before it was inserted in the glass. A medieval treatise prescribed in place of sand a fine-ground black-marble dust, boiled nine times in wine. At each boiling, the scum was skimmed off, and finally the dust was dried in the sun.

---

8   **Chartres:** a city about 55 miles from Paris, famed for its Gothic cathedral.

29   Sandglasses were ill adapted for daylong timekeeping. Either they had to be made too large for convenience—like the sandglass Charlemagne[9] ordered which was so large that it had to be turned only once in twelve hours—or, if they were small, they had to be turned frequently at the precise moment when the last grain had dropped. Some had a little dial attached with a pointer that could be advanced with each turn of the glass. But the sandglass did serve better than a water clock for measuring the shortest intervals when no other device was yet known. Columbus on his ships noted the passing time by a half-hour sandglass that was turned as it emptied to keep track of the seven "canonical" hours.[10] By the sixteenth century the sandglass was already being used to measure short intervals in the kitchen. Or to help a preacher (and his congregation!) regulate the length of his sermon. An English law of 1483 was said to require clocks to be placed *over* pulpits, since congregations could not otherwise see the "sermon-glass." The House of Commons kept a two-minute glass to time the ringing of bells to announce divisions for voting. Stonemasons and other craftsmen used a glass to count their hours of work. Teachers brought their hourglass along to measure the duration of their lecture or the length of the students' prescribed study period. An Oxford don in Elizabethan times[11] once threatened his idle pupils "that if they did not doe their exercise better he would bring an Hower-glass two howers long."

30   The unique use of the sandglass, after the sixteenth century, was measuring a ship's speed. Knots were tied at seven-fathom intervals on a line tied to a log chip that would float astern. A sailor dropped the log chip off the end of the speeding ship and counted off the number of knots paid out while a small sandglass measured a half-minute. If five knots passed in the interval, the ship was making five nautical miles an hour. Throughout the nineteenth century, sailing vessels still "heaved the log" every hour to keep track of the speed.

31   In the long run the sandglass was not much use in measuring the hours of the night, for it was inconvenient to keep the glass turning. From time to

---

9 **Charlemagne:** Charles I (742–814), also known as "Charles the Great," was King of the Franks from 768–814; in 800, he was crowned emperor of the Romans.

10 **"canonical" hours:** the times of day prescribed by the Church's canons, or rules, for prayer. According to Boorstin, "distinct prayers were to be said at first light or dawn, with the sunrise, at mid-morning, noon, mid-afternoon, sunset, and nightfall."

11 **Oxford don in Elizabethan times:** In Queen Elizabeth I's time (1533–1603), England had two universities, one located in Cambridge, the other in Oxford; a *don* is the English term for a faculty member.

time, as a way of solving this problem, people tried to combine a time-piece with a lighting device. For centuries, ingenuity was lavished on the effort to use the fire that illuminated the night also to measure the passing hours of darkness. The inventions, however original, were not practical. They were costly, sometimes dangerous, and never succeeded in aligning night hours with day hours. So long as "hours" remained elastic, a fire clock, like a sandglass, would measure off a short, fixed unit but could not be widely used for daylong timekeeping.

32 A famous candle clock was that reputedly designed to help the pious Alfred the Great (849–899), king of the West Saxons, keep the vow he made when he was a fugitive from his native country. He swore that if his king-dom was restored, he would devote a full third of each day to the service of God. According to legend, when he was back in England he ordered a can-dle clock. From seventy-two pennyweight of wax, six twelve-inch candles were made, all uniform in thickness, each marked in one-inch divisions. The candles were lit in rotation, and the six candles were said to last a full twenty-four hours. They were protected by transparent horn panels set into wooden frames to prevent the light from being extinguished by a draft. If King Alfred devoted the time of two full candle lengths to his religious duties, he could be assured that he was fulfilling his vow.

33 Other sovereigns who could afford to use candles or lamp oil for the purpose of timekeeping—King Alfonso X of Castile (c. 1276), King Charles V of France (the Wise, 1337–1380), King Philip I of Spain (1478–1506)—ex-perimented with clock lamps. The search for a practical portable clock lamp led a Milanese physician, Girolamo Cardano (1501–1576), to invent a fountain-feeding device that used the principle of the vacuum to draw in a constant flow of oil. Cardano's lamp provided a convenient and popular lighting device until the late eighteenth century.

34 Even after mechanical clocks came into general use, restless inventors continued to try all sorts of expedients—some using the flame of an oil lamp to propel the mechanism of a clock, others using the consumption of oil indicated on a calibrated transparent container, still others using the changing shadow of a diminishing candle cast on a scale that marked the changing night hours—to conquer both night and time with the same de-vice.

35 In China, Japan, and Korea, the use of fire to measure time took quite another turn. The custom of burning incense gave them a clue to a range of ingenious and beautiful devices. These produced a pleasing aroma while a continuous trail of powdered incense was burned in an elaborate seal. The time was indicated by the place within the seal that was reached by the fire. One of the most intricate of these—the "hundred-gradations incense

seal"—was invented in China in 1073, when a drought had dried up the wells and so made it impossible to use the customary water clocks. The Chinese aromatic clock, in turn, inspired later generations to find newly vivid and elaborate ways to use a fire clock to measure time into temporary hours, which varied with the seasons. The charming intricacy of the Chinese designs was a delightful by-product of the effort to make a virtue of the variant hour.

36   There seems no end to the desperate ingenuity spent on ways to count the passing hours of the night before inexpensive artificial illumination became universal. After the invention of the mechanical clock the striking hour was the obvious way of conquering darkness. A clever French inventor in the late seventeenth century, M. de Villayer, tried using the sense of taste. He designed a clock so arranged that when he reached for the hour hand at night, it guided him to a small container with a spice inserted in place of numbers, a different spice for each hour of the night. Even when he could not see the clock, he could always taste the time.

Looking Back

1. Boorstin writes: "Anything that would flow, that would be consumed or would consume has been tried somewhere or another as a measure of time." Cite examples from the essay of each.

2. What time device or devices fall in none of the categories cited in the quotation in question 1?

3. Boorstin's writing is filled with allusions and examples from the areas of religion, literature, history and historical personages, and geography. Working in small groups, find specific samples of each and indicate what they tell the reader about Boorstin.

4. Boorstin writes of our "loss of the sense of contrast between day and night, light and dark." Discuss how people might have regarded the night before the invention of artificial light. What perils would night and darkness have held?

5. Discuss the extent to which you are or are not dependent upon clocks and watches in your daily life. Do you think you are typical or unusual in that respect?

Looking Into

1. Imagine how your life would change had the world no way to "measure the dark hours." Make a list of at least five specific changes, then write a paragraph explaining the one that would have the greatest impact on you and why.

2. Draw or construct an ancient sundial according to Boorstin's description.

Anosmia

DIANE ACKERMAN

Poet and science writer Diane Ackerman was born in Waukegan, Illinois, in 1948. After graduating from Pennsylvania State University, she earned both a master's and a doctorate from Cornell University in Ithaca, New York, where she has occasionally taught. In 1976, she published her first of five volumes of poetry: *The Planets: A Cosmic Pastoral*. In 1979, she went to the Southwest to research contemporary cowboy life, an experience that resulted in *Twilight of the Tenderfoot* (1980). A subsequent book was *On Extended Wings* (1985), a book about learning to fly and "not being a passenger in life." Fascinated by "all the textures in life," she explored the senses in *A Natural History of the Senses* (1990), the book from which the essay in this book is taken.

In 1991, she published two works: *The Moon by Whale Light*, a collection of prose portraits of four animals—penguins, whales, alligators and bats; and a collection of poems, *Jaguar of Sweet Laughter*. Her latest book is *The Natural History of Love* (1994). Ackerman is not content to rely on libraries for her research, although about libraries she said, "I tend to graze in them, enchanted by all the different things people have chosen to write about"; three or four times a year she travels all over the world to experience first hand "tagging seals, or swimming with whales, or raising penguins." Ackerman's fascination with the world makes her one of the rare twentieth century writers "to bridge science and art."

Looking Ahead

In her introduction to *A Natural History of the Senses*, a book she describes as "an act of celebration," Diane Ackerman notes that in the book she wishes to explore "the origin and evolution of the senses, how they vary from culture to culture, their range and reputation, their folklore and science. . . ." In the chapter on smell, she tells of the peculiar condition known as anosmia from which some two million Americans suffer.

[1]	*O*ne rainy night in 1976, a thirty-three-year-old mathematician went out for an after-dinner stroll. Everyone considered him not just a gourmet

but a wunderkind, because he had the ability to taste a dish and tell you all the ingredients with shocking precision. One writer described it as a kind of "perfect pitch." As he stepped into the street, a slow-moving van ran into him and he hit his head on the pavement when he fell. The day after he got out of the hospital, he discovered to his horror that his sense of smell was gone.

2   Because his taste buds still worked, he could detect foods that were salty, bitter, sour, and sweet, but he had lost all of the heady succulence of life. Seven years later, still unable to smell and deeply depressed, he sued the driver of the van and won. It was understood, first, that his life had become irreparably impoverished and, second, that without a sense of smell his life was endangered. In those seven years, he had failed to detect the smell of smoke when his apartment building was on fire; he had been poisoned by food whose putrefaction he couldn't smell; he could not smell gas leaks. Worst of all, perhaps, he had lost the ability of scents and odors to provide him with heart-stopping memories and associations. "I feel empty, in a sort of limbo," he told a reporter. There was not even a commonly known name for his nightmare. Those without hearing are labeled "deaf," those without sight "blind," but what is the word for someone without smell? What could be more distressing than to be sorely afflicted by an absence without a name? "Anosmia" is what scientists call it, a simple Latin/Greek combination: "without" + "smell." But no casual term—like "smumb," for instance—exists to give one a sense of community or near-normalcy.

3   The "My Turn" column in *Newsweek* of March 21, 1988, by Judith R. Birnberg, contains a deeply moving lament about her sudden loss of smell. All she can distinguish is the texture and temperature of food. "I am handicapped: one of 2 million Americans who suffer from anosmia, an inability to smell or taste (the two senses are physiologically related). . . . We so take for granted the rich aroma of coffee and the sweet flavor of oranges that when we lose these senses, it is almost as if we have forgotten how to breathe." Just before Ms. Birnberg's sense of smell disappeared, she had spent a year sneezing. The cause? Some unknown allergy. "The anosmia began without warning. . . . During the past three years there have been brief periods—minutes, even hours—when I suddenly became aware of odors and knew that this meant that I could also taste. What to eat first? A bite of banana once made me cry. On a few occasions a remission came at dinner time, and my husband and I would dash to our favorite restaurant. On two or three occasions I savored every miraculous mouthful through an entire meal. But most times my taste would be gone by the time we parked the car." Although there are centers for treating smell and taste dysfunction

(of which Monell[1] is probably the best known), little can be done about anosmia. "I have had a CAT scan, blood tests, sinus cultures, allergy tests, allergy shots, long-term zinc therapy, weekly sinus irrigations, a biopsy, cortisone injections into my nose and four different types of sinus surgery. My case has been presented to hospital medical committees. . . . I have been through the medical mill. The consensus: anosmia caused by allergy and infection. There can be other causes. Some people are born this way. Or the olfactory nerve is severed as a result of concussion. Anosmia can be the result of aging, a brain tumor or exposure to toxic chemicals. Whatever the cause, we are all at risk in detecting fires, gas leaks and spoiled food." Finally, she took a risky step and allowed a doctor to give her prednisone, an anti-inflammatory steroid, in an effort to shrink the swelling near olfactory nerves. "By the second day, I had a brief sense of smell when I inhaled deeply. . . . The fourth day I ate a salad at lunch, and I suddenly realized that I could taste everything. It was like the moment in 'The Wizard of Oz' when the world is transformed from black and white to Technicolor. I savored the salad: one garbanzo bean, a shred of cabbage, a sunflower seed. On the fifth day I sobbed—less from the experience of smelling and tasting than from believing the craziness was over."

4   At breakfast the next day, she caught her husband's scent and "fell on him in tears of joy and started sniffing him, unable to stop. His was a comfortable familiar essence that had been lost for so long and was now rediscovered. I had always thought I would sacrifice smell to taste if I had to choose between the two, but I suddenly realized how much I had missed. We take it for granted and are unaware that *everything* smells: people, the air, my house, my skin. . . . Now I inhaled all odors, good and bad, as if drunk." Sadly, her pleasures lasted only a few months. When she began reducing the dosage of prednisone, as she had to for safety's sake (prednisone causes bloating and can suppress the immune system, among other unpleasant side effects), her ability to smell waned once more. Two new operations followed. She's decided to go back on prednisone, and yearns for some magical day when her smell returns as mysteriously as it vanished.

5   Not everyone without a sense of smell suffers so acutely. Nor are all smell dysfunctions a matter of loss; the handicap can take strange forms. At Monell, scientists have treated numerous people who suffer from "persistent odors," who keep smelling a foul smell wherever they go. Some walk around with a constant bitter taste in their mouths. Some have a deformed

---

1 **Monell:** The Monell Chemical Senses Center is in Philadelphia, Pennsylvania.

or distorted sense of smell. Hand them a rose, and they smell garbage. Hand them a steak and they smell sulfur. Our sense of smell weakens as we get older, and it's at its peak in middle age. Alzheimer's patients often lose their sense of smell along with their memory (the two are tightly coupled); one day Scratch-and-Sniff tests may help in diagnosis of the disease.

6   Research done by Robert Henkin, from the Center for Sensory Disorders at Georgetown University, suggests that about a quarter of the people with smell disorders find that their sex drive disappears. What part does smell play in lovemaking? For women, especially, a large part. I am certain that, blindfolded, I could recognize by smell any man I've ever known intimately. I once started to date a man who was smart, sophisticated, and attractive, but when I kissed him I was put off by a faint, cornlike smell that came from his cheek. Not cologne or soap: It was just his subtle, natural scent, and I was shocked to discover that it disturbed me viscerally. Although men seldom report such detailed responses to their partner's natural smell, women so often do that it's become a romantic cliché: When her lover is away, or her husband dies, an anguished woman goes to his closet and takes out a bathrobe or shirt, presses it to her face, and is overwhelmed by tenderness for him. Few men report similar habits, but it's not surprising that women should be more keenly attuned to smells. Females score higher than males in sensitivity to odors, regardless of age group. For a time scientists thought estrogen[2] might be involved, since there was anecdotal evidence[3] that pregnant women had a keener sense of smell, but as it turned out prepubescent girls were better sniffers than boys their age, and pregnant women were no more adept at smelling than other women. Women in general just have a stronger sense of smell. Perhaps it's a vestigial bonus from the dawn of our evolution, when we needed it in courtship, mating, or mothering; or it may be that women have traditionally spent more time around foods and children, ever on the sniff for anything out of order. Because females have often been responsible for initiating mating, smell has been their weapon, lure, and clue.

---

2 **estrogen**: steroid hormones produced chiefly by the ovary and responsible for the development and maintenance of female secondary sex characteristics.

3 **anecdotal evidence**: evidence based not on controlled experiments but on the stories, anecdotes, that people tell.

Looking Back

1. In a small group, discuss which of the following literary techniques Ackerman uses to tell about anosmia—short narrative anecdotes, extended metaphors or analogies, examples, literary allusions or references?

2. Judith R. Birnberg is quoted as saying that being deprived of the sense of smell would be worse than being deprived of the sense of taste? What sense would you least like to lose? Why?

3. One of the most famous literary works of the twentieth century is *Remembrance of Things Past*, a series of seven novels written by the French writer Marcel Proust. In the first volume, the protagonist bites into a madeleine, a small rich cake baked in the shape of a shell and one that instantly reminds him of memories of his childhood. Scan through your own sensory memories for an odor associated with some incident in your own childhood. Be prepared to relate that incident in class.

4. The word *nose* appears in numerous idiomatic expressions in English: "look down one's nose," "keep one's nose clean," "keep one's nose to the grindstone," "put one's nose out of joint," and others. Choose another of the sensory organs—eye or ear—and list as many expressions as you can think of. In class, list those expressions on the board. Then decide, as a class which of the five senses seems to be the richest source.

Looking Into

1. The sense of smell is one of our ways of knowing our world. Keep a diary for one day in which you record all the things you smell. Then try describing one particular odor in detail.

2. Study the appropriate ads in a fashion magazine, noting the names manufacturers have chosen for perfumes or after-shave lotions. Think of a brand name that would be marketable and devise an ad campaign for both radio and print (magazines, newspapers) markets. Record the radio script; present a graphic of the print campaign.

3. Write a paragraph in which you describe what it's like to try to eat one of your favorite foods when your sense of smell is impaired.

On Smells

MICHEL DE MONTAIGNE

Michel de Montaigne was born in 1533 in the family chateau not far from the seaport of Bordeaux in southwestern France. Raised to speak Latin as his mother tongue, he attended school in Bordeaux from the age of six, began studying law, probably in Toulouse, when he was thirteen, and at the age of twenty-one became a counsellor in the Bordeaux *parlement* and, later, a magistrate. In 1571, after some years as a courtier in both Paris and Rouen, he abruptly retired from public life, returned to his chateau, and began his literary life. Montaigne, perhaps the most famous and prolific essayist who ever lived, was the creator of, and the first to name, the essay, which is derived from the French *essai* meaning "trial."

His intent in writing his essays, as he noted in a prefatory statement to his book, was to leave his friends and relatives "some traits of my conditions and humors [character or personality], and by that means preserve more whole, and more life-like, the knowledge they had of me." His first two collections were first published in 1580, when Montaigne was forty-seven. In 1581, under royal pressure, Montaigne became mayor of the town of Bordeaux, but in 1586, he retired permanently to his estates to revise and add to the essays of his first two collections and to complete the third and last volume; it was published in 1588, four years before his death.

Looking Ahead

Writing in the sixteenth century, Montaigne, like Ackerman, also had some things to say about smells. "On Smells" is taken from his first book of essays, and its leisurely pace, its classical allusions, its extensive personal experiences and thoughts are typical of Montaigne's style.

1 It is recorded of some men, among them Alexander the Great, that their sweat exhaled a sweet odor, owing to some rare and extraordinary

property, of which Plutarch[1] and others sought to find out the cause. But the common run of bodies are quite otherwise, and the best state they can be in is to be free from odor. Even the purest breath can be no sweeter or more excellent than to lack all offensive odors, as healthy children do. That is why, says Plautus,

Mulier tum bene olet, ubi nibil olet,[2]

a woman smells most perfectly when she does not smell at all, just as her deeds are said to smell sweetest when they are unnoticed and unheard. And those fine foreign perfumes are rightly regarded as suspicious in those who use them; it may be thought that their purpose is to cover some natural defect in that quarter. Thence proceed those paradoxes of the ancient poets, that to smell sweet is to stink.

Rides nos, Coracine, nil olentes,
malo quam bene olere, nil olere.[3]

And again:

Posthume, non bene olet, qui bene semper olet.[4]

² Yet I very much like to be regaled with good smells, and particularly loathe bad ones, which I can detect at a greater distance than anyone else:

Namque sagacius unus odoror,
Polypus, an gravis birsutis cubet bircus in alis,
quam canis acer ubi lateat sus.[5]

---

1 **Plutarch:** a Greek biographer and philosopher whose great work *Parallel Lives* presents a series of paired biographies of eminent Greeks and Romans. His biography of the Greek general Alexander the Great, for example, was paired with the greatest Roman general, Julius Caesar.

2 **Mulier tum bene olet, ubi nibil olet:** This quotation, translated in the essay itself, is a quotation from *Mostellaria* (The Ghost), a comedy by the Roman playwright Plautus.

3 **Rides . . . nil olere:** "You laugh at me, Coracinus, because I use no scent. I had rather smell of nothing than smell sweet." The quotation is from Martial, a Roman epigrammatist, or writer of short pithy sayings.

4 **Posthume . . . olet:** "Posthumus, the man who always smells sweet does not smell sweet"; this, too, is another epigram from Martial.

5 **Namque . . . lateat sus:** "For my nose is sharper, Polypus, at smelling the rank goatsmell of hairy armpits, than a dog at scenting out hidden game." The quotation is from the Roman lyric poet and satirist, Horace.

3   The simplest and most natural smells seem to me the most pleasant; and this applies chiefly to the ladies. In the heart of barbarism, the women of Scythia[6] are accustomed, after bathing, to powder and plaster their whole body and face with a certain sweet-smelling herb that grows in their country; and when they remove this paint to come to their husbands, they remain both sleek and perfumed.

4   Whatever the odor, it is remarkable how it clings to me, and how prone my skin is to absorb it. He who reproaches nature for failing to furnish man with the means of bringing smells to his nose is wrong, for they bring themselves. But in my case it is my moustache, which is thick, that performs that duty. If I touch it with my gloves or my handkerchief, it holds the scent for the whole day. It betrays the place where I have been. The close, luscious, greedy, long-drawn kisses of youth would adhere to it in the old days, and would remain for several hours afterwards. And yet I do not find myself much prone to epidemic diseases, which are either caught by contact, or arise from the contagion of the air; I have escaped those of my time, of which there have been several varieties in our cities and our armies. We read of Socrates[7] that, though he never left Athens during the many visitations of plague that affected the city, he alone was never the worse for them.

5   Physicians might, I believe, make greater use of scents than they do, for I have often noticed that they cause changes in me, and act on my spirits according to their qualities; which make me agree with the theory that the introduction of incense and perfume into churches, so ancient and widespread a practice among all nations and religions, was for the purpose of raising our spirits, and of exciting and purifying our senses, the better to fit us for contemplation.

6   To form a better opinion of this, I should like to have tried the art of those cooks who are able to blend foreign odors with the flavor of their meats, as was particularly noticed of those in the service of that King of Tunis who landed at Naples in our own day to confer with the Emperor Charles.[8] His meats were stuffed with sweet-smelling herbs at such expense that to dress a peacock and two pheasants in this way cost a hundred

---

6   **Scythia**: a region in southeast Europe near the Don and Dniepper Rivers in present day Ukraine.
7   **Socrates**: Greek philosopher.
8   **Emperor Charles**: Roman emperor and (as Charles I) king of Spain from 1518 until his abdication in 1555; he was the grandson of Ferdinand and Isabella of Spain. Charles's army had defeated the King of Tunis in a decisive battle.

ducats; and when they were carved, not only the banqueting hall but every room in the palace, and even the near-by houses, were filled with a very sweet vapor, which did not disappear for some time afterwards.

7   My chief precaution in choosing my lodgings is to avoid a heavy and unwholesome atmosphere. The affection that I have for those beautiful cities Venice and Paris is lessened by their offensive smells, which arise from the marshes of the former and the mud of the latter.

Looking Back

1. How does Montaigne's technique for writing about smells differ from Ackerman's in "Anosmia"?

2. What does Montaigne say about the theory surrounding the introduction of incense and perfume in churches? What do you think of this theory?

3. In small discussion groups, compare Montaigne's essay with one or two others in this book and make a list of the ways in which the essay form has changed.

Looking Into

1. From this essay what do we discover about Montaigne the man?

2. In the past, students often learned to write by modeling; that is, by copying the style and form of a writer acknowledged to be a master. Choose a topic and in two or three pages emulate Montaigne's style. To determine the elements of Montaigne's style, you may wish to review your answers to questions 1 and 3 in the "Looking Back" section.

3. What must it have been like to live in a time when there were no deodorants or toothpastes, when people did not bathe regularly or attend carefully to personal hygiene, when there was not yet refrigeration or other means of preserving foods and keeping them fresh? The world must have been more alive with smells. Write a letter to a fastidious friend in which you describe some of the smells you might have encountered in an average day had you lived four hundred years ago.

The Man with No Endorphins

JAMES GORMAN

Born in 1949, James Gorman majored in English at Princeton University. In his first job he wrote for the *St. John Valley Times*, a newspaper in Madawaska, Maine. Subsequently, he began writing witty and often irreverent columns for *Discover*, a science magazine. He has also been a contributor of book reviews to the *New York Times Book Review* section, and articles to *The Atlantic* and *Audubon* magazines and to the *New York Times Magazine*. His first book was *First Aid for Hypochondriacs* (1981); his second, *The Man with No Endorphins: and Other Reflections on Science* (1988), is a compilation of articles originally published in *Discover* magazine; his most recent is *The Total Penguin* (1990).

Looking Ahead

In the following title essay from his book, Gorman muses less on the neurochemical phenomena of opiate receptors than on his apparent lack of them, particularly in the kind of stressful situations to which a citizen living in the advanced First World is subjected. Gorman's style is characterized by a wry and self-deprecating wit.

[1] *A* neurochemical vignette: There's a man, running in the rain, wearing loafers, in Baltimore—it's me. I'm not happy. I'm late for a talk on opiate receptors in the brain because I've been in traffic, then in the new Baltimore subway (which I must say works a lot better than my central nervous system), and finally in the rain, risking life and limb and ruining my shoes. I desperately want to learn more about endorphins and enkephalins, the brain's own opiates, which are supposed to ease pain and produce pleasure, but I know I'm going to be late, and probably wet. (I can never remember: Do you stay drier going faster, or standing very straight under the umbrella and taking tiny steps?) My heart is pounding, my anxiety rising, and my toes are damp. One thought is foremost in my mind. I'm thinking: "Where are my endorphins when I need them?"

2   I've always been fond of neurochemistry; a field that brings you the opiates of the brain is hard not to like. But neurochemistry hasn't treated me well. I'm sure some brains manufacture these great chemicals, and that the people who have these brains experience runner's high and other pleasant effects. But as near as I can tell my brain doesn't *do* endorphins. When I run I get shin splints and twisted ankles. The most I've ever gotten out of running, in emotional terms, was a momentary absence of anxiety, which I attributed to complete physical exhaustion. It was O.K., but it wasn't that different from being depressed. Runners tell me I never ran far enough. But I happen to know that earthworms have endorphins. Earthworms don't jog. And if invertebrates don't have to run to be happy, I don't see why a higher (or at least taller) vertebrate like myself should have to.

3   The truth is I'm not even interested in getting high. I'm not greedy. I was happy enough with the mild depression that followed running in the park to continue jogging for years. I stopped only because my twisted ankles refused to heal. What I'm really looking for is absence of pain, a certain kind of pain, which I'll define. There is traditional physical pain: cuts and bruises, having your head chopped off. I'm not talking about that. There is traditional psychological pain: Oedipus and Electra complexes, schizophrenia, anxiety neuroses. I'm not talking about that. I'm talking about another class of pain, which occurs in huge quantities every day in my neighborhood. This kind of pain is caused by computers, customer service personnel at banks, medical insurance and expense account forms, and airline baggage personnel, not to mention airlines. Let's call it First World pain.

4   I know that good people, when their taxes are due or their computers fail, realize that there are people in the world who have schistosomiasis[1] so that it would be incredibly selfish and insensitive to whine about capital gains or the loss of a great sentence when they still get to eat an unconscionably large amount of protein at dinner, which they don't have to share with blood flukes. Unfortunately, a lot of us aren't good people. A lot of us are bad. A lot of us are so wrapped up in our own little First World lives that taxes and computer failure seem, to us, to cause intense pain, to us.

5   Out of this sort of selfishness—I myself pay taxes, and have recently experienced computer failure which induced in me not only extreme pain, but guilt for not curing, or having, schistosomiasis—I went to Baltimore to

---

1 **schistosomiasis**: a tropical and often mortal disease caused when a schistosome—a parasite worm, also called a "blood fluke"—infests the blood.

the talk on brain chemicals. Other reporters, I'm sure, were at the conference to report to the public news that would affect their health and welfare, to educate them. I went because I thought I might learn how to find and use my own endorphins. No such luck. Most of the news was about pain messengers—not the people who bring bills and rejection slips in the mail, but peptides that relay the news of tissue damage to the nerve endings so they can send the news to the brain and the brain can cause the mouth of the person with the tissue damage (i.e., a finger that has had the door of a Coupe de Ville slammed shut on it) to howl in pain and indignation. The first messenger in this system is called bradykinin. Bradykinin, according to Solomon Snyder of Johns Hopkins, whose talk I was late for, is the strongest pain-causing substance there is. Fortunately, bradykinin antagonists have been developed to bind the bradykinin before it gets to the nerve endings. Since bradykinin apparently carries messages about arthritis as well as bruised fingers, the anatagonist could be rubbed on an arthritic knee (this is all speculative) like old-time liniment, and it would scarf up all the bradykinin and stop the pain. What this could mean to millions of pain sufferers is obvious. What it means to me is that, in neurochemistry, sometimes it does make sense to kill the messenger.[2]

6   However, to get back to my own pain, which, sad to say, is the subject of greatest interest to me, I have figured out why endorphins don't work on it. The reason is that human beings were not designed, by evolution, to fill out tax forms, use computers, or fly on commercial airplanes. Now, we weren't designed to play the violin either, as I keep telling a friend of mine when he hauls out his fiddle and starts talking about Paganini.[3] But when it comes to fiddling we do have what biologists call a pre-adaptation: fingers. They didn't evolve for fiddling; they evolved, as we all know, to play the guitar. But if you've got good ones, they can be used to do hot licks on a Guarneri as well as a Gibson.[4] There is, however, no similar pre-adaptation for dealing with the IRS or airline baggage personnel.

---

2   **kill the messenger**: In ancient, and not so ancient, times, the illogical response to bad news was occasionally the killing of the messenger who brought such news.
3   **Paganini**: "Paganini, on the other hand—on both hands in fact—had long spidery fingers, perhaps because of a genetic aberration called Marfan's syndrome. He *was* designed to play the violin"—J.G.
4   **Guarneri . . . Gibson**: Andrea Guarneri (1626-1698), along with his two sons, was a famed Italian violin maker. The Gibson is a brand of guitar favored by rock musicians and others.

7   Skeptics among you may be mumbling that there's this tribe that's known for its incredible patience in hunting the dik-dik,[5] but the dik-dik is a more appealing quarry than an old Samsonite suitcase, and the rain forest is preferable to the baggage carousel, even during fever season. In airports, not only do proselytizers try to convert you to obscure religions (opiates, opiates everywhere)[6] but there are crowds of other people whose endorphins are also failing them, and who, for all you know, are about to pull Uzi submachine guns from under their coats and relieve their own pain by causing you to have some. Faced with this situation, the brain is at a loss. It doesn't recognize the pain you're undergoing as something endorphins can take care of, so it lets them sleep and leaves you to fend for yourself, unopiated.

8   It can be done, assuming, of course, that sooner or later the luggage stumbles through those flaps and the "There's-my-suitcase" neuron lights up. Sometimes that doesn't happen. And now we come to the airline personnel. At an earlier point in my life, when I was in the process of trying to summon up my endorphins, or at least distract myself, by crude means like exercise, I also tried breathing. To be precise, I tried Lamaze, not while giving birth, but in stressful situations. It didn't work, but it did provide me with a tale whose moral is this: Ask not what your endorphins can do for you,[7] but take your fly rod on the airplane with you.

9   One day a few months before the birth of our second child I was having a fit about some frustrating aspect of home improvement. My wife suggested to me that if Lamaze could get a woman through childbirth, maybe it could get a man through a conversation with an electrician. I tried it. I was never able to find the electrician, and the work is still not done, but I did use controlled breathing to call an airline and get information on flights to Great Falls, Montana. I stayed on the telephone, and kept my voice down for the whole twenty minutes, without benefit of medication.

10   I then went to Great Falls, Montana, with my wife, niece, first child, incipient second child, and last but (I'm ashamed to say) not least, my prized

---

5 **dik-dik**: an extremely small African antelope, so named in mimicry of its cry.
6 **religions (opiates, opiates everywhere)**: an allusion both to Karl Marx's dismissal of religion as "the opium of the people," and, perhaps, to a line from Coleridge's famous poem, "The Rime of the Ancient Mariner"—"Water, water, everywhere / Nor any drop to drink."
7 **"ask not what your endorphins can do for you**: an allusion to a famous line in John F. Kennedy's Inaugural Address—"ask not what your country can do for you; ask what you can do for your country."

fly rod. We were going to hike, fish, and look at dinosaur bones. You know what happened. I checked the fly rod and the airline lost it. I stood at the baggage counter, breathing—in, out, in, out, managing the pain—and filled out a form. (Have I emphasized forms as a source of pain?) We went to the hotel, and four days later I was told, in a telephone conversation (my wife was next to me with a cup of cracked ice, coaching me on my breathing), that the rod had been retrieved from Angola and sent to Kalispell, Montana, on the other side of the continental divide from the Many Glacier Hotel, to which I had been sent. The man from the airline, in the single most infuriating conversation I've ever had, replied to my calm, reasoned statement that I wasn't in Kalispell by telling me that that's where I should have been. There were more frequent flights to that airport, and, he said to me, as I stood there rodless and dumbfounded, the fishing was better over there.

¹¹   I wasn't arrested for what I said into the telephone, but I could have been. Frankly, I don't see why, if these endorphins are going to be so fickle, we can't have more doctors around. When you're all worked up, there's nothing like general anaesthesia. I did eventually get the fly rod back, just as we were about to leave to go dig dinosaurs, and I used it a few more times that summer, back East. Optimists will see in this resolution a benevolent, smiling universe. Realists will see that the paragraph isn't over yet. On my last day of fishing (I didn't know it was my last day of fishing), I put the fly rod on the top of the car and, due to some faulty synapses, drove off. I heard a rattle, and in the side mirror I saw my rod leap into the air, do a barrel roll, and dive under the wheels of a pickup truck. There was nothing left but splinters. My endorphins, as usual, were nowhere to be seen.

Looking Back

1. In the opening paragraph, what indications are there of Gorman's humorous tone?

2. When this book was reviewed in the *New York Times Book Review* section, the reviewer was Diane Ackerman, whose essay on anosmia appears in this section. In small groups, analyze the style of both authors and indicate what literary characteristics they share; then determine what characteristics are peculiar to Gorman.

3. Montaigne asserted that his reason for writing his *essais* was to convey "some traits of my conditions and humors, and by that means preserve more whole, and more life-like, the knowledge [my friends and family] had of me." What personal information about himself does Gorman give directly? What can you infer?

4. Gorman links his thesis—that, at least for him, opiate receptors don't appear to work in all situations—to instances limited to First World residents: filling out tax forms, using computers, flying on commercial airlines. Relate in class a First World situation that caused you particular pain.

Looking Into

1. In a one- to two-page essay, defend the inclusion of Gorman's essay in a unit that focuses on science and technology.

2. In a personal letter of about two pages, tell a friend or relative about a particularly frustrating experience that occurred to you—perhaps one that you recalled for question 4 above.

3. Pain serves a useful function. Write a short paper in which you describe how an inability or reduced ability to perceive pain might be dangerous.

The Scribe

PRIMO LEVI
(translated by Raymond Rosenthal)

Primo Levi was born in 1919 in Turin, an industrial city and the capital of Piedmont, a region in northwestern Italy. After completing a classical high school education, and despite the anti-Semitic laws which prevented Jews from attending institutions of high learning, Levi enrolled in the University of Turin as a chemistry major, graduating with the highest honors in 1941. Levi worked in the laboratory of a Milan pharmaceutical factory until 1943, when Mussolini's government collapsed and the Nazis occupied northern Italy. Along with ten of his friends, Levi fled to the mountains, forming a guerilla band and hoping to join the larger resistance movement. When the group was betrayed in December 1943, Levi identified himself as "an Italian citizen of the Jewish race" and was turned over to the Nazi SS. In February 1944, he was transported to Auschwitz, a concentration camp he survived because of physical strength, his chemistry degree—he was eventually assigned to work in a chemical laboratory—and, above all, luck.

After the war Levi returned to Turin, taking a position as a chemist specializing in paints, enamels, and synthetic resins. At the same time, he wrote a memoir of his camp experiences, *Survival in Auschwitz: The Nazi Assault on Humanity* (1947; American translation, 1961). In 1958, the success of this republished book encouraged Levi to write a sequel: *The Reawakening* (1963; American translation, 1965). Other Levi books translated into English include a collection of autobiographical essays, *The Periodic Table* (1975; American translation, 1984), in which a particular incident or person is linked to one of the chemical elements; a collection of stories, *Moments of Reprieve* (1981; American translation, 1986); and an epic novel *If Not Now, When?* (1982; American translation, 1985). When Primo Levi died in 1987, he was regarded as one of the world's most important and gifted writers.

Looking Ahead

Levi was more than 65 years old when he purchased a word processor. In the following essay, taken from a book of essays titled *Other People's Trades* (1985; American translation, 1989), Levi muses on the wonders of this electronic marvel, his early approaches to mastering it, its similarity to a supernatural Jewish being, and his ultimate satisfaction at having mastered it.

[1]   Several years ago, in September 1984, I bought myself a word processor, that is, a writing tool that returns automatically at the end of a line and makes it possible to insert, cancel, instantaneously change words or entire sentences; in brief, makes it possible to achieve in one leap a finished document, clean, without insertions or corrections. Certainly I'm not the first writer who has decided to take the plunge. Only a year earlier I would have been considered reckless or a snob; today no longer, so fast does electronic time run.

[2]   I hasten to add two clarifications. In the first place: whoever wants to or must write can very well continue with his ballpoint or typewriter: my gadget is a luxury, it is amusing, even exciting, but superfluous. Second, to reassure the uncertain and laymen, I myself was, indeed still am, as I'm writing here on the screen, a layman. My ideas as to what takes place behind the screen are vague. At first contact, this ignorance of mine humiliated me profoundly; a young man rushed in to reassure me and he has guided me, and to start with he said to me: You belong to the austere generation of humanists who still insist on wanting to understand the world around them. This demand has become absurd: leave everything to habit, and your discomfort will disappear. Consider: do you know or do you think you know how the telephone and television work? And yet you use them every day. And with the exception of a few learned men how many know how their hearts and kidneys work?

[3]   Despite this admonition, the first collision with the apparatus was filled with anguish, the anguish of the unknown which for many years I had no longer felt. The computer was delivered to me accompanied by a profusion of manuals; I tried to study them before touching the keys, and I felt lost. It seemed to me that although they were apparently written in Italian, they were in an unknown language; indeed, a mocking and misleading language in which well-known words like "open," "close," and "quit" are used in unusual ways. To be sure, there is a glossary that strives to define them, but proceeds in an opposite direction to that of common dictionaries: these define abstruse terms by having recourse to familiar terms; the glossary would give a new meaning to deceptively familiar terms by having recourse to abstruse terms, and the effect is devastating. How much better it would have been to invent a decisively new terminology for these new things! But once more my young friend intervened and pointed out to me that trying to learn how to use a computer with the help of manuals is as foolish as trying to learn how to swim by reading a treatise

without going into the water; indeed, he specified, without even knowing what water is, having heard only vague talk about it.

4   So I set about working on two fronts: that is, verifying the instructions of the manuals on the equipment, and immediately the legend of the golem[1] came to mind. It is told that centuries ago a magician-rabbi built a clay automaton with Herculean strength[2] and blind obedience so that it would defend the Jews of Prague from the pogroms,[3] but it remained inert, inanimate, until its maker slipped into its mouth a roll of parchment on which was written a verse from the Torah. At that, the clay golem became a prompt and wise servant: it roamed the streets and kept good guard, but turned to stone again when the parchment was removed. I asked myself whether the builders of my apparatus happened to know this strange story (they certainly are cultivated and even witty people): the computer actually has a mouth, crooked, slightly open in a mechanical grimace. Until I introduce the program floppy disk, the computer doesn't compute anything, it is a lifeless metallic box; but, when I turn on the switch a polite luminous signal appears on the small screen: this, in the language of my personal golem, means that he is avid to gulp down the floppy disk. When I have satisfied him, he hums softly, purring like a contented cat, comes alive, and immediately displays his character: he is industrious, helpful, severe with my mistakes, obstinate, and capable of many miracles which I still don't know about and which intrigue me.

5   Provided he's fed the proper program, he can run a warehouse, or an archive, translate a function in his diagram, compile histograms, even play chess: all undertakings that for the moment do not interest me, indeed, make me melancholy and morose, like the pig who was offered pearls. He can also draw, and this for me is a drawback, of the opposite sort: I hadn't drawn anything since elementary school and now, having available a servomechanism[4] which fabricates for me, custom-made, the images that I cannot draw, and at a command even prints them right in front of my nose,

---

1 **golem**: in Jewish folklore, a being who is artificially created and endowed with life by supernatural means.
2 **Herculean strength**: In Greek mythology, Hercules was the son of Zeus and the mortal Alcmene; his extraordinary strength and courage enabled him to perform twelve difficult labors demanded by Hera, Zeus's wife.
3 **pogroms**: a Russian word meaning "like thunder" and referring to the organized and often official massacres or persecution of minorities, especially the Jews.
4 **servomechanism**: a feedback system usually consisting of a sensing element, an amplifier, and a motor used in a mechanical device.

amuses me to an indecent extent and distracts me from more proper uses. I must do violence to myself to "leave" the drawing program and go back to writing.

6   I have noticed that writing in this way one tends to be prolix. The labor of the past, when stone was carved, led to the "lapidary" style:[5] here the opposite takes place, the manual labor is almost nil, and if one doesn't control oneself one inclines to a wasteful expenditure of words; but there is a providential counter and one must keep one's eye on it.

7   If I now analyze my initial anxiety, I realize that it was in great part illogical: it contained an old fear of those who write, the fear that the unique, inestimable text worked at so hard, which will give you eternal fame, might be stolen or end up in a manhole. Here you write, the words appear neatly on the screen, well aligned, but they are shadows: they are immaterial, deprived of the reassuring support of the paper. The written word speaks out; the screen doesn't; when you're satisfied with the text you "put it on disk," where it becomes invisible. Is it still there, absconding to some little corner of the memory disk, or did you destroy it with some mistaken move? Only after days of experience *in corpore vile* (that is, on false texts, not created but copied), you become convinced that the catastrophe of the lost text was foreseen by the talented gnomes who designed the computer: the destruction of a text requires a maneuver which has been made deliberately complicated, and during which the apparatus itself warns you: "Watch out, you're about to commit suicide."

8   Some twenty-five years ago I wrote a not-very-serious short story in which after many deontological hesitations,[6] a professional poet decides to buy an electronic Versifier and successfully delegates to it all his activity. My apparatus for the time being does not do as much, but it lends itself in an excellent fashion to the composing of verses, because it permits me to make numerous changes without the page looking dirty or disorderly, and reduces to a minimum the manual effort of writing: "So one observes in me the counterpart." A literary friend of mine objects that in this way one loses the noble joy of the philologist[7] intent on reconstructing, through successive erasures and corrections, the itinerary which leads to the perfection of Leopardi's *Infinite*:[8] he's right, but one can't have everything.

---

5   **"lapidary" style**: a style, Levi ironically implies, that would refer to writing fine enough to be engraved in stone (in Latin, *lapis* means "stone").
6   **deontological hesitations**: ethical hesitations.
7   **philologist**: one who studies the language of literature.
8   **Leopardi's *Infinite***: Giacomo Leopardi (1798-1837) was an Italian poet; *Infinite* was one of his most famous lyrical poems.

9   As far as I'm concerned, since I've put bridle, bit, and saddle on my computer, the tedium of being a Dinornis,[9] the survivor of an extinct species, has become attenuated in me: the gloom of being "a survivor of his own time"[10] has almost disappeared. The Greeks said about an uncultured man: "He doesn't know how to read or swim"; today one would have to add, "Nor how to use a computer"; I still don't use it well, I'm not an expert, and I don't know if I ever will be, but I am no longer illiterate. And besides, it is a pleasure to be able to add an item to one's list of memorable "firsts": the first time you saw the sea, passed the border, kissed a woman, gave life to a golem.

Looking Back

1. The *Oxford English Dictionary* gives several definitions for a scribe: "a writer"; "one who writes at another's dictation"; "a copyist or transcriber of manuscripts." By titling his essay "The Scribe," is Levi being ironic? You might begin to think about this question by, first, determining who is the scribe—Levi and/or the machine.

2. What stages does Levi go through before he is comfortable with his mechanical "apparatus"?

3. In a small group, discuss what advantages and what disadvantages Levi sees in his word processor. Then compare your own experiences with those of Levi.

4. Why might Levi personify his word processor as a golem?

5. Levi's young friend points out that trying to learn how to use a computer by reading the manual is as foolish as trying to learn how to swim by reading a book without going into the water. Discuss other activities or skills that can only be learned by doing.

---

9 **Dinornis**: an extinct bird of great size, the remains of which have been found in New Zealand.
10 **"a survivor of his own time"**: Levi was interned during World War II in Auschwitz.

Looking Into

1. In an essay of two or three pages, describe your own experiences of becoming comfortable with a new electronic marvel.

2. In his reference to the golem, Levi uses a literary device known as personification—giving an inanimate object human (or in this case, superhuman) characteristics. Choose an object—such as an electric toothbrush, a CD player, a calculator—and in a one-page description personify that object.

3. Write a short page in which you describe how you were able to master a new skill only by doing it, and not by just reading about it.

Looking Around

1. Of the seven writers represented in this section, four are not formally trained as scientists: Boorstin, Ackerman, Montaigne, and Gorman. What personal qualities do they possess that make them effective writers about science? Describe in two or three paragraphs.

2. Whether its focus is literature, history, personal experiences, or science, well-written nonfiction is vivid and concrete. Of the three scientists—Asimov, Margulis/Sagan, and Levi—whose writing best meets the standards of vividness and concreteness? Write a paper in which you support your opinion by citing examples from the essay.

3. In 1942, one of the directors of the National Academy of Sciences asked leading scientists which of eleven fields of scientific study were the most important for the future. Overwhelmingly, the first choice of respondents was studies dealing with man himself—namely human behavior, human biology, and medical problems—and the second or third place choice was future sources of energy. If that same questionnaire were sent today, do you think the answers would be the same? Explain why or why not in a brief essay.

4. Technology often advances faster than man's ability to control the products of invention. Do you think it would be wise to call a halt to scientific activity until some standards of social control are established? Why or why not? Explain in a short paper.

5. What are some ways in which science and technology have contributed to the improvement of the human condition? How have humanity's health, welfare, and knowledge benefitted from scientific knowledge? Write a brief paper in which you explain your position.

PART 6
Values

—∿—

*A*ll our progress is an unfolding, like the vegetable bud. You have first an instinct, then an opinion, then a knowledge, as the plant has root, bud, and fruit. Trust the instinct to the end, though you can render no reason. It is vain to hurry it. By trusting it to the end, it shall ripen into truth and you shall know why you believe.

Ralph Waldo Emerson from "Intellect"

Values are the truths that people believe are important, the ideals or principles that they live by. Sometimes values are enshrined in documents ("We hold these truths to be self-evident. . . ."), sometimes embodied in books of wisdom such as the Bible or Koran, and frequently contained in the hearts and minds of ordinary people. The authors in this section all proclaim their values in persuasive writing.

Paul Fussell argues in "Thank God for the Atom Bomb" that the decision to drop bombs on Hiroshima and Nagasaki in 1945 was ultimately a humane one. In the essay "In Praise of Sunshine Patriots," Garrison Keillor writes that indifference to the American revolutionary cause, particularly on the part of New Yorkers, resulted in the kind of country in which he prefers to live. In "Do He Have Your Number, Mr. Jeffrey?" Gayle Pemberton writes of the values that shaped her life, values learned in spite of the white world of Los Angeles and the movies.

Peter Mayle, in "I'll be Suing You," comments on the proliferation of lawyers and what this means for us all. In "The Glass Half Empty," columnist Anna Quindlen muses on the kind of life her daughter will face as she grows up in a "two-tiered" world.

Thank God for the Atom Bomb

PAUL FUSSELL

The son of an attorney, Paul Fussell was born in Pasadena, California, in 1924. During World War II, he fought with the forty-fifth Infantry Division in Europe; in August, 1945, Fussell was in the process of being sent from Europe to take part in the imminent invasion of Japan. After the war, Fussell finished his undergraduate work at Pomona College, California, and then attended Harvard University where he earned both his M.A. and his Ph.D. in English. Fussell has taught at Connecticut College, Rutgers University, and at the University of Pennsylvania. He has traveled widely in Europe, the Caribbean, the Near East, the Soviet Union, the south Pacific, India, and Asia. Fussell is the author of several books of nonfiction: *Abroad: British Literary Traveling between the Wars* (1980); *The Great War and Modern Memory* (1975), a National Book Award winner; and *Class: A Guide Through the American Status System* (1983), a trenchant examination of America's class structure. His three collections of essays— *The Boy Scout Handbook and Other Observations* (1982), *Thank God for the Atom Bomb and Other Essays* (1988), and *Bad: or The Dumbing of America* (1991)—are wittily provocative. Fussell is also the editor of *The Norton Book of Travel* (1987).

Looking Ahead

In this essay Paul Fussell writes about one of the most far-reaching moral decisions ever made by a nation—the decision by the United States to drop two atom bombs on Japan in 1945 in order to end World War II quickly, a decision that is still being debated. As you read, jot down the main points Fussell makes.

1     $\mathcal{M}$any years ago in New York I saw on the side of a bus a whiskey ad I've remembered all this time. It's been for me a model of the short poem, and indeed I've come upon few short poems subsequently that ex-

hibited more poetic talent. The ad consisted of two eleven-syllable lines of "verse," thus:

> In life, experience is the great teacher.
> In Scotch, Teacher's is the great experience.

For present purposes we must jettison the second line (licking our lips, to be sure, as it disappears), leaving the first to register a principle whose banality suggests that it enshrines a most useful truth. I bring up the matter because, writing on the forty-second anniversary of the atom-bombing of Hiroshima and Nagasaki,[1] I want to consider something suggested by the long debate about the ethics, if any, of that ghastly affair. Namely, the importance of experience, sheer, vulgar experience, in influencing, if not determining, one's views about that use of the atom bomb.

The experience I'm talking about is having to come to grips, face to face, with an enemy who designs your death. The experience is common to those in the marines and the infantry and even the line navy, to those, in short, who fought the Second World War mindful always that their mission was, as they were repeatedly assured, "to close with the enemy and destroy him." *Destroy*, notice: not hurt, frighten, drive away, or capture. I think there's something to be learned about that war, as well as about the tendency of historical memory unwittingly to resolve ambiguity and generally clean up the premises, by considering the way testimonies emanating from real war experience tend to complicate attitudes about the most cruel ending of that most cruel war.

"What did you do in the Great War, Daddy?" The recruiting poster deserves ridicule and contempt, of course, but here its question is embarrassingly relevant, and the problem is one that touches on the dirty little secret of social class in America. Arthur T. Hadley said recently that those for whom the use of the A-bomb was "wrong' seem to be implying "that it would have been better to allow thousands on thousands of American and Japanese infantrymen to die in honest hand-to-hand combat on the beaches than to drop those two bombs." People holding such views, he notes, "do not come from the ranks of society that produce infantrymen or pilots." And there's an eloquence problem: most of those with firsthand ex-

---

1 **forty-second anniversary . . . Nagasaki:** An atom bomb was dropped on the city of Hiroshima August 6 and on the city of Nagasaki August 9, 1945. Japan surrendered August 15.

perience of the war at its worst were not elaborately educated people. Relatively inarticulate, most have remained silent about what they know. That is, few of those destined to be blown to pieces if the main Japanese islands had been invaded went on to become our most effective men of letters or impressive ethical theorists or professors of contemporary history or of international law. The testimony of experience has tended to come from rough diamonds—James Jones[2] is an example—who went through the war as enlisted men in the infantry or the Marine Corps.

4   Anticipating objections from those without such experience, in his book *WWII* Jones carefully prepares for his chapter on the A-bombs by detailing the plans already in motion for the infantry assaults on the home islands of Kyushu (thirteen divisions scheduled to land in November 1945) and ultimately Honshu (sixteen divisions scheduled for March 1946). Planners of the invasion assumed that it would require a full year, to November 1946, for the Japanese to be sufficiently worn down by land-combat attrition to surrender. By that time, one million American casualties was the expected price. Jones observes that the forthcoming invasion of Kyushu "was well into its collecting and stockpiling stages before the war ended." (The island of Saipan was designated a main ammunition and supply base for the invasion, and if you go there today you can see some of the assembled stuff still sitting there.) "The assault troops were chosen and already in training," Jones reminds his readers, and he illuminates by the light of experience what this meant:

> What it must have been like to some old-timer buck sergeant or staff sergeant who had been through Guadalcanal or Bougainville or the Philippines,[3] to stand on some beach and watch this huge war machine beginning to stir and move all around him and know that he very likely had survived this far only to fall dead on the dirt of Japan's home islands, hardly bears thinking about.

Another bright enlisted man, this one an experienced marine destined for the assault on Honshu, adds his testimony. Former Pfc. E. B. Sledge, author

---

2   **James Jones** (1921–1977): American novelist and author of *From Here to Eternity* and *The Thin Red Line*, both about soldiers before and during World War II.

3   **Guadalcanal or Bougainville or the Philippines:** sites of fierce and bloody battles in the Pacific. Guadalcanal and Bougainville are in the Solomon Islands. Marines landed on Guadalcanal August 7, 1942.

of the splendid memoir *With the Old Breed at Peleliu and Okinawa,* noticed at the time that the fighting grew "more vicious the closer we got to Japan," with the carnage of Iwo Jima and Okinawa[4] worse than what had gone before. He points out that

> what we had *experienced* [my emphasis] in fighting the Japs (pardon the expression) on Peleliu and Okinawa caused us to formulate some very definite opinions that the invasion . . . would be a ghastly bloodletting. . . . It would shock the American public and the world. [Every Japanese] soldier, civilian, woman, and child would fight to the death with whatever weapons they had, rifle, grenade, or bamboo spear.

The Japanese pre-invasion patriotic song, "One Hundred Million Souls for the Emperor," says Sledge, "meant just that." Universal national kamikaze[5] was the point. One kamikaze pilot, discouraged by his unit's failure to impede the Americans very much despite the bizarre casualties it caused, wrote before diving his plane onto an American ship, "I see the war situation becoming more desperate. All Japanese must become soldiers and die for the Emperor." Sledge's First Marine Division was to land close to the Yokosuka Naval Base, "one of the most heavily defended sectors of the island." The marines were told, he recalls, that

> due to the strong beach defenses, caves, tunnels, and numerous Jap suicide torpedo boats and manned mines, few Marines in the first five assault waves would get ashore alive—my company was scheduled to be in the first and second waves. The veterans in the outfit felt we had already run out of luck anyway. . . . We viewed the invasion with complete resignation that we would be killed—either on the beach or inland.

And the invasion was going to take place: there's no question about that. It was not theoretical or merely rumored in order to scare the Japanese. By

---

4 **Iwo Jima and Okinawa:** U.S. forces landed on Iwo Jima on February 9 and on Okinawa, April 1, 1945. Five thousand marines were killed on Iwo Jima and eleven thousand on Okinawa.
5 **kamikaze:** pilot who was assigned to dive an airplane onto a target, often a ship; also, the plane, which contained explosives.

July 10, 1945, the prelanding naval and aerial bombardment of the coast had begun, and the battleships *Iowa, Missouri, Wisconsin,* and *King George V* were steaming up and down the coast, softening it up with their sixteen-inch shells.

5   On the other hand, John Kenneth Galbraith[6] is persuaded that the Japanese would have surrendered surely by November without an invasion. He thinks the A-bombs were unnecessary and unjustified because the war was ending anyway. The A-bombs meant, he says, "a difference, at most, of two or three weeks." But at the time, with no indication that surrender was on the way, the kamikazes were sinking American vessels, the *Indianapolis* was sunk (880 men killed), and Allied casualties were running to over 7,000 per week. "Two or three weeks," says Galbraith. Two weeks more means 14,000 more killed and wounded, three weeks more, 21,000. Those weeks mean the world if you're one of those thousands or related to one of them. During the time between the dropping of the Nagasaki bomb on August 9 and the actual surrender on the 15th, the war pursued its accustomed course: on the 12th of August eight captured American fliers were executed (heads chopped off); the fifty-first United States submarine, *Bonefish,* was sunk (all aboard drowned); the destroyer *Callaghan* went down, the seventieth to be sunk, and the Destroyer Escort *Underhill* was lost. That's a bit of what happened in six days of the two or three weeks posited by Galbraith. What did he do in the war? He worked in the Office of Price Administration in Washington. I don't demand that he experience having his ass shot off. I merely note that he didn't.

6   Likewise, the historian Michael Sherry, author of a recent book on the rise of the American bombing mystique, *The Creation of Armageddon,* argues that we didn't delay long enough between the test explosion in New Mexico and the mortal explosions in Japan. More delay would have made possible deeper moral considerations and perhaps laudable second thoughts and restraint. "The risks of delaying the bomb's use," he says, "would have been small—not the thousands of casualties expected of invasion but only a few days or weeks of relatively routine operations." While the mass murders represented by these "relatively routine operations" were enacting, Michael Sherry was safe at home. Indeed, when the bombs were dropped he was going on eight months old, in danger only of falling out of his pram. In speaking thus of Galbraith and Sherry, I'm aware

---

6 **John Kenneth Galbraith** (b. 1908): American economist.

of the offensive implications *ad hominem*. But what's at stake in an infantry assault is so entirely unthinkable to those without the experience of one, or several, or many, even if they possess very wide-ranging imaginations and warm sympathies, that experience is crucial in this case.

7   In general, the principle is, the farther from the scene of horror, the easier the talk. One young combat naval officer close to the action wrote home in the fall of 1943, just before the marines underwent the agony of Tarawa:[7] "When I read that we will fight the Japs for years if necessary and will sacrifice hundreds of thousands if we must, I always like to check from where he's talking: it's seldom out here." That was Lieutenant (j.g.) John F. Kennedy. And Winston Churchill, with an irony perhaps too broad and easy, noted in Parliament that the people who preferred invasion to A-bombing seemed to have "no intention of proceeding to the Japanese front themselves."

8   A remoteness from experience like Galbraith's and Sherry's, and a similar rationalistic abstraction from actuality, seem to motivate the reaction of an anonymous reviewer of William Manchester's *Goodbye Darkness: A Memoir of the Pacific War* for *The New York Review of Books*. The reviewer naturally dislikes Manchester's still terming the enemy Nips or Japs, but what really shakes him (her?) is this passage of Manchester's:

> After Biak the enemy withdrew to deep caverns. Rooting them out became a bloody business which reached its ultimate horrors in the last months of the war. You think of the lives which would have been lost in an invasion of Japan's home islands—a staggering number of Americans but millions more of Japanese—and you thank God for the atomic bomb.

Thank God for the atom bomb. From this, "one recoils," says the reviewer. One does, doesn't one?

9   And not just a staggering number of Americans would have been killed in the invasion. Thousands of British assault troops would have been destroyed too, the anticipated casualties from the almost 200,000 men in the six divisions (the same number used to invade Normandy) assigned to invade the Malay Peninsula on September 9. Aimed at the reconquest of Singapore, this operation was expected to last until about March 1946—that is, seven more months of infantry fighting. "But for the atomic bombs," a

---

7   **Tarawa:** island in the Pacific.

British observer intimate with the Japanese defenses notes, "I don't think we would have stood a cat in hell's chance. We would have been murdered in the biggest massacre of the war. They would have annihilated the lot of us."

[10] The Dutchman Laurens van der Post had been a prisoner of the Japanese for three and a half years. He and thousands of his fellows, enfeebled by beriberi and pellagra, were being systematically starved to death, the Japanese rationalizing this treatment not just because the prisoners were white men but because they had allowed themselves to be captured at all and were therefore moral garbage. In the summer of 1945 Field Marshal Terauchi issued a significant order: at the moment the Allies invaded the main islands, all prisoners were to be killed by the prison-camp commanders. But thank God that did not happen. When the A-bombs were dropped, van der Post recalls, "This cataclysm I was certain would make the Japanese feel that they could withdraw from the war without dishonor, because it would strike them, as it had us in the silence of our prison night, as something supernatural."

[11] In an exchange of views not long ago in *The New York Review of Books*, Joseph Alsop and David Joravsky set forth the by now familiar argument on both sides of the debate about the "ethics" of the bomb. It's not hard to guess which side each chose once you know that Alsop experienced capture by the Japanese at Hong Kong early in 1942, while Joravsky came into no deadly contact with the Japanese: a young, combat-innocent soldier, he was on his way to the Pacific when the war ended. The editors of *The New York Review* gave the debate the tendentious title "Was the Hiroshima Bomb Necessary?" surely an unanswerable question (unlike "Was It Effective?") and one precisely indicating the intellectual difficulties involved in imposing *ex post facto*[8] a rational and even a genteel ethics on this event. In arguing the acceptability of the bomb, Alsop focuses on the power and fanaticism of War Minister Anami, who insisted that Japan fight to the bitter end, defending the main islands with the same techniques and tenacity employed at Iwo and Okinawa. Alsop concludes: "Japanese surrender could never have been obtained, at any rate without the honor-satisfying bloodbath envisioned by . . . Anami, if the hideous destruction of Hiroshima and Nagasaki had not finally galvanized the peace advocates into tearing up the entire Japanese book of rules." The Japanese plan to deploy the undefeated bulk of their ground forces, over two million men, plus 10,000

---

8 **ex post facto:** Latin for something done or made after the fact.

kamikaze planes, plus the elderly and all the women and children with sharpened spears they could muster in a suicidal defense makes it absurd, says Alsop, to "hold the common view, by now hardly challenged by anyone, that the decision to drop the two bombs on Japan was wicked in itself, and that President Truman and all others who joined in making or who [like Robert Oppenheimer][9] assented to this decision shared in the wickedness." And in explanation of "the two bombs," Alsop adds: "The true, climactic, and successful effort of the Japanese peace advocates . . . did not begin in deadly earnest until *after* the second bomb had destroyed Nagasaki. The Nagasaki bomb was thus the trigger to all the developments that led to peace." At this time the army was so unready for surrender that most looked forward to the forthcoming invasion as an indispensable opportunity to show their mettle, enthusiastically agreeing with the army spokesman who reasoned early in 1945, "Since the retreat from Guadalcanal, the Army has had little opportunity to engage the enemy in land battles. But when we meet in Japan proper, our Army will demonstrate its invincible superiority." This possibility foreclosed by the Emperor's post-A-bomb surrender broadcast, the shocked, disappointed officers of one infantry battalion, anticipating a professionally impressive defense of the beaches, killed themselves in the following numbers: one major, three captains, ten first lieutenants, and twelve second lieutenants.

[12] David Joravsky, now a professor of history at Northwestern, argued on the other hand that those who decided to use the A-bombs on cities betray defects of "reason and self-restraint." It all needn't have happened, he says, "if the U.S. government had been willing to take a few more days and to be a bit more thoughtful in opening up the age of nuclear warfare." I've already noted what "a few more days" would mean to the luckless troops and sailors on the spot, and as to being thoughtful when "opening up the age of nuclear warfare," of course no one was focusing on anything as portentous as that, which reflects a historian's tidy hindsight. The U.S. government was engaged not in that sort of momentous thing but in ending the war conclusively, as well as irrationally Remembering Pearl Harbor with a vengeance. It didn't know then what everyone knows now about leukemia and various kinds of carcinoma and birth defects. Truman was not being sly or coy when he insisted that the bomb was "only another weapon." History, as Eliot's "Gerontion"[10] notes,

---

9 **Robert Oppenheimer** (1904–1967): American physicist who led the Manhattan Project, an atomic bomb research and development center in Los Alamos, New Mexico.

10 **Eliot's "Gerontion":** T. S. Eliot's poem, "Gerontion," written in 1920, is about old age and the necessity for salvation from the world's spiritual malaise.

... has many cunning passages, contrived corridors
And issues, deceives with whispering ambitions,
Guides us by vanities. . . .
                              Think
Neither fear nor courage saves us. Unnatural vices
Are fathered by our heroism. Virtues
Are forced upon us by our impudent crimes.

Understanding the past requires pretending that you don't know the pre-sent. It requires feeling its own pressure on your pulses without any *ex post facto* illumination. That's a harder thing to do than Joravsky seems to think.

[13] The Alsop-Joravsky debate, reduced to a collision between experience and theory, was conducted with a certain civilized respect for evidence. Not so the way the scurrilous, agitprop[11] *New Statesman* conceives those justifying the dropping of the bomb and those opposing. They are, on the one hand, says Bruce Page, "the imperialist class-forces acting through Harry Truman" and, on the other, those representing "the humane, demo-cratic virtues"—in short, "fascists" as opposed to "populists." But ironi-cally the bomb saved the lives not of any imperialists but only of the low and humble, the quintessentially democratic huddled masses—the con-scripted enlisted men manning the fated invasion divisions and the sailors crouching at their gun mounts in terror of the kamikazes. When the war ended, Bruce Page was nine years old. For someone of his experience, phrases like "imperialist class forces" come easily, and the issues look per-fectly clear.

[14] He's not the only one to have forgotten, if he ever knew, the unspeak-able savagery of the Pacific war. The dramatic postwar Japanese success at hustling and merchandising and tourism has (happily, in many ways) ef-faced for most people the vicious assault context in which the Hiroshima horror should be viewed. It is easy to forget, or not to know, what Japan was like before it was first destroyed, and then humiliated, tamed, and constitutionalized by the West. "Implacable, treacherous, barbaric"—those were Admiral Halsey's characterizations of the enemy, and at the time few facing the Japanese would deny that they fit to a T. One remembers the captured American airmen—the lucky ones who escaped decapitation—

---

11 **agitprop:** propagandistic. The word is formed from the Russian *agitatsiya*, meaning "agitation," and *propaganda*.

locked for years in packing crates. One remembers the gleeful use of bayonets on civilians, on nurses and the wounded, in Hong Kong and Singapore. Anyone who actually fought in the Pacific recalls the Japanese routinely firing on medics, killing the wounded (torturing them first, if possible), and cutting off the penises of the dead to stick in the corpses' mouths. The degree to which Americans register shock and extraordinary shame about the Hiroshima bomb correlates closely with lack of information about the Pacific war.

15   And of course the brutality was not just on one side. There was much sadism and cruelty, undeniably racist, on ours. (It's worth noting in passing how few hopes blacks could entertain of desegregation and decent treatment when the U.S. Army itself slandered the enemy as "the little brown Jap.") Marines and soldiers could augment their view of their own invincibility by possessing a well-washed Japanese skull, and very soon after Guadalcanal it was common to treat surrendering Japanese as handy rifle targets. Plenty of Japanese gold teeth were extracted—some from still living mouths—with Marine Corps Ka-Bar knives, and one of E. B. Sledge's fellow marines went around with a cut-off Japanese hand. When its smell grew too offensive and Sledge urged him to get rid of it, he defended his possession of this trophy thus: "How many Marines you reckon that hand pulled the trigger on?" (It's hardly necessary to observe that a soldier in the ETO[12] would probably not have dealt that way with a German or Italian—that is, a "white person's"—hand.) In the Pacific the situation grew so public and scandalous that in September 1942, the Commander in Chief of the Pacific Fleet issued this order: "No part of the enemy's body may be used as a souvenir. Unit Commanders will take stern disciplinary action. . . ."

16   Among Americans it was widely held that the Japanese were really subhuman, little yellow beasts, and popular imagery depicted them as lice, rats, bats, vipers, dogs, and monkeys. What was required, said the Marine Corps journal *The Leatherneck* in May 1945, was "a gigantic task of extermination." The Japanese constituted a "pestilence," and the only appropriate treatment was "annihilation." Some of the marines landing on Iwo Jima had "Rodent Exterminator" written on their helmet covers, and on one American flagship the naval commander had erected a large sign enjoining all to "KILL JAPS! KILL JAPS! KILL MORE JAPS!" Herman Wouk

---

12   **ETO:** European Theater of Operations.

remembers the Pacific war scene correctly while analyzing Ensign Keith in *The Caine Mutiny:* "Like most of the naval executioners of Kwajalein, he seemed to regard the enemy as a species of animal pest." And the feeling was entirely reciprocal: "From the grim and desperate taciturnity with which the Japanese died, they seemed on their side to believe that they were contending with an invasion of large armed ants." Hiroshima seems to follow in natural sequence: "This obliviousness of both sides to the fact that the opponents were human beings may perhaps be cited as the key to the many massacres of the Pacific war." Since the Jap vermin resist so madly and have killed so many of us, let's pour gasoline into their bunkers and light it and then shoot those afire who try to get out. Why not? Why not blow them all up, with satchel charges or with something stronger? Why not, indeed, drop a new kind of bomb on them, and on the un-uniformed ones too, since the Japanese government has announced that women from ages of seventeen to forty are being called up to repel the invasion? The intelligence officer of the U.S. Fifth Air Force declared on July 21, 1945, that "the entire population of Japan is a proper military target," and he added emphatically, *"There are no civilians in Japan."* Why delay and allow one more American high school kid to see his own intestines blown out of his body and spread before him in the dirt while he screams and screams when with the new bomb we can end the whole thing just like that?

[17] On Okinawa, only weeks before Hiroshima, 123,000 Japanese and Americans *killed* each other. (About 140,000 Japanese died at Hiroshima.) "Just awful" was the comment on the Okinawa slaughter not of some pacifist but of General MacArthur. On July 14, 1945, General Marshall sadly informed the Combined Chiefs of Staff—he was not trying to scare the Japanese—that it's "now clear . . . that in order to finish with the Japanese quickly, it will be necessary to invade the industrial heart of Japan." The invasion was definitely on, as I know because I was to be in it.

[18] When the atom bomb ended the war, I was in the Forty-fifth Infantry Division, which had been through the European war so thoroughly that it had needed to be reconstituted two or three times. We were in a staging area near Rheims, ready to be shipped back across the United States for refresher training at Fort Lewis, Washington, and then sent on for final preparation in the Philippines. My division, like most of the ones transferred from Europe, was to take part in the invasion of Honshu. (The earlier landing on Kyushu was to be carried out by the 700,000 infantry already in the Pacific, those with whom James Jones has sympathized.) I was a twenty-one-year-old second lieutenant of infantry leading a rifle platoon. Although still officially fit for combat, in the German war I had al-

ready been wounded in the back and the leg badly enough to be adjudged, after the war, 40 percent disabled. But even if my leg buckled and I fell to the ground whenever I jumped out of the back of a truck, and even if the very idea of more combat made me breathe in gasps and shake all over, my condition was held to be adequate for the next act. When the atom bombs were dropped and news began to circulate that "Operation Olympic" would not, after all, be necessary, when we learned to our astonishment that we would not be obliged in a few months to rush up the beaches near Tokyo assault-firing while being machine-gunned, mortared, and shelled, for all the practiced phlegm of our tough facades we broke down and cried with relief and joy. We were going to live. We were going to grow to adulthood after all. The killing was all going to be over, and peace was actually going to be the state of things. When the *Enola Gay* dropped its package, "There were cheers," says John Toland, "over the intercom; it meant the end of the war." Down on the ground the reaction of Sledge's marine buddies when they heard the news was more solemn and complicated. They heard about the end of the war

> with quiet disbelief coupled with an indescribable sense of relief. We thought the Japanese would never surrender. Many refused to believe it. . . . Sitting in stunned silence, we remembered our dead. So many dead. So many maimed. So many bright futures consigned to the ashes of the past. So many dreams lost in the madness that had engulfed us. Except for a few widely scattered shouts of joy, the survivors of the abyss sat hollow-eyed and silent, trying to comprehend a world without war.

These troops who cried and cheered with relief or who sat stunned by the weight of their experience are very different from the high-minded, guilt-ridden GIs we're told about by J. Glenn Gray in his sensitive book *The Warriors*. During the war in Europe Gray was an interrogator in the Army Counterintelligence Corps, and in that capacity he experienced the war at Division level. There's no denying that Gray's outlook on everything was admirably noble, elevated, and responsible. After the war he became a much-admired professor of philosophy at Colorado College and an esteemed editor of Heidegger. But *The Warriors*, his meditation on the moral and psychological dimensions of modern soldiering, gives every sign of error occasioned by remoteness from experience. Division headquarters is miles—*miles*—behind the line where soldiers experience terror and madness and relieve those pressures by crazy brutality and sadism. Indeed, unless they actually encountered the enemy during the war, most "soldiers" have very little idea what "combat" was like. As William Manchester says, "All who wore uniforms are called veterans, but more than 90 percent of them are as uninformed about the killing zones as those on the home front." Manchester's fellow marine E. B. Sledge thoughtfully and responsibly invokes the terms *drastically* and *totally* to underline the differences in experience between front and rear, and not even the far rear, but the close rear. "Our code of conduct toward the enemy," he notes, "differed drastically from that prevailing back at the division CP."[13] (He's describing gold-tooth extraction from still-living Japanese.) Again he writes: "We existed in an environment totally incomprehensible to men behind the lines . . . ," even, he would insist, to men as intelligent and sensitive as Glenn Gray, who missed seeing with his own eyes Sledge's marine friends sliding under fire down a shell-pocked ridge slimy with mud and liquid dysentery shit into the maggoty Japanese and USMC corpses at the bottom, vomiting as the maggots burrowed into their own foul clothing. "We didn't talk about such things," says Sledge. "They were too horrible and obscene even for hardened veterans. . . . Nor do authors normally write about such vileness; unless they have seen it with their own eyes, it is too preposterous to think that men could actually live and fight for days and nights on end under such terrible conditions and not be driven insane." And Sledge has added a comment on such experience and the insulation provided by even a short distance: "Often people just behind our rifle companies couldn't understand what we knew." Glenn Gray was not in a rifle company, or even just behind one. "When the news of the atomic bombing of Hiroshima and Nagasaki came," he asks us to believe, "many an American soldier felt shocked and ashamed." Shocked, OK, but why ashamed? Because we'd destroyed civilians? We'd been doing that for years, in raids on Hamburg and Berlin and Cologne and Frankfurt and Mannheim and Dresden,[14] and Tokyo, and besides, the two A-bombs wiped out 10,000 Japanese troops, not often thought of now, John Hersey's[15] kindly physicians and Jesuit priests being more touching. If around division headquarters some of the

---

13 **CP:** command post.
14 **Hamburg . . . Dresden:** all cities in Germany.
15 **John Hersey** (1914–1993): author of *Hiroshima,* an account of the atom bomb blast effect on six survivors.

people Gray talked to felt ashamed, down in the rifle companies no one did, despite Gray's assertions. "The combat soldier," he says,

> knew better than did Americans at home what those bombs meant in suffering and injustice. The man of conscience realized intuitively that the vast majority of Japanese in both cities were no more, if no less, guilty of the war than were his own parents, sisters, or brothers.

I find this canting nonsense. The purpose of the bombs was not to "punish" people but to stop the war. To intensify the shame Gray insists we feel, he seems willing to fiddle the facts. The Hiroshima bomb, he says, was dropped "without any warning." But actually, two days before, 720,000 leaflets were dropped on the city urging everyone to get out and indicating that the place was going to be (as the Potsdam Declaration[16] has promised) obliterated. Of course few left.

[19] Experience whispers that the pity is not that we used the bomb to end the Japanese war but that it wasn't ready in time to end the German one. If only it could have been rushed into production faster and dropped at the right moment on the Reich Chancellery or Berchtesgaden[17] or Hitler's military headquarters in East Prussia (where Colonel Stauffenberg's July 20 bomb didn't do the job because it wasn't big enough), much of the Nazi hierarchy could have been pulverized immediately, saving not just the embarrassment of the Nuremberg trials but the lives of around four million Jews, Poles, Slavs, and gypsies, not to mention the lives and limbs of millions of Allied and German soldiers. If the bomb had only been ready in time, the young men of my infantry platoon would not have been so cruelly killed and wounded.

[20] All this is not to deny that like the Russian Revolution, the atom-bombing of Japan was a vast historical tragedy, and every passing year magnifies the dilemma into which it has lodged the contemporary world. As with the

---

16 **Potsdam Declaration:** The last meeting of the three allied leaders, Harry Truman, Clement Attlee (replacing Churchill), and Josef Stalin, was held in Potsdam, Germany, in July 1945. There, President Truman warned Japan to surrender or face "prompt and utter destruction."

17 **Reich . . . Berchtesgaden:** The Reich was the German state during the Nazi period, usually called the Third Reich. Berchtesgaden was the Alpine retreat of Adolf Hitler, chancellor of Nazi Germany.

Russian revolution, there are two sides—that's why it's a tragedy instead of a disaster—and unless we are, like Bruce Page, simplemindedly unimaginative and cruel, we will be painfully aware of both sides at once. To observe that from the viewpoint of the war's victims-to-be the bomb seemed precisely the right thing to drop is to purchase no immunity from horror. To experience both sides, one might study the book *Unforgettable Fire: Pictures Drawn by Atomic Bomb Survivors,* which presents a number of amateur drawings and watercolors of the Hiroshima scene made by middle-aged and elderly survivors for a peace exhibition in 1975. In addition to the almost unbearable pictures, the book offers brief moments of memoir not for the weak-stomached:

> While taking my severely wounded wife out to the river bank . . . ,
> I was horrified indeed at the sight of a stark naked man standing
> in the rain with his eyeball in his palm. He looked to be in great
> pain but there was nothing that I could do for him. I wonder
> what became of him. Even today, I vividly remember the sight. I
> was simply miserable.

These childlike drawings and paintings are of skin hanging down, breasts torn off, people bleeding and burning, dying mothers nursing dead babies. A bloody woman holds a bloody child in the ruins of a house, and the artist remembers her calling. "Please help this child! Someone, please help this child. Please help! Someone, please." As Samuel Johnson said of the smothering of Desdemona,[18] the innocent in another tragedy, "It is not to be endured." Nor, it should be noticed, is an infantryman's account of having his arm blown off in the Arno Valley in Italy in 1944:

> I wanted to die and die fast. I wanted to forget this miserable
> world. I cursed the war, I cursed the people who were responsi-
> ble for it, I cursed God for putting me here . . . to suffer for some-
> thing I never did or knew anything about.

[21] (A good place to interrupt and remember Glenn Gray's noble but hopelessly one-sided remarks about "injustice," as well as "suffering.")

---

18 **Samuel Johnson . . . Desdemona:** English writer and lexicographer commenting on Shakespeare's *Othello,* in which Othello strangles his wife, Desdemona, in a fit of jealousy.

22   "For this was hell," the soldier goes on,

> and I never imagined anything or anyone could suffer so bitterly.
> I screamed and cursed. Why? What had I done to deserve this?
> But no answer came. I yelled for medics, because subconsciously
> I wanted to live. I tried to apply my right hand over my bleeding
> stump, but I didn't have the strength to hold it. I looked to the
> left of me and saw the bloody mess that was once my left arm; its
> fingers and palm were tuned upward, like a flower looking to
> the sun for its strength.

The future scholar-critic who writes *The History of Canting in the Twentieth Century* will find much to study and interpret in the utterances of those who dilate on the special wickedness of the A-bomb-droppers. He will realize that such utterance can perform for the speaker a valuable double function. First, it can display the fineness of his moral weave. And second, by implication it can also inform the audience that during the war he was not socially so unfortunate as to find himself down there with the ground forces, where he might have had to compromise the purity and clarity of his moral system by the experience of weighing his own life against someone else's. Down there, which is where the other people were, is the place where coarse self-interest is the rule. When the young soldier with the wild eyes comes at you, firing, do you shoot him in the foot, hoping he'll be hurt badly enough to drop or mis-aim the gun with which he's going to kill you, or do you shoot him in the chest (or, if you're a prime shot, in the head) and make certain that you and not he will be the survivor of that mortal moment?

23   It would be not just stupid but would betray a lamentable want of human experience to expect soldiers to be very sensitive humanitarians. The Glenn Grays of this world need to have their attention directed to the testimony of those who know, like, say, Admiral of the Fleet Lord Fisher, who said, "Moderation in war is imbecility," or Sir Arthur Harris, director of the admittedly wicked aerial-bombing campaign designed, as Churchill put it, to "de-house" the German civilian population, who observed that "War is immoral," or our own General W. T. Sherman: "War is cruelty, and you cannot refine it." Lord Louis Mountbatten, trying to say something sensible about the dropping of the A-bomb, came up only with "War is crazy." Or rather, it requires choices among crazinesses. "It would seem even more crazy," he went on, "if we were to have more casualties on our side to save the Japanese." One of the unpleasant facts for anyone in the

ground armies during the war was that you had to become pro tem a subordinate of the very uncivilian George S. Patton and respond somehow to his unremitting insistence that you embrace his view of things. But in one of his effusions he was right, and his observation tends to suggest the experiential dubiousness of the concept of "just wars." "War is not a contest with gloves," he perceived. "It is resorted to only when laws, which are rules, have failed." Soldiers being like that, only the barest decencies should be expected of them. They did not start the war, except in the terrible sense hinted at in Frederic Manning's observation based on his front-line experience in the Great War:[19] "War is waged by men; not by beasts, or by gods. It is a peculiarly human activity. To call it a crime against mankind is to miss at least half its significance; it is also the punishment of a crime." Knowing that unflattering truth by experience, soldiers have every motive for wanting a war stopped, by any means.

[24] The stupidity, parochialism, and greed in the international mismanagement of the whole nuclear challenge should not tempt us to misimagine the circumstances of the bomb's first "use." Nor should our well-justified fears and suspicions occasioned by the capture of the nuclear-power trade by the inept and the mendacious (who have fucked up the works at Three Mile Island, Chernobyl, etc.) tempt us to infer retrospectively extraordinary corruption, imbecility, or motiveless malignity in those who decided, all things considered, to drop the bomb. Times change. Harry Truman was not a fascist but a democrat. He was as close to a genuine egalitarian as anyone we've seen in high office for a long time. He is the only President in my lifetime who ever had experience in a small unit of ground troops whose mission it was to kill people. That sort of experience of actual war seems useful to presidents especially, helping to inform them about life in general and restraining them from making fools of themselves needlessly—the way Ronald Reagan did in 1985 when he visited the German military cemetery at Bitburg containing the SS graves.[20] The propriety of this visit he explained by asserting that no Germans who fought in the war remain alive and that "very few . . . even remember the war." Reagan's ignorance or facile forgetfulness are imputed by Arthur Schlesinger to his total lack of serious experience of war—the Second World War or any other. "Though he

---

19 **Great War:** World War I.
20 **Bitburg . . . SS graves:** President Ronald Reagan visited the graves of the elite guard (Schutzstaffel) of Nazis who were in charge of exterminating Jews, homosexuals, and other "undesirables."

often makes throwaway references to his military career," says Schlesinger, "Mr. Reagan in fact is the only American president who was of military age during the Second World War and saw no service overseas. He fought the war on the film lots of Hollywood, slept in his own bed every night and apparently got many of his ideas of what happened from subsequent study of the *Reader's Digest.*"

25   Truman was a different piece of goods entirely. He knew war, and he knew better than some of his critics then and now what he was doing and why he was doing it. "Having found the bomb," he said, "we have used it. . . . We have used it to shorten the agony of young Americans."

26   The past, which as always did not know the future, acted in ways that ask to be imagined before they are condemned. Or even simplified.

Looking Back

1. What is the main thesis of this essay?

2. According to the author, what does the "dirty little secret of social class in America" have to do with the views of those who think dropping the A-bomb was wrong?

3. Summarize paragraph 5 on page 313 beginning "On the other hand, John Kenneth Galbraith. . . ." What is Fussell's strongest supporting point in this paragraph?

4. How does Fussell anticipate arguments that the Japanese were not the only forces characterized by Admiral Halsey's term "barbaric"?

5. How does Fussell anticipate the likely charge that he downplays the horror of the effects of the bomb?

6. In a small group, discuss Frederic Manning's observation that "to call it [war] a crime against mankind is to miss at least half of its significance; it is also the punishment of a crime." What does he mean?

Looking Into

1. Write a persuasive essay on a current national question such as the controversy over whether the United States should seek to stop wars when they occur in other countries.

2. Find a counter argument to Fussell's argument about the atom bomb and summarize it in three or four paragraphs.

3. Imagine that you were an advisor to the president in 1945. Write a brief summary of your arguments either for or against using the atomic bomb against Japan.

In Praise of Sunshine Patriots

GARRISON KEILLOR

Garrison Keillor is widely known for his stories of Lake Wobegon, a fictional place based on his memories of growing up in Anoka, Minnesota. Originally he told the stories on his radio show, "A Prairie Home Companion," which was produced by Minnesota Public Radio and was an amalgam of music, skits, and Keillor's monologues about Lake Wobegon. Keillor also wrote the commercials for the "sponsors" of the show, including Ralph's Pretty Good-Grocery, Bertha's Kitty Boutique, and Powdermilk Biscuits that "give shy persons the strength to get up and do what needs to be done." "A Prairie Home Companion" was broadcast from 1974–1987 and was followed two years later by "Garrison Keillor's American Radio Company of the Air," a similar show.

Keillor received his B.A. degree from the University of Minnesota in 1966 and did graduate study there from 1966–1968. He began his radio career as a writer for KUOM Radio in Minneapolis. He won a George Foster Peabody Broadcasting Award in 1980 and the Edward R. Murrow Award from the Corporation for Public Broadcasting in 1985.

His books include *Happy to Be Here: Stories and Comic Pieces* (1982); *Lake Wobegon Days* (1985), which received a *Los Angeles Times* Book Award nomination; *Leaving Home: a Collection of Lake Wobegon Stories* (1987); *We Are Still Married: Stories and Letters* (1989); *WLT: a Radio Romance* (1991); and *A Book of Guys* (1993).

He has also produced many recordings, including "Lake Wobegon Days," which won a Grammy Award for best non-musical recording in 1987. He is a frequent contributor to the *New Yorker, Harper's,* and *Atlantic Monthly.*

Looking Ahead

Thomas Paine coined the term "sunshine patriot" in 1776. "These are the times that try men's souls," he wrote, "the summer soldier and the sunshine patriot will, in this crisis, shrink from the service of their country. . . ." Garrison Keillor, however, has some kind words for these sunshine patriots.

1   *I*n the summer of 1776, truck farms lay along the dirt road called Broad Way on Manhattan Island where Times Square is now. Herds of cows grazed among the apple orchards, and by July the vegetables were ripening in the fenced gardens. On the west side of the road, where this newspaper[1] is published today on 43rd Street, stood Frog Hall, a big country house on a thousand-acre farm owned by a rabid loyalist[2] and lawyer named Daniel Horsmanden. He got the farm when he married Anne Jevon, who inherited the place from her brother Joseph Haynes, who had bought it from a Dutch farmer, Wolfert Webber, who got it when he married Grietje Stille, the daughter of the previous owner.

2   From the Horsmanden farm on 43rd, the city of New York appeared as a few church spires on the horizon. The population was slightly more than 20,000 mostly living below Wall Street, and down there, on July 18, a crowd gathered at City Hall to hear the Declaration of Independence proclaimed from the steps, the bold document that had been adopted by the Continental Congress on July 2d and that was evidence enough in His Majesty's court to hang any one of the signers. There, in the bright summer sun, with horses whinnying nearby and dogs barking, pigs rooting around in the garbage in the streets, a man read the famous words about unalienable rights.

3   There were loud cheers towards the end—"That these United Colonies are, and of Right ought to be Free and Independent States"—and the American flag was raised for the first time in New York, and then gangs of patriots ran through the streets doing such property damage as seemed appropriate to them.

4   Out in the country on Broad Way, Daniel Horsmanden had no reason to feel alarmed, though. New York was no hotbed of revolution like Boston or Philadelphia. Despite a decade of high-handed and corrupt English bureaucrats, despite the drafting of colonials into the British Army and the peremptory taxes that led to the outbreak of fighting at Lexington and Concord in April 1775, the citizens of New York were profoundly unmoved by it all. When Washington came to the city in 1776 to engage the British Army, one of his generals, Nathanael Greene, told him that two-thirds of New York was loyal to the King and therefore the city was not worth fighting for.

---

1   **this newspaper:** the *New York Times.*
2   **loyalist:** person loyal to King George III.

5   The great indifference of the population to the Great Cause is a fact lightly noted by historians, but it weighed heavily on the Founding Fathers. John Adams estimated that in all the Colonies taken together, only a third of the people favored independence—a third were loyal to King George and a third were indifferent to the outcome. Alexander Hamilton, who fought in the New York Artillery Company, wrote, "Our countrymen have all the folly of the ass and all the passiveness of the sheep . . . they are determined not to be free." Washington's army suffered at times from wholesale desertions; men simply walked away from the American Revolution when they got tired or felt homesick or when it was time to go home and harvest the potatoes.

6   In August 1776, General Washington commandeered Frog Hall for an army hospital, and the Horsmandens joined their loyalist friends in the city. A few weeks later, the Battle of Long Island was fought at Flatbush. The Americans were whipped by General Howe, and the remnants of Washington's army straggled up Broad Way in "a miserable, disorderly retreat," according to one of the officers. The British lines advanced to what is now 107th Street. On Sept. 16 the Americans were defeated again, in the Battle of Harlem Heights, where Columbia University stands.

7   Washington pulled back to White Plains, then retreated across New Jersey, his New York militia deserting him by the hundreds, and New York remained a loyalist stronghold for the duration of the war. It was a city of opulence and some considerable hustle, and it was glad to be out of the war, safely in British hands, waiting to see what the outcome would be.

8   After the British defeat at Yorktown in 1781, and the King's grudging decision to give up the war, about a third of the population of New York left for Canada, including, presumably, Daniel Horsmanden and his wife, Anne. The only Revolutionary hero to emerge from New York was Capt. Nathan Hale, who volunteered for a reconnaissance mission behind British lines after the Battle of Harlem Heights and who was captured and hanged by the British after he made a gallows speech that may have included the line, "I regret that I have but one life to lose for my country."

9   If Nathan Hale felt that way about his life, certainly most New Yorkers preferred to use their one life to pursue happiness, to make money, patronize taverns, to dance, to flirt, to attend shows. They could care less about great truths, even self-evident ones. They mainly wanted to enjoy the good life.

10   Later, when independence was won, New York flew the flag, cheered the troops and welcomed Washington when he came to bid farewell to his officers. Soon, a patriotic mythology was fashioned that included Nathan

Hale, John Hancock's bold signature, Bunker Hill and the whites of their eyes, Washington crossing the Delaware, Washington on his knees at Valley Forge, Betsy Ross, Paul Revere ("One if by land and two if by sea"), Molly Pitcher taking her husband's place at the cannon and John Paul Jones on the burning deck of the *Bonhomme Richard* saying, "I have not yet begun to fight"—a mythology in which the American people rose up as one and defeated the British redcoats, the Hessian mercenaries and the loyalist traitors.

[11] But the truth was that a clear majority of the colonists did not support independence, and surely this fact was painfully obvious when New York became the national capital (1785 to 1790), the seat of Congress and the site of George Washington's inauguration as the first President under the new Constitution.

[12] Everywhere the great men looked, they saw a city indifferent to them and bent on commerce. Congress complained of the noise around Federal Hall, where it met, and the city council closed off the streets, but of course New York could never offer politicians a stage so grand as L'Enfant's new city where the streets radiated from the centers of power, where the Capitol would stand shining on a hill, looking down a broad green promenade. A city that would hum with excitement at times of crisis real or imagined. A city whose only business would be politics.

[13] Indifference, however, is the rule now as it was then—yawning indifference to great causes, noble truths, and the pronouncements of great men. One man's indifference is another man's sanity. The Declaration proclaimed the right of the people to revolt, a dubious right indeed, and most people aren't in favor of it. The crowd of New Yorkers who cheered on July 18, 1776, were sunshine patriots, out for a good time, and when it came to giving their lives for their country, they were more interested in the price of coffee, the future of real estate values and whether it would rain on the 19th.

[14] Such indifference probably helped to save the Republic from a permanent revolution, in which Hamilton might have led an army against Jefferson, in which Americans would pick up their muskets whenever sacred principle was in danger. A nation of heroes would be awfully hard on the rest of us. So we are a nation of civilians.

[15] On the 4th of July, I raise my beer can to Washington, the man who more than any other made our country possible and to New York, the city that ignores revolutions. A country in which our great patriotic holiday is celebrated with food, beer, softball and small talk is exactly the country most of us would prefer to live in.

Looking Back

1. Keillor says that "a patriotic mythology was fashioned" after the American Revolution and mentions people and events that make up this mythology. Study some of the dictionary definitions of *myth* and *mythology* and tell the purpose of this patriotic mythology in the United States.

2. Explain how "indifference probably helped to save the Republic."

3. Considering the strife in various countries in the world today, could an argument be made for more indifference on the part of civilians? Why or why not? Discuss in a small group.

Looking Into

1. In a talk or paper defend Keillor's main thesis against the arguments of someone who declares that this essay is un-American and unpatriotic.

2. In two to four paragraphs, tell how indifference might be a threat to the Republic today.

3. The Irish poet William Butler Yeats once observed in a different context that, "the best lack all conviction, while the worst / Are full of passionate intensity." Write a brief essay in which you apply this quote to the American Revolution and its summer soldiers and sunshine patriots.

Do He Have Your Number, Mr. Jeffrey?

GAYLE PEMBERTON

Gayle Pemberton was born in 1948 and grew up in Minnesota. She earned a B.A. from the University of Michigan and a Ph.D. from Harvard. She has taught at several universities and is currently the director of African-American studies at Princeton University. The essay reprinted below is from her first collection of essays *The Hottest Water in Chicago: On Family, Race, Time, and American Culture* (1993).

Looking Ahead

What comes to mind when you think of Los Angeles or of Southern California? Make a list of the images or ideas that occur to you and then compare them with those in Pemberton's essay.

—❧—

1   During the fall of 1984 I worked for three weekends as a caterer's assistant in Southern California. Like lots of others seeking their fortunes in L.A., I was working by day as a temporary typist in a Hollywood film studio. I was moonlighting with the caterer because, like lots of others, I was going broke on my typist's wages.

2   Though the job was not particularly enjoyable, the caterer and her husband were congenial, interesting people who certainly would have become good friends of mine had I stayed in California. I spent my three weekends in basic scullery work—wiping and slicing mushrooms, mixing batters, peeling apples, tomatoes, and cucumbers, drying plates, glasses, and cutlery. Greater responsibilities would have come with more experience, but I had brushed off California's dust before I learned any real catering secrets or professional gourmet techniques.

3   One exhausting dinner party, given by a rich man for his family and friends, turned out to be among the reasons I brushed off that California

dust. This dinner was such a production that our crew of five arrived the day before to start preparing. The kitchen in this house was larger than some I've seen in fine French restaurants. Our caterer was one of a new breed of gourmet cooks who do all preparation and cooking at the client's home—none of your cold-cut or warming-tray catering. As a result, her clients had a tendency to have loads of money and even more kitchen space.

4   Usually her staff was not expected to serve the meal, but on this occasion we did. I was directed to wear stockings and black shoes and I was given a blue-patterned apron dress, with frills here and there, to wear. Clearly, my academic lady-banker pumps were out of the question, so I invested in a pair of trendy black sneakers—which cost me five dollars less than what I earned the entire time I worked for the caterer. Buying the sneakers was plainly excessive but I told myself they were a necessary expense. I was not looking forward to wearing the little French serving-girl uniform, though. Everything about it and me were wrong, but I had signed on and it would have been unseemly and downright hostile to jump ship.

5   One thing I liked about the caterer was her insistence that her crew not be treated as servants—that is, we worked for her and took orders from her, not from the clients, who might find ordering us around an emboldening and socially one-upping experience. She also preferred to use crystal and china she rented, keeping her employees and herself safe from a client's rage in case a family heirloom should get broken. But on this occasion, her client insisted that we use his Baccarat crystal. We were all made particularly nervous by his tone. It was the same tone I heard from a mucky-muck at my studio typing job: cold, arrogant, a matter-of-fact "you are shit" attitude that is well known to nurses and secretaries.

6   I had never served a dinner before that one—that is, for strangers, formally. I had mimed serving festive meals for friends, but only in a light-hearted way. And, when I was a child, my family thought it a good exercise in etiquette—not to mention in labor savings—to have me serve at formal dinners. "It's really fun, you know," they would say. I never handled the good china, though.

7   I didn't mind cutting up mushrooms or stirring sauce in some foul rich man's kitchen for pennies, but I certainly didn't like the idea of serving at this one's table. I saw our host hold up one of his goblets to a guest, showing off the fine line and texture. There were too many conflicting images for me to be content with the scene. He was working hard on his image for his guests; I was bothered by the way I looked to myself and by what I might have looked like to the assembled crew, guests, and host. I couldn't get the idea of black servility to white power out of my mind.

8   The food was glorious. I recall serving quenelles[1] at one point, followed by a consommé brunoise, a beef Wellington with a carrot and herb based sauce that I stirred for a short eternity, vegetables with lemon butter, and a variety of mouth-watering pastries for dessert. We worked throughout the meal, topping up wine and coffee, removing plates, bumping into each other. As long as I was doing this absurd thing I decided to make some kind of mental work attend it. I made the entire scene a movie, and as I served I created a silent voice-over. At one point, after the quenelles and the entrée and before the coffee, the table of eight sat discussing literature—a discussion of the "what'd you think of . . ." variety. My professorial ears pricked up. I discovered that one member of the party had actually read the book in question, while a few others had skimmed condensed versions in a magazine. My voice-over could have vied, I thought, with the shrillest Bolshevik[2] propaganda ever written.

PEMBERTON (Voice-over)
(haughtily)

You self-satisfied, rich, feeble-brained, idiotic, priggish, filthy
maggots! You, you sit here talking literature—why, you don't
even know what the word means. This is high intellectual dis-
course for you, isn't it? High, fine. You are proud to say, "I
thought the theme honest." What, pray tell, is an honest theme?
It might be better to consider the dishonesty of your disgusting
lives. Why, here I am, a Ph.D in literature, listening to this
garbage, making a pittance, while you illiterate pig-running-
dogs consume food and non-ideas with the same relish.

9   Oh, I did go on. My script was melodramatic, with great soliloquies, flourishes, and, for verisimilitude, an eastern European accent. My comeuppance came as I dried the last of the Baccarat goblets. The crystal, no doubt responding to the dissonance and intensity of my sound track, shattered as I held it in my hand. The rest of the crew said they'd never seen

---

1 **quenelles** (kə nel'): poached dumplings made with ground fish or meat and served with a sauce.
2 **Bolshevik** (bōl'shə vik): member of the radical wing of the party that seized power in the 1917 Russian revolution; any extreme radical.

anyone look as sick as I did at that moment. The goblet was worth more than the price of my trendy sneakers and my night's work combined. I decided to go home.

10   I drove slowly back to my room near Culver City; it was well past midnight. I had the distinct sense that I was the only sober driver on the Santa Monica Freeway that night, but given the weaving pattern of my driving—to avoid the other weavers—I fully expected to be picked up and jailed. Then, some alcohol residue from the broken goblet would have transported itself magically into my bloodstream to make me DWI, just as the goblet had reacted to my thoughts and sacrificed itself in the name of privilege, money, and mean-spiritedness. I made it home, feeling woozy as I left my car.

11   I didn't have to pay for the goblet; the caterer did. She was insured. I worked another party for her—another strange collection of people, but a more festive occasion—and I didn't have to wear the French maid's outfit. I got to stand happily behind a buffet, helping people serve themselves. I think back on my catering experience the way people do who, once something's over, say that they're glad they did it—like lassoing a bull, riding him, then busting ribs and causing permanent sacroiliac distress. The job was just one of many I've had to take to make me believe I could survive when it was obvious that I was going further and further into the hole. I never had more than ten dollars in my wallet the entire time I lived in L.A., and not much more than that in the bank. Perhaps there's something about L.A. that makes working unlikely jobs—jobs your parents send you to college to keep you from having to do—all right and reasonable, since very little makes sense there anyway, and surviving means bellying up to the illusion bar and having a taste with everyone else.

12   L.A. has been like that for a long time. It did not occur to me that night, as I moved from one dinner guest to another dressed in that ludicrous outfit, that I might have created some other kind of scenario—linking what I was doing to what my mother had done nearly fifty years before, probably no farther than ten miles away.

13 It was in the middle thirties, Los Angeles. My mother's employers supplied her with a beige uniform with a frilled bib, short puff sleeves, and a narrow, fitted waist. The skirt of the dress was narrow, stopping just below the knee. She wore seamed stockings and low pumps, black. And her job, as far as she could ascertain, was to just be, nothing else. The couple who employed her—the husband wrote screenplays—had no children, and did not require her services to either cook or clean. I suppose they thought that having a maid was a requirement of their social position. So, Mother got

the job. She is fair-skinned, and at that time she wore her dark, wavy hair long, in large curls that gathered just below her neck. I've seen pictures from those days and see her most enviable figure, an old-fashioned size ten, held up by long legs that, doubtless, were enhanced by the seamed stockings and pumps. Her employers were quite proud of her and thought she looked, they said, "just like a little French girl." When I was very young and filled with important questions, Mother explained to me that she thought it "damned irritating that whites who knew full well who they were hiring and talking to went to such lengths to try to make blacks into something else. If they wanted a little French girl, why didn't they go out and get one?" Ah, the days before *au pairs*.[3] Well, I knew the answer to that one too.

14   Mother had moved to L.A. with her mother. Nana had decided to leave Papa, tired of his verbal abusiveness and profligacy. There were various cousins in California, and I am sure the appeal of the West and new beginnings at the start of the Depression made the choice an easy one. Both of my parents told me that they didn't feel the Depression all that much; things had never been financially good and little changed for them after Wall Street fell. The timing seemed right to Nana. Her other daughter, my aunt, had recently married. My mother had finished her third year at the university and, I bet, got an attack of wanderlust. She went with Nana to help her—and also to get some new air. The circumstances accommodated themselves.

15   I remember my shock when I learned that Mother had worked as a maid. I had always known that she had lived in California, but as a child, it never occurred to me that she would have had to "do something" there. It was not so much that my middle-class feathers were ruffled by the revelation as that I found it difficult to see her in a role that, on screen at least, was so demeaning and preposterous. Mother simply did not fit the stereotype I had been fed. And, to make matters worse, Grandma had taken pains to inform my sister and me when we were little girls that we should avoid—at all costs—rooming with whites in college or working in their homes. Her own stints as a dance-hall matron had convinced her, she said, that whites were the filthiest people on earth. The thought of my mother cleaning up after them made me want to protect her, to undo the necessity for that kind of work by some miraculous feat of time travel, to rescue her from the demeaning and the dirty.

---

3   *au pairs* (o pär): foreign girls who work as domestics for a family in exchange for room and board and learning the language.

16   Mother's attitude about her past employment was more pragmatic, of course. She explained to me—as if I didn't know—that there were really no avenues for black women apart from "service," as it was called, prostitution, and, perhaps, schoolteaching. Nana had no higher education and Mother's was incomplete, so service was the only route they could take. Mother also assured me that she had not cleaned unimaginable filth, but rather, with nothing else to do, had sat all day long reading novels, memorably *Anthony Adverse* by Hervey Allen, a big best-seller of 1934. My image of Mother became brighter, but in some ways more curious: there she was, imagined as a French maid by her employers, but really a black coed, lolling around a Los Angeles home reading *Anthony Adverse.* That's one far cry from Butterfly McQueen as Prissy in *Gone with the Wind.*

17   All good things must come to an end, as they say, and Mother's job did one day. She had been dating a man, she says, "who was very handsome, looked Latin, like Cesar Romero,[4] but he was black too." Talk about images. He arrived to pick her up for a date as she got off work. He inquired after her at the front door—oops—and there went the job. Seems the little French maid's Spanish-looking boyfriend should have realized that no matter what black might appear to be, it better not act other than what it was. A slip in racial protocol, a lost novel-reading employ. "So it went," Mother said. After that incident she decided to look for a different kind of work and she began selling stockings for the Real Silk Hosiery Company, door-to-door.

18   Mother was lucky. I suspect that she and Nana might have had a tougher time if they had been brown-skinned, for contrary to many images from movies, white employers—if they were going to hire blacks at all—preferred the lighter-skinned variety. This was true of professions as diverse as chorus girls, maids, schoolteachers, waitresses, and shop clerks, an implied greater worth as blackness disappears drop by drop into ginger, to mocha, to "high yellow," to white. This scale was intraracially internalized too, making a shambles of black life from the earliest slave days to the present. These gradations also made color-line crossing a popular black sport, particularly since white America seemed to be at once so secure and satisfied in its whiteness and so ignorant of who's who and who's what. Blacks existed only as whites saw them, blackness affirming white racial self-consciousness and nothing else. This is what Ralph Ellison's invisibility is all about; it is what we have all lived.

---

4   **Cesar Romero:** suave movie actor of the 1940s and 1950s.

19   In the evenings and on weekends, Mother and Nana used to go to the movies; they both were hooked and on location for Hollywood's Golden Age. I love movies too. It is on the gene, as I frequently remind myself as I sit watching a vintage B from the forties for the fifth time or so when I ought to be reading a book. A major chunk of my misspent youth involved watching them. When I should have been reading, or studying mathematics, or learning foreign languages—like my more successful academic friends—I was hooked on three-reelers.

20   During my youth Mother was my partner in all this. When I was in kindergarten and first grade on half-day shifts, I never missed a morning movie. When we watched together I would barrage her with important questions: "Who is that?" "Is he dead?" "Is she dead?" "Who was she married to?" "Is this gonna be sad?" Mother was never wrong, except once. We were watching an early Charles Bickford movie and I asked the standard heady question: "Is he dead?" Mother said, "Oh, Lord, yes. He died years ago." Several years later I came home triumphantly from a drive-in and announced that I had seen Bickford in *The Big Country* and that he looked just fine and alive to me.

21   Of course, hopeless romanticism is the disease that can be caught from the kind of movie-going and movie-watching my mother and I have done. There she was, with her mother, frequently a part of the crowd being held behind the barricades at Hollywood premieres, sighing and pointing with agitation as gowned and white-tied stars glided from limousines into rococo movie-houses. Both she and Nana read screen magazines—the forerunners to our evening news programs—that detailed the romantic, hedonistic public and private exploits of Hollywood's royalty. It was a time when my mother, as French maid reading *Anthony Adverse,* had to wait only a few months before the novel burst onto the screen, with glorious illusionary history and Frederic March swashbuckling his way into the hearts of screaming fans. The stars were part of the studio system and could be counted on to appear with frequency, even if the roles appeared to be the same and only the titles, and a few plot twists, changed. (I am convinced, for example, that the 1934 *Imitation of Life* was remade as *Mildred Pierce* in 1945, the major change being that the relatively good daughter of the former becomes the monster of the latter. Louise Beavers and Fredi Washington in the black theme of *Imitation of Life* only slightly alter the major plot.)

22   Mother's was the perfect generation to see Hollywood movies when they were fresh, new, and perhaps more palpable than they are now—when comedies of remarriage, as Stanley Cavell calls them, and historical adventures and melodramas dominated the screen, when westerns and

political dramas were self-consciously mythologizing the American past and present, and when young French maids and their mothers, along with the impoverished, the disillusioned, the lost, and even the comfortable and secure, could sit before the silver screen and see a different world projected than the one they lived in. And they could dream. Mother loves to sketch faces and clothing, using an artistic talent inherited from Papa. She marveled at the stars and their sculpted (sometimes) faces, and would draw from memory the costume designs that made the likes of Edith Head, Cecil Beaton, and Irene famous.

23   Hopeless romanticism was the threat, but neither Nana nor Mother—nor I completely—succumbed to it. They never confused reality with anything they saw on either the big or the small screen. And they taught me what they believed. They both warned me, in different ways and at different times, to be wary of the type of people who wake up to a new world every day (and I've met some)—people with no memory, ingenuous, incapable of seeing either the implications or the connections between one event and another, people who willingly accept what the world makes of them on a Tuesday, forget as night falls, and wake up on Wednesday ready to make the same mistakes. It might have been some of that ingenuousness that produced my feelings of discomfort when I learned that Mother had been a maid, and she understood how I felt.

24   My mother always deplored the depiction of blacks on screen. She saw their roles as demeaning and designed to evoke either cheap sentimentality, cheap laughter, or cheap feelings of superiority in the white audiences they were aimed at. And, although she says she didn't see many of them, Mother loathed the all-black B movies Hollywood made for the "colored" audience, where the stereotypes were broader and more offensive to her, and where the musical interludes did no justice to real talent, she said, but trivialized it. She even hated musical interludes featuring black performers in the standard white A and B movies. She was—and still is—cold to arguments that say talented black performers needed to take any work they could get, and that black audiences were encouraged and happy to see black Hollywood stars no matter what they were doing. Mother countered that Hattie McDaniel's acceptance speech, when she won an Oscar for her role as Mammy in *Gone with the Wind*, was written for her, and that McDaniel was denied the status of eating dinner with her peers that night.

25   We have talked about all of this many, many times, particularly when I have felt it necessary to sort out my own complex and conflicting reactions to Hollywood movies. Like Mother, I have seen as nothing but illusion the world projected on the screen. But as Michael Wood notes in *America in the Movies:* "All movies mirror reality in some way or other.

There are no escapes, even in the most escapist pictures. . . . The business of films is the business of dreams . . . but then dreams are scrambled messages from waking life, and there is truth in lies, too." Mother may have recoiled from black images on screen because they affirmed a reality she did not like. She could suspend her disbelief at white characters and their predicaments, she could enter the dream worlds of aristocrats and chorus girls living happily ever after, or dying romantic, drawn-out deaths, because there was some measure of inner life given these portrayals. The audience demanded some causal foundation to acts ranging from heroism and self-sacrifice to murder, duplicity, and pure cussedness. But black characters on screen, no matter how polished their roles, were ultimately as invisible as she was in her own role as French maid—a projection only of what the white world wanted to see, robbed of the implication of inner lives, nothing but glorified surfaces that really said everything about whiteness and nothing at all about blackness. It didn't matter to Mother if the characters were maids or butlers, lawyers or doctors, simpletons or singers. I knew there was an inner life, a real person in my mother—passionate and shy, lacking self-confidence but projecting intense intelligence and style—and that she had no business being anybody's French girl. The "truth in lies" was that Hollywood rent from us our human dignity while giving us work, as it sought to defuse and deflect our real meaning—a potentially dangerous meaning—in American life.

[26] Mother found these invisible blacks painful to watch because they were so effective as images created in white minds. These complex feelings are on the gene too. I find Shirley Temple movies abominable, notwithstanding the dancing genius of Bill "Bojangles" Robinson. In *The Little Colonel* young Shirley has just been given a birthday party; there are hats and horns and all sorts of scrubbed white children celebrating with her. At some moment—I refuse to watch the film again to be precise—she gets up and takes part of her cake to a group of dusty and dusky children who are waiting outside in the backyard of the house. The only reason for their existence is to be grateful for the crumbs and to sing a song. There can be no other motivation, no reason to exist at all, except to show the dear Little Colonel's largesse and liberal-mindedness, befitting someone not quite to the manor born but clearly on her way to the manor life.

[27] I was watching an Alfred Hitchcock festival not long ago. Hitchcock films are some of Mother's favorites. She likes the illusions and twists of plots, the scrambling of images light and dark. I realized that I hadn't seen *Rear Window* since I was a little girl, and that at the time I hadn't understood much of what had taken place in the movie. I was very interested in it this

time around. There was James Stewart, as Jeffries, in the heaviest makeup ever, with his blue eyes almost enhanced out of his face, looking at evil Raymond Burr through binoculars in the apartment across the way. I was letting the film take me where it would; I created an *explication de texte,*[5] noting how the film raises questions about voyeurism and images. Indeed, Stewart, in looking at the world from his temporary infirmity, is only content when he places a narrative line on the lives of the people on the other side of his binoculars. He is, in a sense, reacting to images and attempting to order them—as we all do.

28   At a crucial moment in the movie, Stewart realizes that he is in danger. The evil wife-murderer and dismemberer, Burr, knows that Stewart has figured out the crime. Stewart hobbles to the telephone, trying to reach his friend, Wendell Corey. Corey isn't in, but Stewart gets the baby-sitter on the line—who speaks in a vaudevillian black accent. He asks her to have Corey call him when he returns. The baby-sitter asks, "Do he have your number, Mr. Jeffrey?"

29   I called my mother to tell her that I had an interesting bit of trivia from *Rear Window.* She became angry when she heard it, said she was appalled. "He should have been ashamed of himself," she said of Hitchcock. Into the white world of *Rear Window* and questions of imagery, it was necessary to place a familiar black image—and this time it didn't even have a face.

30   Mother and Nana left L.A. in 1937. Working in service and selling silk stockings could not provide enough money for them to survive. They went back to the frozen North. Mother married in 1939; Nana returned to Papa and stayed with him until he died in 1967.

31   Nana and Papa both moved to L.A. in 1950, Papa then a semi-retired architect. They had a beautiful home on West Fourth Avenue. It was right in the middle of a two-block area that became part of the Santa Monica Freeway. One morning, on my way to a catering job, I drove my car as far as I could, to the fence above the freeway. I got out and thought long and hard about what had been lost—beyond a house, of course, but their lives gone, part of my youth as a little girl visiting in summers, and dreams about what life could be in the semi-tropical paradise of Southern California where they made dreams that seduced the whole world.

---

5   *explication de texte*: kind of literary criticism involving detailed analysis of a work.

Looking Back

1. What were the reasons for Pemberton's response to her job as caterer's assistant?

2. Pemberton says that neither she nor her mother or grandmother ever succumbed to the disease of hopeless romanticism caught from movie watching. Why does she use the word *disease* and what is wrong with hopeless romanticism?

3. The author says that "black characters on screen . . . were ultimately . . . invisible. . . ." Explain what she means.

Looking Into

1. Describe and analyze the image of blacks on the screen today in a one- or two-page paper.

2. What values and whose values does this essay explore? Discuss this question in a paragraph or two.

3. In paragraph 8, Pemberton presents a voice-over she imagines delivering to the guests at the dinner party. Imagine that you are one of those guests. Write a response to Pemberton in which you point out that her view is one-sided.

I'll Be Suing You

PETER MAYLE

Peter Mayle lives in France, and his extremely popular books include *A Year in Provence* (1990), which won the British Book Award for Best Travel Book of the Year; *Toujours Provence* (1991); *Hotel Pastis: a Novel of Provence* (1993); and *Up the Agency* (1993).

Mayle was in the advertising business in New York for fifteen years as a copywriter and executive before deciding in 1975 to become a full-time writer.

Looking Ahead

In this essay, which originally appeared in *GQ* magazine and was later included in a volume entitled *Expensive Habits* (which helps to explain the first sentence), Peter Mayle is candid about his views on lawyers. Why do we need lawyers, according to Mayle, and what two secret weapons do lawyers have?

1   *I*t is normally my pleasant duty to report on the little extravagances that make life worth living and a dollar worth earning—the civilized rewards available to anyone with a healthy streak of self-indulgence and a good credit rating. This month, however, we shall be looking at one expensive habit—alas, becoming more widespread every day—that offers no enjoyment of any kind to the millions of poor wretches who are forced to pay for it. In theory, it is the pursuit of justice. In practice, it consists of handing over large sums of money to the kind of people you wouldn't want to meet in your neighborhood bar.

2   There is something horribly wrong with a world in which there are more lawyers than good chefs, and yet every year the law schools unleash a further plague of them, letting them loose on the streets to jabber about malpractice, malfeasance, alimony, palimony, torts and suits, and God knows what else, causing dread and apprehension in the hearts of simple, honest citizens like you and me. Indeed, there are several office buildings

in midtown Manhattan (lawyers have a liking for choice real estate) where you risk an injunction merely by stepping on someone's foot in a crowded elevator. The foot turns out to be attached to a pillar of the legal profession, and before you know it you're facing charges of attempted grievous bodily harm as defined in and pursuant to the case of *Schulz* v. *Donoghue*, 1923.

3   I am not alone in my misgivings. Lawyers have been the object of heartfelt invective ever since man developed the intelligence to spell "litigation." "A peasant between two lawyers is like a fish between two cats," says the Spanish proverb. "Lawyers and painters can soon change black to white," says the Danish proverb. "The first thing we do, let's kill all the lawyers," says Shakespeare. Benjamin Franklin, Thoreau, Emerson, and many other good men and true have also expressed themselves in pungent and unflattering terms on the subject of our learned friends. How can it be, then, that despite centuries of well-deserved unpopularity there are more of them around than ever before?

4   There are many contributory factors, but perhaps the most basic is the language problem. For their own obvious ends, lawyers have perfected an exclusive form of communication. It has a passing resemblance to English mixed with a smattering of dog Latin, but to the man in the street, it might just as well be Greek. Thus, when he receives a writ or a subpoena or one of the other countless arrows in the legal quiver, he is completely mystified. What does it mean? What can he do? What else but hire an interpreter— who is, of course, a lawyer. And there we have the kind of situation that lawyers love: the two sides can settle down to a protracted exchange of mumbo jumbo, most of it unintelligible to their clients and all of it charged at an hourly rate that defies belief.

5   Then there is the law, not made by man but dictated by human nature, that requires that idle hands find mischievous employment. When there is not enough work for the legal population, you might reasonably expect the number of lawyers to decrease, with the less successful leaving to try their luck at something useful, like plumbing. Not a chance. If there is not enough work to go around, more work is created. Subdivisions of the law and their specialists spring up to make daily life more complicated for us and more remunerative for them. The result is that you find yourself having to deal with not one lawyer but a whole platoon of them.

6   The first, let's say, specializes in real estate. He will uncover the booby traps hidden (by another lawyer) in the fine print of your apartment lease. You will need a second to explain the subtleties built into your contract of employment, a third if you should disagree with the IRS about the size of your contributions to the national economy, a fourth if your doctor makes a slip of the scalpel, a fifth if you get divorced, a sixth. . . . But the list is al-

ready too long and too depressing, and we haven't even begun to venture into criminal law or that most overpopulated branch of an overpopulated profession, corporate law. Lawyers are everywhere except under the bed, and that might not be too far away if their numbers continue to increase.

7   And why do we need them? Self-defense. Because the other side—be it landlord, employer, ex-wife, or whoever—has elected to have a long and expensive argument rather than a quick, cheap one, and has retained a professional representative to do it. It's no good thinking that you, a rank amateur, can conduct your own case. Innocence will get you nowhere these days, and ignorance will cost you dear. You wouldn't be able to under-stand more than one word in ten anyway. There is no alternative but to fight fire with fire and to employ your own legal bodyguard.

8   So we have to assume that lawyers are necessary. But that doesn't ex-plain why they are so heartily detested, so frequently reviled, and even, dare I say it, distrusted. To understand why these attitudes exist, we must look into the mind of the beast himself and see what it is that makes the lawyer tick.

9   His guiding principle, drummed into him from his first days as a cal-low student, is never, under any circumstances, to admit to being wrong, partly because his professional reputation for omniscience would suffer and partly because it might expose him to the awful possibility of a negli-gence suit. Now, it is obviously easier to avoid being wrong if you can avoid stating a clear opinion that may later prove to be arrant nonsense. This is why there is great fondness in legal circles for two well-tried secret weapons that have enabled generations of lawyers to retain the appear-ance of wisdom without the effort of original thought.

10   The vaguer of the two is the Gray Area, into which the lawyer dives like a rabbit down a burrow if anyone should threaten him with a loaded question. On the face of it, he says, you seem to have a strong case. He nods encouragingly and peers at you over the top of his half glasses. But there are some aspects of it, some mitigating factors, some imponderables, one or two possible extenuations—no, it's not quite as cut and dried as it looks to the layman. In fact, he says, this particular instance is rather a Gray Area.

11   The law, as you subsequently discover if you're unfortunate enough to be involved with it often, is almost entirely made up of Gray Areas, and lawyers are deeply, deeply valued for providing opportunities to say ab-solutely nothing in a highly professional manner. The only glimmers of clarity in this fog of obfuscation occur when your case happens to be an exact replica of another case on which judgment was pronounced fifty

years ago and hasn't been challenged since. This is when the second secret weapon is triumphantly produced.

12 Precedent! What a wonderful, labor-saving, *definitive* thing it is. When a lawyer is stuck for an answer, he consults precedent. When he wants to flatten an opponent, he quotes precedent. When he disagrees with some proposed legal novelty, he argues that there's no precedent for it. But what exactly is precedent? Somebody's opinion, grown old and respectable with the passage of time, but still only an opinion. "Precedent" is probably the most popular word in the legal dictionary, and it has a great advantage over the Gray Area because it permits lawyers to be decisive without having to take any responsibility for the decision.

13 But enough of these disparaging comments on the devious nature of the legal personality. Let us now move on to the matter of fees and costs, because it is here more than anywhere that the ordinary man's attitude toward the legal man changes from mild suspicion to violent outrage.

14 We have all read about cases where the costs run into hundreds of thousands of dollars and the settlements into millions. But those figures are so ridiculously overblown, like the budget deficit, that it is impossible to take them seriously. They're not real. They do, however, provide us with dramatic examples of that compulsion, common to all lawyers, for extracting every last cent from a situation. This is not necessarily to make the punishment fit the crime or to put a true and proper value on justice. It is the natural and inevitable consequence of the pound-of-flesh mentality.[1]

15 All lawyers have it. They can't help it; it's in their genes, and it shows itself at every level from the multimillion-dollar lawsuit down to the smallest, most fleeting incident. If a pound of flesh isn't immediately available, a couple of ounces will suffice. I myself have been charged $250 for a cup of coffee and a ten-minute chat, but at least the chat took place in an office. A friend of mine was actually billed for a phone call he made to his lawyer inviting him out to dinner. I didn't ask if there was a further charge for time spent eating the free dinner, but it wouldn't have surprised me.

16 I don't have the exact figures, but I am told that the current growth rate in the legal profession is, in relative terms, far greater than the growth in population. Lawyers are being hatched like chickens, and it is only a

---

1 **pound-of-flesh mentality:** an allusion to Shakespeare's play, *The Merchant of Venice,* in which Shylock, a money lender, promises to extract a pound of Antonio's flesh if he is not repaid the money he lends Antonio.

matter of time before the entire country is overrun. Everywhere will become like those parts of Los Angeles where lawyers outnumber people. The more affluent families will have live-in attorneys. Litigation, once the hobby of the rich, will take over from baseball and football as a leisure activity, and Berlitz will offer courses in Legalese. I have seen the future, and it's a Gray Area.

Looking Back

1. In your opinion, what does the number of lawyers now practicing imply about the values of American society?

2. Compare the tone of Mayle's essay with the tones of Keillor's and Pemberton's essays. How much do you think tone affects a reader's attitude toward a topic?

3. What other groups of people use jargon that is largely incomprehensible to anyone outside that group? What is the effect?

4. All of the lawyers Mayle mentions seem to be men. Did he mean not to include women? Are female lawyers different from men professionally? Does he assume that his use of male pronouns is understood to include women as well? Discuss.

Looking Into

1. Write an essay about another profession or job with which you have had experience, using the same tone that Mayle uses.

2. Write a defense of lawyers and the legal profession. Imagine that you are a lawyer. Explain why your services are useful to society.

The Glass Half Empty

ANNA QUINDLEN

Born in Philadelphia, Anna Quindlen began her writing career with the *New York Post* as a reporter in 1974, the same year she received her B.A. degree from Barnard College. She then went to work for the *New York Times* where she was a city hall and general assignment reporter from 1977 to 1981, the author of a column, "About New York" from 1981 to 1983, deputy metropolitan editor until 1985, author of a weekly column, "Life in the 30's" for two years, and author of a biweekly syndicated column, "Public & Private," beginning in 1990.

She is married to a lawyer and they have three children. "Life in the 30's" was chiefly about her life and family. "Public & Private" won a Pulitzer Prize for commentary in 1992, and Quindlen has been honored by Women in Communications and the Associated Press.

Two collections of her columns have been published: *Living Out Loud* and *Thinking Out Loud*, from which the column that follows is taken. She has also written a novel, *Object Lessons* (1991), and a children's book, *The Tree That Came to Stay* (1992). She has been called "a national treasure," "the laureate of real life," and "the most eloquent voice" of her generation.

Looking Ahead

On her daughter's second birthday, columnist Anna Quindlen had some trenchant thoughts about what the future holds for her. This column appeared in 1990. Do Quindlen's thoughts seem less or more relevant today?

1   My daughter is two years old today. She is something like me, only better. Or at least that is what I like to think. If personalities had colors, hers would be red.

2   Little by little, in the twenty years between my eighteenth birthday and her second one, I had learned how to live in the world. The fact that women were now making 67 cents for every dollar a man makes—well, it was better than 1970, wasn't it, when we mere making only 59 cents? The

constant stories about the underrepresentation of women, on the tenure track in the film industry, in government, everywhere, had become commonplace. The rape cases. The sexual harassment stories. The demeaning comments. Life goes on. Where's your sense of humor?

3   Learning to live in the world meant seeing the glass half full. Ann Richards was elected governor of Texas instead of a good ol' boy who said that if rape was inevitable, you should relax and enjoy it. The police chief of Houston is a pregnant woman who has a level this-is-my-job look and a maternity uniform with stars on the shoulder. There are so many opportunities unheard of when I was growing up.

4   And then I had a daughter and suddenly I saw the glass half empty. And all the rage I thought had cooled, all those how-dare-you-treat-us-like-that days, all of it comes back when I look at her, and especially when I hear her say to her brothers, "Me too."

5   When I look at my sons, it is within reason to imagine all the world's doors open to them. Little by little some will close, as their individual capabilities and limitations emerge. But no one is likely to look at them and mutter: "I'm not sure a man is right for a job at this level. Doesn't he have a lot of family responsibilities?"

6   Every time a woman looks at her daughter and thinks, She can be anything, she knows in her heart, from experience, that it's a lie. Looking at this little girl, I see it all, the old familiar ways of a world that still loves Barbie. Girls aren't good at math, dear. He needs the money more than you, sweetheart; he's got a family to support. Honey—this diaper's dirty.

7   It is like looking through a telescope. Over the years I learned to look through the end that showed things small and manageable. This is called a sense of proportion. And then I turned the telescope around, and all the little tableaux rushed at me, vivid as ever. That's called reality.

8   We soothe ourselves with the gains that have been made. There are many role models. Role models are women who exist—and are photographed often—to make other women feel better about the fact that there aren't really enough of us anywhere, except in the lowest-paying jobs. A newspaper editor said to me not long ago, with no hint of self-consciousness, "I'd love to run your column, but we already run Ellen Goodman." Not only was there a quota; there was a quota of one.

9   My daughter is ready to leap into the world, as though life were chicken soup and she a delighted noodle. The work of Professor Carol Gilligan of Harvard suggests that sometime after the age of eleven this will change, that even this lively little girl will pull back, shrink, that her constant refrain will become "I don't know." Professor Gilligan says the culture sends a

message: "Keep quiet and notice the absence of women and say nothing." A smart thirteen-year-old said to me last week, "Boys don't like it if you answer too much in class."

10   Maybe someday, years from now, my daughter will come home and say, "Mother, at college my professor acted as if my studies were an amusing hobby and at work the man who runs my department puts his hand on my leg and to compete with the man who's in the running for my promotion who makes more than I do I can't take time to have a relationship but he has a wife and two children and I'm smarter and it doesn't make any difference and some guy tried to jump me after our date last night." And what am I supposed to say to her?

11   I know?

12   You'll get used to it?

13   No. Today is her second birthday and she has made me see fresh this two-tiered world, a world that, despite all our nonsense about post-feminism, continues to offer less respect and less opportunity for women than it does for men. My friends and I have learned to live with it, but my little girl deserves better. She has given me my anger back, and I intend to use it well.

14   That is her gift to me today. Some birthday I will return it to her, because she is going to need it.

Looking Back

1. Explain Quindlen's allusions to empty and full glasses and the simile "it is like looking though a telescope."

2. From your experience, is it true that boys don't like it if girls answer too much in class? If so, why do boys feel that way? If not, do you think this statement was ever true? Discuss.

3. What does Quindlen mean by a "two-tiered world"?

Looking Into

1. Compare and contrast Quindlen's views on the treatment of women with Pemberton's views on the treatment of blacks.

2. Write an informal essay on some occasion such as your birthday, a holiday, the last (or first) day of school—any day that is different from the usual ones. Assume that it could be published in a daily paper.

Looking Around

1. Is there value in evaluating a past event from a modern perspective as Paul Fussell and Garrison Keillor do? If so, what is the value? If not, why not? State your opinion in a brief essay.

2. Americans frequently hold widely differing views on politics, education, religion, and the best solutions to various social problems. Is it possible for the U.S. or Canada to continue to accommodate different value systems, or is there a real possibility that either country could break into separate states or provinces? Discuss in a paper of two or three pages.

3. What influence does the media, of which several writers in this section are a part, have on society's values? Discuss in a small group and present your findings in a paper.

4. What values have shaped your life so far? How did you learn these values? Using one or two illustrations from your past, write a paper about at least two of your most important values.

PART 7
Travel

—∭—

I am an offensive traveller. I do not mean that I arrive in a foreign country in a state of arrogance and start complaining about the beds, the plumbing, the food, the transport, the prices. I do not refuse to drink the water; I do not see bacteria everywhere. I do not say: "The country is wonderful, but you can have the people." I do not suspect everyone who speaks a foreign language of being a thief. I do not scream that I cannot get a good steak in Morocco—steak travellers are the hypochondriacs of motion—a decent haggis in Naples, or an edible chop suey on Ascension Island. I do not complain of the lack of Night Life in English villages or of the absence of thatch in Ohio. . . . By "being offensive" I mean that I travel, therefore I offend. I represent that ancient enemy of all communities: the stranger. Neapolitan girls have crossed themselves to avert the evil eye at the sight of me. And rightly: We are looking on the private life of another people, a life which is entirely their business, with an eye that, however friendly it may be, is alien. We are seeing people as they do not see themselves.

V. S. Pritchett from *The Offensive Traveller*

The ancients—Herodotus, Strabo, Pausanius—traveled, but the books they wrote were more often called histories or geographies, not travel books. Marco Polo (1254–1324) was perhaps the first genuine traveler; his trip—from his native Venice, across Persia (present-day Iran) and Afghanistan, to the court of Kublai Khan, and his later voyages to Japan, India, and the islands of Zanzibar and Madagascar—resulted in one of the first true travel books. By the eighteenth century, travel had become a must for those wealthy enough and intrepid enough to put up with the rigors of rutted and muddy roads, accidents, delays, inadequate inns, and brigands.

Paul Fussell, whose essay "On Travel and Travel Writing" begins this section, suggests that the popularity of travel in the eighteenth century might derive from an influential essay by the English philosopher John Locke: *Essay Concerning Human Understanding* (1690).

By the nineteenth century, travelers were interested in more exotic lands—the Middle East, Africa, the South Seas, Asia, America—and many combined travel with scientific exploration. In the 1890s, Mary Kingsley ventured into West Africa in search of fish specimens. *Travels in West Africa*, an account of her experiences with a tribe of reputed cannibals called the Fans, was published in 1894; Kingsley's deft narrative and lively prose style is evident in the excerpt presented.

One of today's premier travel writers is Paul Theroux. His essay "The Boat Train to Dalian: Number 92" chronicles his encounter with an insouciant young Chinese woman at the northern Chinese port city of Dalian. In the opening chapters of her book *Nothing to Declare: Memoirs of a Woman Traveling Alone*, Mary Morris describes her feelings and impressions upon first arriving in Mexico.

The humorist Calvin Trillin, in "Defying Mrs. Tweedie," visits the Sicilian resort town of Taormina and views it partly through the eyes of "a rather severe travel writer of late Victorian times," Mrs. Tweedie.

The final author in this section, Suzanne Berne, argues in her essay "Traveling Close, Very Close, to Home" that "while some believe traveling means going far away—imagining that a trip to Bangkok is travel while a trip to the park is not—others recognize that travel, like relaxation, is mostly a state of mind." Berne might almost call herself an armchair traveler, a person described by Henry Wadsworth Longfellow as one who "travels by the fireside . . . while journeying with another's feet."

On Travel and Travel Writing

Paul Fussell

The son of an attorney, Paul Fussell was born in Pasadena, California, in 1924. During World War II, he fought with the Forty-fifth Infantry Division in Europe; in August, 1945, Fussell was in the process of being sent from Europe to take part in the imminent invasion of Japan. After the war, Fussell finished his undergraduate work at Pomona College, California, and then attended Harvard University where he earned both his M.A. and his Ph.D. in English. Fussell has taught at Connecticut College, Rutgers University, and at the University of Pennsylvania. He has traveled widely in Europe, the Caribbean, the Near East, the Soviet Union, the south Pacific, India, and Asia. Fussell is the author of several books of nonfiction: *Abroad: British Literary Traveling between the Wars* (1980); *The Great War and Modern Memory* (1975), a National Book Award winner; and *Class: A Guide Through the American Status System* (1983), a trenchant examination of America's class structure. His three collections of essays—*The Boy Scout Handbook and Other Observations* (1982), *Thank God for the Atom Bomb and Other Essays* (1988), and *Bad: or The Dumbing of America* (1991)—are wittily provocative. Fussell is also the editor of *The Norton Book of Travel* (1987).

Looking Ahead

In this introduction to *The Norton Book of Travel*, an anthology of travel pieces, Fussell muses first on the lure of travel and, then, on the difference between a genuine travel book and a guidebook. Often, Fussell asserts, the qualities that make travel books last are a skillful combination of the auto-biographical, the eccentric, and the pedagogical.

1   *W*hy is travel so exciting? Partly because it triggers the thrill of escape, from the constriction of the daily, the job, the boss, the parents. "A great part of the pleasure of travel," says Freud, "lies in the fulfillment of . . . early wishes to escape the family and especially the father." There is

thus about travel almost the *frisson* of the unlawful.[1] The escape is also from the traveler's domestic identity, and among strangers a new sense of selfhood can be tried on, like a costume. The anthropologist Claude Lévi-Strauss notes that a traveler takes a journey not just in space and time (most travel being to places more ancient than the traveler's home) but "in the social hierarchy as well"; and he has noticed repeatedly that upon arriving in a new place, he has suddenly become rich (travelers to Mexico, China, or India will know the feeling). The traveler's escape, at least since the Industrial Age, has also been from the ugliness and racket of Western cities, and from factories, parking lots, boring turnpikes, and roadside squalor. Every travel poster constitutes an implicit satire on the modern scene, testifying to the universal longing to escape. The most "advanced" societies prove the most loathsome, and as Nancy Mitford[2] has said, "North Americans very naturally want to get away from North America."

But if travel offers the thrill of quasi-felonious escape, it also conveys the pleasure of learning new things, and as Aristotle observed over 2,300 years ago, not only philosophers but people in general like learning things, even if the learning comes disguised as "entertainment." It is as learners that explorers, tourists, and genuine travelers, otherwise so different in motives and behavior, come together. Explorers learn the contours of undiscovered shorelines and mountains, tourists learn exchange rates and where to go in Paris for the best hamburgers, and travelers learn—well, what they learn can be inferred in detail from the selections in this book, especially the selections in the middle. Travelers learn not just foreign customs and curious cuisines and unfamiliar beliefs and novel forms of government. They learn, if they are lucky, humility. Experiencing on their senses a world different from their own, they realize their provincialism and recognize their ignorance. "Traveling makes one modest," says Flaubert.[3] "You see what a tiny place you occupy in the world." Travel at its truest is thus an ironic experience, and the best travelers—and travel-writers—seem to be those able to hold two or three inconsistent ideas in their minds at the same time, or able to regard themselves as at once serious persons and clowns.

But the irony of traveling can sometimes end in melancholy. Flaubert observes how sad it is to experience a foreign place that is wonderful and

---

1 the *frisson* of the unlawful: In French, *frisson* means "thrill, shiver, or tremor."
2 Nancy Mitford (1904–1973): English novelist and social commentator.
3 [Gustave] Flaubert (1821–1880): French novelist and one of the giants of modern literature; best known for his first novel, *Madame Bovary*.

to know that you will never return to it. All the pathos and irony of leaving one's youth behind is thus implicit in every joyous moment of travel: one knows that the first joy can never be recovered, and the wise traveler learns not to repeat successes but tries new places all the time. The *mélancolies du voyage*—Flaubert's term—are as much a part of travel (but never, significantly, of tourism) as its more obvious delights. When the ship carrying the young Evelyn Waugh[4] was returning to England at the end of his first serious trip to the Mediterranean, he did something he found hard to understand. He was at a farewell party enjoying himself mightily, but "after a time," he remembers in his first travel book *Labels (1930),*

> I went out from the brightly lighted cabin on to the dark boat-deck. . . . I was carrying my champagne glass in my hand, and for no good reason that I can now think of, I threw it out over the side, watched it hover for a moment in the air as it lost momentum and was caught by the wind, then saw it flutter and tumble into the swirl of water. This gesture . . . has become oddly important to me. . . .

[4] In addition, travel sharpens the senses. Abroad, one feels, sees, and hears things in an abnormal way. Thus D. H. Lawrence,[5] one cold morning in Sardinia, all by himself, finds the simple experience of standing alone on a strange road "wonderful":

> Wonderful to go out on a frozen road. . . . Wonderful the bluish, cold air, and things standing up in cold distance. . . . I am so glad, on this lonely naked road, I don't know what to do with myself. . . .

Lord Byron[6] likewise, who held that "the great object of life is . . . to feel that we exist," discovered that feeling in three things: gambling, battle, and travel, all of them "intemperate but keenly felt pursuits . . . whose

---

4 **Evelyn Waugh** (1903–1966): renowned writer of satiric novels, but also a journalist and a travel writer, especially about Africa and South America.
5 **D. H. Lawrence** (1885–1930): English novelist who wrote four travel books.
6 **Lord Byron** (1788–1824): English lord, poet, and indefatigable traveler to Portugal, Spain, Italy, and Greece, where he died fighting for Greek independence from Turkey.

principal attraction is the agitation inseparable from their accomplishment." And the deeply romantic emotion of travel has been felt by Paul Bowles,[7] always searching for a "magic place" which would yield its secrets and grant him "wisdom and ecstasy"—and even, he says, death. Which is to realize that travel—the word derives from *travail*[8]—as a form of heightened experience is like normal experience in not being entirely joyous. Homesickness is one of the traveler's ailments, and so is loneliness. Fear—of strangers, of being embarrassed, of threats to personal safety—is the traveler's usual, if often unadmitted, companion. The sensitive traveler will also feel a degree of guilt at his alienation from ordinary people, at the unearned good fortune that has given him freedom while others labor at their unexciting daily obligations. If a little shame doesn't mingle with the traveler's pleasure, there is probably going to be insufficient ironic resonance in his perceptions.

5   Just as tourism is not travel, the guidebook is not the travel book. The guidebook is to be carried along and to be consulted frequently for practical information. How many *rials* are you allowed to bring in? How expensive is that nice-looking hotel over there? The travel book, on the other hand, is seldom consulted during a trip. Rather, it is read either before or after, and at home, and perhaps most often by a reader who will never take the journey at all. Guidebooks belong to the world of journalism, and they date; travel books belong to literature, and they last. Guidebooks are not autobiographical but travel books are, and if the personality they reveal is too commonplace and un-eccentric, they will not be very readable. Norman Douglas,[9] both a notable eccentric and a notable traveler, knows what he's talking about when he says that

> the reader of a good travel book is entitled not only to an exterior voyage, to descriptions of scenery and so forth, but to an interior, a sentimental or temperamental voyage, which takes place side by side with that outer one; . . . the ideal book of this kind offers us, indeed, a triple opportunity of exploration—abroad, into the author's brain, and into our own. The writer should therefore

---

7 **Paul Bowles:** American composer and novelist who became an expatriate, living most of his professional life in Tangier but traveling widely to such places as India, Ceylon, Turkey.

8 **travail:** trouble, suffering, hardship.

9 **Norman Douglas** (1868–1952): writer of one novel, *South Wind,* but chiefly known for his travel books about Capri, Tunisia, and Calabria.

possess a brain worth exploring; some philosophy of life . . . and the courage to proclaim it and put it to the test; he must be naïf and profound, both child and sage.

And the ideal travel writer is consumed not just with a will to know. He is also moved by a powerful will to teach. Inside every good travel writer there is a pedagogue—often a highly moral pedagogue—struggling to get out.

6   But the pedagogic impulse is not sufficient to make a great travel writer. Neither are acute senses, powerful curiosity, physical and intellectual stamina, and a lively historical, political, and social imagination. A commitment to language and to literary artifice must also be there, and the impulse to write must equal the impulse to travel. T. E. Lawrence[10] once asked Charles Doughty why he'd gone on the laborious journey he wrote about in *Arabia Deserta* (1888). Doughty replied that he had traveled in order "to redeem the English language from the slough into which it had fallen since the time of Spenser."[11] In the heyday of travel writing, in the nineteenth century, excesses even crept in. Then, so many people were making books out of moving around and noticing things and then writing about them that William Makepeace Thackeray[12] devised the term "the letterpress landscape" to suggest the way a given sight might look to a lettered observer. Which was the object of interest, the scene itself or its description in scores of travel books? Was the landscape the attraction, or the language used to memorialize it?

7   The autobiographical narrative at the heart of a travel book will use many of the devices of fiction, which is why a travel diary, whose sequential entries are innocent of what's coming next, is less interesting than a full-fledged travel book, which can create suspense and generate irony by devices of concealment and foreshadowing. The ancient geographer Strabo was convinced that anyone telling about his travels must be a liar, and in a sense he was right, for if a traveler doesn't visit his narrative with the spirit and techniques of fiction, no one will want to hear it. Even if a travel

---

10   **T. E. Lawrence (1888–1935)** and **Charles Doughty** (1843–1926): famed World War I English soldier who became known as "Lawrence of Arabia." Doughty was the author of *Travels in Arabia Deserta,* the record of his Arabian trek (1876–1878) which, when it was republished in 1921, featured an introduction by Lawrence.

11   **[Sir Edward] Spenser** (c. 1552–1599): English poet much admired for his style.

12   **William Makepeace Thackeray** (1811–1863): English novelist and man of letters whose most famous work is *Vanity Fair.*

account does not, like the works of Sir John Mandeville[13] and Marco Polo, trade largely in wonders, it will still resemble the literary form of the *romance*[14] by containing more than a mere *novel's* share of anomalies and scandals and surprises and incredibilities. Travel romances differ from the more overtly fictional ones not in delivering fewer wonders but in being careful to locate their wonders within an actual, verifiable, and often famous topography.

8   Successful travel writing mediates between two poles: the individual physical things it describes, on the one hand, and the larger theme that it is "about," on the other. That is, the particular and the universal. A travel book will make the reader aware of a lot of *things*—ships, planes, trains, donkeys, sore feet, hotels, bizarre customs and odd people, unfamiliar weather, curious architecture, risky food. At the same time, a travel book will reach in the opposite direction and deal with these data so as to suggest that they are not wholly inert and discrete but are elements of a much larger meaning, a meaning metaphysical, political, psychological, artistic, or religious—but always, somehow, ethical. Stendhal[15] seems to be hinting at something similar when he observes that "It is not enough for a landscape to be interesting in itself. Eventually there must be a moral and historic interest." (A reason, perhaps, why the National Parks are less interesting to the real traveler than, say, the D-Day beaches of Normandy.) The travel book is about two things at once. As the critic Samuel Hynes points out, it is "a dual-plane work with a strong realistic surface, which is yet a parable." And the parable most often takes the form of a metaphor of understanding, and understanding by a process of intellectual kinesis, of the mind in motion.

---

13   **Sir John Mandeville** (14th century): purported author of *The Travels of Sir John Mandeville*, a famous travel book whose stated aim was to be a guide book for pilgrims to the Holy Land but that veered off into such areas as Turkey, Arabia, India, and Egypt. The work was published in France in c. 1356–1357 and its description of fabulous wonders influenced both Chaucer and Shakespeare. The author was probably English but virtually nothing is known about him or, indeed, if he ever traveled further than the library of the monastery at St. Alban's north of London.

14   **romance:** The precursor of the novel, a "romance" was a narrative that emphasized exotic adventures—wars, kidnappings, and sundry catastrophes—rather than realistic characterization. The medieval romance, written in verse or prose, usually dealt with the legends about King Arthur, or Charlemagne, and their knights, and emphasized the power of love and the virtues—courage, grace, honor—of chivalry.

15   **Stendhal** (1783–1842): pseudonym of Henri Beyle, French novelist, critic, and travel writer.

⁹   I am aware that everyone's favorite travel piece is not included in this book, and I am sorry. There is so much good travel writing that a library couldn't contain it all, and this is merely one book of selections. Separating out the best requires draconic standards. I have tried to choose people who are not just admirable travelers, sensitive, indefatigable, and if possible, ironic and even funny when appropriate, but admirable writers as well, equally interested in traveling and making lively sentences out of it. And I hope no one will take the amount of space accorded each writer as an indication of his or her value. Some writers write short, some long, and it is this fact, together with the exigencies of natural divisions, that has determined the length of the selections.

Looking Back

1. According to Fussell, what reasons prompt people to travel? To what extent do your own travel experiences bear out his assertions?

2. What significant contemporary reason for traveling does Fussell ignore and why?

3. Fussell differentiates between the guidebook and the travel book. Find a copy of Richard Haliburton's *The Royal Road to Romance* or Mark Twain's book *Innocents Abroad* or another work approved by your teacher, read a chapter, and in small discussion groups classify the chapter as either a guidebook or a travel book.

4. Fussell also differentiates between "explorers, tourists, and genuine travelers." How are they alike? How different? Ask yourself which category you probably fit in at this point in your life.

Looking Into

1. Fussell writes that the genuine traveler must have "acute senses, powerful curiosity, physical and intellectual stamina, and a lively historical, political, and social imagination." In three or four paragraphs,

describe the one person among your acquaintances who best fits this description. Use specific supporting examples.

2. Many writers convey their impressions about a place on postcards or in letters. Write a two-page letter to a friend in which you use, in Fussell's sense, "the devices of fiction" to make a person, a place, or an incident come alive.

3. Write a short paper about the one place in the world you would most like to visit. Explain why you want to go there and what specific things you would expect to see.

from Travels in West Africa

MARY KINGSLEY

Mary Kingsley was born in London in 1862, the daughter of an eccentric physician and amateur anthropologist who traveled widely in Asia, the South Seas, and America. Kingsley led a relatively secluded life until 1892, when her sickly parents died within six months of each other. Through an uncle she met scientists who gave her the idea of collecting fish in Africa and thus contributing to scientific knowledge. Still, as she despondently wrote to a friend, "Dead tired, and feeling no one had need of me any more . . . I went down to West Africa to die." On her first trip, in 1893, she traveled through Cabinda, off the coast of Angola; Old Calabar in southeast Nigeria; an island near the Cameroon coast; and the lower Congo River.

In December 1894, she returned to Africa, this time outfitted by the British Museum for collecting additional specimens in French Congo, Nigeria, and in Gabon, where she went up the Ogowe river through the tribal country of the Fan. She returned to England a year later, in December 1895, with a valuable natural history collection that included a fish, new to the scientific world, from the Ogowe. She subsequently lectured throughout England on Africa and the conditions of the Africans under colonial rule, and wrote the first of her two books about Africa: *Travels in West Africa* (1897). Two years later she published her influential *West African Studies* (1899), an examination of the culture and mores of the peoples of West Africa, both natives and colonials.

According to J. E. Flint, a historian at the University of Nigeria, Kingsley's two books "helped to change in a profound way the attitude of European colonial administrators towards their African subjects." In 1900, Kingsley was planning a third expedition to Africa when the Boer War in South Africa broke out. Postponing her trip, she offered her services to the British government in South Africa as a nurse. The government sent her to a camp for Boer prisoners. Two months later, in June 1900, she died in the camp of fever.

Looking Ahead

As keepers of the home and raisers of children, few women before the twentieth century had the opportunity to travel—except in the company of their husbands or families. Among the notable exceptions was Mary Kingsley. Her literary heritage—her uncle Charles Kingsley was the author of such beloved nineteenth-century English novels as *Westward Ho!* and *The Water Babies*—is evident in her detailed, often ironic narrative and in her delight and awe at the fearsome and impressive animals of West Africa.

[1]   *M*y main aim in going to Congo Francais[1] was to get up above the tide line of the Ogowe River[2] and there collect fishes; for my object on this voyage was to collect fish from a river north of the Congo. I had hoped this river would have been the Niger, for Sir George Goldie[3] had placed at my disposal great facilities for carrying on work there in comfort; but for certain private reasons I was disinclined to go from the Royal Niger Protectorate into the Royal Niger Company's territory; and the Calabar, where Sir Claude MacDonald[4] did everything he possibly could to assist me, I did not find a good river for me to collect fishes in. These two rivers failing me, from no fault of either of their own presiding genii,[5] my only hope of doing anything now lay on the South West Coast river, the Ogowe. . . .

[2]   There is an uniformity in the habits of West Coast rivers, from the Volta to the Coanza, which is, when you get used to it, very taking. Excepting the Congo, the really great river comes out to sea with as much mystery as possible; lounging lazily along among its mangrove swamps in a what's-it-matter when-one-comes-out and where's-the-hurry style, through quantities of channels inter-communicating with each other. Each channel, at first sight as like the other as peas in a pod, is bordered on either side by green-black walls of mangroves, which Captain Lugard[6] graphically de-

1 **Congo Francais:** known in Kingsley's time as French Equatorial Africa.

2 **Ogowe River:** a north-south tributary of the Congo, now spelled Ogooue.

3 **Sir George Goldie** (1846–1925): English administrator who was the founder/creator of the Royal Niger Company, a commercial company which, in 1900, eventually sold its African interests, including control of the entire Niger River, to Britain, thus increasing Britain's imperial territories.

4 **Sir Claude MacDonald** (1852–1915): British soldier and diplomat who, as a British government commissioner, established a stable government in Nigeria in the late 1800s.

5 **genii:** The plural of genie, protective spirits.

6 **Captain Lugard:** "A colonial administrator who served in the British East Africa Company."—M. K. [Mangrove swamps are comprised of tropical trees or shrubs that grow along estuaries, salt marshes or on muddy coasts. In low tide, the roots are above ground and, to a well-bred Victorian man such as Lugard, might suggest ankles, a part of the anatomy which a proper Victorian male would not mention nor a female reveal.]

scribed as seeming "as if they had lost all count of the vegetable proprieties, and were standing on stilts with their branches tucked up out of the wet, leaving their gaunt roots exposed in mid-air." High-tide or low-tide, there is little difference in the water; the river, be it broad or narrow, deep or shallow, looks like a pathway of polished metal; for it is as heavy weighted with stinking mud as water e'er can be, ebb or flow, year out and year in. But the difference in the banks, though an unending alternation between two appearances, is weird.

[3] At high-water you do not see the mangroves displaying their ankles in the way that shocked Captain Lugard. They look most respectable, their foliage rising densely in a wall irregularly striped here and there by the white line of an aerial root, coming straight down into the water from some upper branch as straight as a plummet, in the strange, knowing way an aerial root of a mangrove does, keeping the hard straight line until it gets some two feet above water-level, and then spreading out into blunt fingers with which to dip into the water and grasp the mud. Banks indeed at high water can hardly be said to exist, the water stretching away into the mangrove swamps for miles and miles, and you can then go, in a suitable small canoe, away among these swamps as far as you please.

[4] This is a fascinating pursuit. For people who like that sort of thing it is just the sort of thing they like, as the art critic of a provincial town wisely observed anent an impressionist picture recently acquired for the municipal gallery. But it is a pleasure to be indulged in with caution; for one thing, you are certain to come across crocodiles. Now a crocodile drifting down in deep water, or lying asleep with its jaws open on a sandbank in the sun, is a picturesque adornment to the landscape when you are on the deck of a steamer, and you can write home about it and frighten your relations on your behalf; but when you are away among the swamps in a small dug-out canoe, and that crocodile and his relations are awake—a thing he makes a point of being at flood tide because of fish coming along—and when he has got his foot upon his native heath—that is to say, his tail within holding reach of his native mud—he is highly interesting, and you may not be able to write home about him—and you get frightened on your own behalf. For crocodiles can, and often do, in such places, grab at people in small canoes. I have known of several natives losing their lives in this way; some native villages are approachable from the main river by a short cut, as it were, through the mangrove swamps, and the inhabitants of such villages will now and then go across this way with small canoes instead of by the constant channel to the village, which is almost always winding. In addition to this unpleasantness you are liable—until you realize the danger from experience, or have native advice on the point—to get tide-trapped

away in the swamps, the water falling round you when you are away in some deep pool or lagoon, and you find you cannot get back to the main river. For you cannot get out and drag your canoe across the stretches of mud that separate you from it, because the mud is of too unstable a nature and too deep, and sinking into it means staying in it, at any rate until some geologist of the remote future may come across you, in a fossilized state, when that mangrove swamp shall have become dry land. Of course if you really want a truly safe investment in Fame, and really care about Posterity, and Posterity's Science, you will jump over into the black batter-like, stinking slime, cheered by the thought of the terrific sensation you will produce 20,000 years hence, and the care you will be taken of then by your fellow-creatures, in a museum. But if you are a mere ordinary person of a retiring nature, like me, you stop in your lagoon until the tide rises again; most of your attention is directed to dealing with an "at home"[7] to crocodiles and mangrove flies, and with the fearful stench of the slime round you. What little time you have over you will employ in wondering why you came to West Africa, and why, after having reached this point of absurdity, you need have gone and painted the lily and adorned the rose,[8] by being such a colossal ass as to come fooling about in mangrove swamps. Twice this chatty little incident, as Lady MacDonald[9] would call it, has happened to me, but never again if I can help it. On one occasion, the last, a mighty Silurian,[10] as *The Daily Telegraph* would call him, chose to get his front paws over the stern of my canoe, and endeavored to improve our acquaintance. I had to retire to the bows, to keep the balance right,[11] and fetch him a clip on the snout with a paddle, when he withdrew, and I paddled into the very middle of the lagoon, hoping the water there was too deep for him or any of his friends to repeat the performance. Presumably it was, for no one did it again. I should think that crocodile was eight feet

---

7 **"at home":** in Victorian times, a morning or afternoon time when the lady of the house was "at home" to any visitors who wanted to drop in for conversation, a cup of tea, and some sandwiches or cakes. Kingsley is being ironic in her use of the term.

8 **painted the lily and adorned the rose:** Since lilies were often thought to be uniquely beautiful, to 'gild' or paint the lily, or adorn a rose, is a metaphor expressing unnecessary additional decoration.

9 **Lady MacDonald:** presumably the wife of commissioner MacDonald.

10 **Silurian:** The crocodile was associated with this third period of the Paleozoic Age, a geological age dating some 425,000,000 years ago.

11 **to keep the balance right;** "It is no use saying because I was frightened, for this miserably understates the case."—M. K.

long; but don't go and say I measured him, or that this is my outside mea-surement for crocodiles. I have measured them when they have been killed by other people, fifteen, eighteen, and twenty-one feet odd. This was only a pushing young creature who had not learnt manners.

* * *

5   You often hear the utter lifelessness of mangrove-swamps commented on; why I do not know, for they are fairly heavily stocked with fauna, though the species are comparatively few. There are the crocodiles, more of them than any one wants; there are quantities of flies, particularly the big silent mangrove-fly which lays an egg in you under the skin; the egg be-comes a maggot and stays there until it feels fit to enter into external life. Then there are "slimy things that crawl with legs upon a slimy sea," and any quantity of hopping mud-fish, and crabs, and a certain mollusc, and in the water various kinds of cat-fish. Birdless they are save for the flocks of gray parrots that pass over them at evening, hoarsely squarking; and save for this squarking of the parrots the swamps are silent all the day, at least during the dry season; in the wet season there is no silence night or day in West Africa, but that roar of the descending deluge of rain that is more monotonous and more gloomy than any silence can be. In the morning you do not hear the long, low mellow whistle of the plantain-eaters calling up the dawn, nor in the evening the clock-bird nor the Handel-Festival-sized choruses of frogs, or the crickets, that carry on their vesper contro-versy of "she did"—"she didn't" so fiercely on hard land.

6   But the mangrove-swamp follows the general rule for West Africa, and night in it is noisier than the day. After dark it is full of noises; grunts from I know not what, splashes from jumping fish, the peculiar whirr of rushing crabs, and quaint creaking and groaning sounds from the trees; and—above all in eeriness—the strange whine and sighing cough of crocodiles. I shall never forget one moonlight night I spent in a mangrove-swamp. I was not lost, but we had gone away into the swamp from the main river, so that the natives of a village with an evil reputation should not come across us when they were out fishing. We got well in, on to a long pool or lagoon; and dozed off and woke, and saw the same scene around us twenty times in the night, which thereby grew into an eon, until I dreamily felt that I had somehow got into a world that was all like this, and always had been, and was always going to be so. Now and again the strong musky smell came that meant a crocodile close by, and one had to rouse up and see if all the crews' legs were on board. . . . On one examination I found the leg of one of my most precious men ostentatiously sticking out over the side of

the canoe. I woke him with a paddle, and said a few words regarding the inadvisability of wearing his leg like this in our situation; and he agreed with me, saying he had lost a valued uncle, who had been taken out of a canoe in this same swamp by a crocodile. His uncle's ghost had become, he said, a sort of devil which had been a trial to the family ever since; and he thought it must have pulled his leg out in the way I complained of, in order to get him to join him by means of another crocodile. I thanked him for the information and said it quite explained the affair, and I should do my best to prevent another member of the family from entering the state of devildom by aiming blows in the direction of any leg or arm I saw that uncle devil pulling out to place within reach of the crocodiles.

* * *

[7] It is a strange, wild, lonely bit of the world we are now in, apparently a lake or broad[12]—full of sandbanks, some bare and some in the course of developing into permanent islands by the growth on them of that floating coarse grass, any joint of which being torn off either by the current, a passing canoe, or hippos, floats down and grows wherever it settles. . . .

[8] We skirt alongside a great young island of this class; the sword grass some ten or fifteen feet high. It has not got any trees on it yet, but by next season or so it doubtless will have. The grass is stubbled down into paths by hippos, and just as I have realized who are the road-makers, they appear in person. One immense fellow, hearing us, stands up and shows himself about six feet from us in the grass, gazes calmly, and then yawns a yawn a yard wide and grunts his news to his companions. . . . We put our helm paddles hard a starboard and leave that bank. These hippos always look to me as if they were the first or last creations in the animal world. At present I am undecided whether Nature tried "her 'prentice hand"[13] on them in her earliest youth, or whether, having got thoroughly tired of making the delicately beautiful antelopes, corallines, butterflies, and orchids, she just said: "Goodness! I am quite worn out with this finicking work. Here, just put these other viscera into big bags—I can't bother any more."

---

12 **broad:** marsh land.
13 **"her 'prentice hand":** a part of a Robert Burns' poem, "To the Guidwife of Wauchope-House"; the word *'prentice* is a shortened form of the word *apprentice*. The stanza reads: "Auld nature swears, the lovely dears / Her noblest work she classes O; / Her prentice han' she tried on man, / An' then she made the lasses O."

[9] Our hasty trip across to the bank of the island on the other side being accomplished, we, in search of seclusion and in the hope that out of sight would mean out of mind to hippos, shot down a narrow channel between semi-island sandbanks, and those sandbanks, if you please, are covered with specimens—as fine a set of specimens as you could wish for—of the West African crocodile. These interesting animals are also having their siestas, lying sprawling in all directions on the sand, with their mouths wide open. One immense old lady has a family of lively young crocodiles running over her, evidently playing like a lot of kittens. The heavy musky smell they give off is most repulsive, but we do not rise up and make a row about this, because we feel hopelessly in the wrong in intruding into these family scenes uninvited, and so apologetically pole ourselves along rapidly, not even singing.

* * *

[After traveling up river, Kingsley's party begins its land journey.]

[10] Our first day's march was a very long one. Path in the ordinary acceptance of the term there was none. Hour after hour, mile after mile, we passed on, in the under-gloom of the great forest. The pace made by the Fans, who are infinitely the most rapid Africans I have ever come across, severely tired the Ajumba,[14] who are canoe men, and who had been as fresh as paint, after their exceedingly long day's paddling from Arevooma to M'fetta. Ngouta, the Igalwa interpreter, felt pumped, and said as much, very early in the day. . . . The Fans were evidently quite at home in the forest, and strode on over fallen trees and rocks with an easy, graceful stride. What saved us weaklings was the Fans' appetites; every two hours they sat down, and had a snack of a pound or so of meat and aguma[15] apiece, followed by a pipe of tobacco. We used to come up with them at these halts. Ngouta and the Ajumba used to sit down and rest with them, and I also, for a few minutes, for a rest and chat, and then I would go on alone, thus getting a good start. I got a good start, in the other meaning of the word, on the afternoon of the first day when descending into a ravine.

[11] I saw in the bottom, wading and rolling in the mud, a herd of five elephants. I am certain that owing to some misapprehension among the Fates

---

14 **Fans and Ajumba:** two of the tribes in this part of West Africa.
15 **aguma:** a paste-like meal made from the root of the manioc plant.

I was given a series of magnificent sporting chances, intended as a special treat for some favorite Nimrod[16] of those three ladies, and I know exactly how I ought to have behaved. I should have felt my favorite rifle fly to my shoulder, and then, carefully sighting for the finest specimen, have fired. The noble beast should have stumbled forward, recovered itself, and shedding its life blood behind it have crashed away into the forest. I should then have tracked it, and either with one well-directed shot have given it its quietus, or have got charged by it, the elephant passing completely over my prostrate body; either termination is good form, but I never have these things happen, and never will. (In the present case I remembered, hastily, that your one chance when charged by several elephants is to dodge them round trees, working down wind all the time, until they lose smell and sight of you, then to lie quiet for a time, and go home.) It was evident from the utter unconcern of these monsters that I was down wind now, so I had only to attend to dodging, and I promptly dodged round a tree, thinking perhaps a dodge in time saves nine—and I lay down. Seeing they still displayed no emotion on my account, and fascinated by the novelty of the scene, I crept forward from one tree to another, until I was close enough to have hit the nearest one with a stone, and spats of mud, which they sent flying with the stamping and wallowing came flap, flap among the bushes covering me.

[12] One big fellow had a nice pair of 40 lb. or so tusks on him, singularly straight, and another had one big curved tusk and one broken one. If I were an elephant I think I would wear the tusks straight; they must be more effective weapons thus, but there seems no fixed fashion among elephants here in this matter. Some of them lay right down like pigs in the deeper part of the swamp, some drew up trunkfuls of water and syringed themselves and each other, and every one of them indulged in a good rub against a tree. Presently when they had had enough of it they all strolled off up wind, a way elephants have;[17] but why I do not know, because they know the difference, always carrying their trunk differently when they are going up wind to what they do when they are going down—arrested mental development, I suppose. They strolled through the bush in Indian file, now and then breaking off a branch, but leaving singularly little dead water for their tonnage and breadth of beam. One laid his trunk affectionately on the back of the one in front of him, which I believe to be the elephant equiv-

---

16 **Nimrod:** Noah's great-grandson who, in Genesis 10: 8–10, is a mighty hunter.
17 **a way elephants have:** "Foolish, because natives always attack them in the rear."—M. K.

alent to walking arm-in-arm. When they had gone I rose up, turned round to find the men, and trod on Kiva's back then and there, full and fair, and fell sideways down the steep hillside until I fetched up among some roots.

[13] It seems Kiva had come on, after his meal, before the others, and seeing the elephants, and being a born hunter, had crawled like me down to look at them. He had not expected to find me there, he said. I do not believe he gave a thought of any sort to me in the presence of these fascinating creatures, and so he got himself trodden on. I suggested to him we should pile the baggage, and go and have an elephant hunt. He shook his head reluctantly, saying "Kor, kor," like a depressed rook, and explained we were not strong enough; there were only three Fans—the Ajumba, and Ngouta did not count—and moreover that we had not brought sufficient ammunition owing to the baggage having to be carried, and the ammunition that we had must be saved for other game than elephant, for we might meet war before we met the Rembwe River.

* * *

[Kingsley and her party trek on into more mountainous country with forests of both ebony and "thin spindly stemmed trees of great height," and past timber falls "with more snakes and centipedes among it than you had any immediate use for, even though you were a collector."]

[14] When we got into the cool forest beyond it was delightful; particularly if it happened to be one of those lovely stretches of forest, gloomy down below, but giving hints that far away above us was a world of bloom and scent and beauty which we saw as much of as earthworms in a flower-bed. Here and there the ground was strewn with great cast blossoms, thick, wax-like, glorious cups of orange and crimson and pure white, each one of which was in itself a handful, and which told us that some of the trees around us were showing a glory of color to heaven alone. Sprinkled among them were bunches of pure stephanotis-like flowers.

* * *

[15] The first day in the forest we came across a snake—a beauty with a new red-brown and yellow-patterned velvety skin, about three feet six inches long and as thick as a man's thigh. Ngouta met it, hanging from a bough, and shot backwards like a lobster, Ngouta having among his many weaknesses a rooted horror of snakes. This snake the Ogowe natives all hold in great aversion. For the bite of other sorts of snakes they profess to

have remedies, but for this they have none. If, however, a native is stung by one he usually conceals the fact that it was this particular kind, and tries to get any chance the native doctor's medicine may give. The Duke[18] stepped forward and with one blow flattened its head against the tree with his gun butt, and then folded the snake up and got as much of it as possible into the bag, while the rest hung dangling out. Ngouta, not being able to keep ahead of the Duke, his Grace's pace being stiff, went to the extreme rear of the party, so that other people might be killed first if the snake returned to life, as he surmised it would. We had the snake for supper, that is to say the Fan and I; the others would not touch it, although a good snake, properly cooked, is one of the best meats one gets out here, far and away better than the African fowl.

[16]   The Fan also did their best to educate me in every way; they told me their names for things, while I told them mine. I found several European words already slightly altered in use among them, such as "Amuck"—a mug, "Alas"—a glass, a tumbler. I do not know whether their "Ami"—a person addressed, or spoken of—is French or not. It may come from "Anwe"—M'Pongwe for "Ye," "you." They use it as a rule in addressing a person after the phrase they always open up conversation with, "Azuna"—Listen, or I am speaking.

[17]   They also showed me many things: how to light a fire from the pith of a certain tree, which was useful to me in after life, but they rather overdid this branch of instruction one way and another; for example, Wiki had . . . a mania for bush-ropes and a marvelous eye and knowledge of them; he would pick out from among the thousands surrounding us now one of such peculiar suppleness that you could wind it round anything, like a strip of cloth, and as strong withal as a hawser; or again another which has a certain stiffness, combined with a slight elastic spring, excellent for hauling, with the ease and accuracy of a lady who picks out the particular twisted strand of embroidery silk from a multi-colored tangled ball. He would go into the bush after them while other people were resting, and particularly after the sort which, when split is bright yellow, and very supple and excellent to tie round loads.

[18]   On one occasion, between Egaja and Esoon, he came back from one of these quests and wanted me to come and see something, very quietly: I

---

18 **the Duke:** an ironic name Kingsley gives to a tribesman who has accompanied the Kingsley expedition just "to see the fun." She describes him as a "Fan gentleman with the manners of a duke."

went, and we crept down into a rocky ravine, on the other side of which lay one of the outermost Egaja plantations. When we got to the edge of the cleared ground, we lay down, and wormed our way, with elaborate caution, among a patch of Koko; Wiki first, I following in his trail.

[19]   After about fifty yards of this, Wiki sank flat, and I saw before me some thirty yards off, busily employed in pulling down plantains, and other depredations, five gorillas: one old male, one young male, and three females. One of these had clinging to her a young fellow, with beautiful wavy black hair with just a kink in it. The big male was crouching on his haunches, with his long arms hanging down on either side, with the backs of his hands on the ground, the palms upwards. The elder lady was tearing to pieces and eating a pine-apple, while the others were at the plantains destroying more than they ate.

[20]   They kept up a sort of a whinnying, chattering noise, quite different from the sound I have heard gorillas give when enraged, or from the one you can hear them giving when they are what the natives call "dancing" at night. I noticed that their reach of arm was immense, and that when they went from one tree to another, they squattered across the open ground in a most inelegant style, dragging their long arms with the knuckles downwards. I should think the big male and female were over six feet each. The others would be from four to five. I put out my hand and laid it on Wiki's gun to prevent him from firing, and he, thinking I was going to fire, gripped my wrist.

[21]   I watched the gorillas with great interest for a few seconds, until I heard Wiki make a peculiar small sound, and looking at him saw his face was working in an awful way as he clutched his throat with his hand violently.

[22]   Heavens! think I, this gentleman's going to have a fit; it's lost we are entirely this time. He rolled his head to and fro, and then buried his face into a heap of dried rubbish at the foot of a plantain stem, clasped his hands over it, and gave an explosive sneeze. The gorillas let go all, raised themselves up for a second, gave a quaint sound between a bark and a howl, and then the ladies and the young gentleman started home. The old male rose to his full height (it struck me at the time this was a matter of ten feet at least, but for scientific purposes allowance must be made for a lady's emotions) and looked straight towards us, or rather towards where that sound came from. Wiki went off into a paroxysm of falsetto sneezes the like of which I have never heard; nor evidently had the gorilla, who . . . went off after his family with a celerity that was amazing the moment he touched the forest, and disappeared as they had, swinging himself along through it from bough to bough, in a way that convinced me that, given the

necessity of getting about in tropical forest, man has made a mistake in getting his arms shortened. I have seen many wild animals in their native wilds, but never have I seen anything to equal gorillas going through bush; it is a graceful, powerful, superbly perfect hand-trapeze performance.[19]

23   After this sporting adventure, we returned, as I usually return from a sporting adventure, without measurements of the body.

* * *

[Kingsley also had a series of encounters with leopards.]

24 I must say the African leopard is an audacious animal, although it is ungrateful of me to say a word against him, after the way he has let me off personally, and I will speak of his extreme beauty as compensation for my ingratitude. I really think, taken as a whole, he is the most lovely animal I have ever seen; only seeing him, in the one way you can gain a full idea of his beauty, namely in his native forest, is not an unmixed joy to a person, like myself, of a nervous disposition. I may remark that my nervousness regarding the big game of Africa is of a rather peculiar kind. I can confidently say I am not afraid of any wild animal—until I see it—and then—well I will yield to nobody in terror. . . . Whenever I have come across an awful animal in the forest and I know it has seen me, I take Jerome's advice, and instead of relying on the power of the human eye rely upon that of the human leg, and effect a masterly retreat in the face of the enemy. If I know it has not seen me I sink in my tracks and keep an eye on it, hoping that it will go away soon. Thus I once came upon a leopard. I had got caught in a tornado in a dense forest. The massive, mighty trees were waving like a wheat-field in an autumn gale in England, and I dare say a field mouse in a wheat-field in a gale would have heard much the same uproar. The tornado shrieked like ten thousand vengeful demons. The great trees creaked and groaned and strained against it and their bush-rope cables groaned and smacked like whips, and ever and anon a thundering crash with snaps like pistol shots told that they and their mighty tree had

---

19 **hand-trapeze performance:** "I have no hesitation in saying that the gorilla is the most horrible wild animal I have seen. I have seen at close quarters specimens of the most important big game of Central Africa, and, with the exception of snakes, I have run away from all of them; but although elephants, leopards, and pythons give you a feeling of alarm, they do not give that feeling of horrible disgust that an old gorilla gives on account of its hideousness of appearance."—M. K.

strained and struggled in vain. The fierce rain came in a roar, tearing to shreds the leaves and blossoms and deluging everything. I was making bad weather of it, and climbing up over a lot of rocks out of a gully bottom where I had been half drowned in a stream, and on getting my head to the level of a block of rock I observed right in front of my eyes, broadside on, maybe a yard off, certainly not more, a big leopard. He was crouching on the ground, with his magnificent head thrown back and his eyes shut. His fore-paws were spread out in front of him and he lashed the ground with his tail, and I grieve to say, in face of that awful danger—I don't mean me, but the tornado—that depraved creature swore, softly, but repeatedly and profoundly. I did not get all these facts up in one glance, for no sooner did I see him than I ducked under the rocks, and remembered thankfully that leopards are said to have no power of smell. But I heard his observation on the weather, and the flip-flap of his tail on the ground. Every now and then I cautiously took a look at him with one eye round a rock-edge, and he remained in the same position. My feelings tell me he remained there twelve months, but my calmer judgment puts the time down at twenty minutes; and at last, on taking another cautious peep, I saw he was gone. . . .

25 I have never hurt a leopard intentionally; I am habitually kind to animals, and besides I do not think it is ladylike to go shooting things with a gun. Twice, however, I have been in collision with them. On one occasion a big leopard had attacked a dog, who, with her family, was occupying a broken-down hut next to mine. The dog was a half-bred boarhound, and a savage brute on her own account. I, being roused by the uproar, rushed out into the feeble moonlight, thinking she was having one of her habitual turns-up with other dogs, and I saw a whirling mass of animal matter within a yard of me. I fired two mushroom-shaped native stools in rapid succession into the brown of it, and the meeting broke up into a leopard and a dog. The leopard crouched, I think to spring on me. I can see its great, beautiful, lambent eyes still, and I seized an earthen water-cooler and flung it straight at them. It was a noble shot; it burst on the leopard's head like a shell and the leopard went for bush one time. Twenty minutes after people began to drop in cautiously and inquire if anything was the matter, and I civilly asked them to go and ask the leopard in the bush, but they firmly refused. We found the dog had got her shoulder slit open as if by a blow from a cutlass, and the leopard had evidently seized the dog by the scruff of her neck, but owing to the loose folds of skin no bones were broken and she got round all right after much ointment from me, which she paid me for with several bites. Do not mistake this for a sporting adventure. I no more thought it was a leopard than that it was a lotus when I joined the fight. My other leopard was also after a dog. Leopards always come

after dogs, because once upon a time the leopard and the dog were great friends, and the leopard went out one day and left her whelps in the charge of the dog, and the dog went out flirting, and a snake came and killed the whelps, so there is ill-feeling to this day between the two. For the benefit of sporting readers whose interest may have been excited by the mention of big game, I may remark that the largest leopard skin I ever measured myself was, tail included, 9 feet 7 inches. It was a dried skin, and every man who saw it said, "It was the largest skin he had ever seen, except one that he had seen somewhere else."

Looking Back

1. Working in small groups, determine what three adjectives best describe Mary Kingsley.

2. Fussell might rightfully categorize Kingsley as an explorer, but in what ways does she also fit his concept of the genuine traveler?

3. Kingsley describes her encounters with crocodiles, elephants, gorillas and leopards. Is her attitude toward each of these creatures the same? Support your answer with specifics from the text.

4. What evidence is there in the excerpt that Kingsley is interested in the natives for reasons beyond their practical contributions to her expedition? What does this evidence tell about Kingsley herself?

5. Kingsley speaks a number of times of the fear and worry she experienced as a traveler. What qualities in her seem to have balanced the fear and made her capable of undertaking her extraordinary adventures?

Looking Into

1. Two of the "devices of literature" that Kingsley uses are allusion and various figures of speech. Make a list of any examples in the first four pages of allusions and of similes, metaphors, and personification. In a paragraph comment on one or two that you find particularly appropriate.

2. In a travel magazine or in a source such as *National Geographic Magazine,* find a foreign landscape containing as much detail as possible. Put yourself somewhere in the picture and write a 250- to 300-word descriptive paragraph that focuses on at least three of the five senses. In addition, try to incorporate figurative language and, if possible, allusion. Your aim is to re-create for the reader the total experience you are having.

3. Have you ever had a dangerous or frightening encounter with an animal? It doesn't have to be a crocodile or leopard—a dog or cat will do. Write a brief description of the encounter, providing as many details as you can remember. Your treatment of the subject may be serious or humorous.

from The Boat Train to Dalian: Number 92

PAUL THEROUX

Of French-Canadian descent, Paul Theroux was born in Medford, Massachusetts, in 1941, the third of seven children in a working-class family. He began his undergraduate work at the University of Maine and finished his B.A., in 1963, at the University of Massachusetts. Almost immediately, he joined the Peace Corps and from 1963–1965 taught at Soche Hill College, Limbe, Malawi. After being deported from Malawi, on the questionable charge of spying, and expelled from the Peace Corps, he returned to Africa as a lecturer at Makerere University, Kampala, Uganda, 1965–1968.

In 1968, Theroux took a teaching position at the University of Singapore. In 1971, having published five novels, he became a professional writer. His first novel, *Waldo*, was published in 1967, and has been followed by a novel, a collection of short stories or essays, or a travel book nearly every year since.

His novels include *Saint Jack* (1973) and *The Mosquito Coast* (1982), both of which were made into films, and *O-Zone* (1986); his most recent is *Millman the Magician* (1994). In addition to such travel books as *The Great Railway Bazaar* (1975), *The Old Patagonian Express* (1979), and *Riding the Iron Rooster* (1988), he has written *Sailing through China* (1984), a short account of a boat trip down the Yangtze River, and *The Kingdom by the Sea: A Journey Around the Coast of Britain* (1983). In an essay in *Sunrise with Seamonsters: Travels and Discoveries* (1985), he writes: "Travel is a creative act—not simply loafing and inviting your soul, but feeding the imagination, accounting for each fresh wonder, memorizing and moving on. The discoveries the traveler makes in broad daylight—the curious problems of the eye he solves—resemble those that thrill and sustain a novelist in his solitude."

Looking Ahead

Paul Theroux's first travel book, *The Great Railway Bazaar,* was an account of a railway trip through Asia on such once-glorious trains as the Orient Express, the Khyber Mail, and the Trans-Siberian Express. Four years later he published *The Old Patagonian Express: By Train through the Americas,* a trip that took him from Boston to the southern tip of South America. In the 1980s, Theroux spent nearly a year exploring China by rail; this excerpt from his book *Riding the Iron Rooster: By Train Through China* (1988) finds him being met by an eager guide at Dalian, a port city about 300 miles east of Beijing, after a trip through Inner Mongolia and Manchuria. Theroux's eye, and ear, for the incongruous makes his encounter with Cherry Blossom a satiric delight.

—〰—

[1] The train continued through the flat, snowy fields, all of them showing plow marks and furrows and stubble beneath the ice crust. There were factories, and they looked beautiful, blurred and softened and silvered by frost and the vapor from their chimneys.

[2] There might have been berths on this train, but if so, I didn't see them. I was afraid that if I got up someone would snatch my seat—I had seen it happen. I did not want to stand for six hours—it was almost 300 miles more to Dalian. As it was we were jammed in, shoulder to shoulder—the smokers, the noodle eaters, the spitters, the bronchial victims, the orange peelers.

[3] There was no dining car. A woman wearing a nightcap came around with a pushcart, selling dried fish and heavy blobs of sponge cake—the favorite snacks of the Chinese traveler. I chose the fish. It was tough and tasted (and looked) like an old innersole—a Chinese innersole, and a minority one[1] at that. On the wrapper it was described as "Dried Fish With Minority Flavor."

[4] I was still cold. The cold was mystifying. I hated it like boredom or bad air. It was like aches and pains—perhaps a fear of death informed my feeling and made the cold frightening, because degree zero is death. I found it dehumanizing, and my heart went out to the people who had to live and work in Mongolia, Heilongjiang, Jilin and Liaoning. And yet it is well known that the spirit among the people in these provinces is especially bright—the hinterland of China is famous for having high morale, the people regarding themselves as pioneers.

[5] But the cold affected me. It is a blessing that cold is hard to describe and impossible to remember clearly. I certainly have no memory for low

---

1 **a minority one:** China is composed of one majority people, the Han, and over 50 minorities, including Mongolians, Manchurians, Tibetans, and many others. Theroux, of course, is being ironic in labeling an innersole a "minority one."

temperatures. And so afterwards I had no memorable sensations of the month-long freeze I had been through—only the visual effects: frosty faces, scarves with frozen spit on them, big bound feet, and mittens, and crimson faces, flecks of ice on that crow-black Chinese hair, the packed snow, the vapor that hung over the larger cities and made even the grimmest city magical, and the glittering frost—the special diamondlike shimmer that you get when it's thirty below.

6   After a few hundred miles the snow grew thinner and finally with an odd abruptness, at the town of Wangfandian there was none. The landscape had the shabby and depressed look that places have when you are used to seeing them covered with snow. There was something drastic about there being no more snow.

7   The symmetry and twiggy patterns of bare, brown orchards below the Qian Shan, and the stone cottages not far from Dalian, gave these hills the look of Scotland and its ruined crofts.

8 A young Chinese woman smiled at me as I stepped onto the platform at Dalian. She was very modern, I could see. Her hair had been waved into a mass of springy curls. She wore sunglasses. Her green coat had a fur collar—rabbit. She said she had been sent to meet me. Her name was Miss Tan.

9   "But please call me Cherry."

10   "Okay, Cherry."

11   "Or Cherry Blossom."

12   It was hard to include those two words in an ordinary sentence. "What is the fare to Yantai,[2] Cherry Blossom?" But I managed, and she always had a prompt reply, usually something like, "It will cost you one arm and one leg." She had a fondness for picturesque language.

13   She led me outdoors, and as we stood on the steps of Dalian Station, she said, "So what do you think of Dalian so far?"

14   "I have only been here seven minutes," I said.

15   "Time flies when you're having fun!" Cherry Blossom said.

16   "But since you asked," I went on, "I am very impressed with what I see in Dalian. The people are happy and industrious, the economy is buoyant, the quality of life is superb. I can tell that morale is very high. I am sure

---

2   **fare to Yantai:** At the time Theroux was in China, travelers within China could not buy a round trip ticket on any kind of transportation; tickets could be bought only from city A to city B. After arriving in city B, travelers then had to ask the government guide assigned to meet them to secure a ticket from city B to city C, a process both frustrating and time-consuming.

it is the fresh air and prosperity. The port is bustling, and I'm sure the markets are filled with merchandise. What I have seen so far only makes me want to see more."

[17] "That is good," Cherry Blossom said.

[18] "And another thing," I said. "Dalian looks like South Boston, in Massachusetts."

[19] It did, too. It was a decaying port, made out of bricks, with wide streets, cobblestones and trolley tracks, and all the paraphernalia of a harbor—the warehouses, dry docks and cranes. I had the impression that if I kept walking I would eventually come to The Shamrock Bar and Grill. It was also Boston weather—cold and partly sunny under blowing clouds—and Boston architecture. Dalian was full of big brick churches that had probably once been called Saint Pat's, Saint Joe's and Saint Ray's—they were now kindergartens and nurseries, and one was the Dalian Municipal Library. But reform had come to Dalian and with it such businesses as The Hot Bread Bakery and the Hong Xing (Red Star) Cut and Perma.

[20] "And also men hurry to Hong Xing to get a perma," Cherry Blossom said. "They go lickety-split."

[21] The streets looked like Boston's streets. Never mind that the main thoroughfare in Dalian was called Stalin Road (Sidalin Lu). It looked like Atlantic Avenue.

[22] At the turn of the century the Russians had schemed to make Dalny (as they called it; it means "far away" in Russian) a great port for the tsar's ships. It was valuable for fighting the Japanese because, unlike Vladivostok, it would not freeze in the winter. After the Russo-Japanese war, when the Japanese flew kites in Dairen[3]—each kite saying *The Russians Have Surrendered!*—this port city was handed to the Japanese. They simply completed the Russian plan for turning what had been a fishing village into a great port. It prospered until the Second World War, and when the Japanese were defeated, the Russians were given the city under the Yalta terms. The Russians remained until well after the Chinese Liberation, when the Chinese renamed the city Dalian (Great Link). I liked it for its salt air and sea gulls.

[23] "What desires do you entertain in Dalian?" Cherry Blossom said.

[24] I told her that I had come here to get warm after the freeze in Dongbei, the Northeast. And I needed a ticket on the ship that traveled from Dalian across the Bohai Gulf to Yantai.[4] Could she get that for me?

---

3   **Dairen:** an old name for Dalian.
4   **Bohai Gulf to Yantai:** between northern China and the Korean peninsula is Liaoning peninsula; Dalian is at its southern end and from its port boats cross the Bohai Gulf to the northern coast of china, east of Beijing.

25   "Keep your fingers crossed," she said.

26   She vanished after that. I found an old hotel—Japanese prewar baronial; but I was turned away. I was accepted at the dreary new Chinese hotel, a sort of Ramada Inn with a stagnant fish pond in the lobby. I spent the day looking for an antique shop, and the only one I found was disappointing. A man tried to sell me a trophy awarded to the winner of a schoolboys' javelin competition in 1933 at a Japanese high school. "Genuine silver," he whispered. "Qing Dynasty."[5]

27   The next day I saw Cherry Blossom. She had no news about my ticket.

28   "You will just have to keep your hopes up!"

29   We agreed to meet later, and when we did she was smiling.

30   "Any luck?" I asked.

31   "No!" She kept smiling. And with this bad news I noticed that she had a plump and slightly pimply face. She was wearing an arsenic-green wool scarf to match the wool cap she herself had knitted in the dormitory (she had four roommates) at the Working Women's Unit.

32   "I have failed completely!"

33   Then why was she smiling? God, I hated her silly hat.

34   "But," she said, wiggling her fingers, "wait!"

35   She had a sharp way of speaking that made every sentence an exclamation. She reached into her plastic handbag.

36   "Here is the ticket! It has been a total success!"

37   Now she wagged her head at me and made her tight curls vibrate like springs.

38   I said, "Were you trying to fool me, Cherry Blossom?"

39   "Yes!"

40   I wanted to hit her.

41   "Is that a Chinese practical joke?"

42   "Oh, yes," she said, with a giggle.

43   But then aren't all practical jokes exercises in sadism?

44   I went to the free market—open since 1979. Every sort of fish, shellfish and seaweed was on display—a pound of big, plump prawns was five dollars, but that was the most expensive item. They also sold squid, abalone, oysters, conch, sea slugs and great stacks of clams and flatfish. The fishermen did not look Chinese; they had a flatheaded Mongolian appearance and might have been Manchus, of whom there are five or six million in this peninsula and in the north. The market gave me an appetite, and that night I had abalone stir-fried in garlic sauce: delicious.

---

5 **Qing Dynasty** (1644–1912): the last of the imperial dynasties.

45 Cherry Blossom said that foreign cruise ships stopped in Dalian in the summer. The tourists stayed for half a day.

46 "What can you see in Dalian in half a day?"

47 She said they all got on a bus and visited the shell-carving factory, the glassware factory, a model children's school (the kids sang songs from *The Sound of Music*) and then it was back to the ship and on to Yantai or Qing-dao.

48 "I'd like to see Stalin Square," I said.

49 We went there. In the center of it was a statue to the Russian army, which had occupied the city after the war.

50 "There are no Stalin Squares in the Soviet Union, Cherry Blossom. Did you know that?"

51 She said, no, she was surprised to hear it. She asked why.

52 "Because some people think he made a few mistakes," I said, though I did not mention the pogroms,[6] the secret police, purges, or the mustached brute's[7] ability to plan large-scale famines in order to punish dissenting regions.

53 "Is there a Mao Zedong Square in Dalian, Cherry Blossom?"

54 "No," she said, "because he made a few mistakes.[8] But don't cry over spilled milk!"

55 I told her that I had read somewhere that the evil genius Lin Biao—China's Trotsky[9]—had lived in Dalian. She said no, this was not so. She had lived her whole life in Dalian, and no one had ever mentioned Lin's connection.

56 But the driver was older. He said yes, Lin Biao had lived there in Dalian. Lin Biao, a great military tactician, was now maligned because he had done so much to build up Mao—it was Lin who devised the Little Red Book[10] and chose all the quotations; and in the end (so it was said) he had plotted to assassinate Mao, when Mao was weak and at his heffalump

---

6 **pogroms:** an organized and often officially sanctioned massacre of a particular group, associated with but not limited to Russia in the 1930s.

7 **mustached brute:** an allusion to Joseph Stalin under whose rule in the 1930s millions of citizens were exterminated.

8 **a few mistakes:** "She had the reason wrong. Mao was the mover of a resolution to forbid the naming of provinces, cities, towns or Squares for himself of other living leaders (*Selected Works of Mao Zedong*, vol. IV, p. 380)."—P. T.

9 **Trotsky:** Leon Trotsky (1877–1940), Russian revolutionist and statesman whom Stalin banished in 1929; he was assassinated in Mexico in 1940, probably at Stalin's behest.

10 **Little Red Book:** ostensibly, a collection of the wise sayings of Chairman Mao Ze Dong, bound in red, which was widely bought and memorized by Chinese Communists during the Cultural Revolution (1966–1976).

stage; and Lin, in trying to flee the country by plane ("seeking protection from his Moscow masters . . . as a defector to the Soviet revisionists in betrayal of the Party and the country"), had crashed in dear old Undur Khan, in the People's Republic of Mongolia. Foul play was never mentioned. It was regarded as natural justice that this heliophobe should meet an untimely death.

57 It was his heliophobia that made me want to see his house. This weedy little man had a horror of the sun. I thought his house might not have any windows, or perhaps special shutters; or maybe he lived in a bomb shelter in the basement.

58 Cherry Blossom was saying in Chinese to the driver, "I did not know that Lin Biao lived in Dalian," and then to me in English, "It's too dark to find his house. Let's go to the beach instead."

59 We headed for the south part of Dalian, to a place called Fu's Village Beach. Because of the cliffs and the winding road, the driver went very slowly.

60 Cherry Blossom said, "This car is as slow as cold molasses in January."

61 "You certainly know a lot of colorful expressions, Cherry."

62 "Yes. I am queer as a fish." And she giggled behind her hand.

63 "You should be as happy as a clam," I said.

64 "I like that one so much! I feel like a million dollars when I hear that."

65 These colloquial high jinks could have been tiresome, but it was such a novelty for a Chinese person to be playful I enjoyed it. And I liked her for not taking herself too seriously. She knew she was mildly excruciating.

66 Meanwhile we were descending to Fu's Village—great rocky cliffs and an empty beach of yellow sand, with the January wind off the sea beating the waves against it. Offshore there were five bloblike islands floating blackly on the gulf. A couple was canoodling on the beach, out of the wind—the Chinese do it standing up, usually behind a rock or a building, and they hug each other very tightly. It is all smooching. These two ran away when they saw me. A drunken fisherman staggered across the beach, towards his big wooden row-boat that was straight off an ancient scroll: a sharply rockered bottom, very clumsy, the shape of a wooden shoe, probably very seaworthy.

67 I asked Cherry Blossom whether she took her tourists here. She said there wasn't time.

68 "Some of the people have funny faces," she said.

69 "What is the funniest face you have ever seen, Cherry?"

70 She shrieked "Yours!" and clapped her hands over her eyes and laughed.

71   "Another of your saucy jokes, Cherry Blossom!"

72   She became rather grave and said, "But truly, the Tibetans have the funniest faces. They are so funny I get frightened."

73   "What about American faces?"

74   "Americans are wonderful."

75   We had tea at a vast, empty restaurant. We were the only customers. It was at the top of one of Fu's cliffs, with a panoramic view.

76   "Do you want to see the Dragon Cave?"

77   I said yes and was taken upstairs to see a restaurant decorated to resemble a cave. It had fiberglass walls, bulging brown plastic rocks, lights shining through plastic stalactites, and each table was fixed in a greeny-black cleft, with fake moss and boulders around it. The idea was perhaps not a bad one, but this was a vivid example of the Chinese not knowing when to stop. It was shapeless, artless, grotesquely beyond kitsch;[11] it was a complicated disfigurement, wrinkled and stinking, like a huge plastic toy that had begun to melt and smell. You sat on those wrinkled rocks and bumped your head on the stalactites and ate fish cheeks with fresh ginger.

78   Cherry Blossom said, "Do you think it's romantic?"

79   "Some people might find it romantic," I said. And I pointed out the window. "That's what I find romantic."

80   The tangerine sun had settled into the Gulf of Bohai, coloring the little islands and the cliffs of Dalian and the long stretch of empty beach.

81   Cherry Blossom said, "Let your imagination fly!"

82   We left the Dragon Cave (and I thought: It must have a counterpart in California). I said, "I understand there are recuperation tours. People come to this province to try out Chinese medicine."

83   "Yes. It is like a fat farm."

84   "Where did you learn that, Cherry Blossom?"

85   "My teachers at the institute were Americans. They taught me so many things!"

86   She had loved her years at the Dalian Foreign Languages Institute. She was now only twenty-two, but she intended to go on studying and working. She had no intention of getting married, and in explaining why, she lost her jokey manner and became distressed.

87   Her decision not to marry was the result of a trip to Peking. She had taken a group of visiting doctors to see a Chinese hospital—how it worked,

---

11   **kitsch:** excessive, often sentimental and tasteless overdecoration.

how the patients were treated, the progress of surgical procedures; and so forth. The doctors expressed an interest in seeing a delivery. Cherry Blossom witnessed this and, so she said, almost went into shock at the sight of the baby, with its squashed head and its bloody face, issuing forth and streaming water. The mother had howled and so had the baby.

88   In all respects it was a completely normal birth.

89   "It was a mess," she said, and touched her plump cheeks in disgust. "I was afraid. I hated it. I would never do it—never. I will never get married."

90   I said, "You don't have to have babies just because you get married."

91   She was shaking her head. The thought was absurd—she couldn't take it in. The whole point of marriage these days was to produce one child. Even though the Party was now stressing that the best marriages were work related, the husband and wife joint members of a work unit, a busy little team, Cherry Blossom could not overcome the horror of what she had seen in the delivery room of Capital Hospital in Peking. She said she intended to remain in the dormitory of the Working Women's Unit and go on knitting.

92   It was late at night when we crossed Dalian to get to the harbor, where I intended to take the ship to Yantai. We passed through the old bourgeois suburbs that had been built by the Japanese and the Russians. On the sloping streets of these neighborhoods there were seedy semidetached villas[12] and stucco bungalows under the bare trees. I had not seen anything quite like them in China. They were appropriate to the suburban streets, the picket fences and the brick walls; and then I saw the laundry in the front yards and the Chinese at the windows.

93   I often passed down streets like this, seeing big gloomy villas with gables and jutting eaves and mullioned windows; but always in nightmares. They were the sort of houses that first looked familiar in the dream, and then I saw evil faces at the windows, and I realized that I was no longer safe. How often in nightmares I had been chased down streets like these.

94   "I am sorry to see you go," Cherry Blossom said, when we arrived at the boat.

95   She was the only person in China who ever said that to me. In her old-fashioned way, with her old-fashioned clichés, she was very nice. I wished

---

12   **seedy semidetached villas:** A villa is a one-story residence; semidetached refers to two residences that share a common wall; seedy implies they are rundown, shabby.

her well, and we shook hands. I wanted to tell her that I was grateful to her for looking after me. I started to say it, but she cut me off.

96   "Keep the wind at your back, Paul," she said, and giggled again, delighted with her own audacity.

—⁂—

Looking Back

1. Some travel writers are prepared to like, or at least "understand," everything they see, everyone they meet. Theroux—who travels with a clear head and honest, unromantic eyes—clearly belongs to a new breed of traveler, a kind that Pritchett, the author of the unit page quotation, might truly find "offensive." Working in small discussion groups, determine what Theroux points out about China that seems to offend him. What does he seem to like?

2. Theroux combines sharp observation with occasional scholarship. What evidence in this essay is there of his having done some research?

3. Why does Theroux devote so much space to Cherry Blossom?

4. When Cherry Blossom asks what Theroux thinks of Dalian, he eventually responds: "I am very impressed with what I see in Dalian. The people are happy and industrious, the economy is buoyant, the quality of life is superb. I can tell that morale is very high. I am sure it is the fresh air and prosperity. The port is bustling, and I'm sure the markets are filled with merchandise. What I have seen so far only makes me want to see more." He then adds, "And another thing," I said, "Dalian looks like South Boston, in Massachusetts." Is Theroux genuinely impressed?

Looking Into

1. What characteristics of Theroux's writing would encourage you to read other books he has written? Make a list of those characteristics and write a paragraph explaining which is the most important to you and why.

2. In your own travels—and they need not be foreign—what person have you met that made a strong impression on you? Working in a minimum

of description and a maximum of dialogue, convey this person's character in an essay of two or three pages. Be prepared to read your response aloud.

3. As an official guide for foreigners, Cherry Blossom would probably have to write a report for her superiors on her encounter with Theroux, a report that might differ significantly from that of Theroux. Write that report from Cherry Blossom's point of view, focusing on both a description of the events described in this selection and on Theroux himself.

from Nothing to Declare: Memoirs of a Woman Traveling Alone

MARY MORRIS

Mary Morris was born in Chicago, Illinois, in 1947. She attended Tufts University, where she earned her B.A. in 1969; she has both an M.A. and an M. Phil. from Columbia University. From 1981–1987, she was a lecturer in creative writing at Princeton University; in 1989, she was again a lecturer in creative writing at New York University in New York City. Morris is the author of three volumes of short stories: *Vanishing Animals and Other Stories* (1979), *The Bus of Dreams and Other Stories* (1985), and *A Mother's Love* (1993); and two novels: *Crossroads* (1983) and *The Waiting Room* (1989). In addition to *Nothing to Declare: Memoirs of a Woman Traveling Alone* (1988), her first travel book, Morris has written *Wall-to-Wall: From Beijing to Berlin by Rail* (1991). Her newest book, *Maiden Voyages: Writings of Women Travelers* (1993), is an anthology of the travel writings of more than fifty writers. Morris has also been published in such periodicals as the *New York Times, New Woman, Redbook,* and *Vogue.*

Looking Ahead

In 1981, Mary Morris left New York City "in search of a place where the land and the people and the time in which they lived were somehow connected." But once she arrives in San Miguel de Allende, a high desert village some four hours north of Mexico City, she begins to question the wisdom of so abrupt and dramatic a choice. In the excerpt that follows, the first three sections of her book *Nothing to Declare,* Morris conveys her initial impressions of the country and the village, her sense of isolation and foreignness, and her introduction to her neighbor, her neighbor's children, her neighbor's rooster, and the family lamb.

1   There are only two ways to get to San Miguel. One is to drive north from Mexico City. The other is to drive south from Laredo. There is also a

train but I only saw it once in the time I lived there, and it was two hours late. The road north from Mexico City is unremarkable—a superhighway to Laredo, lined with Pemex stations,[1] auto part shops, tire retailers. It is also lined with many foreign factories, such as John Deere Tractors, Singer, Volkswagen, Pepsi, companies that find prices right and labor cheap south of the border.

2   If you are driving north from Mexico City, after about four hours you reach a turn. If you miss the turn, you can go straight back to America in about ten hours flat. But if you leave that main road and turn left, toward the west in the direction of San Miguel, as I did one summer in what seems now like a long time ago, you enter a different world. The kind of world you might read about in the works of Latin American writers such as Fuentes, Rulfo, García Márquez.[2] Macondo[3] could be out there.

3   You come to the old Mexico, a lawless land. It is a landscape that could be ruled by bandits or serve as a backdrop for the classic Westerns, where all you expect the Mexicans to say is *"hombre"* and *"amigo"* and *"sí, señor."* It is a land with colors. Desert colors. Sand and sienna, red clay and cactus green, scattered yellow flowers. The sky runs all the ranges of purple and scarlet and orange. You can see dust storms or rain moving toward you. Rainbows are frequent. The solitude is dramatic.

4   You come abruptly to the high desert, where people travel on the backs of burros and everything slows down. Cactuses are huge and resemble men in agony, twisted and wild; it is a trail of crucifixions.

5 I have a friend named Brenda Reynolds who was living in Mexico City, and it was Brenda who drove me to San Miguel the first time. She was preparing to move back to the States just as I was arriving, but she offered to take me to San Miguel, spend a night, and help me get my bearings. Brenda was one of the people who suggested San Miguel when I told her I wanted to live away from the United States for a while. Brenda said it was a perfect place and that the weather was wonderful. I had heard other things about San Miguel as well. Americans who want to get away often go there. It is a place of exile.

---

1 **Pemex stations:** gasoline stations; Pemex is the Mexican government's oil company.
2 **Fuentes, Rulfo, Garcia Marquez:** Carlos Fuentes and Juan Rulfo are contemporary Mexican writers; Garcia Marquez is a contemporary Colombian writer and winner of the Nobel Prize for Literature.
3 **Macondo:** name of the imaginary town in which Garcia Marquez has set several of his most famous novels.

6   I had grown weary of life in New York and had some money from a grant, so I felt ready for a change. With a terrible feeling of isolation and a growing belief that America had become a foreign land, I headed south. I went in search of a place where the land and the people and the time in which they lived were somehow connected—where life would begin to make sense to me again.

7   When I arrived in Mexico City, Brenda served me black zapotes. A black zapote is a fruit somewhat like a giant prune which, when mashed with sugar and lemon juice, with the skin and seeds removed (an incredibly arduous task), tastes like something they'd serve in heaven. There is no comparable way to describe this dish except to say that it was the first thing I tasted when I arrived at Brenda's house in Mexico and I thought then that I had come to paradise.

8   This was before driving to San Miguel, before I traveled down that very dusty road with Brenda, laughing the whole way until we approached San Miguel. Then I grew serious, struck by the reality of the place to which I had come. As we twisted on those hairpin turns, a street sign appeared. It contained the silhouette of a full-bodied woman and beneath her the words *curva peligrosa*—dangerous curves. . . .

9   I never saw pictures of San Miguel before I moved there, but I went with a very clear sense of what everything should look like, a cross between New York and my hometown and the island of Crete—exciting, familiar, and foreign all at the same time.

10   The Buddhists are right in their belief that expectation is one of the great sources of suffering. We try to direct the scripts in our heads and are miserable when we fail. We often wonder why things go better—parties, journeys, love—when we have no expectations. What I saw as we drove into San Miguel bore little relation to what I'd thought I'd find. A dusty town rose out of a hill, with a salmon-pink church spire and pale stucco buildings. Buses were everywhere, idling near the center of town, sending up exhaust that would make me choke whenever I walked past. Their drivers shouted the names of destinations unknown to me—Celaya, Guanajuato, Dolores. Tortilla ladies and avocado ladies sold sandwiches near the buses as blind beggars and naked children, broken-spirited donkeys and starving dogs, filled the streets.

11   I was missing the fine points. Expectation does that to you. I missed the bougainvillea, the colonial buildings, the cobblestone streets. It is easy to miss all of that once the panic sets in. I only saw the dust and the donkeys and the strangers and a place that seemed so distant from anything I thought I could ever call home.

[12] That night Brenda and I checked into a hotel where I drifted into despair. I had no idea how I was going to live in this place. I couldn't believe that I'd packed myself up and moved to a strange country where I barely spoke the language and didn't know a soul. My purpose seemed vague, and walking those streets for the first time, I told myself that I should just get back in the car and go home. We had dinner and strolled, hardly speaking. I was quiet, withdrawn, and Brenda, who has always respected my privacy, did not pry. Perhaps she suspected that something had happened to me before I left, but she did not ask and I didn't say.

[13] In the morning we went to a hot spring nearby called Taboada, a place I would frequent on Sundays because the hotel there served a wonderful brunch. The Mexicans frolicked with their families, often fat, happy, splashing out of control, and I longed to be that carefree again. Afterward we drove back to the hotel and Brenda was ready to go. Like a scoutmaster sending a boy out on a survival training course, she left me with a Spanish-English dictionary, a few extra pens, and the name of the woman who ran the Blue Door Bakery, who supposedly had rooms to rent.

[14] I was on my own. I had no idea what to do with myself. It grew dark early and I wasn't ready for bed. Instead I went out for a walk. The streets were dark and cobbled and smelled of garbage. I didn't know my way as I wandered through the back alleys and narrow roads. I passed restaurants with crowded tables and lighted rooms where families stared into the blue light of miniature TVs. Old women, grasping babies, sat telling stories and laughing on doorsteps. I searched for a movie house, a coffee shop with guitar music, but all I found were dozens of bars filled with men, and I wasn't ready to go into one alone.

[15] I walked to the center of town, to a square lined with benches and trees, which in most parts of Mexico is called the *zócalo*, but in San Miguel is called the *jardín*, where an odd procession passed in front of me. A circle of girls walked in the clockwise direction around the perimeters of the jardín, perhaps half the distance of a square city block. There were at least a hundred of them. And encircling them, moving counterclockwise, was a group of young men. Hesitating, I cut through their circle and sat down on a bench, where I watched as the single men and women of the town encircled each other on and on into the darkness in this ritualized form of courtship—called the promenade—which would occur every night at the hour when the birds came home to rest in the trees of the jardín.

[16] They flirted and giggled and pretended to ignore one another, but as darkness fell, some wandered off, boy leading girl away to a more secluded spot in a darkened street, an alleyway. I imagined them whispering

each other's names and thought of how far I was from someone who might whisper mine.

17   The church bells rang. From the steeple clock that seemed to rule over this town and mark the monotony of the days, I saw that it was only nine o'clock. I still had much of the evening ahead of me and no place to go. Then I noticed the people entering church. Toothless old men and corpulent women with babies wrapped in shawls shuffled in. Girls in miniskirts with white blouses held the hands of boys in green or cranberry polyester pants; others in blue jeans, black hair slicked back, lingered in the alcoves.

18   In this town of shrieking birds and promenading lovers, I could think of nothing else to do, so I went to church. I walked hesitantly into the large Gothic stone building and down an aisle toward the apse. Slipping into a pew off to the side, I sat beside a campesino family,[4] the woman with a child suckling at her exposed breast, the children in freshly ironed shirts, the father, in a sombrero, keeping a toddler from running away.

19   I sat down with a blind man and with wide-eyed children, with the toothless, the ancients, the impoverished, the illegitimate mothers, the crippled, the drunk, the miserable, the lost. I prayed with the beggar who had no hands and with the woman whose eyes were empty sockets. I prayed with the contrite and the forlorn, with *los desdichados*—the unlucky, the misfortunate. I prayed until the tears came down my face and I was crying in that church on that Sunday night, my first night alone in Mexico, praying that the reason for this journey would be made clear to me, oblivious of the Mexicans who watched with troubled eyes, moved by my inexplicable grief.

20   The woman who ran the Blue Door Bakery did have rooms to rent and at dusk the next day she took me to see them. We drove down the hill away from the center of town. We left the cobbled streets with bougainvillea vines and turned up a dirt road lined with mud huts, garbage, diseased animals, children in tattered rags. When I asked where we were going, she replied, "San Antonio." And that was all.

21   She was a cold, calculating person whom I would simply call "the Señora" and who'd take only cash for rent. In the middle of these slums in the neighborhood called San Antonio, the Señora had built some town houses. One of them had been vacated recently, and she showed it to me. It had a living room, kitchen, and small patio on the ground floor. Two bed-

---

4   **campesino family:** country or farm family.

rooms upstairs. Upstairs the front of the town house had French doors and a small balcony, but the back wall had no windows. I should have suspected that someone was building a house on the other side, but I did not. The sound of construction would punctuate my days. A small, winding staircase went to the roof, where I'd read and do the wash in the afternoons. From the roof I could see the sierra—the pale lavender hills and the stretch of high desert, the cactus men and wildflowers.

22   It was the only place I considered. "I'll take it," I said.

23   I never would have moved to the neighborhood called San Antonio if I'd known better. For that part of town was different from the other parts. Very few Americans lived there. It was too far from the center of things. I would have to walk half an hour up a dusty hill to get to market. It was the poorest part; it was where the servants who served the wealthy lived and where others struggled just to get by. It was the dustiest, dirtiest place, where the Mexicans would call me *"gringita"*[5] and my own mother, when she heard me describe it, would beg me to leave. I had no idea what I was doing when I moved into San Antonio. But I am grateful for the mistake I made.

24 I had come to Mexico with two suitcases and an electric typewriter, and the next day I brought them by taxi to my town house, whose name I noticed as I dragged my belongings from the cab: the *Departamentos Toros* (bull apartments). I am a Taurus and as I stood beneath the sign with the name of the apartment, I thought this must be a good omen, to move into a place named after my astrological sign. I spent the day settling in. But as dusk came, I realized I knew no one, was about a mile from town, and had no food in the house.

25   Climbing the winding stairs to the roof terrace, I saw the vast Mexican desert stretching before me, the sun setting in strips of brilliant scarlet across the horizon. The town with the pink steeple of the church seemed far away. I saw the birds—large, black, noisy birds—which every evening at dusk flew to the center of the town to stand guard over the promenade. And then, as I'd do many evenings after that, struck by the prospect of the evening alone, I followed them.

26   I changed my clothes, put on a pair of walking shoes, and headed up the hill—a climb I'd never get used to. But I went to the place where the birds were going. It seems I have always followed the birds, or have wanted to follow them. The loud chirps, thousands of them, grew piercing as I approached the jardín.

---

5 *gringita:* a disparaging word for a female foreigner.

27   The birds were bedding down for the night and the promenade was in process. I sat on a bench to watch. It is odd to sit in a place where you know absolutely no one. There was not a familiar face, not even the possibility of someone passing whom I might know. I was here a perfect stranger.

28   After a while I got up and headed down a road. I paused in front of a bar lit in amber. Inside Mexican men drank and laughed. There were no Mexican women, but there were a few Americans, so I thought it would be all right. I went in and ordered a beer. I sat for perhaps half an hour, until it grew dark. People were all around me and I thought to myself how I should try to make conversation, but I found I could think of nothing to say. I was sure that someone would come up to me and say something like, "Been in town long?" or "So where'd you come from?" But no one did. I ordered another beer and nursed it slowly, realizing I did not want to go home. I watched the people around me. Mexicans laughing and talking with blond American women. Other Americans huddled in corners. One man, whom I'd later know as Harold, sat in his pajamas, which he wore when he went on a binge.

29   I took it all in, and then, at about ten o'clock, I walked home. I descended the hill, toward the bus stop, until I reached the turnoff to San Antonio. At the turnoff is the dirt road, about a quarter mile long, it is walled on both sides. If you are attacked while walking down this road, you have no place to go.

30   For the first time, I walked that quarter mile at night alone. Every shadow, every sound, made me turn. I behaved like a hunted thing. It is not easy to move through the world alone, and it is never easy for a woman. You must keep your wits about you. You mustn't get yourself into dark places you can't get out of. Keep money you can get to, an exit behind you, and some language at your fingertips. You should know how to strike a proud pose, curse like a sailor, kick like a mule, and scream out your brother's name, though he may be three thousand miles away. And you mustn't be a fool.

31   Brace yourself for tremendous emptiness and great surprise. Anything can happen. The bad things that have occurred in my travels—and in my life in general—have happened because I wasn't prepared. At times I wonder that I am still alive.

32 A giant white rooster stood on my small balcony at five in the morning, greeting the dawn. He was so loud it seemed as if he were in bed with me. I opened my glass doors and tried to shoo him, but the rooster wouldn't leave. That was when I noticed the yard on the other side of the wall, perhaps only a dozen feet away, where my neighbor lived.

33   In Mexico, there are many walls whose purpose is to keep poor people away from rich people. Often the tops of these walls are decorated with bits of broken bottles—Coke, Pepsi, Seven-Up—to deter people from climbing over them. There was the wall that lined the road to San Antonio. And between my house and the rest of Mexico was a wall eight feet high.

34   From my balcony I looked into the yard and saw lumber, debris, mud, a pig, a lamb, animal droppings, chicks, assorted articles of clothing, and no vegetation. A radio played mariachi music over the sound of running water and scrubbing. Somewhere beneath a makeshift wood-plank shelter a woman was doing the wash under a small light.

35   I put on my robe and went outside. The sky was a deep shade of blue-green and the rooster continued its dialogue with the other roosters of San Antonio. I climbed on a large stone by the wall and pulled myself up as far as I could, shouting. A few moments later a woman peered down at me. I could barely make out her dark face in the blue-green light of morning, but she had thick black hair and weathered skin, a brilliant smile. "Excuse me," I said in my broken one-year-of-college Spanish, "but is that your rooster on my balcony?"

36   She looked up and shook her head. "He is always on the prowl. He hates to stay home," she said in dismay. "Like all men."

37   The next thing I knew she had come around to my side of the wall and we went into my apartment. She seemed to know the place well. Without a word, she went upstairs into the bedroom and onto the balcony, grabbed the rooster by his legs, and carried him, flapping, out of the house.

38   I tried to go back to sleep, but the feathers floating around my head and the sound of the radio and the woman's comment about the rooster and men stuck in my mind. Finally I fell asleep until about ten o'clock, when I heard someone knocking.

39   I opened the door and found two small children. "My mother," one of them whispered, holding out a napkin, "asked me to give you these." I could barely hear her as she handed me the napkin. I opened it and found five corn tortillas, still hot. "What are your names?" I asked them. They said nothing. "Where do you live?" They pointed to the other side of the wall. Then they ran away.

40   That afternoon I climbed the hill to the market to go shopping for the first time. The market was about a mile's hike from San Antonio—a long, steep climb that takes about half an hour. Then suddenly I was bombarded by the market.

41   Honeycombs covered with dead bees were thrust into my face. Huge chucks of brown mescal that look like caramel, red and black zapotes, pa-

payas and mangoes cut open for sampling, cactus ears, cheese, garlic, long-stemmed gladiolas, juice stands, polyester dresses, pottery, watermelon. I paused at the herbalist who sells his bark and wood chips, dried grasses and flowers, roots and herbal teas, to cure your insomnia, kidney failure, weight loss, tension, headache, infertility. I was struck by it all, from the flowers to the stench of the butcher's unrefrigerated meats. There was beauty and filth everywhere as wasps buzzed the candy man and sucked the exposed sugar, and diseased children, selling corn, flicked maggots from their eyes.

42 I bought chicken, rice, avocados, beans, wild honey, and mangoes, which was more than I could carry. After a few blocks, I had to stop at the jardín to rest. I had not been there long when a man sat down beside me. He was a handsome Mexican with a camera around his neck. "So how long've you been in town?" he asked in good English. I told him I was new. He introduced himself. "Guillermo Gonzalez," he said. He was a photographer and offered to help me with my bags. He carried them down the hill as far as the turnoff to San Antonio. And then he said, "Why don't I pick you up tonight and take you to La Fragua."

43 "La Fragua?"

44 "Yes, it is the place where most people go. I'll pick you up at six and introduce you to some people I know."

45 I made myself an early dinner and got dressed up. At six he had not shown, so I read. I read until seven, then seven-thirty. When he still had not shown, I decided to go into town on my own. I was not yet accustomed to Mexican time, nor to being stood up. I put on lipstick and headed out the door.

46 I was ready to climb the hill when the rains broke. They came out of nowhere and I rushed back inside. Within moments torrents had fallen on my enclosed patio. My windows were a sheet of rain. I went up to the roof and from the small shelter where I would do the wash, I watched it come down. Gray rain swept across the high desert, a rain that would bring incredible wildflowers and turn the hills into an easel of color with cornflowers, primrose, buttercups, and lavender thistle, but I didn't know this at the time. I went downstairs as dusk fell and the rain continued and I sat reading, waiting for the rain to cease. But it did not. It kept coming. It came longer than any rain should have come. And then, just as the night began, the electricity failed. The lights went, leaving me in darkness.

47 I was caught completely unprepared. I had no light to read by, no candles, no batteries for my flashlight. I had no television or radio or phone. No one to talk to, no one to see, no plans for seeing anyone, no way back to the life I had known.

⁴⁸   I listened to the endless buzzing of mosquitoes as they bit me. I listened to my own breath. I told myself that in a few hours it would be morning. All I had to do was sleep. Instead I listened to the whisper of two lovers who sought refuge beneath the awning of my porch. I was perhaps no more than five feet away from them. They did not know I was there as they panted and caressed and made sounds like animals into the night.

⁴⁹ I woke to the sound of sweeping and the bleating of a lamb, so I stumbled downstairs and opened the door. There I saw a woman with a distended belly and strong, crablike arms and legs. Her skin was dark and her thick hair was tied up in a loose bun. She wore a miniskirt, to which a small child clung. It took me a moment to recognize her as the woman who lived on the other side of the wall.

⁵⁰   I wished them good morning. The children hid their faces and giggled. The one ducked beneath the lamb, hiding her face in its fleece. The woman brushed the strands of hair off her face. We introduced ourselves. Her name was Lupe and she said she took care of the property of the señora who ran the Blue Door Bakery. Her youngest daughters were Lisa, who was four, and Cristina, who was two, nicknamed Pollo because she was scrawny like a chicken. The lamb was Pancha.

⁵¹   I was not sure what to say in this first conversation, so I asked Lupe if she knew where I could buy plants for my house. "Flowers?" she asked. And I said yes, flowers. I told her I wanted flowers. Living things.

⁵²   Lupe said she would take me if I'd wait while she changed her clothes. I had wanted to work that morning, but since she was offering, I felt I could not say no. I asked her if it was far and she said no, *"No muy lejos."* Not very far. She dragged Pollo off with her and left me with Lisa and the lamb.

⁵³   I asked Lisa, "Is that your lamb?"

⁵⁴   And Lisa said, "Yes."

⁵⁵   "Is he your friend?"

⁵⁶   And she said, "Yes, he's my friend."

⁵⁷   "What will you do when he gets big?"

⁵⁸   And she said, "We're going to eat him."

⁵⁹   In a few moments Lupe returned in a clean dress, her hair combed neatly, pushing a wheelbarrow into which she plunked Pollo. She grabbed Lisa by the hand and told me to follow. Thus Lupe, Pollo, Lisa, me, and the doomed lamb, Pancha, set off with wheelbarrow in search of the elusive flower lady.

⁶⁰   We climbed up a hill over cobblestones, across the open sewer that would bring typhoid and dysentery and in some instances death to those

who drank from it. In the heat and dry sun of the morning we climbed, farther and farther, into the poorest section of San Miguel, deeper into San Antonio, past mud-and-plank shacks where hungry children sat and scrawny dogs with open sores begged until I thought I could stand it no longer, and after about half an hour I asked, "Is it much farther?" and Lupe responded, "No muy lejos."

61   While I sweated and ached just from moving up and down hills, Lupe pushed and laughed and trudged. I have no idea where she took me or how long we walked, but eventually we reached a dusty road and there, along the side of the road, sat a one-eyed old woman in a shawl, selling flowers and plants at a good price. I picked a half dozen or so and felt suddenly embarrassed as I pulled money out of my wallet. The plants cost less than ten dollars, but I was slowly realizing that ten dollars would feed all Lupe's children (she had six at the time) for a week.

62   But I bought the flowers because that was what we'd come for, and we surrounded Pollo in bougainvillea and some house plants and a rose bush. Then Lupe proceeded to push the wheelbarrow back to where we'd come from. When I offered to help, she laughed. She said I was weak and she was strong. She made a muscle and made me feel it. She told me she was old but strong. I asked her how old and she said thirty-six. I told her I was thirty-two. She laughed and said I was old, too.

Looking Back

1. In one significant respect, Morris is not a typical traveler: she intends to live in, not visit, Mexico. Trace and account for her initial reactions to Mexico in light of that fact.

2. Does Morris seem to be a traveler more in the Kingsley or the Theroux tradition?

3. What kind of a person is Lupe?

4. What do you expect will be the relationship between the author and her neighbor Lupe and why?

5. Morris writes, "The Buddhists are right in their belief that expectation is one of the great sources of suffering. We try to direct the scripts in our heads and are miserable when we fail." Discuss why this might be so.

Looking Into

1. The *Time* magazine review of Morris' book noted that Morris had "an eye for the brutal, the garish, the silly, and the bizarre." What images in this excerpt bear out that judgment? What images did you find particularly vivid?

2. Recall a time when you were in an unfamiliar place—a new neighborhood, a new school, a summer camp. Using details and vivid images, recreate your feelings about that place.

Defying Mrs. Tweedie

CALVIN TRILLIN

Calvin Trillin was born in Kansas City, Missouri, in 1935. He attended Yale University, graduating with a B.A. in 1957. In 1960, he began his short career as a reporter with *Time* magazine in Atlanta, Georgia, and in New York City. In his first book, *An Education in Georgia* (1964), he reflects on his early days there as a reporter. Since 1963, Trillin has been a staff writer with the *New Yorker* magazine, writing a variety of pieces under the general heading of "U. S. Journal." In these regional pieces, Trillin typically focuses on people who are rarely famous or important, on events that have little apparent "news value." *U. S. Journal,* a collection of these articles, was published in 1971. In 1978, Trillin also accepted a position as humor columnist for *Nation* magazine. Trillin defined his column, "Uncivil Liberties," as "a thousand words every three weeks for saying whatever's on my mind, particularly if what's on my mind is marginally ignoble." Trillin's two books, *Uncivil Liberties* (1982) and *With All Disrespect: More Uncivil Liberties* (1985), are published collections of his *Nation* columns.

Three books which combine his passion for both food and its necessary corollary travel are *American Fried: Adventures of a Happy Eater* (1974), *Alice, Let's Eat: Further Adventures of a Happy Eater* (1978)—nominated for a National Book Award—and *Third Helpings* (1983), a book in which Trillin argues for changing the national Thanksgiving dish from turkey to spaghetti carbonara, "a dish," Trillin asserts, "the Indians learned how to make from Christopher Columbus." Trillin's most recent book is *Remembering Denny* (1993), a memoir of the poignant fate of a talented college friend.

Looking Ahead

A writer for *New Yorker* magazine, but one who rarely writes about New York; a resident of New York City, a city that prides itself on splendid restaurants, but one whose idea of a truly fine feast is a Chicago deep-dish pizza or Crawford County, Kansas, chicken or Kansas City pit barbecue; a generally pacific man, but one who compiled a book of his *New Yorker* pieces on the small-town murders of unremarkable people—Calvin Trillin is a gentle ironist, capable of finding the incongruous in any topic, and a first-rate humorist. In the following essay, taken from his book *Travels with*

Alice, Trillin, his wife Alice, and their friends the Mackintoshes are visiting Taormina, Sicily, a once-trendy resort now somewhat fallen on the hard times of "mass tourism."

———〰———

[1] $\mathcal{B}$efore Alice and I left for a visit to the Sicilian resort town of Taormina, I consulted *Sunny Sicily* for the observations of Mrs. Alec Tweedie, a rather severe travel writer of late Victorian times who was also the author of *Through Finland in Carts* and, before she caught on to the value of a snappy title, *Danish Versus English Butter Making.* I can't imagine why some people say that I don't have a scholarly approach to travel.

[2]   Writing in 1904, Mrs. Tweedie summed up Taormina like this: "The place is being spoilt." It's the sort of comment that can give pause to a traveler who is considering a visit to Taormina somewhat later in the century. Mrs. Tweedie's conclusion that Taormina was being ruined by an influx of English and Americans must have been made, after all, at about the same time the Wright brothers took off at Kitty Hawk—and neither she nor the Wright brothers could have had any notion of the impact of Super-APEX fares. There was no way for me to know whether or not Mrs. Tweedie had been one of those people who simply seem to take great pleasure in telling you that they can recall the time when the place you're about to visit—any place you're about to visit—was actually O.K. ("Pity about the Marquesas. I remember thinking years ago that if that semimonthly prop service from Fiji[1] ever started, that would be it.")

[3]   Still, even though Mrs. Tweedie complained bitterly that "the natives have lost their own nice ways," she had to admit that Taormina was "one of the most beautiful spots on earth," an ancient town perched high on a mountain overlooking the Ionian Sea. Also, I had reason to believe that Mrs. Tweedie's standards in matters of spoilage were stricter than my own. She sounded as if she might fit comfortably among those travelers whose measure of authenticity is so exacting that they tend to find even the ruins ruined.

[4]   Taormina, in fact, happens to have a noted ruin—a Greek theater where what must have been the cheap seats command such a spectacular

---

1   **prop service from Fiji:** prop service refers to propeller airplanes, presumably coming from the South Sea island of Fiji.

view of Mount Etna and the sea and ninety thousand bougainvillea that I can imagine Aristophanes and Euripides[2] sitting around some playwrights' hangout commiserating with each other on how hard it is to hold a Taormina audience's attention. As a matter of fact, Mrs. Tweedie did find that ruin ruined. The Greek theater, she wrote, "is really Roman, as the Romans completely altered it." I have nothing against the Romans myself. How is it possible to dismiss a culture that handed down spaghetti carbonara? Although I don't have much interest in gazing upon volcanic mountains from afar—I find it preferable only to gazing upon them up close—I was, of course, traveling with a connoisseur of views. I always seem to be particularly intent on pleasing Alice during Italian vacations, even if that requires taking in what I would think of as a plethora of views. It may have grown out of my custom of calling her the *principessa*[3] whenever we're traveling in Italy. At some point I found that it improved the service at the hotels.

5   By Mrs. Tweedie's standards, the natives of Taormina must have lost their own nice ways years before she marched briskly into the piazza, wearing, as I have always envisioned her, a tweed suit, sensible walking shoes, and an authoritative expression. At the time of Mrs. Tweedie's first inspection, the British had been coming to Taormina for thirty years, presumably attracted by an assortment of feasts for the eye—from the long view of Etna and the sea to the constant sight of flowers tumbling over the walls of medieval stone buildings to the sudden surprising slice of sea visible through an alley so narrow that the flower-bedecked balconies on either side almost meet overhead. Those are the sorts of vistas, of course, that only arouse suspicion in somebody with Mrs. Tweedie's keen eye. "Somehow the scene never looks quite real," she complained after taking in a view she found irritatingly gorgeous.

6   When Mrs. Tweedie was probably still skidding around Finland in a cart, Taormina already had a grand hotel: the San Domenico Palace, which was opened in 1895 in a converted sixteenth-century monastery. Apparently, a visit by Wilhelm II of Prussia made Taormina popular with all sorts of royalty, Vanderbilts and Rothschilds as well as Hohenzollerns[4]—all the

---

2   **Aristophanes and Euripedes:** two Greek dramatists, fifth century B.C.
3   *principessa:* Italian for "princess."
4   **Vanderbilts . . . Hohenzollerns:** The wealthy Vanderbilts made their money in American finance in the nineteenth century; the even wealthier Rothschilds, as bankers of the House of Rothschild, established in the eighteenth century; the Hohenzollerns were a German royal family. 1415–1918, rulers of Prussia and Brandenberg.

more reason to believe, it seemed to me, that the operators of the San Domenico, where we stayed, would know how to treat someone referred to incessantly by her escort as the *principessa*.

7   Taormina also picked up a reputation as a place that appealed to writers and artists and assorted genteel bohemians.[5] It almost goes without saying that D. H. Lawrence once lived there. Having had D. H. Lawrence residences pointed out to me all over the world, I can only wonder how he got any writing done, what with packing and getting steamship reservations and having to look around for a decent plumber in every new spot. I suspect, though, that Taormina's reputation for harboring exotics comes less from Lawrence than from a German nobleman named Wilhelm von Gloeden, who arrived at about the same time as Wilhelm II and started taking what became well-known photographs of Sicilian boys—some dressed as ancient Greeks, some dressed as girls, and some not dressed at all.

8   Late in the evening, as I sat in one of the outdoor cafés on Taormina's principal piazza, where one café uses enlargements of von Gloeden photographs to decorate its walls, my thoughts sometimes turned from Sicilian almond pastry to the possibility that von Gloeden and Mrs. Tweedie met in Taormina. The street that dominates the town—the Corso Umberto, a strolling street that bans cars except during early-morning delivery hours— couldn't have changed much from the days when there were no cars to ban, except that in Mrs. Tweedie's time the industrial revolution had not progressed to the point of providing Corso Umberto shops with souvenir T-shirts that say I MAFIOSI TAORMINA. The piazza, known as Piazza Nove Aprile, is a wide spot about halfway down the Corso Umberto where a gap in the buildings along one side of the street for a few hundred feet presents a stunning view of the sea. The jacaranda trees must have been there then, and I suspect the bench alongside the sixteenth-century church was lined with the very same nineteenth-century old folks, sternly watching the evening strollers as if collecting vicarious sins to confess the next day.

9   I could easily imagine the encounter. Suddenly a man at one of the cafés stands up, trying to keep his composure while gathering up the bulky cameras and tripod he always carries with him. "I really don't see what concern it is of yours, madam," he says in heavily accented English.

10   Too late. Mrs. Tweedie is bearing down on him, brandishing the umbrella that made a porter in Palermo sorry that he complained about what

---

5 **bohemians:** those with artistic or literary tastes whose behavior is deliberately unconventional.

had been a perfectly adequate sixpence tip. Von Gloeden bolts from the café, knocking down a portly mustachioed man (Wilhelm II of Prussia) and caroming off an ice cream vendor as he races down the street. Mrs. Tweedie is gaining on him.

11   "Shame! Shame!" she shouts as she waves the lethal umbrella above her head. "Shame on you, you wicked, wicked man!"

12 Mrs. Tweedie couldn't have been the last person to find Taormina spoiled. I suspect that Tweedie-like comments have been made about the place pretty steadily ever since. They are based partly on the belief that Taormina is a European outpost that is almost unrelated to what Lawrence Durrell[6] called "the wild precincts of Sicily." It has always been seen as a worldly resort that, by some accident of history, happens to be on the east coast of Sicily instead of on the Riviera or the Argentario.[7] All of that is true, of course, even though Taormina seemed stuffed full of things Sicilian—a vast variety of Sicilian ice cream and Sicilian marzipan and Sicilian pastry, weekly performances of the traditional Sicilian puppet show, an annual festival celebrating the intricately painted Sicilian horse cart, and, now and then, that bracing, life-enhancing smell of pure garlic.

13   It may be, though, that Taormina has survived as a resort partly because it always served as a comfortable outpost of Europe on what has traditionally been thought of as a harsh, almost North African island. The precincts of Sicily are not nearly as wild as they once were, but the tourist amenities are still spread pretty thin. A tourist traveling around the island to take in its Greek and Roman and Byzantine treasures has reason to be grateful for a place that openly specializes in what the American army used to call Rest and Rehabilitation. The person who has been doing the driving on a tour of Sicily may arrive in Taormina suffering from the sort of nervous exhaustion once associated with soldiers arriving for R & R in Tokyo from a tour as artillery spotters in Korea. It is not true, as is often heard in Europe, that Sicilian drivers are unpredictable: they can be counted on to pass. On the highway, Sicilians pass on straightaways, they pass on hills, they pass on curvy hills and hilly curves. In a large city like Palermo or Catania or Messina, a traveler trapped in a motionless line of cars on

---

6 **Lawrence Durrell** (1913–1990): English novelist and traveler, especially in the Mediterranean countries.
7 **Riviera or the Argentario:** coastal resort areas in southern France and eastern Italy.

a conventional two-lane street can suddenly find himself being passed on both the left and the right at the same time.

14   In Taormina there is no need to drive at all. The layout of the town seems designed for the stroll. The logical way to get to Mazzarò, the beach at the foot of the mountain, is on a funicular,[8] which can't be passed on either side. The big decisions made by visitors to Taormina are on the order of deciding whether to have the grilled shrimp or the grilled swordfish, or deciding whether to take an evening stroll along the Corso Umberto or in the public gardens, where spaces for the benches have been cut out of thick bushes of bougainvillea.

15   Some friends of ours named Tony and Mary Mackintosh had joined us in Taormina. Mary, a college friend of Alice's, married Tony, who's English, not long after graduation, and they've lived in England ever since. We see them in London or in New York or, now and then, in some third country. As travelers we've always been compatible. They're not the sort of people who are going to push for a stroll in the Corso Umberto if you happen to feel like going to the public gardens instead—they'll just catch up with you in the café later—nor the sort of people who find it troubling that the venue of the evening stroll is the big decision of the day. Which is to say, I suppose, that they're easily entertained themselves.

16   It should be said that once we had made the strolling decision each evening, we did have a couple of other matters to settle. We had to select an appropriate ice cream cone for Alice, and we had to collect entries for our private marzipan contest. As it happens, Alice is even more interested in *gelato*—Italian ice cream—than she is in views. In Taormina we often spent a good part of the evening systematically checking out the various *gelaterias*, with Alice inspecting the *gelati* displays the way Mrs. Tweedie might have run her eye over a Greek façade that she suspected of having Roman alterations. Our marzipan collection had nothing to do with eating. I'm not sure I know anybody who actually likes to eat marzipan. All of us were simply so astonished at the variety of foodstuffs Sicilians can duplicate in pure marzipan—absolutely realistic bananas and oranges and figs and onions and cucumbers and lobsters—that we thought it only appropriate to give a prize for sheer imagination. For a while we figured the prize would go to a shop near the cathedral that displayed miniature provolone cheeses made of marzipan. Then, on a side street, we discovered the winner. The

---

8   **funicular:** a cable railway on a steep incline.

display consisted of a generous helping of spaghetti, including parsley and cloves of garlic, and next to that a fried egg.

[17] I wasn't kidding myself. Even though we had taken on those additional responsibilities, Mrs. Tweedie would have accused us of frittering away our time in Taormina, relaxing in a resort when we could have been inspecting ruins or perhaps even studying the difference between Danish and English butter making. If we'd had the sort of gumption Mrs. Tweedie expected from proper tourists, we could have questioned Tony closely on how the English make butter and then picked up the Danish end on some future trip to Scandinavia.

[18] Sitting in a café, I could sometimes imagine Mrs. Tweedie standing before me, like a stern bus-tour guide of vaguely Germanic origins who is outraged at seeing one of her charges having a quiet drink when he's supposed to be on the tour of the glassmaking factory and the eighteenth-century grist mill. "This is not a free morning," she reminds me, in her voice but von Gloeden's accent.

[19] "But Taormina has existed so long as a resort that you can think of it as a historic site itself," I'd say to Mrs. T., edging out of umbrella range as I said it. "Even the cafés."

[20] It's true—or true enough. For instance, a century in the business has left Taormina with a display of just about every sort of hotel that has attracted people to European resorts through changing times and fashions. Between *gelaterias*, we sometimes found ourselves touring hotels—from peaceful, old-fashioned places that conjure up a European resort of the twenties, to those sleek, hard-edged new Italian beach hotels that must retain a couple of porters to go through regularly and remove anything that looks inviting to sit on. In the first few days in Taormina, I seemed to be taking a tour of the San Domenico every time I tried to find my way back to our room—in the "new section," added to the monastery building in 1926. I would wander through courtyards thick with flowers, down high hallways decorated with an occasional icon that seemed to have been left behind by the previous owners, in and out of public rooms that by size and design appeared to have been built for basketball games between the Wilhelm II Royal Five and the Rothschild Bouncing Bankers. Apparently, a lot of people who were not paying guests wanted to take tours of the San Domenico on purpose. A sign outside said, in four languages, IT IS NOT ALLOWED TO VISIT THE HOTEL.

[21] A resort, like an ancient theater, is altered by succeeding occupations. Despite some lingering reputation for elegance and artiness, Taormina had actually become a place that catered mainly to what its more or less official

guidebook calls "mass tourism." The English and Americans whose presence troubled Mrs. Tweedie were no longer in evidence; they had been replaced by people on group tours from Italy or Germany or Scandinavia. On a summer Saturday night the Corso Umberto appeared to be dominated by middle-class residents of Catania and Messina who had driven over for a day's outing, making Taormina authentically Sicilian in a way Mrs. Tweedie could never have imagined. Although some prosperous Italian families may always return to the San Domenico for the Christmas holidays, the time had passed when Taormina was the place to observe the sort of chic Europeans seen in resorts like Porto Ercole or Cap Ferrat[9]—the men in spotless white pants and espadrilles, the women looking as if they spend half their time at Gucci and the other half at the gym. Like Greek details in what was eventually converted into a Roman theater, though, the marks of their presence could still be seen in a few hotels and shops; the line of souvenir shops on the Corso Umberto was broken now and then by a fairly elegant antique store or the sort of jewelry store in which purchases are made at a desk rather than a counter, in the manner of negotiating a corporate merger.

22   The writers' colony had dissolved over the years, leaving as traces a plaque here and there and an occasional art show and some Taormina people's memories of having met Thomas Mann or having had Truman Capote[10] over for dinner. The local people who talked of Taormina's being spoiled were no longer talking about natives losing their own nice ways but about the chic and exotic going elsewhere.

23   "It used to be much more sophisticated," a man working at one of the hotels told me. "Now the middle classes are traveling more."

24   I nodded in sympathy. "I was saying as much to the *principessa* today," I said, "as she was selecting her *gelati*."

Looking Back

1. Who is Mrs. Tweedie and why does Trillin refer to her so repeatedly?

---

9   **Porto Ercole or Cap Ferrat:** Mediterranean beach resorts in Italy and southern France.

10   **Thomas Mann** (1875–1955) and **Truman Capote** (1924–1984): German novelist and man of letters, Nobel Prize winner; American novelist, playwright, and sometime traveler.

2. At the end of the first paragraph, Trillin archly comments, "I can't imagine why some people say that I don't have a scholarly approach to travel." What evidence in this essay suggests that Trillin has indeed done some research?

3. What do Trillin's occasional flights of fancy contribute to the essay?

4. What topic other than Mrs. Tweedie and the physical attributes of Taormina does Trillin emphasize? What might that tell the reader about him?

5. How does Trillin make the term *principessa,* introduced and repeated early in the essay, "pay off" at the end?

Looking Into

1. Trillin has many strengths as a travel writer. Cite examples that indicate he, like Mary Morris, has a keen eye for detail.

2. A local travel agency is offering a free two-week vacation in Taormina. In fifty words or less, write a paragraph answering the following question: what attractions in Taormina make you want to visit there?

Traveling Close, Very Close, To Home

SUZANNE BERNE

Suzanne Berne was born in 1961 in Washington, D.C., and grew up both there and in Virginia. After attending Wesleyan University in Middletown, Connecticut, she taught expository writing at both Harvard and Radcliffe Colleges and, more recently, at the Harvard University Extension School. She regularly reviews current fiction and nonfiction, primarily for the *New York Times Book Review*. In addition, she has contributed articles to both its Sunday travel section and to the magazine selection. She has also written pieces for the magazine section of the *Boston Globe* and for such other periodicals as *Victoria* and *House Beautiful*. Although she has traveled to Europe, she agrees with Thoreau that the best travel is in one's own back yard—which, in her case, is New England. She has received a grant from the National Endowment for the Arts and has recently completed a novel.

Looking Ahead

Suzanne Berne, in an essay that appeared in the Sunday travel section of the *New York Times*, suggests that travel need not involve elaborate itineraries, multiple pieces of luggage, transoceanic flights, or glamorous and palatial hotels. In fact, she writes, "a person may be a seasoned traveler without necessarily leaving the backyard." Drawing on her own experiences as well as those of such American writers as Emily Dickinson, Henry David Thoreau, Aldo Leopold, and Annie Dillard, Berne writes of the adventures that await each of us if we but "recognize that travel, like relaxation, is mostly a state of mind."

¹ The first time I realized that it was possible to travel at home, I was 6 years old and standing in the linen closet of a rented house on Cape Cod. It was an old drafty house by a bay, full of camphor-smelling eaves and corners and unexpected doorways, and one foggy afternoon I slunk about the shadowy upstairs picturing myself in the Black Forest.¹ My grandfather

---

1 **Black Forest:** a forest in the Bavarian section of southwestern Germany.

had been to the Black Forest, and from his description I envisioned a mossy, Grimm's-fairy-tale sort of place, not so different from the dark upper hall with its peeling fern-colored wallpaper. That afternoon it had taken me an hour to reach the linen closet, which served as a remote Bavarian castle, and by the time I finally arrived after hiking through the hallway I was worn out. When my mother found me recovering by the pillowcases a few minutes later she asked what I'd been doing, and I told her: "Traveling." She seemed to accept this statement at face value and, from that moment on, so did I.

2   What I discovered from those foggy afternoons was that home can be a wide and varied place, and that a person may be a seasoned traveler without necessarily leaving the backyard. While some believe traveling means going far away—imagining that a trip to Bangkok is travel while a trip to the park is not—others recognize that travel, like relaxation, is mostly a state of mind. The wanderer wanders wherever he is. Naturally, the inverse must also be true. Just as some people can't relax, some cannot travel, no matter where they find themselves. Look at the commuter who drives 75 miles a day, then says he hasn't gone anywhere in months. Or the business person who flies to Rome and then never leaves her hotel. And what about the delicate soul who ventures forth only when the weather is clement, the accommodations posh, the sights acclaimed—is this travel, or resting away from home?

3   Travel, in my opinion, is one part locomotion and three parts the desire for discovery. It should set the mind going. Which is why a stroll around the block can be as invigorating a journey for the determined discoverer as a junket around the globe. To know one place well is to travel deeply, continuously. To know one place altogether is impossible; it can take a lifetime, after all, to navigate an acre if you proceed inch by inch. Not that most of us will ever roam that closely, but the opportunity is there. Consider Emily Dickinson, who rarely left her house and yet traveled so extensively inside of it that critics are still retracing her footsteps. A poem about one of her adventures begins:

> *I started early, took my dog,*
> *And visited the sea;*
> *The mermaids in the basement*
> *Came out to look at me.*

4   Dickinson is, perhaps, an extremist, the domestic equivalent of Marco Polo. Yet one doesn't have to be a recluse to voyage at home. While he

lived at Walden Pond, Henry David Thoreau treated his visits to nearby Concord Village as if they were brief sojourns on the continent. "It was very pleasant," he notes, "when I stayed late in town, to launch myself into the night, especially if it was dark and tempestuous, and set sail from some bright village parlor . . . for my snug harbor in the woods." He called the scatter of ponds around Concord "my lake country," and there he wandered, viewing the flora and fauna, keeping a record of strange sights, his Grand Tour on the banks of Walden. One afternoon he might watch ants battle by his woodpile, emerging as shaken and excited as any foreign war correspondent; the next he might sit by the railroad tracks, sniffing the cinder-struck air, musing on the vagaries of international commerce based on a whiff of salt fish. "I have traveled much in Concord," he observed, and it's hard to think of anyone who has ventured farther.

5 Some of the most stirring travel accounts I've ever read, in fact, have been written by people who stayed right at home. Aldo Leopold's "A Sand County Almanac," his description of 12 months on a Wisconsin sand farm, treats each season as its own location, with its own particular attractions, citizenry and customs. He pays special attention to the trees he encounters on his rambles, and reports the startling news that, "There is much small-talk and neighborhood gossip among pines," surely as intriguing a bit of information as anything in Frommer's.[2]

6 A quarter of a century later, Annie Dillard describes her exploration of one "rather tamed valley" in Virginia with a gusto that makes Lewis and Clark seem timid. "It's all a matter of keeping my eyes open," she writes in "Pilgrim at Tinker Creek." And so she turns a morning's saunter into a trek, with starlings, frogs and praying mantis egg cases crowding her rural landscape like so many exotic acquaintances. "I would like to know grasses and sedges—and care," reflects Dillard. "Then my least journey into the world would be a field trip." Once while crouching on a log she became so bedazzled by a spot of Tinker Creek that she fell in.

7 Keeping one's eyes open, occasionally falling in astonishment into a creek or a gutter, obliges one to recall that adventure happens in small places as well as large. "I explore the neighborhood," declares Annie Dillard, with the same passion Columbus must have felt when coming upon the New World. At heart, an expedition is no more than a trip undertaken to see or do something—and what that something is usually matters less than the spirit in which the trip is made. Which is not to say that journeys

---

2 [Arthur] Frommer: the author of a series of guidebooks about various countries.

to France and Peru and the Grand Canyon aren't wonderful, or that everyone should stay at home all the time. Only that where one lives should be treated with the same inquisitiveness as anywhere one might go.

[8] In my own case, although I no longer travel by way of linen closets, I do wander locally for most of my excitement. This has a bit to do with economic considerations, but even more to do with my conviction that if a second look reveals more than the first, then a daily look will reveal something new every time. So I take the same route on my afternoon walks, examining the houses I pass with clinical interest, noting a new garage door here, a bed of pansies there, admiring a weathervane, trying my best to comprehend the inhabitants through their domiciles much as de Tocqueville[3] sought to comprehend America through its politics. To hear another language I traipse down to the Armenian markets not far from my house and listen to the clerks yell over vat-sized bowls of olives. When I am feeling especially venturesome, I climb into the car and drive to a nearby meadow that has a few wild animals, a sketchy stream and a cool fringe of oak forest. These are places I have come to love partly because they are familiar, but mostly because I've learned to see them in detail.

[9] Of course, noting detail enlivens travel afar as well as at home. Last summer, I visited friends on Deer Isle, a chip of an island off the coast of northern Maine. Half swallowed by pine trees, their cottage perched on a rocky spur overlooking a scatter of smaller islands and beyond, the sea. At night we sat on their porch, watching the sun set over the water, feeling those black pines close in behind us, admiring and dreading the moment when the sun slipped past the brim of the world and left us alone in the dark. On those nights I couldn't help thinking of earlier residents in this lonely place, especially the fishermen's wives. So often solitary, an ocean at their doorsteps, trees at their backs, those women must have braced for the evenings, watching the same light vanishing. How far they must have traveled. Because it seems to me, finally, that travel truly lies in yearning, the outward gaze that lends one the hope that anything may still happen, that there is so much yet to see.

---

3   [Alexis] de Tocqueville (1805–1859): a French writer and traveler whose book *Democracy in America* (1835) examined America with great insight.

Looking Back

1. What interpretations does Berne give to the word *traveling*?

2. Working in groups of two, determine what, as travelers, Dickinson, Thoreau, Leopold, Dillard, and Berne have in common?

3. Berne observes that some people "cannot travel, no matter where they find themselves." How does she support this observation? Do you agree with it?

4. Berne says that "travel truly lies in yearning," yet many people travel for business, some for academic reasons, some for family emergencies. The people about whom Berne writes are traveling for none of those reasons. What is it they yearn for that they hope travel can provide?

Looking Into

1. Following Berne's example, take the same walk in an unfamiliar neighborhood for three or four days in a row; be observant of the residences you see and try "to see them in detail." Then, try to "comprehend the inhabitants through their domiciles much as de Tocqueville sought to comprehend America through its politics." Make a list of the details you notice about two or three of the residences and speculate about the inhabitants of each.

2. The French painter Monet produced a series of nearly thirty pictures of haystacks painted at different times of the day and at different times of the year. Choose a familiar place near your home and in a series of four paragraphs recreate that place. Focus particularly on the changes of color, texture, size, or activity.

Looking Around

1. The writers in this section are both male and female. Can you discern any significant difference in their approach to travel or travel writing? Describe in a brief essay.

2. If, like Mary Morris, you were to decide to move to another country, which country would be your first choice and why? How might you avoid her initial feelings of isolation and aloneness? Explain in a few paragraphs.

3. With which of these writers would you most like to travel? With which would you least like to travel? Explain your choices in a brief paper.

4. What qualities do you possess that would make you the ideal traveler? What qualities do you think you would need to develop? Describe these qualities in a short paper.

5. Most travelers are quite disdainful toward "tourists," whom they see as a decidedly different and clearly inferior breed of wanderer. Which, if any, of the writers in this section seem to be more tourist than traveler? Explain your choices in a short paper.

PART 8
Writers on Writing

—⁂—

I think there are four great motives for writing, at any rate for writing prose. They exist in different degrees in every writer, and in any one writer the proportions will vary from time to time, according to the atmosphere in which he is living, They are:

(1) Sheer egoism. Desire to seem clever, to be talked about, to be remembered after death, to get your own back on grown-ups who snubbed you in childhood, etc. etc. . . .

(2) Aesthetic enthusiasm. Perception of beauty in the external world or, on the other hand, in words and their right arrangement. Pleasure in the impact of one sound on another, in the firmness of good prose or the rhythm of a good story. Desire to share an experience which one feels is valuable and ought not to be missed. . . .

(3) Historical impulse. Desire to see things as they are, to find out true facts and store them up for the use of posterity.

(4) Political purpose—using the word "political" in the widest possible sense. Desire to push the world in a certain direction, to alter other people's idea of the kind of society that they should strive after. Once again, no book is genuinely free from political bias. The opinion that art should have nothing to do with politics is itself a political attitude.

George Orwell from "Why I Write."

The best writers are invariably wordstruck. Indeed, writers are devoted lovers of language—its rhythms, its peculiarities, its humor, its connotations, its variations, its richness. For writers, weaving words into phrases and sentences and paragraphs provides both emotional and intellectual delight, as satisfying—and as demanding—as shooting hoops, solving arcane mathematical problems, or constructing a model railroad.

In an excerpt from *One Writer's Beginnings* novelist and short-story writer Eudora Welty reflects on her early childhood in Jackson, Mississippi, and the many influences, both human and inanimate, that contributed to making her a writer. Chief among them was her early development as a listener.

Simon J. Ortiz writes in "The Language We Know" about growing up in two cultures: the once-threatened oral tradition of his Acoma Indian heritage and the written tradition of the Western, English-speaking world he was forced to master, and how the combination of those two cultures has been critical to both what and how he writes.

Amy Tan also grew up in a dual culture, and in "Mother Tongue" she muses on the various "Englishes" she had to contend with before she found a voice that could bring together her various worlds and appeal to one particular reader.

James Baldwin, too, had barriers to contend with, but his were centered not in language, but in the experiences of being a black man in America. In his "Autobiographical Notes," Baldwin asserts that "The difficulty then, for me, of being a Negro writer was the fact that I was, in effect, prohibited from examining my own experience too closely by the tremendous demands and the very real dangers of my social situation."

Finally, in "The Parable of the Cave: or, In Praise of Watercolors," novelist Mary Gordon writes angrily of the penalties of being a woman writer and, thus, being inevitably relegated to a minor rather than a major status in the eyes of literary critics.

from One Writer's Beginnings

EUDORA WELTY

Born in 1909, the oldest of three children, Eudora Welty is a lifelong resident of Jackson, Mississippi. In 1929, she received a B.A. from the University of Wisconsin; she briefly attended the Graduate School of Business at Columbia University but soon returned to Mississippi to write for a local radio station and a newspaper. During the Depression, Welty accepted a job as a publicity agent for the Mississippi office of the Works Progress Administration (WPA), a position that enabled her to travel throughout Mississippi's eighty-two counties and that "was the real germ of my wanting to become a real writer, a true writer." Nearly forty years later, she published *One Time, One Place: Mississippi in the Depression/A Snapshot Album* (1971), a collection of the pictures she had taken during her travels. In an introduction to that book, Welty wrote: "I learned quickly enough when to click the shutter, but what I was becoming aware of more slowly was a story-writer's truth: the thing to wait on, to reach there in time for, is the moment in which people reveal themselves." Welty's pictures were exhibited in New York in 1936, the same year her first story—"Death of a Traveling Salesman"—was published.

Her first short story collection, *A Curtain of Green, and Other Stories,* was published in 1941. Two years later she published a second collection, *The Wide Net, and Other Stories.* Two other collections include *The Golden Apples* (1949), a group of connected stories, and *The Bride of the Innisfallen* (1955). *The Collected Stories of Eudora Welty* was published in 1980. Although Welty acknowledges that she is by inclination a short-story writer, she has also written several novels: *The Robber Bridegroom* (1942), which was made into a Broadway musical, *Delta Wedding* (1946), *The Ponder Heart* (1954), *Losing Battles* (1970), and the Pulitzer Prize-winning *The Optimist's Daughter* (1972). Among her many honors and awards are the Presidential Medal of Freedom, awarded in 1980, and the National Medal of Arts, 1987.

Looking Ahead

In April, 1983, Eudora Welty delivered three lectures at Harvard, later published in the book *One Writer's Beginnings* (1984). The lectures, chiefly autobiographical and chronological, focused on Welty's development as a writer and were titled "Listening," "Learning to See," and "Finding a

Voice." The following excerpt, from the opening of the first lecture, emphasizes the importance of Welty's early "listenings."

[1]	*I*n our house on North Congress Street in Jackson, Mississippi, where I was born, the oldest of three children, in 1909, we grew up to the striking of clocks. There was a mission-style oak grandfather clock standing in the hall, which sent its gong-like strokes through the livingroom, diningroom, kitchen, and pantry, and up the sounding board of the stairwell. Through the night, it could find its way into our ears: sometimes, even on the sleeping porch, midnight could wake us up. My parents' bedroom had a smaller striking clock that answered it. Though the kitchen clock did nothing but show the time, the diningroom clock was a cuckoo clock with weights on long chains, on one of which my baby brother, after climbing on a chair to the top of the china closet, once succeeded in suspending the cat for a moment. I don't know whether or not my father's Ohio family, in having been Swiss back in the 1700s before the first three Welty brothers came to America, had anything to do with this: but we all of us have been time-minded all our lives. This was good at least for a future fiction writer, being able to learn so penetratingly, and almost first of all, about chronology. It was one of a good many things I learned almost without knowing it; it would be there when I needed it.

[2]	My father loved all instruments that would instruct and fascinate. His place to keep things was the drawer in the "library table" where lying on top of his folded maps was a telescope with brass extensions, to find the moon and the Big Dipper after supper in our front yard, and to keep appointments with eclipses. There was a folding Kodak[1] that was brought out for Christmas, birthdays, and trips. In the back of the drawer you could find a magnifying glass, a kaleidoscope and a gyroscope kept in a black buckram box, which he would set dancing for us on a string pulled tight. He had also supplied himself with an assortment of puzzles composed of metal rings and intersecting links and keys chained together, impossible for the rest of us, however patiently shown, to take apart; he had an almost childlike love of the ingenious.

1	**folding Kodak:** an early camera made by the Kodak company.

[3] In time, a barometer was added to our diningroom wall; but we didn't really need it. My father had the country boy's accurate knowledge of the weather and its skies. He went out and stood on our front steps first thing in the morning and took a look at it and a sniff. He was a pretty good weather prophet.

[4] "Well, I'm *not*," my mother would say with enormous self-satisfaction.

[5] He told us children what to do if we were lost in a strange country. "Look for where the sky is brightest along the horizon," he said. "That reflects the nearest river. Strike out for a river and you will find habitation." Eventualities were much on his mind. In his care for us children he cautioned us to take measures against such things as being struck by lightning. He drew us all away from the windows during the severe electrical storms that are common where we live. My mother stood apart, scoffing at caution as a character failing. "Why, I always loved a storm! High winds never bothered me in West Virginia! Just listen at that! I wasn't a bit afraid of a little lightning and thunder! I'd go out on the mountain and spread my arms wide and *run* in a good big storm!"

[6] So I developed a strong meteorological sensibility. In years ahead when I wrote stories, atmosphere took its influential role from the start. Commotion in the weather and the inner feelings aroused by such a hovering disturbance emerged connected in dramatic form. (I tried a tornado first, in a story called "The Winds.")

[7] From our earliest Christmas times, Santa Claus brought us toys that instruct boys and girls (separately) how to build things—stone blocks cut to the castle-building style, Tinker Toys, and Erector sets. Daddy made for us himself elaborate kites that needed to be taken miles out of town to a pasture long enough (and my father was not afraid of horses and cows watching) for him to run with and get up on a long cord to which my mother held the spindle, and then we children were given it to hold, tugging like something alive at our hands. They were beautiful, sound, shapely box kites, smelling delicately of office glue for their entire short lives. And of course, as soon as the boys attained anywhere near the right age, there was an electric train, the engine with its pea-sized working headlight, its line of cars, tracks equipped with switches, semaphores, its station, its bridges, and its tunnel, which blocked off all other traffic in the upstairs hall. Even from downstairs and through the cries of excited children, the elegant rush and click of the train could be heard through the ceiling, running around and around its figure eight.

[8] All of this, but especially the train, represents my father's fondest beliefs—in progress, in the future. With these gifts he was preparing his children.

9   And so was my mother with her different gifts.

10   I learned from the age of two or three that any room in our house, at any time of day, was there to read in, or to be read to. My mother read to me. She'd read to me in the big bedroom in the mornings, when we were in her rocker together, which ticked in rhythm as we rocked, as though we had a cricket accompanying the story. She'd read to me in the diningroom on winter afternoons in front of the coal fire, with our cuckoo clock ending the story with "Cuckoo," and at night when I'd got in my own bed. I must have given her no peace. Sometimes she read to me in the kitchen while she sat churning,[2] and the churning sobbed along with *any* story. It was my ambition to have her read to me while *I* churned; once she granted my wish, but she read off my story before I brought her butter. She was an expressive reader. When she was reading, "Puss in Boots," for instance, it was impossible not to know that she distrusted *all* cats.

11   It had been startling and disappointing to me to find out that story books had been written by *people,* that books were not natural wonders, coming up of themselves like grass. Yet regardless of where they came from, I cannot remember a time when I was not in love with them—with the books themselves, cover and binding and the paper they were printed on, with their smell and their weight and with their possession in my arms, captured and carried off to myself. Still illiterate, I was ready for them, committed to all the reading I could give them.

12   Neither of my parents had come from homes that could afford to buy many books, but though it must have been something of a strain on his salary, as the youngest officer in a young insurance company, my father was all the while carefully selecting and ordering away for what he and Mother thought we children should grow up with. They bought first for the future.

13   Besides the bookcase in the livingroom, which was always called "the library," there were the encyclopedia tables and dictionary stand under windows in our diningroom. Here to help us grow up arguing around the diningroom table were the Unabridged Webster, the Columbia Encyclopedia, Compton's Pictured Encyclopedia, the Lincoln Library of Information, and later the Book of Knowledge.[3] And the year we moved into our new house, there was room to celebrate it with the new 1925 edition of the

---

2 **churning:** agitating milk in a container called a churn in order to make butter.
3 **Book of Knowledge:** a multi-volumed set of books that contained not only encyclopedia-type information but stories and fables.

Britannica, which my father, his face always deliberately turned toward the future, was of course disposed to think better than any previous edition.

[14]   In "the library," inside the mission-style bookcase with its three diamond-latticed glass doors, with my father's Morris chair[4] and the glass-shaded lamp on its table beside it, were books I could soon begin on—and I did, reading them all alike and as they came, straight down their rows, top shelf to bottom. There was the set of Stoddard's Lectures, in all its late nineteenth-century vocabulary and vignettes of peasant life and quaint beliefs and customs, with matching halftone illustrations: Vesuvius erupting, Venice by moonlight, gypsies glimpsed by their campfires. I didn't know then the clue they were to my father's longing to see the rest of the world. I read straight through his other love-from-afar: the Victrola Book of the Opera, with opera after opera in synopsis, with portraits in costume of Melba, Caruso, Galli-Curci, and Geraldine Farrar,[5] some of whose voices we could listen to on our Red Seal records.[6]

[15]   My mother read secondarily for information; she sank as a hedonist into novels. She read Dickens[7] in the spirit in which she would have eloped with him. The novels of her girlhood that had stayed on in her imagination, besides those of Dickens and Scott[8] and Robert Louis Stevenson, were *Jane Eyre, Trilby, The Woman in White, Green Mansions, King Solomon's Mines.* Marie Corelli's[9] name would crop up but I understood she had gone out of favor with my mother, who had only kept *Ardath* out of loyalty. In time she absorbed herself in Galsworthy, Edith Wharton, above all in Thomas Mann of the *Joseph* volumes.[10]

[16]   *St. Elmo* was not in our house; I saw it often in other houses. This wildly popular Southern novel is where all the Edna Earles in our population

---

4   **Morris chair:** a large easy chair with arms and a movable back, designed by the English architect, writer, designer William Morris (1834–1896).

5   **Melba, Caruso, Galli-Curci, and Geraldine Farrar:** opera singers of the late nineteenth and early twentieth centuries.

6   **Red Seal records:** the label of a famous 78 r.p.m. record company, now owned by RCA.

7   **[Charles] Dickens** (1812–1870): preeminent Victorian novelist whose works were as avidly read in the United States as in his native England.

8   **[Sir Walter] Scott** (1771–1832): Scottish poet and novelist, today best remembered for his medieval novel *Ivanhoe* but as celebrated in his day as Charles Dickens.

9   **Marie Corelli** (1855–1924): English novelist wildly popular at the end of the nineteenth century but who became ridiculed for the exuberance of her imagination.

10   **Joseph volumes:** a four-volume novel about the biblical figure of Joseph written by the German Writer Thomas Mann (1875–1955) between 1933–1943.

started coming from. They're all named for the heroine, who succeeded in bringing a dissolute, sinning roué and atheist of a lover (St. Elmo) to his knees. My mother was able to forgo it. But she remembered the classic advice given to rose growers on how to water their bushes long enough: "Take a chair and *St. Elmo.*"

17   To both my parents I owe my early acquaintance with a beloved Mark Twain. There was a full set of Mark Twain and a short set of Ring Lardner in our bookcase; and those were the volumes that in time united us all, parents and children.

18   Reading everything that stood before me was how I came upon a worn old book without a back that had belonged to my father as a child. It was called *Sanford and Merton.* Is there anyone left who recognizes it, I wonder? It is the famous moral tale written by Thomas Day in the 1780s, but of him no mention is made on the title page of *this* book; here it is *Sanford and Merton in Words of One syllable* by Mary Godolphin. Here are the rich boy and the poor boy and Mr. Barlow, their teacher and interlocutor, in long discourses alternating with dramatic scenes—danger and rescue allotted to the rich and the poor respectively. It may have only words of one syllable, but one of them is "quoth." It ends with not one but two morals, both engraved on rings: "Do what you ought, come what may," and "If we would be great, we must first learn to be good."

19   This book was lacking its front cover, the back held on by strips of pasted paper, now turned golden, in several layers, and the pages stained, flecked, and tattered around the edges; its garish illustrations had come unattached but were preserved, laid in. I had the feeling even in my heedless childhood that this was the only book my father as a little boy had had of his own. He had held onto it, and might have gone to sleep on its coverless face: he had lost his mother when he was seven. My father had never made any mention to his own children of the book, but he had brought it along with him from Ohio to our house and shelved it in our bookcase.

20   My mother had brought from West Virginia that set of Dickens: those books looked sad, too—they had been through fire and water before I was born, she told me, and there they were, lined up—as I later realized, waiting for *me.*

21   I was presented, from as early as I can remember, with books of my own, which appeared on my birthday and Christmas morning. Indeed, my parents could not give me books enough. They must have sacrificed to give me on my sixth or seventh birthday—it was after I became a reader for myself—the ten-volume set of Our Wonder World. These were beautifully made, heavy books I would lie down with on the floor in front of the diningroom hearth, and more often than the rest volume 5, *Every Child's Story*

Book, was under my eyes. There were the fairy tales—Grimm, Andersen, the English, the French, "Ali Baba and the Forty Thieves"; and there was Aesop and Reynard the Fox; there were the myths and legends, Robin Hood, King Arthur, and St. George and the Dragon, even the history of Joan of Arc; a whack of *Pilgrim's Progress* and a long piece of *Gulliver.* They all carried their classic illustrations. I located myself in these pages and could go straight to the stories and pictures I loved; very often "The Yellow Dwarf" was first choice, with Walter Crane's Yellow Dwarf in full color making his terrifying appearance flanked by turkeys. Now that volume is as worn and backless and hanging apart as my father's poor *Sanford and Merton.* The precious page with Edward Lear's "Jumblies" on it has been in danger of slipping out for all these years. One measure of my love for Our Wonder World was that for a long time I wondered if I would go through fire and water for it as my mother had done for Charles Dickens; and the only comfort was to think I could ask my mother to do it for me.

22   I believe I'm the only child I know of who grew up with this treasure in the house. I used to ask others. "Did you have Our Wonder World?" I'd have to tell them The Book of Knowledge could not hold a candle to it.

23   I live in gratitude to my parents for initiating me—and as early as I begged for it, without keeping me waiting—into knowledge of the word, into reading and spelling, by way of the alphabet. They taught it to me at home in time for me to begin to read before starting to school. I believe the alphabet is no longer considered an essential piece of equipment for traveling through life. In my day it was the keystone to knowledge. You learned the alphabet as you learned to count to ten, as you learned "Now I lay me" and the Lord's Prayer and your father's and mother's name and address and telephone number, all in case you were lost.

24   My love for the alphabet, which endures, grew out of reciting it but, before that, out of seeing the letters on the page. In my own story books, before I could read them for myself, I fell in love with various winding, enchanted-looking initials drawn by Walter Crane at the heads of fairy tales. In "Once upon a time," an "O" had a rabbit running it as a treadmill, his feet upon flowers. When the day came, years later, for me to see the Book of Kells,[11] all the wizardry of letter, initial, and word swept over

---

11 **Book of Kells:** an illuminated copy of the Gospels in Latin created in eighth century Ireland. The term *illuminated* refers to the hand-coloring or gilding of a page, often in bands of vines enclosing the text; typically, the first letter of the first word on a page is greatly enlarged and ornately decorated, often with miniature pictures of animals or people.

me a thousand times over, and the illumination, the gold, seemed a part of the word's beauty and holiness that had been there from the start.

25 Learning stamps you with its moments. Childhood's learning is made up of moments. It isn't steady. It's a pulse.

26 In a children's art class, we sat in a ring on kindergarten chairs and drew three daffodils that had just been picked out of the yard; and while I was drawing, my sharpened yellow pencil and the cup of the yellow daffodil gave off whiffs just alike. That the pencil doing the drawing should give off the same smell as the flower it drew seemed part of the art lesson—as shouldn't it be? Children, like animals, use all their senses to discover the world. Then artists come along and discover it the same way, all over again. Here and there, it's the same world. Or now and then we'll hear from an artist who's never lost it.

27 In my sensory education I include my physical awareness of the *word*. Of a certain word, that is; the connection it has with what it stands for. At around age six, perhaps, I was standing by myself in our front yard waiting for supper, just at that hour in a late summer day when the sun is already below the horizon and the risen full moon in the visible sky stops being chalky and begins to take on light. There comes the moment, and I saw it then, when the moon goes from flat to round. For the first time it met my eyes as a globe. The word "moon" came into my mouth as though fed to me out of a silver spoon. Held in my mouth the moon became a word. It had the roundness of a Concord grape Grandpa took off his vine and gave me to suck out of its skin and swallow whole, in Ohio.

28 This love did not prevent me from living for years in foolish error about the moon. The new moon just appearing in the west was the rising moon to me. The new should be rising. And in early childhood the sun and moon, those opposite reigning powers, I just as easily assumed rose in east and west respectively in their opposite sides of the sky, and like partners in a reel they advanced, sun from the east, moon from the west, crossed over (when I wasn't looking) and went down on the other side. My father couldn't have known I believed that when, bending behind me and guiding my shoulder, he positioned me at our telescope in the front yard and, with careful adjustment of the focus, brought the moon close to me.

29 The night sky over my childhood Jackson was velvety black. I could see the full constellations in it and call their names; when I could read, I knew their myths. Though I was always waked for eclipses, and indeed carried to the window as an infant in arms and shown Halley's Comet in my sleep, and though I'd been taught at our diningroom table about the solar system and knew the earth revolved around the sun, and our moon

around us, I never found out the moon didn't come up in the west until I was a writer and Herschel Brickell, the literary critic, told me after I misplaced it in a story. He said valuable words to me about my new profession: "Always be sure you get your moon in the right part of the sky."

30 My mother always sang to her children. Her voice came out just a little bit in the minor key. "Wee Willie Winkie's" song was wonderfully sad when she sang the lullabies.

31   "Oh, but now there's a record. She could have her own record to listen to," my father would have said. For there came a Victrola[12] record of "Bobby Shafftoe" and "Rock-a-Bye Baby," all of Mother's lullabies, which could be played to take her place. Soon I was able to play her my own lullabies all day long.

32   Our Victrola stood in the diningroom. I was allowed to climb onto the seat of a diningroom chair to wind it, start the record turning, and set the needle playing. In a second I'd jumped to the floor, to spin or march around the table as the music called for—now there were all the other records I could play too. I skinned back onto the chair just in time to lift the needle at the end, stop the record and turn it over, then change the needle. That brass receptacle with a hole in the lid gave off a metallic smell like human sweat, from all the hot needles that were fed it. Winding up, dancing, being cocked to start and stop the record, was of course all in one the act of *listening*—to "Overture to *Daughter of the Regiment*." "Selections from *The Fortune Teller*," "Kiss Me Again," "Gypsy Dance from *Carmen*," "Stars and Stripes Forever," "When the Midnight Choo-Choo Leaves for Alabam," or whatever came next. Movement must be at the very heart of listening.

33   Ever since I was first read to, then started reading to myself, there has never been a line read that I didn't *hear*. As my eyes followed the sentence, a voice was saying it silently to me. It isn't my mother's voice, or the voice of any person I can identify, certainly not my own. It is human, but inward, and it is inwardly that I listen to it. It is to me the voice of the story or the poem itself. The cadence, whatever it is that asks you to believe, the feeling that resides in the printed word, reaches me through the reader-voice. I have supposed, but never found out, that this is the case with all readers—to read as listeners—and with all writers, to write as listeners. It may be part of the desire to write. The sound of what falls on the page begins the process of testing it for truth, for me. Whether I am right to trust so

---

12 **Victrola:** the trademark name of an early phonograph.

far I don't know. By now I don't know whether I could do either one, reading or writing, without the other.

³⁴   My own words, when I am at work on a story, I hear too as they go, in the same voice that I hear when I read in books. When I write and the sound of it comes back to my ears, then I act to make my changes. I have always trusted this voice.

³⁵ In that vanished time in small-town Jackson, most of the ladies I was familiar with, the mothers of my friends in the neighborhood, were busiest when they were sociable. In the afternoons there was regular visiting up and down the little grid of residential streets. Everybody had calling cards, even certain children; and newborn babies themselves were properly announced by sending out their tiny engraved calling cards attached with a pink or blue bow to those of their parents. Graduation presents to high-school pupils were often "card cases." On the hall table in every house the first thing you saw was a silver tray waiting to receive more calling cards on top of the stack already piled up like jackstraws; they were never thrown away.

³⁶   My mother let none of this idling, as she saw it, pertain to her; she went her own way with or without her calling cards, and though she was fond of her friends and they were fond of her, she had little time for small talk. At first, I hadn't known what I'd missed.

³⁷   When we at length bought our first automobile, one of our neighbors was often invited to go with us on the family Sunday afternoon ride. In Jackson it was counted an affront to the neighbors to start out for anywhere with an empty seat in the car. My mother sat in the back with her friend, and I'm told that as a small child I would ask to sit in the middle, and say as we started off, "Now *talk*."

³⁸   There was dialogue throughout the lady's accounts to my mother. "I said" . . . "He said" . . . "And I'm told she very plainly said" . . . "It was midnight before they finally heard, and what do you think it *was?*"

³⁹   What I loved about her stories was that everything happened in *scenes*. I might not catch on to what the root of the trouble was in all that happened, but my ear told me it was dramatic. Often she said, "The crisis had come!"

⁴⁰   This same lady was one of Mother's callers on the telephone who always talked a long time. I knew who it was when my mother would only reply, now and then, "Well, I declare," or "You don't say so," or "Surely not." She'd be standing at the wall telephone, listening against her will, and I'd sit on the stairs close by her. Our telephone had a little bar set into the handle which had to be pressed and held down to keep the connec-

tion open, and when her friend had said good-bye, my mother needed me to prize her fingers loose from the little bar; her grip had become paralyzed. "What did she say?" I asked.

41   "She wasn't *saying* a thing in this world," sighed my mother. "She was just ready to talk, that's all."

42   My mother was right. Years later, beginning with my story "Why I Live at the P.O.," I wrote reasonably often in the form of a monologue that takes possession of the speaker. How much more gets told besides!

43   This lady told everything in her sweet, marveling voice, and meant every word of it kindly. She enjoyed my company perhaps even more than my mother's. She invited me to catch her doodlebugs; under the trees in her backyard were dozens of their holes. When you stuck a broom straw down one and called, "Doodlebug, doodlebug, your house is on fire and all your children are burning up," she believed this is why the doodlebug came running out of the hole. This was why I loved to call up her doodlebugs instead of ours.

44   My mother could never have told me her stories, and I think I knew why even then: my mother didn't believe them. But I could listen to this murmuring lady all day. She believed everything she heard, like the doodlebug. And so did I.

45   This was a day when ladies' and children's clothes were very often made at home. My mother cut out all the dresses and her little boys' rompers, and a sewing woman would come and spend the day upstairs in the sewing room fitting and stitching them all. This was Fannie. This old black sewing woman, along with her speed and dexterity, brought along a great provision of up-to-the-minute news. She spent her life going from family to family in town and worked right in its bosom, and nothing could stop her. My mother would try, while I stood being pinned up. "Fannie, I'd rather Eudora didn't hear that." "That" would be just what I was longing to hear, whatever it was, "I don't want her exposed to gossip"—as if gossip were measles and I could catch it. I did catch some of it but not enough. "Mrs. O'Neil's oldest daughter she had her wedding dress *tried on,* and all her fine underclothes featherstitched and ribbon run in and then—" "I think that will do, Fannie," said my mother. It was tantalizing never to be exposed long enough to hear the end.

46   Fannie was the worldliest old woman to be imagined. She could do whatever her hands were doing without having to stop talking; and she could speak in a wonderfully derogatory way with any number of pins struck in her mouth. Her hands steadied me like claws as she stumped on her knees around me, tacking me together. The gist of her tale would be lost on me, but Fannie didn't bother about the ear she was telling it to; she just

liked telling. She was like an author. In fact, for a good deal of what she said, I daresay she *was* the author.

47   Long before I wrote stories, I listened for stories. Listening *for* them is something more acute than listening *to* them. I suppose it's an early form of participation in what goes on. Listening children know stories are *there.* When their elders sit and begin, children are just waiting and hoping for one to come out, like a mouse from its hole.

48   It was taken entirely for granted that there wasn't any lying in our family, and I was advanced in adolescence before I realized that in plenty of homes where I played with schoolmates and went to their parties, children lied to their parents and parents lied to their children and to each other. It took me a long time to realize that these very same everyday lies, and the stratagems and jokes and tricks and dares that went with them, were in fact the basis of the *scenes* I so well loved to hear about and hoped for and treasured in the conversation of adults.

49   My instinct—the dramatic instinct—was to lead me, eventually, on the right track for a storyteller: the *scene* was full of hints, pointers, suggestions, and promises of things to find out and know about human beings. I had to grow up and learn to listen for the unspoken as well as the spoken—and to know a truth, I also had to recognize a lie.

Looking Back

1. As a child, what did Welty listen to? What effect did her various "listenings" have on her eventual career as a writer?

2. What evidence in the piece indicates that Welty's parents were good parents?

3. Why does Welty focus so extensively on her father's book *Sanford and Merton?* What does it seem to represent to her?

4. Working in small groups, make as long a list as possible in answer to the following question: What aspects of Welty's early life are "things of the past" to us today?

5. What are some of the key characteristics of Welty's style?

Looking Into

1. Welty writes about an incident that happened when she was six and that first enabled her to understand "the connection [a word] had with what it stands for." Think of a moment in your own life when you had a sudden insight into the meaning of a particular word. Recreate that moment in no more than a paragraph.

2. Eudora Welty was over seventy when she looked back on her life and discerned the influences that had made her a writer. Imagine yourself as either a writer, a teacher, a fire fighter, or a professional athlete. Make a list of some of the characteristics you would need to be successful in that career you choose. Then scan your own life for influences comparable to those Welty talks about. Be prepared to discuss one of those influences.

The Language We Know

SIMON J. ORTIZ

Native-American Simon J. Ortiz, an Acoma Indian, was born in 1941 in Albuquerque, New Mexico, and grew up primarily in McCartys, New Mexico. He attended Fort Lewis College, Colorado, for one year before going into the U.S. Army, 1963–1966, where he became specialist 5. From 1966–1969, he attended the University of New Mexico and the University of Iowa. Ortiz has worked as a public relations worker, a newspaper editor, an instructor at such institutions as San Diego State University, the Institute of American Arts, the College of Marin, the University of New Mexico, and Lewis and Clark College.

He has been the consulting editor of both the Navajo Community College Press, Tsaile, Arizona, and the Pueblo of Acoma Press, New Mexico. In 1990, he became the arts coordinator of the Metropolitan Arts Commission, Portland. The majority of Ortiz's publications have been volumes of poetry: *Naked in the Wind* (1971), *Going for the Rain* (1976), *A Good Journey* (1977), *From Sand Creek: Rising in This Heart Which Is Our America* (1981), and *A Poem Is a Journey* (1981). In addition to two children's books—*The People Shall Continue* (1977) and *Blue and Red* (1982)—Ortiz has written *Howbah Indians* (1978) and *Fightin': New and Collected Stories* (1983), two collections of short fiction. Ortiz's most recent works are *Woven Stone: A 3-in-1 Volume of Poetry and Prose* (1991) and *After and Before the Lightning* (1991), a collection of poetry.

Looking Ahead

Some sixty miles west of the city of Albuquerque lies Acoma Pueblo, a settlement located atop a 365-foot-high mesa. Since its founding is estimated between 800 and 1150 A.D., it is the oldest continuously inhabited village in the United States. The people of Acoma—the *Aaquumeh hano*—are probably most noted for their distinctive pottery with its black and white, and occasionally sienna-colored, designs. In Simon J. Ortiz, they have a strong spokesman for the preservation of their cultural values. In this essay, Ortiz talks about the importance to his development as a writer of the oral tradition in which he grew up.

¹ I don't remember a world without language. From the time of my earliest childhood, there was language. Always language, and imagination, speculation, utters of sound. Words, beginnings of words. What would I be without language? My existence has been determined by language, not only the spoken but the unspoken, the language of speech and the language of motion. I can't remember a world without memory. Memory, immediate and far away in the past, something in the sinew, blood, ageless cell. Although I don't recall the exact moment I spoke or tried to speak, I know the feeling of something tugging at the core of the mind, something unutterable uttered into existence. It is language that brings us into being in order to know life.

² My childhood was the oral tradition of the Acoma Pueblo people—Aaqumeh hano—which included my immediate family of three older sisters, two younger sisters, two younger brothers, and my mother and father. My world was our world of the Aaquumeh in McCartys, one of the two villages descended from the ageless mother pueblo of Acoma. My world was our Eagle clan-people among other clans. I grew up in Deetziyamah, which is the Aaquumeh name for McCartys, which is posted at the exit off the present interstate highway in western New Mexico. I grew up within a people who farmed small garden plots and fields, who were mostly poor and not well schooled in the American system's education. The language I spoke was that of a struggling people who held ferociously to a heritage, culture, language, and land despite the odds posed them by the forces surrounding them since 1540 A.D., the advent of Euro-American colonization. When I began school in 1948 at the BIA (Bureau of Indian Affairs) day school in our village, I was armed with the basic ABC's and the phrases "Good morning, Miss Oleman" and "May I please be excused to go to the bathroom," but it was an older language that was my fundamental strength.

³ In my childhood, the language we all spoke was Acoma, and it was a struggle to maintain it against the outright threats of corporal punishment, ostracism, and the invocation that it would impede our progress towards Americanization. Children in school were punished and looked upon with disdain if they did not speak and learn English quickly and smoothly, and so I learned it. It has occurred to me that I learned English simply because I was forced to, as so many other Indian children were. But I know, also, there was another reason, and this was that I loved language, the sound, meaning, and magic of language. Language opened up vistas of the world around me, and it allowed me to discover knowledge that would not be possible for me to know without the use of language. Later, when I began

to experiment with and explore language in poetry and fiction, I allowed that a portion of that impetus was because I had come to know English through forceful acculturation. Nevertheless, the underlying force was the beauty and poetic power of language in its many forms that instilled in me the desire to become a user of language as a writer, singer, and story-teller. Significantly, it was the Acoma language, which I don't use enough of today, that inspired me to become a writer. The concepts, values, and philosophy contained in my original language and the struggle it has faced have determined my life and vision as a writer.

4 In Deetziyamah, I discovered the world of the Acoma land and people firsthand through my parents, sisters and brothers, and my own percep-tions, voiced through all that encompasses the oral tradition, which is age-less for any culture. It is a small village, even smaller years ago, and like other Indian communities it is wealthy with its knowledge of daily event, history, and social system, all that make up a people who have a many-dimensioned heritage. Our family lived in a two-room home (built by my grandfather some years after he and my grandmother moved with their daughters from Old Acoma), which my father added rooms to later. I re-member my father's work at enlarging our home for our growing family. He was a skilled stoneworker, like many other men of an older Pueblo generation who worked with sandstone and mud mortar to build their homes and pueblos. It takes time, persistence, patience, and the belief that the walls that come to stand will do so for a long, long time, perhaps even forever. I like to think that by helping to mix mud and carry stone for my father and other elders I managed to bring that influence into my con-sciousness as a writer.

5 Both my mother and my father were good storytellers and singers (as my mother is to this day—my father died in 1978), and for their genera-tion, which was born soon after the turn of the century, they were rela-tively educated in the American system. Catholic missionaries had taken both of them as children to a parochial boarding school far from Acoma, and they imparted their discipline for study and quest for education to us children when we started school. But it was their indigenous sense of gain-ing knowledge that was most meaningful to me. Acquiring knowledge about life was above all the most important item; it was a value that one had to have in order to be fulfilled personally and on behalf of his com-munity. And this they insisted upon imparting through the oral tradition as they told their children about our native history and our community and culture and our "stories." These stories were common knowledge of act, event, and behavior in a close-knit pueblo. It was knowledge about

how one was to make a living through work that benefited his family and everyone else.

6   Because we were a subsistence farming people, or at least tried to be, I learned to plant, hoe weeds, irrigate and cultivate corn, chili, pumpkins, beans. Through counsel and advice I came to know that the rain which provided water was a blessing, gift, and symbol and that it was the land which provided for our lives. It was the stories and songs which provided the knowledge that I was woven into the intricate web that was my Acoma life. In our garden and our cornfields I learned about the seasons, growth cycles of cultivated plants, what one had to think and feel about the land; and at home I became aware of how we must care for each other: all of this was encompassed in an intricate relationship which had to be maintained in order that life continue. After supper on many occasions my father would bring out his drum and sing as we, the children, danced to themes about the rain, hunting, land, and people. It was all that is contained within the language of oral tradition that made me explicitly aware of a yet unarticulated urge to write, to tell what I had learned and was learning and what it all meant to me.

7   My grandfather was old already when I came to know him. I was only one of his many grandchildren, but I would go with him to get wood for our households, to the garden to chop weeds, and to his sheep camp to help care for his sheep. I don't remember his exact words, but I know they were about how we must sacredly concern ourselves with the people and the holy earth. I know his words were about how we must regard ourselves and others with compassion and love; I know that his knowledge was vast, as a medicine man and an elder of his kiva, and I listened as a boy should. My grandfather represented for me a link to the past that is important for me to hold in my memory because it is not only memory but knowledge that substantiates my present existence. He and the grandmothers and grandfathers before him thought about us as they lived, confirmed in their belief of a continuing life, and they brought our present beings into existence by the beliefs they held. The consciousness of that belief is what informs my present concerns with language, poetry, and fiction.

8 My first poem was for Mother's Day when I was in the fifth grade, and it was the first poem that was ever published, too, in the Skull Valley School newsletter. Of course I don't remember how the juvenile poem went, but it must have been certain in its expression of love and reverence for the woman who was the most important person in my young life. The poem didn't signal any prophecy of my future as a poet, but it must have come

from the forming idea that there were things one could do with language and writing. My mother, years later, remembers how I was a child who always told stories—that is, tall tales—who always had explanations for things probably better left unspoken, and she says that I also liked to perform in school plays. In remembering, I do know that I was coming to that age when the emotions and thoughts in me began to moil to the surface. There was much to experience and express in that age when youth has a precociousness that is broken easily or made to flourish. We were a poor family, always on the verge of financial disaster, though our parents always managed to feed us and keep us in clothing. We had the problems, unfortunately ordinary, of many Indian families who face poverty on a daily basis, never enough of anything, the feeling of a denigrating self-consciousness, alcoholism in the family and community, the feeling that something was falling apart though we tried desperately to hold it all together.

9   My father worked for the railroad for many years as a laborer and later as a welder. We moved to Skull Valley, Arizona, for one year in the early 1950s, and it was then that I first came in touch with a non-Indian, non-Acoma world. Skull Valley was a farming and ranching community, and my younger brothers and sisters and I went to a one-room school. I had never really had much contact with white people except from a careful and suspicious distance, but now here I was, totally surrounded by them, and there was nothing to do but bear the experience and learn from it. Although I perceived there was not much difference between *them* and *us* in certain respects, there was a distinct feeling that we were not the same either. This thought had been inculcated in me, especially by an Acoma expression—*Gaimuu Mericano*—that spoke of the "fortune" of being an American. In later years as a social activist and committed writer, I would try to offer a strong positive view of our collective Indianness through my writing. Nevertheless, my father was an inadequately paid laborer, and we were far from our home land for economic-social reasons, and my feelings and thoughts about that experience during that time would become a part of how I became a writer.

10   Soon after, I went away from my home and family to go to boarding school, first in Santa Fe and then in Albuquerque. This was in the 1950s, and this had been the case for the past half-century for Indians: we had to leave home in order to become truly American by joining the mainstream, which was deemed to be the proper course of our lives. On top of this was termination, a U.S. government policy which dictated that Indians sever their relationship to the federal government and remove themselves from their lands and go to American cities for jobs and education. It was an era which bespoke the intent of U.S. public policy that Indians were no longer

to be Indians. Naturally, I did not perceive this in any analytical or purposeful sense; rather, I felt an unspoken anxiety and resentment against unseen forces that determined our destiny to be un-Indian, embarrassed and uncomfortable with our grandparents' customs and strictly held values. We were to set our goals as American working men and women, single-mindedly industrious, patriotic, and unquestioning, building for a future which ensured that the U.S. was the greatest nation in the world. I felt fearfully uneasy with this, for by then I felt the loneliness, alienation, and isolation imposed upon me by the separation from my family, home, and community.

[11]   Something was happening; I could see that in my years at Catholic school and the U.S. Indian school. I remembered my grandparents' and parents' words: educate yourself in order to help your people. In that era and the generation who had the same experience I had, there was an unspoken vow: we were caught in a system inexorably, and we had to learn that system well in order to fight back. Without the motive of a fight-back we would not be able to survive as the people our heritage had lovingly bequeathed us. My diaries and notebooks began then, and though none have survived to the present, I know they contained the varied moods of a youth filled with loneliness, anger, and discomfort that seemed to have unknown causes. Yet at the same time, I realize now, I was coming to know myself clearly in a way that I would later articulate in writing. My love of language, which allowed me to deal with the world, to delve into it, to experiment and discover, held for me a vision of awe and wonder, and by then grammar teachers had noticed I was a good speller, used verbs and tenses correctly, and wrote complete sentences. Although I imagine that they might have surmised this as unusual for an Indian student whose original language was not English, I am grateful for their perception and attention.

[12] During the latter part of that era in the 1950s of Indian termination and the Cold War, a portion of which still exists today, there were the beginnings of a bolder and more vocalized resistance against the current U.S. public policies of repression, racism, and cultural ethnocide. It seemed to be inspired by the civil rights movement led by black people in the U.S. and by decolonization and liberation struggles worldwide. Indian people were being relocated from their rural homelands at an astonishingly devastating rate, yet at the same time they resisted the U.S. effort by maintaining determined ties with their heritage, returning often to their native communities and establishing Indian centers in the cities they were removed to. Indian rural communities, such as Acoma Pueblo, insisted on their land claims and began to initiate legal battles in the areas of natural and social,

political and economic human rights. By the retention and the inspiration of our native heritage, values, philosophies, and language, we would know ourselves as a strong and enduring people. Having a modest and latent consciousness of this as a teenager, I began to write about the experience of being Indian in America. Although I had only a romanticized image of what a writer was, which came from the pulp rendered by American popular literature, and I really didn't know anything about writing, I sincerely felt a need to say things, to speak, to release the energy of the impulse to help my people.

¹³ My writing in my late teens and early adulthood was fashioned after the American short stories and poetry taught in the high schools of the 1940s and 1950s, but by the 1960s, after I had gone to college and dropped out and served in the military, I began to develop topics and themes from my Indian background. The experience in my village of Deetziyamah and Acoma Pueblo was readily accessible. I had grown up within the oral tradition of speech, social and religious ritual, elders' counsel and advice, countless and endless stories, everyday events, and the visual art that was symbolically representative of life all around. My mother was a potter of the well-known Acoma clayware, a traditional art form that had been passed to her from her mother and the generations of mothers before. My father carved figures from wood and did beadwork. This was not unusual, as Indian people know; there was always some kind of artistic endeavor that people set themselves to, although they did not necessarily articulate it as "Art" in the sense of Western civilization. One lived and expressed an artful life, whether it was in ceremonial singing and dancing, architecture, painting, speaking, or in the way one's social-cultural life was structured. When I turned my attention to my own heritage, I did so because this was my identity, the substance of who I was, and I wanted to write about what that meant. My desire was to write about the integrity and dignity of an Indian identity, and at the same time I wanted to look at what this was within the context of an America that had too often denied its Indian heritage.

¹⁴ To a great extent my writing has a natural political-cultural bent simply because I was nurtured intellectually and emotionally within an atmosphere of Indian resistance. Aacquu did not die in 1598 when it was burned and razed by European conquerors,[1] nor did the people become hopeless

---

1 **European conquerors:** In 1598, Juan de Zaldivar, the nephew of New Mexico's first Spanish colonizer, was killed when he marched on Acoma and demanded tribute. In response, Juan's brother Vicente and seventy soldiers attacked the Acoma Pueblo, killing some 800 residents and destroying the village.

when their children were taken away to U.S. schools far from home and new ways were imposed upon them. The *Aaquumeh hano,* despite losing much of their land and surrounded by a foreign civilization, have not lost sight of their native heritage. This is the factual case with most other Indian peoples, and the clear explanation for this has been the fight-back we have found it necessary to wage. At times, in the past, it was outright armed struggle, like that of present-day Indians in Central and South America with whom we must identify; currently, it is often in the legal arena, and it is in the field of literature. In 1981, when I was invited to the White House for an event celebrating American poets and poetry, I did not immediately accept the invitation. I questioned myself about the possibility that I was merely being exploited as an Indian, and I hedged against accepting. But then I recalled the elders going among our people in the poor days of the 1950s, asking for donations—a dollar here and there, a sheep, perhaps a piece of pottery—in order to finance a trip to the nation's capital. They were to make another countless appeal on behalf of our people, to demand justice, to reclaim lost land even though there was only spare hope they would be successful. I went to the White House realizing that I was to do no less than they and those who had fought in the Pueblo Revolt of 1680,[2] and I read my poems and sang songs that were later described as "guttural" by a Washington, D.C., newspaper. I suppose it is more or less understandable why such a view of Indian literature is held by many, and it is also clear why there should be a political stand taken in my writing and those of my sister and brother Indian writers.

[15] The 1960s and afterward have been an invigorating and liberating period for Indian people. It has been only a little more than twenty years since Indian writers began to write and publish extensively, but we are writing and publishing more and more; we can only go forward. We come from an ageless, continuing oral tradition that informs us of our values, concepts, and notions as native people, and it is amazing how much of this tradition is ingrained so deeply in our contemporary writing, considering the

---

2 **Pueblo Revolt of 1680:** In 1610, the first Spanish colonizers came to the Rio Grande valley. Over the next seventy years the Native Americans of the area were either persuaded or forced to convert to Christianity. In 1675, the Spanish seized some forty-seven tribal religious leaders on the charge of "practicing witchcraft." After most were flogged and three were hanged, one of the survivors eventually organized the pueblos into a revolt which swept across New Mexico. Priests were massacred, churches destroyed, and baptized Indians were washed with soapweed to purify them. In 1692, the Spanish recaptured the province with a force of some 300 men.

brutal efforts of cultural repression that was not long ago outright U.S. policy. We were not to speak our languages, practice our spiritual beliefs, or accept the values of our past generations; and we were discouraged from pressing for our natural rights as Indian human beings. In spite of the fact that there is to some extent the same repression today, we persist and insist in living, believing, hoping, loving, speaking, and writing as Indians. This is embodied in the language we know and share in our writing. We have always had this language, and it is the language, spoken and unspoken, that determines our existence, that brought our grandmothers and grandfathers and ourselves into being in order that there be a continuing life.

Looking Back

1. Why is language in general important to Ortiz?

2 Why is the Acoma language especially important to Ortiz?

3. What were Ortiz's experiences with people not of his clan or culture? What was the effect of those experiences on him?

4. Ortiz describes his writing as having "a natural political-cultural bent." What evidence in his essay indicates that that "bent" animates his writings? To what extent would Orwell (the author of the part-opening quote) approve of Ortiz's "bent"?

Looking Into

1. Early in his essay, Ortiz alludes to the BIA. The Bureau of Indian Affairs was established in 1824 under the Department of War. Toward the end of the nineteenth century it was transferred to the Department of the Interior and given the purpose of overseeing the care of Native Americans, most of whom had been relocated to reservations. Ownership of land, grazing and trading rights, schooling—indeed all issues pertaining to Indians—became the province of the BIA. Officials at the BIA denied Native Americans the right to be citizens (and thus to vote), forcibly removed their children from home and sent them away to be

educated at church- or government-run boarding schools, and outlawed their religious ceremonies. In the 1950s, as Ortiz mentions, the government began a new policy toward Native Americans, a policy Ortiz refers to as "termination." Working in small groups, research the policy of "termination" and what it meant for Native Americans such as Ortiz. Write a report in which you explain the policy and its effect; conclude by commenting on the justness of such a policy.

2. Native Americans have long suffered from being stereotyped in movies. View two or more movies that depict Native Americans, one made between 1935 and 1955 and another between 1965 and the present. Write an argumentative paper in which you respond to the following questions. Has the portrayal of Native Americans in films changed in the last sixty years? If so, in what ways? Are those changes in your opinion good or bad?

Mother Tongue

AMY TAN

Like Simon J. Ortiz, Amy Tan grew up in two cultures and two quite different languages. Tan's parents were Chinese immigrants who left China in the late 1940s and settled in northern California. Born in 1952, Tan grew up in Oakland, Fresno, Berkeley, and several other San Francisco suburbs before her parents settled in Santa Clara, California. As she told one interviewer, "I moved every year, so I was constantly adjusting . . . living in my own imagination." After both her father and her brother Peter died, eight months apart, of brain tumors, Tan's mother took her family to the Netherlands and then to Montreux, Switzerland, where Tan finished high school. In 1969, Tan enrolled in a pre-med course at Linfield College, a small Baptist college in Oregon—Tan's father had been both an electrical engineer and a Baptist minister. A year later she transferred to San Jose State, California, changing her major from pre-med to English. She graduated with a B.A. in 1973, earned her M.A. in 1974, and spent two years in postgraduate study at the University of California, Berkeley.

Her first work experience was as a consultant to programs for disabled children. She also worked as a reporter, a managing editor, and an associate publisher for *Emergency Room Reports,* now called *Emergency Medicine Reports.* From 1983–1987, she worked as a freelance technical writer, writing speeches for salespeople and executives. Tan's first published novel, *The Joy Luck Club* (1989), a novel that was an instant critical and popular success, received nominations for the prestigious National Book Award, has been translated into seventeen languages, including Chinese, and has been made into a movie. In 1991, Tan published her second novel: *The Kitchen God's Wife,* a book that received even greater praise than her first, a rare achievement for most novelists. Tan has also published two children's books, *The Moon Lady* (1992), and most recently *The Chinese Siamese Cat* (1994).

Looking Ahead

In this autobiographical essay, Tan talks about the various "Englishes" she knows, the attitude of people toward those who do not speak "perfect" English, the possible effect of growing up in a family where "perfect" English is not spoken, and her growth from embarrassment *about* to appreciation *of* her "mother's tongue."

—m—

[1]   *I* am not a scholar of English or literature. I cannot give you much more than personal opinions on the English language and its variations in this country or others.

[2]   I am a writer. And by that definition, I am someone who has always loved language. I am fascinated by language in daily life. I spend a great deal of my time thinking about the power of language—the way it can evoke an emotion, a visual image, a complex idea, or a simple truth. Language is the tool of my trade. And I use them all—all the Englishes I grew up with.

[3]   Recently, I was made keenly aware of the different Englishes I do use. I was giving a talk to a large group of people, the same talk I had already given to half a dozen other groups. The nature of the talk was about my writing, my life, and my book, *The Joy Luck Club*. The talk was going along well enough, until I remembered one major difference that made the whole talk sound wrong. My mother was in the room. And it was perhaps the first time she had heard me give a lengthy speech, using the kind of English I have never used with her. I was saying things like, "The intersection of memory upon imagination" and "There is an aspect of my fiction that re-lates to thus-and-thus"—a speech filled with carefully wrought grammat-ical phrases, burdened, it suddenly seemed to me, with nominalized forms, past perfect tenses, conditional phrases, all the forms of standard English that I had learned in school and through books, the forms of English I did not use at home with my mother.

[4]   Just last week, I was walking down the street with my mother, and I again found myself conscious of the English I was using, the English I do use with her. We were talking about the price of new and used furniture and I heard myself saying this: "Not waste money that way." My husband was with us as well, and he didn't notice any switch in my English. And then I realized why. It's because over the twenty years we've been togeth-er I've often used that same kind of English with him, and sometimes he even uses it with me. It has become our language of intimacy, a different sort of English that relates to family talk, the language I grew up with.

[5]   So you'll have some idea of what this family talk I heard sounds like, I'll quote what my mother said during a recent conversation which I video-taped and then transcribed. During this conversation, my mother was talk-ing about a political gangster in Shanghai who had the same last name as her family's, Du, and how the gangster in his early years wanted to be adopted by her family, which was rich by comparison. Later, the gangster

became more powerful, far richer than my mother's family, and one day showed up at my mother's wedding to pay his respects. Here's what she said in part:

6   "Du Yusong having business like fruit stand. Like off the street kind. He is Du like Du Zong—but not Tsung-ming Island people. The local people call putong, the river east side, he belong to that side local people. That man want to ask Du Zong father take him in like become own family. Du Zong father wasn't look down on him, but didn't take seriously, until that man big like become a mafia. Now important person, very hard to inviting him. Chinese way, came only to show respect, don't stay for dinner. Respect for making big celebration, he shows up. Mean gives lots of respect. Chinese custom. Chinese social life that way. If too important won't have to stay too long. He come to my wedding. I didn't see, I heard it. I gone to boy's side, they have YMCA dinner. Chinese age[1] I was nineteen."

7   You should know that my mother's expressive command of English belies how much she actually understands. She reads the *Forbes*[2] report, listens to *Wall Street Week*,[3] converses daily with her stockbroker, reads all of Shirley MacLaine's books[4] with ease—all kinds of things I can't begin to understand. Yet some of my friends tell me they understand 50 percent of what my mother says. Some say they understand 80 to 90 percent. Some say they understand none of it, as if she were speaking pure Chinese. But to me, my mother's English is perfectly clear, perfectly natural. It's my mother tongue. Her language, as I hear it, is vivid, direct, full of observation and imagery. That was the language that helped shape the way I saw things, expressed things, made sense of the world.

8   Lately, I've been giving more thought to the kind of English my mother speaks. Like others, I have described it to people as "broken" or "fractured" English. But I wince when I say that. It has always bothered me that I can think of no way to describe it other than "broken," as if it were damaged and needed to be fixed, as if it lacked a certain wholeness and soundness. I've heard other terms used, "limited English," for example.

---

1   **Chinese age:** All Chinese children, no matter what day of the year they are born, automatically become one year old on the following Lunar New Year.
2   *Forbes:* a prominent American financial magazine.
3   *Wall Street Week:* a weekly public television program that focuses on the American financial scene.
4   **Shirley MacLaine's books:** Film star Shirley MacLaine has written a series of books about her belief that she has lived several earlier lives.

But they seem just as bad, as if everything is limited, including people's perceptions of the limited English speaker.

9   I know this for a fact, because when I was growing up, my mother's "limited" English limited *my* perception of her. I was ashamed of her English. I believed that her English reflected the quality of what she had to say. That is, because she expressed them imperfectly her thoughts were imperfect. And I had plenty of empirical evidence to support me: the fact that people in department stores, at banks, and at restaurants did not take her seriously, did not give her good service, pretended not to understand her, or even acted as if they did not hear her.

10   My mother has long realized the limitations of her English as well. When I was fifteen, she used to have me call people on the phone to pretend I was she. In this guise, I was forced to ask for information or even to complain and yell at people who had been rude to her. One time it was a call to her stockbroker in New York. She had cashed out her small portfolio and it just so happened we were going to go to New York the next week, our very first trip outside California. I had to get on the phone and say in an adolescent voice that was not very convincing, "This is Mrs. Tan."

11   And my mother was standing in the back whispering loudly, "Why he don't send me check, already two weeks late. So mad he lie to me, losing me money."

12   And then I said in perfect English, "Yes, I'm getting rather concerned. You had agreed to send the check two weeks ago, but it hasn't arrived."

13   Then she began to talk more loudly. "What he want, I come to New York tell him front of his boss, you cheating me?" And I was trying to calm her down, make her be quiet, while telling the stockbroker, "I can't tolerate any more excuses. If I don't receive the check immediately, I am going to have to speak to your manager when I'm in New York next week." And sure enough, the following week there we were in front of this astonished stockbroker, and I was sitting there red-faced and quiet, and my mother, the real Mrs. Tan, was shouting at his boss in her impeccable broken English.

14   We used a similar routine just five days ago, for a situation that was far less humorous. My mother had gone to the hospital for an appointment, to find out about a benign brain tumor a CAT scan had revealed a month ago. She said she had spoken very good English, her best English, no mistakes. Still, she said, the hospital did not apologize when they said they had lost the CAT scan and she had come for nothing. She said they did not seem to have any sympathy when she told them she was anxious to know the exact diagnosis, since her husband and son had both died of brain tumors. She said they would not give her any more information until the next time and she would have to make another appointment for that. So

she said she would not leave until the doctor called her daughter. She wouldn't budge. And when the doctor finally called her daughter, me, who spoke in perfect English—lo and behold—we had assurances the CAT scan would be found, promises that a conference call on Monday would be held, and apologies for any suffering my mother had gone through for a most regrettable mistake.

15   I think my mother's English almost had an effect on limiting my possibilities in life as well. Sociologists and linguists probably will tell you that a person's developing language skills are more influenced by peers. But I do think that the language spoken in the family, especially in immigrant families which are more insular, plays a large role in shaping the language of the child. And I believe that it affected my results on achievement test, IQ tests, and the SAT. While my English skills were never judged as poor, compared to math, English could not be considered my strong suit. In grade school I did moderately well, getting perhaps, B's, sometimes B-pluses, in English and scoring perhaps in the sixtieth or seventieth percentile on achievement tests. But those scores were not good enough to override the opinion that my true abilities lay in math and science, because in those areas I achieved A's and scored in the ninetieth percentile or higher.

16   This was understandable. Math is precise; there is only one correct answer. Whereas, for me at least, the answers on English tests were always a judgment call, a matter of opinion and personal experience. Those tests were constructed around items like fill-in-the-blank sentence completion, such as, "Even though Tom was——, Mary thought he was——." And the correct answer always seemed to be the most bland combinations of thoughts, for example, "Even though Tom was shy, Mary thought he was charming," with the grammatical structure "even though" limiting the correct answer to some sort of semantic opposites, so you wouldn't get answers like, "Even though Tom was foolish, Mary thought he was ridiculous." Well, according to my mother, there were very few limitations as to what Tom could have been and what Mary might have thought of him. So I never did well on tests like that.

17   The same was true with word analogies, pairs of words in which you were supposed to find some sort of logical, semantic relationship—for example, "*Sunset* is to *nightfall* as —— is to ——." And here you would be presented with a list of four possible pairs, one of which showed the same kind of relationship: *red* is to *stoplight, bus* is to *arrival, chills* is to *fever, yawn* is to *boring.* Well, I could never think that way. I knew what the tests were asking, but I could not block out of my mind the images already created by the first pair, "*sunset* is to *nightfall*"—and I would see a burst of colors against a darkening sky, the moon rising, the lowering of a curtain of stars.

And all the other pairs of words—red, bus, stoplight, boring—just threw up a mass of confusing images, making it impossible for me to sort out something as logical as saying: "A sunset precedes nightfall" is the same as "a chill precedes a fever." The only way I would have gotten that answer right would have been to imagine an associative situation, for example, my being disobedient and staying out past sunset, catching a chill at night, which turns into feverish pneumonia as punishment, which indeed did happen to me.

[18] I have been thinking about all this lately, about my mother's English, about achievement tests. Because lately I've been asked, as a writer, why there are not more Asian Americans represented in American literature. Why are there few Asian Americans enrolled in creative writing programs? Why do so many Chinese students go into engineering? Well, these are broad sociological questions I can't begin to answer. But I have noticed in surveys—in fact, just last week—that Asian students, as a whole, always do significantly better on math achievement tests than in English. And this makes me think that there are other Asian-American students whose English spoken in the home might also be described as "broken" or "limited." And perhaps they also have teachers who are steering them away from writing and into math and science, which is what happened to me.

[19] Fortunately, I happen to be rebellious in nature and enjoy the challenge of disproving assumptions made about me. I became an English major my first year in college, after being enrolled as pre-med. I started writing nonfiction as a freelancer the week after I was told by my former boss that writing was my worst skill and I should hone my talents toward account management.

[20] But it wasn't until 1985 that I finally began to write fiction. And at first I wrote using what I thought to be wittily crafted sentences, sentences that would finally prove I had mastery over the English language. Here's an example from the first draft of a story that later made its way into *The Joy Luck Club*, but without this line: "That was my mental quandary in its nascent state." A terrible line, which I can barely pronounce.

[21] Fortunately, for reasons I won't get into today, I later decided I should envision a reader for the stories I would write. And the reader I decided upon was my mother, because these were stories about mothers. So with this reader in mind—and in fact she did read my early drafts—I began to write stories using all the Englishes I grew up with: the English I spoke to my mother, which for lack of a better term might be described as "simple"; the English she used with me, which for lack of a better term might be described as "broken"; my translation of her Chinese, which could cer-

tainly be described as "watered down"; and what I imagined to be her translation of her Chinese if she could speak in perfect English, her internal language, and for that I sought to preserve the essence, but neither an English nor a Chinese structure. I wanted to capture what language ability tests can never reveal: her intent, her passion, her imagery, the rhythms of her speech and the nature of her thoughts.

22   Apart from what any critic had to say about my writing, I knew I had succeeded where it counted when my mother finished reading my book and gave me her verdict: "So easy to read."

Looking Back

1. What is the play on words of the title, "Mother Tongue"? Why is it particularly appropriate for this essay?

2. What effect did her mother's English have on Tan when she was growing up?

3. Now that she is a grown woman, does Tan still feel embarrassed by her mother's English?

4. What serious observations does Tan offer on the academic problems of many children of immigrants?

5. To what extent do Tan's experiences compare to or contrast with those of Ortiz?

Looking Into

1. To convey to the reader an accurate sense of her mother's speech, Tan transcribed a paragraph from a videotape. Read paragraph six of the essay again. Then, working with a partner, "translate" Mrs. Tan's words into standard written English. (NOTES: The Whangpoo River divides the Putong industrial district from the rest of the city of Shanghai; Tsung Ming Island (now written Chongming) is an island at the mouth of the Yangtse River some 14 miles downriver from Putong; since in China, a

person's surname appears first, *Du* is a family name while *Yu* and *song* are first and second names.)

2. Tan writes that she had "plenty of empirical evidence" that "people in department stores, at banks, and at restaurants did not take her [mother] seriously, did not give her good service, pretended not to understand her, or even acted as if they did not hear her." To what extent do you think people's language affects the way they are treated? What evidence can you give for your opinion? Write a two- or three-page paper in which you discuss the following question. Have you ever been discriminated against for your language, or appearance, or some other factor over which you have little control?

Autobiographical Notes

JAMES BALDWIN

Born in 1924 to an angry, imperious, and impoverished evangelical preacher and factor worker, James Baldwin grew up in Harlem, the oldest and most precocious of nine children. At the age of fourteen, he himself became a preacher, but by the age of seventeen he had turned his back on both his home and a Christianity whose "tenets had, in essence, been used to enslave [blacks]." While moving through a series of jobs such as handyman, dishwasher, waiter, office boy, and defense plant worker, he began writing a novel which was deemed promising enough to earn him a fellowship grant; he also began writing book reviews for various New York City periodicals.

In 1948, he moved to Paris, France, where he stayed until 1977. There, he finished his first and—in the opinion of many critics—his best novel: *Go Tell It on the Mountain* (1953), an autobiographical work based on his experiences as a youthful junior preacher at the Fireside Pentecostal Assembly. Subsequent novels—*Giovanni's Room* (1956), *Another Country* (1962), *Tell Me How Long the Train's Been Gone* (1968) and *If Beale Street Could Talk* (1974)—explore the "psychological implications of racism for both the oppressed and the oppressor." Baldwin also wrote three passionately angry works of nonfiction, all of which emphasized his ability to be an important witness to America's policy of "institutionalized race discrimination": *Notes of a Native Son* (1955), *Nobody Knows My Name: More Notes of a Native Son* (1961), and *The Fire Next Time* (1963). Two plays, *The Amen Corner* (1955) and *Blues for Mr. Charlie* (1964), had moderately successful Broadway runs. In 1985, Baldwin published *The Price of the Ticket: Collected Non-Fiction, 1948–1985*; in 1986, *Evidence of Things Not Seen*, an analysis of the Atlanta child murders.

Baldwin received numerous fellowships and grants which supported him while he was writing; his last award was the Commander of the Legion of Honor given to him in 1986 by the French government. Writing after Baldwin's death in 1987, Juan Williams wrote in the *Washington Post:* "The success of Baldwin's effort as the witness is evidenced time and again by the people, black and white, gay and straight, famous and anonymous, whose humanity he unveiled in his writings. America and the literary world are far richer for his witness."

Looking Ahead

Baldwin's book *Notes of a Native Son*, which begins with the following essay, was published in the mid-fifties, a time when the focus of the country was on economic recovery from World War II, when social attitudes seemed immutable, when no Civil Rights Law seemed possible. Baldwin's title pays homage to Richard Wright, whose book *Native Son* had brought him international fame as a spokesman for the plight of the black man in America. Baldwin's despair that the racial issue in America will never be resolved, much less eliminated, is mirrored in a parallel despair that his passionate inveighings against racism probably will not change attitudes. Still, in his essays as well as in his novels, Baldwin indeed recreated "out of the disorder of life that order which is art."

[1]   *I* was born in Harlem thirty-one years ago. I began plotting novels at about the time I learned to read. The story of my childhood is the usual bleak fantasy, and we can dismiss it with the unrestrained observation that I certainly would not consider living it again. In those days my mother was given to the exasperating and mysterious habit of having babies. As they were born, I took them over with one hand and held a book with the other. The children probably suffered, though they have since been kind enough to deny it, and in this way I read *Uncle Tom's Cabin* and *A Tale of Two Cities*[1] over and over and over again; in this way, in fact, I read just about everything I could get my hands on—except the Bible, probably because it was the only book I was encouraged to read. I must also confess that I wrote—a great deal—and my first professional triumph, in any case, the first effort of mine to be seen in print, occurred at the age of twelve or thereabouts, when a short story I had written about the Spanish revolution[2] won some sort of prize in an extremely short-lived church newspaper. I remember the story was censored by the lady editor, though I don't remember why, and I was outraged.

[2]   Also wrote plays, and songs, for one of which I received a letter of congratulations from Mayor La Guardia,[3] and poetry, about which the less

---

1 *Uncle Tom's Cabin . . . A Tale of Two Cities:* novels by American novelist Harriet Beecher Stowe (1811–1896) and English novelist Charles Dickens (1812–1870), the first about slavery; the second, about the French Revolution.
2 **Spanish revolution:** a Spanish civil war occurring between 1936–1939.
3 **Mayor [Fiorello] La Guardia** (1882–1947): mayor of the City of New York from 1934–1945.

said, the better. My mother was delighted by all these goings-on, but my father wasn't; he wanted me to be a preacher. When I was fourteen I became a preacher, and when I was seventeen I stopped. Very shortly thereafter I left home. For God knows how long I struggled with the world of commerce and industry—I guess they would say they struggled with *me*—and when I was about twenty-one I had enough done of a novel to get a Saxton Fellowship. When I was twenty-two the fellowship was over, the novel turned out to be unsalable, and I started waiting on tables in a Village restaurant[4] and writing book reviews—mostly, as it turned out, about the Negro problem, concerning which the color of my skin made me automatically an expert. Did another book, in company with photographer Theodore Pelatowski, about the store-front churches in Harlem. This book met exactly the same fate as my first—fellowship, but no sale. (It was a Rosenwald Fellowship.) By the time I was twenty-four I had decided to stop reviewing books about the Negro problem—which, by this time, was only slightly less horrible in print than it was in life—and I packed my bags and went to France, where I finished, God knows how, *Go Tell It on the Mountain.*

3 Any writer, I suppose, feels that the world into which he was born is nothing less than a conspiracy against the cultivation of his talent—which attitude certainly has a great deal to support it. On the other hand, it is only because the world looks on his talent with such a frightening indifference that the artist is compelled to make his talent important. So that any writer, looking back over even so short a span of time as I am here forced to assess, finds that the things which hurt him and the things which helped him cannot be divorced from each other; he could be helped in a certain way only because he was hurt in a certain way; and his help is simply to be enabled to move from one conundrum to the next—one is tempted to say that he moves from one disaster to the next. When one begins looking for influences one finds them by the score. I haven't thought much about my own, not enough anyway; I hazard that the King James Bible, the rhetoric of the store-front church, something ironic and violent and perpetually understated in Negro speech—and something of Dickens' love for bravura—have something to do with me today; but I wouldn't stake my life on it. Likewise, innumerable people have helped me in many ways; but finally, I suppose, the most difficult (and most rewarding) thing in my life has been the fact that I was born a Negro and was forced, therefore, to

---

4 **Village restaurant:** Greenwich Village, a section of Manhattan, New York City.

effect some kind of truce with this reality. (Truce, by the way, is the best one can hope for.)

4   One of the difficulties about being a Negro writer (and this is not special pleading, since I don't mean to suggest that he has it worse than anybody else) is that the Negro problem is written about so widely. The bookshelves groan under the weight of information, and everyone therefore considers himself informed. And this information, furthermore, operates usually (generally, popularly) to reinforce traditional attitudes. Of traditional attitudes there are only two—For or Against—and I, personally, find it difficult to say which attitude has caused me the most pain. I am perfectly aware that the change from ill-will to good-will, however motivated, however imperfect, however expressed, is better than no change at all.

5   But it is part of the business of the writer—as I see it—to examine attitudes, to go beneath the surface, to tap the source. From this point of view the Negro problem is nearly inaccessible. It is not only written about so widely; it is written about so badly. It is quite possible to say that the price a Negro pays for becoming articulate is to find himself, at length, with nothing to be articulate about. ("You taught me the language," says Caliban to Prospero,[5] "and my profit on't is I know how to curse.") Consider: The tremendous social activity that this problem generates imposes on whites and Negroes alike the necessity of looking forward, of working to bring about a better day. This is fine, it keeps the waters troubled; it is all, indeed, that has made possible the Negro's progress. Nevertheless, social affairs are not generally speaking the writer's prime concern, whether they ought to be or not; it is absolutely necessary that he establish between himself and these affairs a distance that will allow, at least, for clarity, so that before he can look forward in any meaningful sense, he must first be allowed to take a long look back. In the context of the Negro problem neither whites nor blacks, for excellent reasons of their own, have the faintest desire to look back; but I think that the past is all that makes the present coherent, and further, that the past will remain horrible for exactly as long as we refuse to assess it honestly.

6   I know, in any case, that the most crucial time in my own development came when I was forced to recognize that I was a kind of bastard of the West; when I followed the line of my past I did not find myself in

---

5   **Caliban to Prospero:** Caliban is an evil monster; Prospero is his benign master in Shakespeare's final play, *The Tempest*.

Europe but in Africa. And this meant that in some subtle way, in a really profound way, I brought to Shakespeare, Bach, Rembrandt, to the stones of Paris, to the cathedral at Chartres, and to the Empire State Building, a special attitude. These were not really my creations, they did not contain my history; I might search in them in vain forever for any reflection of myself. I was an interloper; this was not my heritage. At the same time I had no other heritage which I could possibly hope to use—I had certainly been unfitted for the jungle or the tribe. I would have to appropriate these white centuries, I would have to make them mine—I would have to accept my special attitude, my special place in this scheme—otherwise I would have no place in *any* scheme. What was the most difficult was the fact that I was forced to admit something I had always hidden from myself, which the American Negro has had to hide from himself as the price of his public progress; that I hated and feared white people. This did not mean that I loved black people; on the contrary, I despised them, possibly because they failed to produce Rembrandt. In effect, I hated and feared the world. And this meant, not only that I thus gave the world an altogether murderous power over me, but also that in such a self-destroying limbo I could never hope to write.

7 One writes out of one thing only—one's own experience. Everything depends on how relentlessly one forces from this experience the last drop, sweet or bitter, it can possibly give. This is the only real concern of the artist, to recreate out of the disorder of life that order which is art. The difficulty then, for me, of being a Negro writer was the fact that I was, in effect, prohibited from examining my own experience too closely by the tremendous demands and the very real dangers of my social situation.

8 I don't think the dilemma outlined above is uncommon. I do think, since writers work in the disastrously explicit medium of language, that it goes a little way towards explaining why, out of the enormous resources of Negro speech and life, and despite the example of Negro music, prose written by Negroes has been generally speaking so pallid and so harsh. I have not written about being a Negro at such length because I expect that to be my only subject, but only because it was the gate I had to unlock before I could hope to write about anything else. I don't think that the Negro problem in America can be even discussed coherently without bearing in mind its context; its context being the history, traditions, customs, the moral assumptions and preoccupations of the country; in short, the general social fabric. Appearances to the contrary, no one in America escapes its effects and everyone in America bears some responsibility for it. I believe this the more firmly because it is the overwhelming tendency to speak of this problem as though it were a thing apart. But in the work of Faulkner, in the

general attitude and certain specific passages in Robert Penn Warren, and, most significantly, in the advent of Ralph Ellison,[6] one sees the beginnings—at least—of a more genuinely penetrating search. Mr. Ellison, by the way, is the first Negro novelist I have ever read to utilize in language, and brilliantly, some of the ambiguity and irony of Negro life.

9   About my interests: I don't know if I have any, unless the morbid desire to own a sixteen-millimeter camera and make experimental movies can be so classified. Otherwise, I love to eat and drink—it's my melancholy conviction that I've scarcely ever had enough to eat (this is because it's *impossible* to eat enough if you're worried about the next meal)—and I love to argue with people who do not disagree with me too profoundly, and I love to laugh. I do *not* like bohemia, or bohemians,[7] I do not like people whose principal aim is pleasure, and I do not like people who are *earnest* about anything. I don't like people who like me because I'm a Negro; neither do I like people who find in the same accident grounds for contempt. I love America more than any other country in the world, and, exactly for this reason, I insist on the right to criticize her perpetually. I think all theories are suspect, that the finest principles may have to be modified, or may even be pulverized by the demands of life, and that one must find, therefore, one's own moral center and move through the world hoping that this center will guide one aright. I consider that I have many responsibilities, but none greater than this: to last, as Hemingway says, and get my work done.

10   I want to be an honest man and a good writer.

Looking Back

1. Welty, Ortiz, and Tan all chiefly credit their development as writers to the influence of spoken language. To what extent do you think Baldwin's early experiences might make him agree or disagree?

---

6 **Robert Penn Warren . . . Ralph Ellison.** two American writers: Warren (1905–1989), a novelist, critic, and poet; Ellison (1914–1994), primarily a novelist.

7 **bohemia, or bohemians:** a place where artists and writers [i.e., bohemians] live in an unconventional, carefree way.

2. In paragraph three, Baldwin writes, ". . . the most difficult (and most rewarding) thing in my life has been the fact that I was born a Negro and was forced, therefore, to effect some kind of truce with this reality." Why might Baldwin paradoxically assert that being a Negro was "the most difficult (and most rewarding) thing in [his] life"?

3. What do you think Baldwin means when he writes that he was "forced to effect some kind of truce with this reality"? Begin your discussion with a consideration of both the denotation and the connotation of the word *truce*.

4. For Baldwin, the resolution of the racial issue was the key to redemption for both blacks and whites in America. When he discusses that question in "Autobiographical Notes," how would you describe his tone— sad? bitter? resigned? truculent? Cite passages to support your answer.

Looking Into

1. In the long paragraph that precedes the final sentence, Baldwin gives a quick thumbnail sketch of himself. Read the paragraph aloud, listening for the rhythms of the sentences. Then write a sketch of yourself, imitating Baldwin's sentence patterns and his increasingly serious tone.

2. Baldwin praises Ralph Ellison for his ability to convey "some of the ambiguity and irony of Negro life." In small groups, examine at least ten news reports about an American minority in newspapers or in such periodicals as *Time, Newsweek,* or any similar publication. Make a list of the ambiguities or ironies discernible in the life of that minority. Then write a proposal to a local government or private agency for the elimination of one of those ironies.

The Parable of the Cave; or In Praise of Watercolors

MARY GORDON

Novelist, short-story writer, and essayist Mary Gordon, the daughter of a legal secretary and a writer and publisher who died when she was young, was born in 1949, in Long Island, New York, grew up in Valley Stream, and graduated from a Roman Catholic high school, an education that has informed and influenced her writing. She won a scholarship to Barnard College, New York, graduating with a B.A. in 1971; in 1973, she earned an M.A. from Syracuse University and began work on a Ph.D. Gordon taught English at Dutchess Community College and at Amherst College, but with the publication of her first novel *Final Payments* in 1978, she became a full-time writer. She has subsequently published three other novels—*The Company of Women* (1980), *Men and Angels* (1985), and *The Other Side* (1990); a collection of short stories, *Temporary Shelter* (1986); and *Good Boys and Dead Girls and Other Essays* (1991), a collection of essays divided into three sections: "On Writers and Writing," "The world, The church, The lives of women," and "Parts of a Journal." Her most recent work, *The Rest of Life* (1993), consists of three novellas.

Looking Ahead

Mankind's oldest artistic efforts stare out from the ceilings and walls of caves deep in the earth: primitive paintings that depict men and animals. Anthropologists surmise that the next art form to be developed was dance, especially ritual dance, followed quickly by poetry and drama. Whatever the art form, throughout the centuries the prime producers and practitioners of art were men. Explanations range from women's first obligation being to the family to women's having little if anything to say. Essayist Mary Gordon discusses the difficulties faced by many women artists, not least of which is the denigration of their efforts by men.

1   *O*nce I was told a story by a famous writer. "I will tell you what women writers are like," he said. The year was 1971. The women's movement had made men nervous; it had made a lot of women write. "Women writers are like a female bear who goes into a cave to hibernate. The male bear shoves a pine cone up her ass, because he knows if she shits all winter, she'll stink up the cave. In the spring, the pressure of all that built-up shit makes her expel the pine cone, and she shits a winter's worth all over the walls of the cave."

2   That's what women writers are like, said the famous writer.

3   He told the story with such geniality; he looked as if he were giving me a wonderful gift. I felt I ought to smile; everyone knows there's no bore like a feminist with no sense of humor. I did not write for two months after that. It was the only time in my life I have suffered from writer's block. I should not have smiled. But he was a famous writer and spoke with geniality. And in truth, I did not have the courage for clear rage. There is no seduction like that of being thought a good girl.

4   Theodore Roethke[1] said that women poets were "stamping a tiny foot against God." I have been told by male but not by female critics that my work was "exquisite," "lovely," "like a watercolor." They, of course, were painting in oils. They were doing the important work. Watercolors are cheap and plentiful; oils are costly: their base—oil—must be bought. And the idea is that oil paintings will endure. But what will they endure against? Fire? Flood? Bombs? Earthquake? Their endurance is another illusion: one more foolish bet against nature, or against natural vulnerabilities; one more scheme, like fallout shelters; one more gesture of illusory safety.

5   There are people in the world who derive no small pleasure from the game of "major" and "minor." They think that no major work can be painted in watercolors. They think, too, that Hemingway writing about boys in the woods is major; Mansfield[2] writing about girls in the house is minor. Exquisite, they will hasten to insist, but minor. These people join up with other bad specters, and I have to work to banish them. Let us pretend these specters are two men, two famous poets saying, "Your experience is an embarrassment; your experience is insignificant."

6   I wanted to be a good girl, so I tried to find out whose experience was not embarrassing. The prototype for a writer who was not embarrassing

---

1   **Theodore Roethke** (1908–1963): American poet.

2   **[Ernest] Hemingway** (1899–1961) and **[Katherine] Mansfield** (1888–1923): American novelist and journalist; English writer of penetrating short stories.

was Henry James.[3] And you see, the two specters said, proffering hope, he wrote about social relationships, but his distance gave them grandeur.

[7] Distance, then, was what I was to strive for. Distance from the body, from the heart, but most of all, distance from the self as writer. I could never understand exactly what they meant or how to do it; it was like trying to follow the directions on a home permanent in 1959.

[8] If Henry James had the refined experience, Conrad[4] had the significant one. The important moral issues were his: men pitted against nature in moments of extremity. There are no important women in Conrad's novels, except for *Victory*, which, the critics tell us, is a romance and an exception. Despite the example of Conrad, it was all right for the young men I knew, according to my specters, to write about the hymens they had broken, the diner waitresses they had seduced. Those experiences were significant. But we were not to write about our broken hearts, about the married men we loved disastrously, about our mothers or our children. Men could write about their fears of dying by exposure in the forest; we could not write about our fears of being suffocated in the kitchen. Our desire to write about these experiences only revealed our shallowness; it was suggested we would, in time, get over it. And write about what? Perhaps we would stop writing.

[9] And so, the specters whispered to me, if you want to write well, if you want us to take you seriously, you must be distant, you must be extreme.

[10] I suppose the specters were not entirely wrong. Some of the literature that has been written since the inception of the women's movement is lacking in style and moral proportion. But so is the work of Mailer, Miller, Burroughs, Ginsberg.[5] Their lack of style and proportion may be called offensive, but not embarrassing. They may be referred to as off the mark, but they will not be called trivial.

[11] And above all I did not wish to be *trivial*; I did not wish to be embarrassing. But I did not want to write like Conrad, and I did not want to

---

3 **Henry James** (1843–1916): American novelist who probed the motivations and interactions of people; died in England, a naturalized British citizen.

4 **[Joseph] Conrad** (1857–1924): Polish adventurer and ship's captain who retired to England, became a naturalized British citizen and wrote chiefly psychological studies of men at sea and under physical and moral stress.

5 **[Norman] Mailer** (1923–), **[Henry] Miller** (1891–1980), **[William] Burroughs** (1914–), **[Allen] Ginsberg** (1926–): American novelist and nonfiction writer; American novelist; American novelist; American "Beat" poet.

write like Henry James. The writers I wanted to imitate were all women: Charlotte Brontë, Woolf, Mansfield, Bowen, Lessing, Olsen.[6] I discovered that what I loved in writing was not distance but radical closeness; not the violence of the bizarre but the complexity of the quotidian.

12   I lost my fear of being trivial, but not my fear of being an embarrassment. And so I wrote my first novel in the third person. No one would publish it. Then a famous woman writer asked why I had written a first-person novel in the third person. She is a woman of abiding common sense, and so I blushed to tell her: "I wanted to sound serious. I didn't want to be embarrassing."

13   Only her wisdom made me write the novel I meant to. I can say it now: I will probably never read Conrad again; what he writes about simply does not interest me. Henry James I will love always, but it is not for his distance that I love him. The notion that style and detachment are necessary blood brothers is crude and bigoted. It is an intellectual embarrassment.

14   And I can say it now: I would rather own a Mary Cassatt[7] watercolor than a Velazquez[8] oil.

15   Here is the good side of being a woman writer: the company of other women writers, dead and living. My writer friends, all women, help me banish the dark specters. So does Katherine Mansfield; so does Christina Rossetti.[9] I feel their closeness to the heart of things; I feel their aptness and their bravery.

16   I think it is lonelier to be a man writer than a woman writer now, because I do not think that men are as good at being friends to one another as women are. Perhaps, since they have not thought they needed each other's protection, as women have known we have needed each other's, they have not learned the knack of helpful, rich concern that centers on a friend's work. They may be worried, since they see themselves as hewers of wood and slayers of animals, about production, about the kind of achievement that sees its success only in terms of another's failure. They may not be as kind to one another; they may not know how. These are the specters that

---

6   **Charlotte Bronte** (1816–1855), **[Virginia] Woolf** (1882–1941), **[Katherine] Mansfield** (see above), **[Elizabeth] Bowen** (1899–1973), **[Doris] Lessing** (1919–), **[Tillie] Olsen** (1913–): The first four women are English novelists and/or short story writers; Lessing, born in Rhodesia, now lives and teaches in England; Olsen is an American novelist and short story writer.

7   **Mary Cassatt** (1845–1926): American impressionist artist.

8   **[Diego] Velasquez** (1599–1660): Spanish court painter.

9   **Christina Rossetti** (1830–1894): English poet.

men now must banish. Our specters may be easier to chase. For the moment. They were not always so.

17 To this tale there should be an appendix, an explanation. Why was I so susceptible to the bad advice of men? What made me so ready to listen? Where did I acquire my genius for obedience?

18 I had a charming father. In many crucial ways, he was innocent of sexism, although he may have substituted narcissism in its place. He wanted me to be like him. He was a writer, an unsuccessful writer, and my mother worked as a secretary to support us. Nevertheless, he was a writer; he could think of himself as nothing else. He wanted me to be a writer too. I may have been born to be one, which made things easier. He died when I was seven. But even in those years we had together I learned well that I was his child, not my mother's. His mind was exalted, my mother's common. That she could earn the money to support us was only proof of the ordinariness of her nature, an ordinariness to which I was in no way heir. So I was taught to read at three, taught French at six, and taught to despise the world of women, the domestic. I was a docile child. I brought my father great joy, and I learned the pleasures of being a good girl.

19 And I earned, as a good girl, no mean rewards. Our egos are born delicate. Bestowing pleasure upon a beloved father is much easier than discovering the joys of solitary achievements. It was easy for me to please my father; and this ease bred in me a desire to please men—a desire for the rewards of a good girl. They are by no means inconsiderable: safety and approval, the warm, incomparable atmosphere created when one pleases a man who has vowed, in his turn, to keep the wolf from the door.

20 But who is the wolf?

21 He is strangers. He is the risk of one's own judgments, one's own work.

22 I have learned in time that I am at least as much my mother's daughter as my father's. Had I been only my mother's daughter, it is very possible that I would never have written: I may not have had the confidence required to embark upon a career so valueless in the eyes of the commonsense world. I did what my father wanted; I became a writer. I grew used to giving him the credit. But now I see that I am the *kind* of writer I am because I am my mother's daughter. My father's tastes ran to the metaphysical. My mother taught me to listen to conversations at the dinner table; she taught me to remember jokes.

23 My subject as a writer has far more to do with family happiness than with the music of the spheres. I don't know what the nature of the universe is, but I have a good ear. What it hears best are daily rhythms, for that is what I value, what I would wish, as a writer, to preserve.

24   My father would have thought this a stubborn predilection for the minor. My mother knows better.

—⟋⟍—

Looking Back

1. What point does the coarse "story [told] by a famous writer" make? Why does Gordon regret that she "did not have the courage for clear rage"?

2. What qualities in the work of male writers earn them, according to Gordon's "specters," the accolade of being "major" writers? What qualities in the work of female writers earn them the patronizing label of being "minor" writers?

3. The first part of Gordon's title not only refers to the bear anecdote, but also hints at a famous passage from Plato's *Republic,* known as the Allegory of the Cave. In this passage Plato depicts a group of people chained together in a cave, their backs to a fire. What they view on the wall before them are shadows of whatever moves behind them and is reflected on the wall by the fire. What the chained see, therefore, are shadows, or specters, of reality. Gordon reinforces her Platonic allusion by creating in paragraph four, two male specters. According to Gordon, these specters reveal to women the "reality" of their inferior position as writers. Gordon initially accepted the "truth" of their distortion of reality. Why did she accept it and why has she changed her mind?

4. What is the significance of the second part of Gordon's title: "In Praise of Watercolors."

Looking Into

1. Gordon makes clear what kind of writing she admires. List the statements she makes in the essay that constitute the objects of her admiration. Then, working in small groups, review the other essays in this unit and name the writer that Gordon might put at the top of an admired list. In one or two paragraphs, defend your choice.

2. In groups of four—two who agree with Gordon's thesis and two who oppose it—make a sentence outline of at least four arguments in favor of your position, each followed by at least two examples. Choose one person representing each position and have that person read the reasons and the supporting examples. As a class, discuss whose arguments seem the stronger.

Looking Around

1. Several of the authors in this section emphasize the importance of listening. In a short paper, describe what a would-be writer might hear that would be useful.

2. From these essays, can you discern what ultimately impelled each of these authors to choose writing as a career? Describe in a brief paper.

3. Several of these writers write in order to preserve or record a part of their cultural heritage. Why might that be important to them? Do you think it should be? Write your answer in an essay.

4. Some people feel that in order to have something worth writing about, an author should engage in exotic or extreme adventures. Would any of the five writers in this section agree? Present your opinion in two or three paragraphs.

5. Select an author whom you particularly admire. Research whether that author has ever written about his or her own development as a writer or what influenced him or her to become a writer. In a short paper, compare those experiences with those of one of the writers in this section.

6. Based on the five essays in this section, which of these authors would you be most inclined to read? In a brief paper, support your choice with two or three reasons.

Acknowledgments

—⁓—

3 Reprinted by permission of Sterling Lord Literistic, Inc. Copyright © 1988 by Barry Lopez.

14 From *There's a Country in My Cellar* by Russell Baker. Copyright © 1990 by Russell Baker. Published by William Morrow. Originally published by The New York Times Company. Reprinted by permission.

18 "Learning from My Grandmothers" in *The Ways of My Grandmothers* by Beverly Hungry Wolf. Copyright © 1980 by Beverly Hungry Wolf. Published by William Morrow & Company, Inc.

23 Copyright © 1993 by The New York Times Company. Reprinted by permission.

29 "Good Housekeeping" first appeared in *Mama Makes Up Her Mind* (Addison-Wesley, 1993) and is reprinted with the permission of The Lazear Agency, Inc. and Addison-Wesley Publishing Company, Inc. © 1993 by Bailey White.

36 From *The Cabin* by David Mamet. Copyright © 1992 by David Mamet. Reprinted by permission of Random House, Inc.

43 From *The Woman Warrior* by Maxine Hong Kingston. Copyright © 1975, 1976 by Maxine Hong Kingston. Reprinted by permission of Alfred A. Knopf, Inc.

55 Reprinted with the permission of Scribner, an imprint of Simon & Schuster from *The Inn of Tranquility* by John Galsworthy. Copyright 1912 Charles Scribner's Sons; copyright renewed 1940 Ada Galsworthy.

63 From *Moving the Mountain: Women Working for Social Change* by Ellen Cantarow. Copyright © 1980 by The Feminist Press. Reprinted by permission of McGraw-Hill, Inc.

72 "Maintenance" originally appeared in *The Georgia Review*, Volume XLIV, Nos. 1 and 2 (Spring/Summer 1990), © 1990 by The University of Georgia, © 1990 by Naomi Shihab Nye. Reprinted by permission of Naomi Shihab Nye and *The Georgia Review.*

82 Copyright © 1982 by David Goldman and Janet Selzer, Trustees. Reprinted by permission of Georges Borchardt, Inc. for Richard Selzer.

96 Mashinini, Emma, "Push Your Arse." Reprinted from *Strikes Have Followed Me All My Life* (1989) by permission of the publisher, Routledge, New York.

107 All pages from "Memorandum" from *One Man's Meat* by E. B. White. Copyright 1941 by E. B. White. Copyright renewed 1969 by E. B. White. Reprinted by permission of HarperCollins Publishers, Inc.

119 From *Secrets of the Universe* by Scott Russell Sanders. Copyright © 1991 by Scott Russell Sanders. Reprinted by permission of Beacon Press.

133 "A Winter Grouse" by Sydney Lea first appeared in *Virginia Quarterly Review.* Reprinted by permission.

141 Reprinted by permission of International Creative Management, Inc. Copyright © 1992 by Donna Tartt.

149 "Running the Table" by Frank Conroy first appeared in *GQ* in 1990. Reprinted by permission of the author.

157 Copyright © 1994 by The New York Times Company. Reprinted by permission.

161 From *Dave Barry Turns 40* by Dave Barry. Copyright © 1990 by Dave Barry. Reprinted by permission of Crown Publishers, Inc.

177 Excerpt from *The Edge of the Sea* by Rachel Carson. Copyright © 1955 by Rachel L. Carson, © renewed 1983 by Roger Christie. Reprinted by permission of Houghton Mifflin Co. All rights reserved.

184 "Living Like Weasels" from *Teaching a Stone to Talk* by Annie Dillard. Copyright © 1982 by Annie Dillard. Reprinted by permission of HarperCollins Publishers, Inc.

189 "The Gall of the Wild" is reprinted by permission of James E. Sheridan, Professor Emeritus of History, Northwestern University.

194 From *Last Chance to See* by Douglas Adams and Mark Carwardine. Copyright © 1991 by Douglas Adams and Mark Carwardine. Reprinted by permission of Crown Publishers, Inc.

208 Copyright © 1993 by The New York Times Company. Reprinted by permission.

221 From *A Country Year: Living the Questions* by Sue Hubbell. Copyright © 1983, 1984, 1985, 1986 by Sue Hubbell. Reprinted by permission of Random House, Inc.

233 Reprinted by permission of Don Congdon Associates, Inc. Copyright © 1968 by Edward Abbey.

245 From *Asimov's New Guide to Science* by Isaac Asimov. Copyright © 1960, 1965, 1972 by Basic Books, Inc. Reproduced by permission of Penguin Books Ltd.

Index of Authors and Titles